Better Homes and Gardens®
BIGGEST BOOK OF
SLOW COOKER RECIPES
VOLUME
2

WILEY

John Wiley & Sons, Inc.

Library of Congress Control Number: 2006921304

ISBN-13: 978-0-696-23052-3

Printed in China.

10 9 8 7 6 5 4

John Wiley & Sons, Inc.
Publisher: Natalie Chapman
Executive Editor: Anne Ficklen

BIGGEST BOOK OF SLOW COOKER RECIPES
Editor: Carrie E. Holcomb
Contributing Project Editor and Indexer: Spectrum Communication Services, Inc.
Contributing Designer: Joyce DeWitt
Contributing Cover Designer: Daniel Pelavin
Copy Chief: Terri Fredrickson
Publishing Operations Manager: Karen Schirm
Senior Editor, Asset and Information Manager: Phillip Morgan
Edit and Design Production Coordinator: Mary Lee Gavin
Editorial Assistant: Cheryl Eckert
Book Production Managers: Pam Kvitne, Marjorie J. Schenkelberg,
   Rick von Holdt, Mark Weaver
Contributing Copy Editor: Sarah Oliver Watson
Contributing Proofreaders: Devin Gentry, Donna Segal, Barbara Simpson
Test Kitchen Director: Lynn Blanchard
Test Kitchen Product Supervisors: Marilyn Cornelius, Jill Moberly
Test Kitchen Home Economists: Elizabeth Burt, R.D.; Marilyn Cornelius;
   Juliana Hale; Laura Marzen, R.D.; Maryellyn Krantz; Jill Moberly; Dianna Nolin;
   Colleen Weeden; Lori Wilson; Charles Worthington

Our Better Homes and Gardens® Test Kitchen seal on the back cover of this book assures you that every recipe in *Biggest Book of Slow Cooker Recipes Volume 2* has been tested in the Better Homes and Gardens® Test Kitchen. This means that each recipe is practical and reliable, and meets our high standards of taste appeal. We guarantee you satisfaction with this book as long as you own it.

TABLE OF CONTENTS

INTRODUCTION

Family Meals Made Easy

With today's hectic schedules, enjoying dinner together as a family may seem like an impossible dream. One way to make those meals happen is to rely on dishes simmered in a slow cooker. Available in a kaleidoscope of new colors, sizes, and shapes, this tried-and-true appliance never goes out of style because it provides ready-when-you-are convenience and helps budget-conscious cooks turn less expensive meats into sensational meals.

No matter whether you've had a slow cooker for years or are just pulling your first one out of the box, you're probably looking for innovative ways to use it. You'll find them in the *Biggest Book of Slow Cooker Recipes Volume 2.* This jam-packed volume goes beyond our first collection of slow-cooker recipes to bring you creative ideas that are right for today's families and busy lifestyles.

The *Biggest Book of Slow Cooker Recipes Volume 2* showcases more than 350 recipes including everything from meat, poultry, and meatless main dishes to soups and stews, side dishes, and desserts. There also are appetizers and beverages to make entertaining easy and fun. And there are two bonus chapters. If you're watching your weight, you can opt for some of the light entrées to help keep calories and fat in check. And for those times when you're cooking on the fly, choose a five-ingredient recipe that goes together in a flash.

For satisfying meals that are ready to serve when you walk in the door, there's no better place to turn for inspiration than the *Biggest Book of Slow Cooker Recipes Volume 2.*

APPETIZERS & BEVERAGES

1

For a mild dip kids will love, make this hearty meat-and-cheese dip without the chipotle peppers and black pepper.

ALMOST-A-MEAL QUESO

PREP:
20 minutes

COOK:
High 1 hour

MAKES:
8 cups

SLOW COOKER:
3½- or 4-quart

1   pound ground beef

1   large onion, chopped

2   cloves garlic, minced

2   pounds American cheese, cubed

½   of a 16-ounce link cooked kielbasa or smoked sausage, quartered lengthwise and sliced

1   14½-ounce can diced tomatoes, undrained

1   4-ounce can diced green chile peppers, undrained

2   to 3 canned chipotle chile peppers in adobo sauce, drained and chopped*

1   tablespoon chili powder

1½   teaspoons Worcestershire sauce

½   teaspoon black pepper

Tortilla chips

1 In a large skillet cook ground beef, onion, and garlic until beef is brown; drain off fat. Add beef to a 3½- or 4-quart slow cooker. Stir in cheese, sausage, undrained tomatoes, undrained chile peppers, chipotle peppers, chili powder, Worcestershire sauce, and black pepper.

2 Cover and cook on high-heat setting for 1 to 2 hours or until cheese melts, stirring after 1 hour. Serve immediately or keep warm, covered, on warm setting or low-heat setting for up to 2 hours, stirring occasionally. Serve with tortilla chips.

Per 2 tablespoons dip: 83 cal., 6 g total fat (4 g sat. fat), 19 mg chol., 263 mg sodium, 1 g carbo., 0 g fiber, 5 g pro.

***NOTE:** Because chile peppers contain volatile oils that can burn your skin and eyes, avoid direct contact with them as much as possible. When working with chile peppers, wear plastic or rubber gloves. If your bare hands do touch the peppers, wash your hands and nails well with soap and warm water.

If you prefer a spicier dip, choose a hot-style bulk pork sausage.

CHEESE-SAUSAGE DIP

8	ounces bulk pork sausage
1	medium red onion, sliced
2	pounds American cheese, cubed
2	10-ounce cans chopped tomatoes and green chile peppers, undrained
1	16-ounce package small, cooked smoked sausage links or cocktail wieners, sliced
	Tortilla chips

1 In a medium saucepan cook bulk pork sausage and onion over medium heat until sausage is brown; drain off fat. Transfer sausage mixture to a 3$^1/_2$- or 4-quart slow cooker. Stir in cheese, undrained tomatoes and green chile peppers, and sliced sausage links or cocktail wieners.

2 Cover and cook on high-heat setting about 1$^1/_2$ hours or until cheese melts, stirring after 1 hour. Serve immediately or keep warm, covered, on warm setting or low-heat setting for up to 1 hour, stirring occasionally. Serve with tortilla chips.

Per ¼ cup dip: 168 cal., 14 g total fat (8 g sat. fat), 41 mg chol., 644 mg sodium, 2 g carbo., 0 g fiber, 9 g pro.

PREP:
15 minutes

COOK:
High 1$^1/_2$ hours

MAKES:
8 cups

SLOW COOKER:
3$^1/_2$- or 4-quart

If you have leftover dip, reheat it to serve over baked potatoes for an easy side dish.

BROCCOLI-CHEESE DIP

PREP:
15 minutes

COOK:
Low 4 hours, High 1½ hours

MAKES:
about 4½ cups

SLOW COOKER:
1½- or 2-quart

1   16-ounce package frozen chopped broccoli, thawed

8   ounces American cheese, cubed

1   10¾-ounce can condensed cream of mushroom soup

3   tablespoons milk or water

¼   teaspoon garlic powder

¼   teaspoon black pepper

     Whole grain crackers

1 In a 1½- or 2-quart slow cooker stir together broccoli, cheese, cream of mushroom soup, milk, garlic powder, and pepper.

2 Cover and cook on low-heat setting for 4 to 5 hours or on high-heat setting for 1½ to 2 hours. If no heat setting is available, cook for 3 to 4 hours. Stir before serving. Serve immediately or keep warm, covered, on warm setting or low-heat setting (if available) for up to 1 hour. Serve with crackers.

Per 3 tablespoons dip: 52 cal., 4 g total fat (2 g sat. fat), 10 mg chol., 235 mg sodium, 2 g carbo., 1 g fiber, 3 g pro.

Green chile peppers and picante sauce add a pleasant kick to this rich dip. Serve it with plenty of tortilla chips or large corn chips.

CHEESY CHILI DIP

1	large onion, chopped
1	tablespoon butter
1	10½-ounce can chili without beans
1	10-ounce can chopped tomatoes and green chile peppers, undrained
1	4-ounce can diced green chile peppers, undrained
¼	cup bottled picante sauce
½	teaspoon cumin seeds, crushed, or ⅛ teaspoon ground cumin
1	pound process cheese spread, cubed
3	cups shredded cheddar cheese (12 ounces)
	Tortilla chips or large corn chips

PREP:
20 minutes

COOK:
Low 4 hours, High 2 hours

MAKES:
6 cups

SLOW COOKER:
2½- to 4-quart

1 In a medium saucepan cook onion in butter about 5 minutes or until tender. Spoon onion mixture into a 2½- to 4-quart slow cooker. Stir in chili, undrained tomatoes and green chile peppers, undrained chile peppers, picante sauce, and cumin seeds. Stir in cheese spread cubes and shredded cheddar cheese.

2 Cover and cook on low-heat setting for 4 to 5 hours or on high-heat setting for 2 to 2½ hours or until cheese melts and mixture is hot, stirring after about 1½ hours. Serve immediately or keep warm, covered, on warm setting or low-heat setting for up to 2 hours. Serve with chips.

Per ¼ cup dip: 153 cal., 11 g total fat (7 g sat. fat), 36 mg chol., 533 mg sodium, 4 g carbo., 0 g fiber, 8 g pro.

It's easier to corral this cheesy, chunky dip with scoop-shaped corn chips.

CREAMY CHILI & ONION DIP

PREP:
15 minutes

COOK:
Low 3½ hours

MAKES:
about 5½ cups

SLOW COOKER:
2½- to 3½-quart

2 8-ounce packages cream cheese, cubed

2 15-ounce cans chili with beans

1 large onion, chopped

¾ cup bottled chipotle salsa or desired salsa

Scoop-shaped corn chips

1 In a 2½- to 3½-quart slow cooker stir together cream cheese, chili, onion, and salsa. Cover and cook on low-heat setting for 3½ to 4 hours. Stir well. Serve immediately or keep warm, covered, on warm setting or low-heat setting for up to 2 hours. Serve with corn chips.

Per ¼ cup dip: 116 cal., 9 g total fat (5 g sat. fat), 31 mg chol., 281 mg sodium, 5 g carbo., 1 g fiber, 5 g pro.

Plan on everyone coming back for seconds of this captivating concoction of crab, mayonnaise, and two cheeses.

CREAMY CRAB DIP

Nonstick cooking spray

12 ounces cream cheese, cut into cubes

½ cup mayonnaise or salad dressing

½ cup finely shredded Parmesan cheese (2 ounces)

¼ cup snipped fresh chives or thinly sliced green onions

1 tablespoon Worcestershire sauce for chicken

2 6-ounce cans crabmeat, drained, flaked, and cartilage removed

Snipped fresh chives or green onions

Pita bread wedges, toasted, or assorted crackers

PREP:
15 minutes

COOK:
Low 1½ hours, High 1 hour

MAKES:
2½ cups

SLOW COOKER:
1½-quart

1 Coat the inside of a 1½-quart slow cooker with nonstick cooking spray; set aside.

2 In a medium bowl combine cream cheese, mayonnaise, Parmesan cheese, the ¼ cup chives or green onions, and the Worcestershire sauce. Stir in crabmeat. Transfer crabmeat mixture to prepared slow cooker.

3 Cover and cook on low-heat setting for 1½ to 2 hours or on high-heat setting for 1 to 1½ hours. If no heat setting is available, cook for 1 to 1½ hours. Stir well before serving. Sprinkle with additional chives or green onions. Serve immediately or keep warm, covered, on warm setting or low-heat setting (if available) for up to 2 hours. Serve with pita bread wedges or assorted crackers.

Per 2 tablespoons dip: 125 cal., 11 g total fat (5 g sat. fat), 37 mg chol., 183 mg sodium, 1 g carbo., 0 g fiber, 6 g pro.

Like things on the spicy side? Use hot-style Italian sausage or chorizo in place of the pork sausage.

SAUSAGE-CHEESE DIP

PREP:
15 minutes

COOK:
Low 2 hours

MAKES:
6 cups

SLOW COOKER:
3½- or 4-quart

1 pound bulk pork sausage

1 14½-ounce can diced tomatoes with garlic and onion, undrained

2 pounds pasteurized prepared cheese product with jalapeño chile peppers, cubed

Thinly sliced baguette-style French bread or pita wedges, toasted

1 In a large skillet cook sausage over medium heat until brown. Drain well. Transfer sausage to a 3½- or 4-quart slow cooker. Stir in undrained tomatoes and cubed cheese.

2 Cover and cook on low-heat setting for 2 to 3 hours, stirring after 1 hour to mix in the cheese. Serve immediately or keep warm, covered, on warm setting or low-heat setting for up to 2 hours, stirring occasionally. Serve with French bread slices or pita wedges.

Per ¼ cup dip: 190 cal., 15 g total fat (9 g sat. fat), 37 mg chol., 671 mg sodium, 4 g carbo., 0 g fiber, 9 g pro.

For a festive presentation, use a combination of red and green sweet pepper for the fondue, and create an eye-catching platter of bread chunks, corn chips, and colorful vegetable dippers.

SOUTHWEST CHEESE FONDUE

2   10¾-ounce cans condensed cream of potato soup

8   ounces American cheese, cubed (2 cups)

½   cup finely chopped red and/or green sweet pepper

⅓   cup milk

½   teaspoon ground cumin

Crusty bread cubes, corn chips, and/or vegetable dippers

Milk (optional)

1 In a 1½- to 2½-quart slow cooker place cream of potato soup; mash any pieces of potato. Stir in cheese, sweet pepper, the ⅓ cup milk, and the cumin.

2 Cover and cook on low-heat setting for 4 to 5 hours, stirring after 3 hours, or on high-heat setting for 2 to 2½ hours, stirring after 2 hours. If no heat setting is available, cook for 2 to 2½ hours, stirring after 2 hours. Serve immediately or keep warm, covered, on warm setting or low-heat setting (if available) for up to 1 hour. Serve with crusty bread cubes, corn chips, and/or vegetable dippers. If mixture becomes too thick, stir in additional milk, 1 tablespoon at a time, until mixture reaches desired consistency.

Per ¼ cup fondue: 101 cal., 6 g total fat (4 g sat. fat), 19 mg chol., 553 mg sodium, 6 g carbo., 0 g fiber, 5 g pro.

PREP:
15 minutes

COOK:
Low 4 hours, High 2 hours

MAKES:
about 3½ cups

SLOW COOKER:
1½- to 2½-quart

This blend of green chile peppers, black olives, and cheese is a real crowd-pleaser.

NACHO CHEESE DIP

PREP:
10 minutes

COOK:
Low 2½ hours, High 1¼ hours

MAKES:
3 cups

SLOW COOKER:
1½-quart

1   10-ounce can diced tomatoes and green chile peppers, undrained

1   8-ounce package pasteurized prepared cheese product, cubed

1   cup shredded Monterey Jack cheese (4 ounces)

1   cup shredded cheddar cheese (4 ounces)

1   teaspoon ground cumin

1   2¼-ounce can sliced pitted ripe olives, drained

    Vegetable dippers and/or tortilla chips

1 Pour undrained tomatoes into a 1½-quart slow cooker; top with cheese product, Monterey Jack cheese, cheddar cheese, and cumin.

2 Cover and cook on low-heat setting for 2½ to 3 hours or on high-heat setting for 1¼ to 1½ hours. If no heat setting is available, cook for 1½ to 2 hours. (Mixture may look slightly curdled.) Stir until smooth.

3 Stir in olives. Serve immediately or keep warm, covered, on warm setting or low-heat setting (if available) for up to 1 hour.* Serve with vegetable dippers and/or tortilla chips.

Per ¼ cup dip: 154 cal., 11 g total fat (7 g sat. fat), 34 mg chol., 488 mg sodium, 3 g carbo., 1 g fiber, 9 g pro.

*NOTE: If dip thickens, stir in enough milk, 1 tablespoon at a time, to make desired consistency.

Kids especially will get a kick out of the "dig in" fondue-style presentation of this hearty snack.

WALKING PIZZA

8   ounces bulk Italian or pork sausage

1   large onion, finely chopped

2   cloves garlic, minced

2   14½-ounce cans diced tomatoes, drained

2   11-ounce cans condensed tomato bisque soup

2   4-ounce cans (drained weight) sliced mushrooms, drained

1   cup chopped pepperoni or Canadian-style bacon

½   cup chopped green sweet pepper

2   teaspoons dried basil or oregano, crushed

8   cups cubed Italian bread
     Finely shredded Parmesan cheese

1 In a large skillet cook sausage, onion, and garlic until meat is brown. Drain off fat. In a 4- to 5-quart slow cooker combine sausage mixture, drained tomatoes, tomato bisque soup, drained mushrooms, pepperoni or Canadian-style bacon, sweet pepper, and basil.

2 Cover and cook on low-heat setting for 4 to 5 hours or on high-heat setting for 2 to 2½ hours, stirring after 1 hour. Serve immediately or keep warm, covered, on warm setting or low-heat setting for up to 2 hours. Spoon into bowls or cups; serve with bread cubes and sprinkle with Parmesan cheese.

Per serving: 173 cal., 8 g total fat (3 g sat. fat), 22 mg chol., 715 mg sodium, 18 g carbo., 2 g fiber, 6 g pro.

PREP:
20 minutes

COOK:
Low 4 hours, High 2 hours

MAKES:
16 servings

SLOW COOKER:
4- to 5-quart

Made with eggplant, onions, and tomatoes, caponata is a Sicilian specialty that can be served as an appetizer, salad, or relish. Be sure to have plenty of bread for scooping up the enchanting medley.

CAPONATA

PREP:
20 minutes

COOK:
Low 6 hours, High 3 hours

STAND:
30 minutes

MAKES:
12 servings

SLOW COOKER:
3½-quart

1	medium eggplant (about 1 pound), peeled and cut into ½-inch pieces (about 5 cups)
1	14½-ounce can diced tomatoes, drained
1	medium onion, chopped
½	cup sliced pitted green olives
2	tablespoons olive oil
2	tablespoons balsamic vinegar
2	tablespoons capers, drained
1	teaspoon dried oregano, crushed
¼	teaspoon crushed red pepper
2	cloves garlic, minced
2	tablespoons pine nuts, toasted
2	tablespoons snipped fresh basil
	Thinly sliced baguette-style French bread, toasted, or pita bread wedges, toasted

1 In a 3½-quart slow cooker combine eggplant, drained tomatoes, onion, olives, olive oil, balsamic vinegar, capers, oregano, crushed red pepper, and garlic. Cover and cook on low-heat setting for 6 to 8 hours or on high-heat setting for 3 to 4 hours.

2 Spoon cooked mixture into a serving bowl. Cover and let stand at room temperature for 30 minutes. Stir in pine nuts and basil. Serve with bread or pita wedges.

Per ¼ cup: 59 cal., 4 g total fat (1 g sat. fat), 0 mg chol., 235 mg sodium, 5 g carbo., 1 g fiber, 1 g pro.

For a terrific side dish serve the no-tend sauce over pasta.

TOMATO SAUCE WITH GARLIC CHEESE BREAD

1   14½-ounce can diced tomatoes with basil, garlic, and oregano, undrained

1½   cups tomato-base pasta sauce

1   4-ounce can (drained weight) sliced mushrooms, drained

¼   cup finely shredded Parmesan cheese (1 ounce)

1   11¾-ounce package frozen garlic cheese bread or garlic bread

PREP:
10 minutes

COOK:
Low 3 hours, High 2 hours

MAKES:
14 servings

SLOW COOKER:
1½-quart

1 In a 1½-quart slow cooker combine undrained tomatoes, pasta sauce, and drained mushrooms.

2 Cover and cook on low-heat setting for 3 to 4 hours or on high-heat setting for 2 to 2½ hours. If no heat setting is available, cook for 2 to 2½ hours. Stir in Parmesan cheese.

3 Prepare garlic cheese bread according to package directions. Cut crosswise into slices.

4 Serve sauce immediately or keep warm, covered, on warm setting or low-heat setting (if available) for up to 1 hour. To serve, dip cheese bread slices into sauce.

Per serving: 107 cal., 4 g total fat (2 g sat. fat), 1 mg chol., 419 mg sodium, 13 g carbo., 1 g fiber, 4 g pro.

Orange marmalade and ginger team up to make these tender, slow-simmered riblets irresistible.

ORANGE-GLAZED RIBS

PREP:
20 minutes

COOK:
Low 5 hours, High 2½ hours

MAKES:
about 16 servings
(about 2 rib pieces each)

SLOW COOKER:
5- to 6-quart

4   pounds pork loin back ribs*

1   medium onion, chopped

½   cup chopped dried apricots or figs

¾   cup orange marmalade

¼   cup lemon juice

¼   cup water

1   tablespoon grated fresh ginger

⅓   cup bottled barbecue sauce

⅓   cup orange marmalade

1 Cut ribs into single-rib portions. Place ribs in a 5- to 6-quart slow cooker. Add onion and apricots or figs to slow cooker. In a small bowl stir together the ¾ cup marmalade, the lemon juice, the water, and ginger. Pour over mixture in slow cooker.

2 Cover and cook on low-heat setting for 5 to 6 hours or on high-heat setting for 2½ to 3 hours.

3 To serve, use a slotted spoon or tongs to transfer ribs to a serving dish. In a small saucepan stir together barbecue sauce and the ⅓ cup orange marmalade. Heat through. Spoon over ribs.

Per serving: 177 cal., 6 g total fat (2 g sat. fat), 48 mg chol., 89 mg sodium, 12 g carbo., 1 g fiber, 20 g pro.

***NOTE:** To make eating the ribs easier, have your butcher saw the ribs in half crosswise (across the bone) for smaller rib portions.

Order the ribs a day or so ahead to give your butcher time to saw the ribs in half crosswise for you.

CURRY-GLAZED PORK RIBS

2½ pounds pork loin back ribs*
½ cup bottled chutney
¾ cup apple juice or apple cider
2 tablespoons quick-cooking tapioca, crushed**
2 teaspoons curry powder
¼ teaspoon salt
⅛ teaspoon black pepper

PREP:
15 minutes

COOK:
Low 5 hours, High 2½ hours

MAKES:
about 24 ribs

SLOW COOKER:
3½- or 4-quart

1 Cut ribs into single-rib portions. Place ribs in a 3½- or 4-quart slow cooker. In a small bowl cut up any large pieces of chutney. Stir in apple juice, tapioca, curry powder, salt, and pepper. Pour over ribs.

2 Cover and cook on low-heat setting for 5 to 6 hours or on high-heat setting for 2½ to 3 hours. Serve immediately or keep warm, covered, on warm setting or low-heat setting for up to 2 hours.

Per rib: 63 cal., 2 g total fat (1 g sat. fat), 14 mg chol., 52 mg sodium, 4 g carbo., 0 g fiber, 7 g pro.

*NOTE: To make eating the ribs easier, have your butcher saw the ribs in half crosswise (across the bone) for smaller rib portions.

**NOTE: Use a mortar and pestle to crush the tapioca.

Crushed red pepper gives these tangy Asian-style wings a lively kick.

POLYNESIAN GLAZED WINGS

PREP:
20 minutes

BROIL:
15 minutes

COOK:
Low 3 hours, High 1½ hours

MAKES:
about 32 servings

SLOW COOKER:
3½- or 4-quart

3 pounds chicken wings (about 16)

1 10-ounce bottle sweet-and-sour sauce (about 1¼ cups)

2 tablespoons soy sauce

2 teaspoons grated fresh ginger

¼ to ½ teaspoon crushed red pepper

1 Use a sharp knife to carefully cut off tips of the wings; discard wing tips. Cut each wing at joint to make 2 pieces. Place wing pieces on the unheated rack of a broiler pan. Broil 4 to 5 inches from heat for 15 to 20 minutes or until chicken is browned, turning once.

2 For sauce, in a 3½- or 4-quart slow cooker combine sweet-and-sour sauce, soy sauce, ginger, and crushed red pepper. Add wing pieces, stirring to coat with sauce.

3 Cover and cook on low-heat setting for 3 to 4 hours or on high-heat setting for 1½ to 2 hours. Serve immediately or keep warm, covered, on warm setting or low-heat setting for up to 1 hour.

Per serving: 61 cal., 5 g total fat (1 g sat. fat), 29 mg chol., 112 mg sodium, 2 g carbo., 0 g fiber, 5 g pro.

Two tablespoons of green curry paste make these saucy wings succulently spicy; three tablespoons add lip-tingling boldness.

GREEN CURRY CHICKEN WINGS

1	small onion, chopped
14	chicken wings (about 3 pounds total)
¾	cup purchased unsweetened coconut milk
3	tablespoons bottled fish sauce
2 to 3	tablespoons green curry paste
2	tablespoons cornstarch
2	tablespoons cold water
¼	cup shredded fresh basil leaves

1 Place onion in a 3½- or 4-quart slow cooker. Use a sharp knife to carefully cut off tips of the wings; discard wing tips. Cut each wing at joint to make 2 pieces. Place wing pieces over onions in slow cooker. In a small bowl stir together coconut milk, fish sauce, and curry paste. Pour over chicken wings.

2 Cover and cook on low-heat setting for 5 to 6 hours or on high-heat setting for 2½ to 3 hours. Using a slotted spoon, remove chicken from slow cooker; cover and set aside. Skim fat from cooking liquid.

3 In a medium saucepan stir together cornstarch and the cold water; stir in the cooking liquid. Cook and stir over medium heat until thickened and bubbly. Cook and stir for 2 minutes more. Stir in basil. Serve over wings.

Per serving: 183 cal., 14 g total fat (5 g sat. fat), 47 mg chol., 488 mg sodium, 3 g carbo., 0 g fiber, 12 g pro.

PREP:
30 minutes

COOK:
Low 5 hours, High 2½ hours

MAKES:
12 servings

SLOW COOKER:
3½- or 4-quart

You can rely on cocktail-size meatballs to disappear fast from an appetizer table. These gems showcase ham, pork, graham crackers, and a ginger-spiked sweet-and-sour sauce.

SWEET & SOUR HAM BALLS

PREP:
20 minutes

BAKE:
15 minutes

COOK:
Low 2 hours, High 1 hour

OVEN:
350°F

MAKES:
30 meatballs

SLOW COOKER:
3½- or 4-quart

1	egg
½	cup finely crushed graham crackers or ¼ cup fine dry bread crumbs
2	tablespoons milk
8	ounces ground cooked ham
8	ounces ground pork
1	9- or 10-ounce bottle sweet-and-sour sauce
⅓	cup unsweetened pineapple juice
⅓	cup packed brown sugar
½	teaspoon ground ginger

1 Preheat oven to 350°F. For meatballs, in a large bowl beat egg with a fork; stir in graham cracker crumbs and milk. Add ground ham and pork; mix well. Shape meat mixture into 30 meatballs. Arrange meatballs in a 15×10×1-inch baking pan. Bake for 15 to 20 minutes or until meatballs are cooked through (160°F). Drain well.

2 Meanwhile, in a 3½- or 4-quart slow cooker stir together sweet-and-sour sauce, pineapple juice, brown sugar, and ground ginger.

3 Add browned meatballs to slow cooker. Gently stir to coat meatballs with sauce. Cover and cook on low-heat setting for 2 to 3 hours or on high-heat setting for 1 to 1½ hours. Serve immediately or keep warm, covered, on warm setting or low-heat setting for up to 2 hours.

Per meatball: 50 cal., 2 g total fat (1 g sat. fat), 15 mg chol., 149 mg sodium, 6 g carbo., 0 g fiber, 3 g pro.

Frozen cooked meatballs make this zesty party dish almost effortless.

CHILI-CRANBERRY MEATBALLS

1	16-ounce can whole cranberry sauce
1	12-ounce bottle chili sauce
½	cup packed brown sugar
2	tablespoons lemon juice
½	teaspoon bottled hot pepper sauce (optional)
2	16-ounce packages frozen cooked meatballs (64 total), thawed

1 In a 3½- or 4-quart slow cooker combine cranberry sauce, chili sauce, brown sugar, lemon juice, and, if desired, hot pepper sauce. Add meatballs.

2 Cover and cook on low-heat setting for 4 hours or on high-heat setting for 2 hours. Serve immediately or keep warm, covered, on warm setting or low-heat setting for up to 2 hours.

Per meatball: 69 cal., 3 g total fat (2 g sat. fat), 9 mg chol., 177 mg sodium, 7 g carbo., 1 g fiber, 3 g pro.

PREP:
15 minutes

COOK:
Low 4 hours, High 2 hours

MAKES:
64 meatballs

SLOW COOKER:
3½- or 4-quart

These appetizers make throwing a party easy. Four ingredients and two hours—that's all you need.

COCKTAIL MEATBALLS

PREP:
10 minutes

COOK:
Low 4 hours, High 2 hours

MAKES:
32 meatballs

SLOW COOKER:
1½- or 2-quart

1	16-ounce package frozen cooked meatballs (32), thawed
½	cup bottled roasted red and/or yellow sweet peppers, cut into 1-inch pieces
⅛	teaspoon crushed red pepper
½	of a 26-ounce jar onion-garlic pasta sauce (1½ cups)

1 In a 1½- or 2-quart slow cooker combine meatballs and roasted peppers. Sprinkle with crushed red pepper. Pour pasta sauce over meatball mixture in slow cooker.

2 Cover and cook on low-heat setting for 4 to 5 hours or on high-heat setting for 2 to 2½ hours. If no heat setting is available, cook for 4 to 5 hours. Skim fat from sauce, if necessary. Stir gently before serving. Serve immediately or keep warm, covered, on warm setting or low-heat setting (if available) for up to 2 hours.

Per meatball: 55 cal., 4 g total fat (2 g sat. fat), 5 mg chol., 161 mg sodium, 3 g carbo., 1 g fiber, 2 g pro.

FOR 3½- OR 4-QUART SLOW COOKER:
Prepare as directed except use two 16-ounce packages meatballs (64 total), thawed; 1 cup bottled roasted red and/or yellow sweet peppers; ¼ teaspoon crushed red pepper; and one 26-ounce jar onion-garlic pasta sauce. Makes 64 meatballs.

A spirited blend of apple jelly, mustard, and whiskey makes these beefy sausage bites irresistible.

SWEET, HOT & SOUR MEATBALLS

2	eggs
½	cup fine dry bread crumbs
1	medium onion, finely chopped
¼	cup milk
½	teaspoon salt
½	teaspoon black pepper
1	pound bulk pork sausage
1	pound ground beef
¾	cup apple jelly
⅓	cup spicy brown mustard
⅓	cup whiskey or apple juice
1½	teaspoons Worcestershire sauce
	Dash bottled hot pepper sauce

PREP:
35 minutes

BAKE:
25 minutes

COOK:
Low 3 hours, High 1½ hours

OVEN:
375°F

MAKES:
36 meatballs

SLOW COOKER:
3½- or 4-quart

1 Preheat oven to 375°F. For meatballs, in a large bowl beat eggs with a fork; stir in bread crumbs, onion, milk, salt, and black pepper. Add pork sausage and ground beef; mix well. Shape into 36 meatballs. Place in a shallow baking pan. Bake for 25 to 30 minutes or until meatballs are cooked through (160°F). Drain well.

2 Place meatballs in a 3½- or 4-quart slow cooker. In a small bowl stir together apple jelly, spicy brown mustard, whiskey or apple juice, Worcestershire sauce, and hot pepper sauce; pour over meatballs. Cover and cook on low-heat setting for 3 to 4 hours or on high-heat setting for 1½ to 2 hours. Serve immediately or keep warm, covered, on warm setting or low-heat setting for up to 2 hours.

Per meatball: 112 cal., 7 g total fat (3 g sat. fat), 28 mg chol., 195 mg sodium, 6 g carbo., 0 g fiber, 5 g pro.

These sausages with colorful cranberry sauce and aromatic allspice are just the thing to serve at a casual holiday gathering.

CRANBERRY-SAUCED SAUSAGES

PREP:
10 minutes

COOK:
Low 4 hours, High 2 hours

MAKES:
16 servings

SLOW COOKER:
3½- or 4-quart

1 16-ounce can jellied cranberry sauce

⅔ cup ketchup

2 tablespoons lemon juice

1 teaspoon dry mustard

¼ teaspoon ground allspice

1 16-ounce package small cooked smoked sausage links

1 In a 3½- or 4-quart slow cooker combine cranberry sauce, ketchup, lemon juice, dry mustard, and allspice. Stir in the smoked sausage links.

2 Cover and cook on low-heat setting for 4 hours or high-heat setting for 2 hours. Serve immediately or keep warm, covered, on warm setting or low-heat setting for up to 2 hours.

Per serving: 134 cal., 7 g total fat (3 g sat. fat), 20 mg chol., 393 mg sodium, 13 g carbo., 1 g fiber, 4 g pro.

You'll love the combination of spicy and sweet in this updated version of an all-time favorite. Orange marmalade, chipotle peppers, and tomato sauce make up the sauce. Use cocktail wieners or small, smoked sausage links—or some of both.

HOT & SWEET COCKTAIL WIENERS

1   16-ounce package cocktail wieners or small, cooked smoked sausage links

1   8-ounce can tomato sauce

¼   cup orange marmalade or apricot jam

1   to 2 tablespoons canned chipotle peppers in adobo sauce, chopped*

1 In a 1½-quart slow cooker combine cocktail wieners, tomato sauce, orange marmalade or apricot jam, and chipotle peppers.

2 Cover and cook on low-heat setting for 4 hours or on high-heat setting for 2 hours. If no heat setting is available, cook for 3 hours. Serve immediately or keep warm, covered, on warm setting or low-heat setting (if available) for up to 1 hour. Serve wieners with toothpicks.

Per serving: 107 cal., 8 g total fat (3 g sat. fat), 17 mg chol., 295 mg sodium, 5 g carbo., 0 g fiber, 3 g pro.

***NOTE:** Because chile peppers contain volatile oils that can burn your skin and eyes, avoid direct contact with them as much as possible. When working with chile peppers, wear plastic or rubber gloves. If your bare hands do touch the peppers, wash your hands and nails well with soap and warm water.

PREP:
5 minutes

COOK:
Low 4 hours, High 2 hours

MAKES:
16 servings

SLOW COOKER:
1½-quart

These tongue-tingling nibbles are great to munch while you're tailgating, at holiday parties, or as you watch a game or movie on TV.

FIERY CHILI MIXED NUTS

PREP:
10 minutes

COOK:
Low 4 hours

MAKES:
7½ cups

SLOW COOKER:
5- to 6-quart

6	cups mixed nuts
1	egg white
1	tablespoon water
½	cup sugar
½	of a 1.25-ounce package taco seasoning mix (about 2 tablespoons)
¼	teaspoon cayenne pepper

1 Place nuts in a 5- to 6-quart slow cooker. In a medium bowl beat egg white and the water with a whisk until frothy. Stir in sugar, taco seasoning mix, and cayenne pepper. Pour over nuts and stir gently to coat.

2 Cover and cook on low-heat setting for 4 to 4½ hours, stirring once halfway through cooking. Spread on waxed paper or foil, separating into small clusters; let cool. Store in a tightly covered container in the refrigerator for up to 1 week or freeze for up to 3 months.

Per ¼-cup serving : 190 cal., 16 g total fat (2 g sat. fat), 0 mg chol., 180 mg sodium, 9 g carbo., 3 g fiber, 5 g pro.

These no-fuss glazed nuts are super easy. Just place toasted nuts, along with a few other ingredients, in the slow cooker for a couple of hours.

SWEET-SPICED NUTS

1⅓	cups whole almonds, toasted
1⅓	cups pecan halves, toasted
1⅓	cups walnuts, toasted
½	cup sugar
⅓	cup butter or margarine, melted
2	teaspoons apple pie spice or ground cinnamon
½	teaspoon salt

1 Place toasted nuts in a 1½- to 4-quart slow cooker. In a small bowl combine sugar, butter, apple pie spice, and salt. Add to slow cooker; stir to coat nuts.

2 Cover and cook on low-heat setting for 2 hours, stirring after 1 hour. If no heat setting is available, cook for 2 hours, stirring after 1 hour.

3 Stir nuts again. Spread in a single layer on waxed paper or foil; let cool for 1 hour. (Nuts may appear soft after cooking, but will crisp upon cooling.) Store in a tightly covered container for up to 3 days.

Per ¼ cup nuts: 248 cal., 22 g total fat (4 g sat. fat), 10 mg chol., 100 mg sodium, 11 g carbo., 3 g fiber, 5 g pro.

PREP:
20 minutes

COOK:
Low 2 hours

COOL:
1 hour

MAKES:
4 cups

SLOW COOKER:
1½- to 4-quart

For a simple garnish, float a very thin apple slice on each serving of this mulled sipper.

BERRY-APPLE CIDER

PREP:
10 minutes

COOK:
Low 4 hours, High 2 hours

MAKES:
8 (8-ounce) servings

SLOW COOKER:
3½- to 5-quart

4	1-inch-long pieces stick cinnamon
1½	teaspoons whole cloves
4	cups apple cider or apple juice
4	cups cranberry-raspberry juice
	Thinly sliced apple (optional)

1 For spice bag, cut a 6-inch square from a double thickness of 100%-cotton cheesecloth. Place cinnamon and cloves in center of cheesecloth square. Bring up corners of cheesecloth and tie closed with clean 100%-cotton string.

2 In a 3½- to 5-quart slow cooker combine spice bag, apple cider or juice, and cranberry-raspberry juice.

3 Cover and cook on low-heat setting for 4 to 6 hours or on high-heat setting for 2 to 2½ hours.

4 Discard spice bag. Serve immediately or keep warm, covered, on warm setting or low-heat setting for up to 2 hours. If desired, garnish individual servings with thinly sliced apple.

Per serving: 128 cal., 0 g total fat (0 g sat. fat), 0 mg chol., 21 mg sodium, 31 g carbo., 0 g fiber, 0 g pro.

Take your choice of dried fruits—a mix of peaches, apricots, and pears is especially tasty.

SPICED FRUIT TEA

6	inches stick cinnamon, broken*
1	tablespoon crystallized ginger, chopped
4	cups brewed black tea
4	cups orange-peach-mango juice or orange juice
1	cup dried fruit (such as dried peaches, apricots, and/or pears)
	Orange slices
	Sugar or honey (optional)

PREP:
15 minutes

COOK:
Low 4 hours, High 2 hours

MAKES:
8 (6-ounce) servings

SLOW COOKER:
3½- or 4½-quart

1 For spice bag, cut a 6- to 8-inch square from a double thickness of 100%-cotton cheesecloth. Place cinnamon and ginger in center of cheesecloth square. Bring up corners of cheesecloth and tie closed with clean 100%-cotton string.

2 In a 3½- to 4½-quart slow cooker combine tea and juice. Add dried fruit and spice bag to tea mixture in slow cooker.

3 Cover and cook on low-heat setting for 4 to 6 hours or on high-heat setting for 2 to 3 hours. Discard spice bag and dried fruit. Ladle tea into cups. Float an orange slice in each cup. If desired, sweeten to taste with sugar or honey.

Per serving: 56 cal., 0 g total fat (0 g sat. fat), 0 mg chol., 14 mg sodium, 14 g carbo., 0 g fiber, 0 g pro.

*NOTE: To break cinnamon sticks, place in a heavy plastic bag and gently pound sticks with the flat side of a meat mallet.

This warming sipper is ideal for welcoming guests at any wintertime party—especially during the holidays.

CHERRY-APPLE CIDER

PREP:
15 minutes

COOK:
Low 4 hours, High 2 hours

MAKES:
about 12 (8-ounce) servings

SLOW COOKER:
5- to 6-quart

11   cups apple cider or apple juice

1   16-ounce package frozen, unsweetened, pitted tart red cherries

1   cup cherry brandy or apple brandy (optional)

¼   cup honey or packed brown sugar

6   inches stick cinnamon

1   teaspoon whole cloves

1 In a 5- to 6-quart slow cooker combine apple cider, cherries, brandy (if desired), honey, cinnamon, and cloves.

2 Cover and cook on low-heat setting for 4 to 6 hours or on high-heat setting for 2 to 2½ hours. Strain cider through a sieve lined with 100%-cotton cheesecloth.

Per serving: 146 cal., 0 g total fat (0 g sat. fat), 0 mg chol., 7 mg sodium, 36 g carbo., 1 g fiber, 1 g pro.

The word wassail comes from an old Norse phrase meaning "be in good health."
This tea-and-cranberry medley is ideal for toasting the well-being of all your guests.

CITRUS WASSAIL

6	inches stick cinnamon, broken
12	whole cloves (about ½ teaspoon)
4	cups freshly brewed hot tea
4	cups cranberry juice
4	cups apple juice or apple cider
2	cups orange juice
1	cup sugar
¾	cup lemon juice
	Orange and lemon slices

1 For spice bag, cut 6-inch square from a double thickness of 100%-cotton cheesecloth. Place cinnamon and cloves in center of cheesecloth square. Bring up corners of cheesecloth and tie closed with a clean 100%-cotton string.

2 In a 5- to 6-quart slow cooker combine tea, cranberry juice, apple juice, orange juice, sugar, and lemon juice. Add the spice bag to the juice mixture in slow cooker.

3 Cover and cook on low-heat setting for 5 to 6 hours or on high-heat setting for 2½ to 3 hours. Remove spice bag, squeezing gently to remove liquid; discard spice bag.

4 Float orange and lemon slices on individual servings.

Per serving: 138 cal., 0 g total fat (0 g sat. fat), 0 mg chol., 4 mg sodium, 35 g carbo., 0 g fiber, 0 g pro.

PREP:
15 minutes

COOK:
Low 5 hours, High 2½ hours

MAKES:
about 15 (8-ounce) servings

SLOW COOKER:
5- to 6-quart

A perfect starter for your next brunch or tailgate party, this sipper has just the right amount of spice. Garnish with celery sticks or dill pickle spears.

SPICY TOMATO SIPPER

PREP:
10 minutes

COOK:
Low 4 hours, High 2 hours

MAKES:
8 (6-ounce) servings

SLOW COOKER:
3 1/2- or 4-quart

1	46-ounce can vegetable juice
1	stalk celery, halved crosswise
2	tablespoons packed brown sugar
2	tablespoons lemon juice
1 1/2	teaspoons prepared horseradish
1	teaspoon Worcestershire sauce
1/2	teaspoon bottled hot pepper sauce

1 In a 3 1/2- or 4-quart slow cooker combine vegetable juice, celery, brown sugar, lemon juice, horseradish, Worcestershire sauce, and hot pepper sauce.

2 Cover and cook on low-heat setting for 4 to 5 hours or on high-heat setting for 2 to 2 1/2 hours.

3 Discard celery. Serve immediately or keep warm on low-heat setting for up to 1 hour.

Per serving: 46 cal., 0 g total fat (0 g sat. fat), 0 mg chol., 456 mg sodium, 10 g carbo., 1 g fiber, 1 g pro.

Citrus juices turn ordinary green tea into a company-special warmer.

GREEN TEA CITRUS SIPPER

6 cups refrigerated citrus juice blend (100% juice)

4 cups water

1 orange, sliced

8 green tea bags

Honey (optional)

1 In a 5- to 6-quart slow cooker stir together citrus juice blend and the water. Add orange slices. Add tea bags.* Cook on low-heat setting for 4 to 6 hours or on high-heat setting for 2 to 3 hours.

2 Remove tea bags, squeezing gently to remove liquid; discard tea bags. If desired, sweeten to taste with honey.

Per serving: 60 cal., 0 g total fat (0 g sat. fat), 0 mg chol., 39 mg sodium, 16 g carbo., 0 g fiber, 0 g pro.

***NOTE:** For easy removal, allow the strings of the tea bags to hang over the side of the slow cooker and use the lid to hold the tea bags in place inside the slow cooker.

PREP:
10 minutes

COOK:
Low 4 hours, High 2 hours

MAKES:
12 (about 8-ounce) servings

SLOW COOKER:
5- to 6-quart

This fruity wassail is bound to become a holiday favorite. Look for mulling spices in the seasoning or beverage aisle of the supermarket.

HOLIDAY WASSAIL

PREP:
10 minutes

COOK:
Low 5 hours, High 2½ hours

STAND:
5 minutes

MAKES:
10 (8-ounce) servings

SLOW COOKER:
3½- to 5-quart

2   tablespoons mulling spices or 2 mulling spice bags

8   cups water

1   12-ounce can frozen cranberry-raspberry juice concentrate, thawed

1   6-ounce can or half of a 12-ounce can frozen apple juice concentrate (¾ cup), thawed

½   cup packed brown sugar

⅓   cup lemon juice

6   tea bags

Cinnamon sticks (optional)

1 If using loose spices, to make a spice bag, cut a 6-inch square from a double thickness of 100%-cotton cheesecloth. Place mulling spices in center of cheesecloth square. Bring up corners of cheesecloth; tie closed with clean 100%-cotton string.

2 In a 3½- to 5-quart slow cooker combine the spice bag(s), the water, cranberry-raspberry juice concentrate, apple juice concentrate, brown sugar, and lemon juice.

3 Cover and cook on low-heat setting for 5 to 6 hours or on high-heat setting for 2½ to 3 hours. Discard spice bag(s). Add tea bags to the slow cooker.* Allow to stand for 5 minutes. Remove tea bags, squeezing gently to remove liquid; discard tea bags.

4 If desired, garnish individual servings with cinnamon sticks.

Per serving: 148 cal., 0 g total fat (0 g sat. fat), 0 mg chol., 27 mg sodium, 37 g carbo., 0 g fiber, 0 g pro.

*NOTE: For easy removal, allow the strings of the tea bags to hang over the side of the slow cooker and use the lid to hold the tea bags in place inside the cooker.

The cinnamon in this soothing sipper adds a tantalizing accent to the bittersweet chocolate.

BITTERSWEET HOT CHOCOLATE

1   quart half-and-half or light cream (4 cups)

1   quart milk (4 cups)

2   3-inch-long cinnamon sticks

1   12-ounce package bittersweet chocolate pieces or two
    6-ounce packages bittersweet chocolate, chopped

1   tablespoon vanilla

    Marshmallows (optional)

1 In a 3- to 4-quart slow cooker combine half-and-half, milk, and cinnamon sticks. Cover and cook on low-heat setting for 5 to 6 hours or on high-heat setting for 2½ to 3 hours. Discard cinnamon sticks. If necessary, skim "skin" from surface; discard. Stir in chocolate pieces; whisk until chocolate is melted and smooth. Stir in vanilla. Serve immediately or keep warm, covered, on warm setting or low-heat setting for up to 2 hours. Serve warm.

2 If desired, float marshmallows on individual servings.

Per serving: 284 cal., 21 g total fat (13 g sat. fat), 36 mg chol., 68 mg sodium, 23 g carbo., 2 g fiber, 7 g pro.

PREP:
5 minutes

COOK:
Low 5 hours, High 2½ hours

MAKES:
12 (6-ounce) servings

SLOW COOKER:
3- to 4-quart

Serve this coffeehouse favorite, warm or iced, any time of year.

CHAI

PREP:
20 minutes

COOK:
Low 4 hours plus 30 minutes,
High 2 hours plus 30 minutes

MAKES:
about 12 (8-ounce) servings

SLOW COOKER:
3½- to 5-quart

6	inches stick cinnamon
6	slices fresh ginger
1	teaspoon whole cloves
5	cups cold water
1	cup sugar
1½	teaspoons ground nutmeg
½	teaspoon ground cardamom
12	tea bags
6	cups milk

1 For spice bag, cut a 6- to 8-inch square from a double thickness of 100%-cotton cheesecloth. Place cinnamon, ginger, and cloves in center of the cheesecloth square. Bring up corners of the cheesecloth; tie closed with a clean 100%-cotton string.

2 In a 3½- to 5-quart slow cooker combine spice bag, the water, sugar, nutmeg, and cardamom.

3 Cover and cook on low-heat setting for 4 to 6 hours or on high-heat setting for 2 to 2½ hours. Add tea bags* and milk. Cover and cook for 30 minutes more. Remove spice bag and tea bags, squeezing gently to remove liquid; discard spice bag and tea bags.

Per serving: 124 cal., 2 g total fat (1 g sat. fat), 10 mg chol., 57 mg sodium, 22 g carbo., 0 g fiber, 4 g pro.

ICED CHAI: Prepare as directed. Transfer to two 2-quart containers. Cover and chill for 2 to 24 hours. Serve over ice.

***NOTE:** For easy removal, allow the strings of the tea bags to hang over the side of the slow cooker and use the lid to hold the tea bags in place inside the cooker.

MEATS

2

Drizzle some of the sweet-and-tangy cooking juices over the meat on the toasted kaiser rolls.

BARBECUE BEEF BRISKET SANDWICHES

PREP:
15 minutes

COOK:
Low 8 hours, High 4 hours

MAKES:
6 to 8 sandwiches

SLOW COOKER:
3½- or 4-quart

1	2- to 3-pound fresh beef brisket
1	teaspoon chili powder
½	teaspoon garlic powder
½	cup ketchup
½	cup bottled chili sauce
¼	cup packed brown sugar
2	tablespoons quick-cooking tapioca
2	tablespoons vinegar
2	tablespoons Worcestershire sauce
1	teaspoon dry mustard
6	to 8 kaiser rolls, split and toasted

1 Trim fat from meat. Sprinkle chili powder and garlic powder evenly over meat; rub in with your fingers. If necessary, cut meat to fit a 3½- or 4-quart slow cooker. Place meat in slow cooker.

2 For sauce, in a small bowl combine ketchup, chili sauce, brown sugar, tapioca, vinegar, Worcestershire sauce, and dry mustard. Pour over meat.

3 Cover and cook on low-heat setting for 8 to 10 hours or on high-heat setting for 4 to 5 hours.

4 Transfer meat to a cutting board. Thinly slice meat across the grain. Arrange meat slices on roll bottoms. Skim fat from cooking juices. Lightly drizzle some of the cooking juices on meat. Add roll tops.

Per sandwich: 471 cal., 10 g total fat (2 g sat. fat), 87 mg chol., 990 mg sodium, 54 g carbo., 3 g fiber, 39 g pro.

Fresh fennel, tomatoes, olives, and Greek or Italian seasoning transform ordinary beef brisket into an exotic Mediterranean treat.

MEDITERRANEAN POT ROAST

1	3-pound fresh beef brisket
3	teaspoons dried Greek or Italian seasoning, crushed
2	medium fennel bulbs, trimmed, cored, and cut into thick wedges; or 4 stalks celery, cut into ½-inch-thick slices, plus ½ teaspoon fennel seeds
1	14½-ounce can diced tomatoes with basil, garlic, and oregano, undrained
½	cup beef broth
1	2¼-ounce can sliced pitted ripe olives, drained
¾	teaspoon salt
½	teaspoon finely shredded lemon peel
¼	teaspoon black pepper
¼	cup cold water
2	tablespoons all-purpose flour
6	cups hot cooked noodles or rice (optional)

PREP:
25 minutes
COOK:
Low 10 hours, High 5 hours
MAKES:
8 servings
SLOW COOKER:
5- to 6-quart

1 Trim fat from meat. If necessary, cut meat to fit in a 5- to 6-quart slow cooker. Sprinkle meat with 1 teaspoon of the Greek or Italian seasoning. Place meat in slow cooker. Top with fennel wedges or sliced celery and fennel seeds.

2 In a medium bowl combine undrained tomatoes, beef broth, olives, salt, lemon peel, pepper, and the remaining 2 teaspoons Greek or Italian seasoning. Pour over meat and vegetables.

3 Cover and cook on low-heat setting for 10 to 11 hours or on high-heat setting for 5 to 5½ hours.

4 Transfer meat to a cutting board; thinly slice meat. Arrange meat and vegetables on a serving platter, reserving cooking liquid. Cover meat and vegetables; keep warm. Pour cooking liquid into a glass measuring cup; skim off fat.

5 For sauce, measure cooking liquid; add water if necessary to make 2 cups total liquid. Transfer to a small saucepan. In a small bowl combine the ¼ cup cold water and the flour; stir into liquid in saucepan. Cook and stir until thickened and bubbly. Cook and stir for 1 minute more. Serve sauce with meat and vegetables. If desired, serve with hot cooked noodles or rice.

Per serving: 287 cal., 11 g total fat (3 g sat. fat), 82 mg chol., 750 mg sodium, 8 g carbo., 6 g fiber, 37 g pro.

The intriguing blend of hoisin sauce and salsa boosts the flavor of beef brisket to new heights.

ORIENTAL BEEF BRISKET

PREP:
20 minutes

COOK:
Low 10 hours, High 5 hours

MAKES:
8 servings

SLOW COOKER:
5- to 6-quart

1   3- to 3½-pound fresh beef brisket

1   pound baking potatoes, peeled and cut into 1-inch cubes

1   pound sweet potatoes, peeled and cut into 1-inch cubes

½   cup bottled hoisin sauce

½   cup purchased salsa

2   tablespoons quick-cooking tapioca

2   cloves garlic, minced

1 Trim fat from meat. Place baking potatoes and sweet potatoes in a 5- to 6-quart slow cooker. Top with meat. In a small bowl combine hoisin sauce, salsa, tapioca, and garlic. Pour salsa mixture over meat; spread evenly.

2 Cover and cook on low-heat setting for 10 hours or on high-heat setting for 5 to 5½ hours.

3 Transfer meat to a cutting board; slice meat across the grain. Serve cooking liquid and potatoes with meat.

Per serving: 344 cal., 11 g total fat (3 g sat. fat), 103 mg chol., 382 mg sodium, 22 g carbo., 2 g fiber, 38 g pro.

Brisket takes on a lively flavor when you serve it with this horseradish-accented gravy.

BEEF BRISKET WITH BEER AND ONIONS

4	large onions, sliced and separated into rings
2	large red sweet peppers, sliced into rings
1	3½-pound fresh beef brisket, trimmed of fat
1	12-ounce can beer
¾	cup bottled chili sauce
3	tablespoons packed brown sugar
2	cloves garlic, minced
1	teaspoon salt
½	teaspoon black pepper
1	tablespoon prepared horseradish
½	cup cold water
¼	cup all-purpose flour

PREP:
30 minutes

COOK:
Low 10 hours, High 5 hours

MAKES:
10 servings

SLOW COOKER:
5- to 6-quart

1 Place onions and sweet peppers in the bottom of a 5- to 6-quart slow cooker. Top with meat.

2 In a medium bowl combine beer, chili sauce, brown sugar, garlic, salt, and black pepper; pour over meat.

3 Cover and cook on low-heat setting for 10 to 12 hours or on high-heat setting for 5 to 6 hours. Transfer meat and vegetables to a serving platter. Cover with foil and keep warm.

4 Pour 2¼ cups of the cooking liquid into a medium saucepan; stir in horseradish. In a small bowl whisk together cold water and flour until combined; stir into cooking liquid mixture in saucepan. Cook and stir over medium heat until thickened and bubbly. Cook and stir for 1 minute more. Thinly slice meat across the grain. Serve meat and vegetables with gravy.

Per serving: 328 cal., 11 g total fat (4 g sat. fat), 99 mg chol., 616 mg sodium, 20 g carbo., 3 g fiber, 34 g pro.

Orange juice and Dijon-style mustard infuse this slow-cooked brisket with delectable flavor.
Be sure to slice it thinly so you can pile the meat high on the kaiser rolls.

CITRUS CORNED BEEF SANDWICHES

PREP:
20 minutes

COOK:
Low 10 hours, High 5 hours

BROIL:
1 minute + 1 minute

MAKES:
8 sandwiches

SLOW COOKER:
3¹/₂- or 4-quart

1   2- to 3-pound corned beef brisket with spice packet

1   cup water

¼   cup Dijon-style mustard

¼   teaspoon finely shredded orange peel

¹/₃ cup orange juice

4   teaspoons all-purpose flour

8   kaiser rolls, split

6   ounces Muenster cheese, sliced

1 Trim fat from meat. Sprinkle spices from spice packet over meat; rub in with your fingers. If necessary, cut meat to fit into a 3¹/₂- or 4-quart slow cooker. Place meat in slow cooker. In a small bowl combine the water and mustard; pour over meat.

2 Cover and cook on low-heat setting for 10 to 12 hours or on high-heat setting for 5 to 6 hours. Transfer meat to a serving platter. Cover with foil and keep warm. Skim fat from cooking juices. Reserve ¼ cup of the cooking juices; discard remaining juices and whole spices.

3 For orange sauce, in a small saucepan stir together orange peel, orange juice, and flour; gradually stir in reserved cooking juices. Cook and stir until thickened and bubbly. Cook and stir for 1 minute more.

4 Preheat broiler. Thinly slice meat across the grain. Arrange rolls, cut sides up, on a baking sheet. Broil 3 inches from heat for 1 to 2 minutes or until toasted. Remove roll tops from baking sheet. Place meat on roll bottoms. Drizzle about 1 tablespoon of the orange sauce over meat on each roll. Top with cheese. Broil for 1 to 2 minutes more or until cheese melts. Add roll tops.

Per sandwich: 455 cal., 22 g total fat (8 g sat. fat), 78 mg chol., 1,382 mg sodium, 34 g carbo., 1 g fiber, 29 g pro.

If you're looking for good old-fashioned pot roast with a twist, this is it: tarragon-seasoned beef, potatoes, mushrooms, and carrots in a creamy sauce.

SUNDAY DINNER POT ROAST

1	1½-pound boneless beef chuck eye roast, eye of round roast, or round rump roast
	Nonstick cooking spray
3	medium potatoes, quartered lengthwise
1	1-pound package peeled baby carrots
1	4-ounce can (drained weight) mushroom stems and pieces, drained
½	teaspoon dried tarragon or basil, crushed
¼	teaspoon salt
1	10¾-ounce can condensed cream of mushroom soup

1 Trim fat from meat. Coat an unheated large skillet with nonstick cooking spray. Preheat skillet over medium-high heat. Add meat; cook until browned, turning to brown evenly.

2 In a 4- to 5-quart slow cooker combine potatoes, carrots, mushrooms, and tarragon. Place browned meat on top of vegetables. Sprinkle with salt. Pour cream of mushroom soup over all.

3 Cover and cook on low-heat setting for 10 to 12 hours or on high-heat setting for 5 to 6 hours.

4 To serve, transfer meat and vegetables to a serving platter. Serve sauce over meat and vegetables.

Per serving: 327 cal., 9 g total fat (3 g sat. fat), 83 mg chol., 800 mg sodium, 29 g carbo., 5 g fiber, 33 g pro.

PREP:
15 minutes

COOK:
Low 10 hours, High 5 hours

MAKES:
5 servings

SLOW COOKER:
4- to 5-quart

A tongue-tingling mix of spices, garlic, and red wine gives this fork-tender beef fabulous flavor.

SPICED-RUBBED POT ROAST

PREP:
20 minutes

COOK:
Low 11 hours, High 5½ hours

MAKES:
6 to 8 servings

SLOW COOKER:
4½- or 5-quart

1   3- to 3½-pound boneless beef chuck pot roast

1   teaspoon salt

½   teaspoon black pepper

½   teaspoon ground mace

¼   teaspoon ground allspice

⅛   teaspoon ground cloves

6   medium carrots, halved crosswise

2   large onions, cut into wedges

2   bay leaves

2   cloves garlic, minced

⅔   cup beef broth

½   cup dry red wine or beef broth

1 Trim fat from meat. If necessary, cut meat to fit into a 4½- or 5-quart slow cooker. In a small bowl combine salt, pepper, mace, allspice, and cloves. Sprinkle salt mixture evenly over meat; rub in with your fingers. Set aside.

2 In the slow cooker combine carrots, onions, and bay leaves. Place meat on top of vegetables. Sprinkle meat with garlic. Pour broth and wine or broth over meat.

3 Cover and cook on low-heat setting for 11 to 12 hours or on high-heat setting for 5½ to 6 hours.

4 Transfer meat to a cutting board. Using a slotted spoon, transfer vegetables to a serving dish. Discard bay leaves. Slice meat and serve with the vegetables. Drizzle with some of the cooking liquid to moisten.

Per serving: 353 cal., 9 g total fat (3 g sat. fat), 135 mg chol., 695 mg sodium, 14 g carbo., 3 g fiber, 50 g pro.

Serve this hearty roast with plenty of crusty French bread to sop up the garlicky thyme-and-wine-flavored cooking juices.

FRENCH-STYLE POT ROAST

1	3-pound boneless beef chuck pot roast
1	pound carrots, cut into 2-inch-long pieces
1	large onion, sliced
1	4-ounce can (drained weight) sliced mushrooms, drained
2	tablespoons quick-cooking tapioca
¾	cup dry red wine or beef broth
4	cloves garlic, minced
2	teaspoons instant beef bouillon granules
¼	teaspoon dried thyme, crushed
¼	teaspoon black pepper
1	14½-ounce can green Italian beans or cut green beans, drained

1 Trim fat from meat. In a 4½- to 6-quart slow cooker combine carrots, onion, and mushrooms. Sprinkle with tapioca. Place meat on vegetables. In a small bowl combine wine or broth, garlic, bouillon granules, thyme, and pepper. Pour over meat.

2 Cover and cook on low-heat setting for 11 to 12 hours or on high-heat setting for 5½ to 6 hours.

3 Remove meat to a serving platter; cover and keep warm. Stir green beans into carrot mixture. Using a slotted spoon, transfer vegetables to a serving platter. Skim fat from cooking liquid. Serve cooking liquid with meat and vegetables.

Per serving: 375 cal., 9 g total fat (3 g sat. fat), 134 mg chol., 662 mg sodium, 17 g carbo., 4 g fiber, 50 g pro.

PREP:
20 minutes

COOK:
Low 11 hours, High 5½ hours

MAKES:
6 to 8 servings

SLOW COOKER:
4½- to 6-quart

Orange peel brings a hint of citrus to this beef chuck roast that features a trio of fall vegetables: parsnips, acorn squash, and onions.

CANADIAN MAPLE-GLAZED POT ROAST

PREP:
20 minutes

COOK:
Low 11 hours, High 5½ hours

MAKES:
8 servings

SLOW COOKER:
4- to 5-quart

1   2½- to 3-pound boneless beef chuck pot roast

1   tablespoon cooking oil

4   medium parsnips and/or carrots, cut into
   3-inch-long pieces

1   medium acorn squash, seeded and cut into
   1-inch-thick slices

2   small onions, cut into wedges

½   cup pure maple syrup or maple-flavored syrup

3   tablespoons quick-cooking tapioca

2   tablespoons white wine vinegar

2   teaspoons finely shredded orange peel

1   teaspoon salt

¼   teaspoon black pepper

4   cups hot cooked noodles

1 Trim fat from meat. If necessary, cut meat to fit in a 4- to 5-quart slow cooker. In a large skillet heat oil over medium-high heat. Brown meat in hot oil, turning to brown on all sides. Drain off fat.

2 In the slow cooker combine parsnips and/or carrots, acorn squash, and onions. Place meat on vegetables. In a small bowl combine maple syrup, tapioca, white wine vinegar, orange peel, salt, and pepper. Pour over meat and vegetables.

3 Cover and cook on low-heat setting for 11 to 12 hours or on high-heat setting for 5½ to 6 hours.

4 Transfer meat and vegetables to a serving platter. Skim fat from cooking liquid. Pass cooking liquid with meat. Serve with hot cooked noodles.

Per serving: 423 cal., 8 g total fat (2 g sat. fat), 110 mg chol., 400 mg sodium, 51 g carbo., 4 g fiber, 36 g pro.

French onion soup is the secret to the captivating flavor of this no-hassle pot roast.

SAVORY ROAST WITH PEPPERS & ONIONS

	Nonstick cooking spray
1	2½- to 3-pound beef chuck pot roast
1	teaspoon dried thyme, crushed
¼	teaspoon cayenne pepper
1	14½-ounce can diced tomatoes with basil, garlic, and oregano, undrained
1	10½-ounce can condensed French onion soup
1	tablespoon Worcestershire sauce
1	16-ounce package frozen (yellow, green, and red) peppers and onion stir-fry vegetables
1½	cups instant rice

1 Lightly coat a 4- to 5-quart slow cooker with nonstick cooking spray. Trim fat from meat. If necessary, cut meat to fit in slow cooker. Place meat in slow cooker. Sprinkle meat with thyme and cayenne pepper. Add undrained tomatoes, French onion soup, and Worcestershire sauce to slow cooker.

2 Cover and cook on low-heat setting for 8 to 9 hours or on high-heat setting for 4 to 4½ hours.

3 If using low-heat setting, turn to high-heat setting. Add stir-fry vegetables and uncooked rice to slow cooker; stir into mixture. Cover and cook for 30 minutes more.

Per serving: 401 cal., 9 g total fat (3 g sat. fat), 90 mg chol., 2,757 mg sodium, 39 g carbo., 4 g fiber, 38 g pro.

PREP:
10 minutes

COOK:
Low 8 hours, High 4 hours; plus 30 minutes on High

MAKES:
8 servings

SLOW COOKER:
4- to 5-quart

Wine, German-style mustard, and cloves combine in this luscious old world-style pot roast.

BAVARIAN BEEF

PREP:
25 minutes

COOK:
Low 8 hours, High 4 hours

MAKES:
8 servings

SLOW COOKER:
3½- or 4-quart

1   2½- to 3-pound boneless beef chuck pot roast

4   carrots, sliced

2   large onions, chopped

¾   cup chopped kosher-style dill pickles

2   stalks celery, sliced

½   cup dry red wine or beef broth

⅓   cup German-style mustard

½   teaspoon coarsely ground black pepper

¼   teaspoon ground cloves

2   bay leaves

¼   cup beef broth or cold water

2   tablespoons all-purpose flour

     Hot cooked spaetzle or cooked noodles (optional)

     Chopped kosher-style dill pickle (optional)

     Crisp-cooked and crumbled bacon (optional)

1 Trim fat from meat. If necessary, cut meat to fit in a 3½- or 4-quart slow cooker.

2 In the slow cooker combine carrots, onions, the ¾ cup pickles, and the celery. Place meat on top of the vegetables.

3 In a small bowl combine wine, mustard, pepper, cloves, and bay leaves. Pour over meat. Cover and cook on low-heat setting for 8 to 10 hours or on high-heat setting for 4 to 5 hours. Transfer meat to a serving platter. Cover meat with foil to keep warm.

4 For gravy, transfer vegetables and cooking liquid to a 2-quart saucepan. Skim off fat. Discard bay leaves. In a small bowl stir together broth or water and flour. Stir into the mixture in saucepan. Cook and stir over medium heat until thickened and bubbly. Cook and stir for 1 minute more. Serve gravy with meat and vegetables. If desired, serve with hot cooked spaetzle or noodles and top with additional chopped pickle and bacon.

Per serving: 238 cal., 6 g total fat (2 g sat. fat), 84 mg chol., 480 mg sodium, 10 g carbo., 2 g fiber, 32 g pro.

A rich gravy made from cooking juices seasoned with vinegar, mustard, allspice, and cloves is the perfect partner for tender slices of moist beef chuck pot roast.

SPICED BEEF POT ROAST

1	2½- to 3-pound boneless beef chuck pot roast
3	medium onions, sliced into rings
2	stalks celery, bias-sliced
¾	cup water
¼	cup vinegar
1	tablespoon packed brown sugar
1	teaspoon dry mustard
1	teaspoon instant beef bouillon granules
½	teaspoon salt
½	teaspoon ground allspice
¼	teaspoon ground cloves
2	bay leaves
⅔	cup cold water
¼	cup all-purpose flour
	Black pepper (optional)
¼	teaspoon browning and flavoring sauce (optional)

PREP:
25 minutes

COOK:
Low 10 hours, High 5 hours

MAKES:
8 to 10 servings

SLOW COOKER:
4- to 5-quart

1 Trim fat from meat. If necessary, cut meat to fit in a 4- to 5-quart slow cooker. Place onions and celery in the slow cooker. Place meat on top of vegetables. In a small bowl combine the ¾ cup water, the vinegar, brown sugar, dry mustard, bouillon granules, salt, allspice, cloves, and bay leaves. Add to slow cooker.

2 Cover and cook on low-heat setting for 10 to 12 hours or on high-heat setting for 5 to 6 hours. Transfer meat, onions, and celery to a serving platter, reserving cooking juices.

3 For gravy, measure cooking juices; skim off fat. If necessary, add enough water to cooking juices to equal 1½ cups total liquid. Pour cooking juices into a medium saucepan. In a small bowl stir the ⅔ cup cold water into the flour. Stir into juices in saucepan. Cook and stir over medium heat until thickened and bubbly. Cook and stir for 1 minute more. Discard bay leaves. If desired, season with pepper. If desired, stir in flavoring sauce for color. Serve gravy with meat and vegetables.

Per serving: 213 cal., 5 g total fat (2 g sat. fat), 84 mg chol., 350 mg sodium, 9 g carbo., 1 g fiber, 31 g pro.

Black bean garlic sauce transforms ordinary pot roast into an exotic delight. Look for the sauce in the Asian section of your supermarket or at an Asian market.

BLACK BEAN POT ROAST

PREP:
30 minutes

COOK:
Low 9 hours, High 4½ hours; plus 15 minutes on High

MAKES:
6 servings

SLOW COOKER:
4- to 5-quart

1	2-pound boneless beef chuck pot roast
1½	cups water
¼	cup black bean garlic sauce
1	tablespoon sugar
1	teaspoon instant beef bouillon granules
12	ounces fresh green beans, trimmed and cut in 2-inch-long pieces
½	of a medium onion, cut into thin strips
3	tablespoons cornstarch
3	tablespoons cold water
1	medium red sweet pepper, cut into thin strips
	Hot cooked rice

1 Trim fat from meat. If necessary, cut meat to fit into a 4- to 5-quart slow cooker.

2 In the slow cooker stir together the 1½ cups water, the garlic sauce, sugar, and bouillon granules. Stir in green beans and onion. Place meat on top of vegetables.

3 Cover and cook on low-heat setting for 9 to 10 hours or on high-heat setting for 4½ to 5 hours.

4 Transfer meat and vegetables to a serving platter; cover meat and keep warm. If using low-heat setting, turn to high-heat setting. For sauce, in a small bowl combine cornstarch and cold water; stir into cooking juices in slow cooker. Stir in sweet pepper strips. Cover and cook about 15 minutes or until sauce is slightly thickened.

5 Using two forks, separate meat into serving-size pieces. Serve meat over hot cooked rice with the sauce and vegetables.

Per serving: 358 cal., 7 g total fat (2 g sat. fat), 89 mg chol., 471 mg sodium, 36 g carbo., 3 g fiber, 37 g pro.

Slow cook beef short ribs with potatoes, butternut squash, and Brussels sprouts and what do you get? A hearty meal for a hungry family.

COLD-WEATHER BEEF SHORT RIBS

1	tablespoon olive oil
1½	pounds boneless beef short ribs
¼	teaspoon black pepper
1	pound new potatoes, halved
1	pound butternut squash, peeled and cut in 1- to 1½-inch cubes (about 1½ cups)
1	large onion, chopped
3	cloves garlic, minced
1	10½-ounce can condensed chicken broth
2	tablespoons cornstarch
2	tablespoons cold water
1	10-ounce package frozen Brussels sprouts
2	tablespoons prepared horseradish
	Snipped fresh parsley (optional)

PREP:
20 minutes

COOK:
Low 8 hours, High 4 hours; plus 45 minutes on High

MAKES:
4 servings

SLOW COOKER:
5- to 6-quart

1 In a large skillet heat oil over medium-high heat. Add short ribs; cook until browned on all sides, turning to brown evenly. Transfer to a 5- to 6-quart slow cooker. Pour any drippings in skillet over short ribs. Sprinkle short ribs with pepper.

2 Add potatoes, butternut squash, onion, and garlic to slow cooker. Pour chicken broth over all. Cover and cook on low-heat setting for 8 to 9 hours or on high-heat setting for 4 to 4½ hours or until meat is nearly tender.

3 If using low-heat setting, turn to high-heat setting. In a small bowl stir together cornstarch and the cold water. Stir cornstarch mixture and Brussels sprouts into short rib mixture in slow cooker. Cover and cook for 45 to 60 minutes or just until vegetables are tender. Stir in horseradish. Transfer ribs and vegetables to a serving platter. If desired, sprinkle with parsley.

Per serving: 485 cal., 18 g total fat (6 g sat. fat), 98 mg chol., 643 mg sodium, 41 g carbo., 7 g fiber, 40 g pro.

Cajun seasoning lends a touch of bayou flavor to slow-simmered round steak.

CAJUN-STYLE STEAKS

PREP:
20 minutes

COOK:
*Low 8 hours, High 4 hours;
plus 30 minutes on High*

MAKES:
4 servings

SLOW COOKER:
3½- or 4-quart

1   pound boneless beef round steak, cut ¾ to 1 inch thick

Salt

Black pepper

Nonstick cooking spray

1   medium onion, sliced and separated into rings

2   tablespoons quick-cooking tapioca

1½ teaspoons dried oregano, crushed

¾   to 1 teaspoon salt-free Cajun seasoning or blackened steak seasoning*

¼   teaspoon salt

1   14½-ounce can diced tomatoes, undrained

1   8-ounce can tomato sauce

2   small green sweet peppers, cut into strips

2   cups hot cooked brown rice

1 Trim fat from meat. Season meat lightly with salt and black pepper. Cut meat into 4 serving-size pieces. Lightly coat an unheated large skillet with nonstick cooking spray. Preheat over medium-high heat. Brown meat in hot skillet, turning to brown on both sides.

2 Meanwhile, place onion in a 3½- or 4-quart slow cooker. Sprinkle with tapioca, oregano, Cajun seasoning, and the ¼ teaspoon salt. Pour undrained tomatoes and tomato sauce over onion. Top with meat.

3 Cover and cook on low-heat setting for 8 to 10 hours or on high-heat setting for 4 to 5 hours.

4 If using low-heat setting, turn to high-heat setting. Add sweet peppers. Cover and cook for 30 minutes more. Serve with hot cooked rice.

Per serving: 324 cal., 4 g total fat (1 g sat. fat), 64 mg chol., 713 mg sodium, 40 g carbo., 4 g fiber, 30 g pro.

*NOTE: To make your own blackened seasoning, in a small bowl combine ½ teaspoon onion powder; ½ teaspoon garlic powder; ½ teaspoon ground white pepper; ½ teaspoon cayenne pepper; ½ teaspoon black pepper; and ½ teaspoon dried thyme, crushed. Store tightly covered in a cool place for up to 6 months. Makes 1 tablespoon.

The Swiss don't actually make Swiss Steak. The recipe name is believed to be English and likely comes from relating the process of "swissing" or smoothing out cloth between rollers to the pounding and flattening of the meat—a step we've skipped in this slow cooker version.

COUNTRY SWISS STEAK

1¼ pounds boneless beef round steak, cut 1 inch thick

1 tablespoon cooking oil

2 links uncooked bratwurst or other sausage, cut into ¾-inch-thick slices

1 small onion, sliced and separated into rings

2 tablespoons quick-cooking tapioca

1 teaspoon dried thyme, crushed

¼ teaspoon salt

¼ teaspoon black pepper

1 14½-ounce can diced tomatoes with basil, oregano, and garlic, undrained

2 cups hot cooked noodles or rice

PREP:
20 minutes

COOK:
Low 8 hours, High 4 hours

MAKES:
4 servings

SLOW COOKER:
3½- or 4-quart

1 Trim fat from beef. Cut beef into 4 serving-size pieces. In a large skillet heat oil over medium-high heat. Brown beef and bratwurst in hot oil; drain off fat. Place onion in a 3½- or 4-quart slow cooker.* Sprinkle with tapioca, thyme, salt, and pepper. Add beef and bratwurst. Pour undrained tomatoes over mixture in slow cooker.

2 Cover and cook on low-heat setting for 8 to 9 hours or on high-heating setting for 4 to 4½ hours. Serve with noodles or rice.

Per serving: 570 cal., 23 g total fat (9 g sat. fat), 145 mg chol., 1,261 mg sodium, 37 g carbo., 2 g fiber, 50 g pro.

*TEST KITCHEN TIP: Since this tomato mixture is thicker and does have a tendency to burn around the edges, we suggest you use a plastic slow cooker liner for this recipe.

You'll want to use every bit of the devilishly tasty sauce—spoon it over noodles or mashed potatoes. You may even be tempted to lick the spoon!

DEVILED STEAK STRIPS

PREP:
15 minutes

COOK:
Low 7 hours, High 3½ hours

MAKES:
6 to 8 servings

SLOW COOKER:
3½- or 4-quart

2   pounds boneless beef round steak

1   15-ounce can tomato sauce

1   large onion, chopped

1   cup water

3   tablespoons quick-cooking tapioca*

3   tablespoons horseradish mustard

3   cloves garlic, minced

2   teaspoons instant beef bouillon granules

¼   teaspoon black pepper

4   to 6 cups hot cooked noodles or mashed potatoes

1 Trim fat from meat. Thinly slice meat across the grain into bite-size strips. In a 3½- or 4-quart slow cooker stir together tomato sauce, onion, water, tapioca, mustard, garlic, bouillon granules, and pepper. Stir meat strips into onion mixture.

2 Cover and cook on low-heat setting for 7 to 9 hours or on high-heat setting for 3½ to 4½ hours. Serve over hot cooked noodles or mashed potatoes.

Per serving: 360 cal., 5 g total fat (1 g sat. fat), 94 mg chol., 756 mg sodium, 39 g carbo., 2 g fiber, 39 g pro.

*NOTE: For a smoother sauce, grind the tapioca in a coffee grinder or blender.

This hearty, satisfying main dish features beef cubes seasoned with garlic, thyme, and lots of Hungarian paprika.

HUNGARIAN GOULASH

1	14½-ounce can diced tomatoes, undrained
1	6-ounce can tomato paste
2	tablespoons quick-cooking tapioca
4	teaspoons Hungarian paprika or regular paprika
3	cloves garlic, minced
½	teaspoon dried thyme, crushed
½	teaspoon salt
½	teaspoon black pepper
1½	pounds beef stew meat cut into 1-inch cubes
1½	cups chopped onion
1	cup coarsely chopped green sweet pepper
1	8-ounce carton dairy sour cream
	Hot cooked noodles

PREP:
15 minutes

COOK:
Low 10 hours, High 5 hours

MAKES:
6 servings

SLOW COOKER:
3½- or 4-quart

1 In a 3½- or 4-quart slow cooker stir together undrained diced tomatoes, tomato paste, tapioca, paprika, garlic, thyme, salt, and pepper. Add meat, onion, and sweet pepper.

2 Cover and cook on low-heat setting for 10 to 12 hours or on high-heat setting for 5 to 6 hours.

3 In a medium bowl combine sour cream and about ¾ cup of the hot cooking liquid. Stir into mixture in slow cooker. Serve over hot cooked noodles.

Per serving: 415 cal., 14 g total fat (7 g sat. fat), 110 mg chol., 429 mg sodium, 40 g carbo., 4 g fiber, 32 g pro.

FOR A 6- TO 7-QUART SLOW COOKER:
Double all ingredients. Makes 12 servings.

Don't skimp on the standing time. It allows the cheese to melt and the pie to cool just enough that it's ready to eat.

TAMALE PIE

PREP:
25 minutes

COOK:
Low 6 hours, High 3 hours; plus 50 minutes on High

STAND:
20 minutes

MAKES:
8 servings

SLOW COOKER:
3½- or 4-quart

2   pounds ground beef

1   large onion, chopped

2   cloves garlic, minced

2   10-ounce cans enchilada sauce

1   11-ounce can whole kernel corn with sweet peppers, drained

1   4½-ounce can diced green chile peppers, undrained

1   8½-ounce package corn muffin mix

1   cup shredded cheddar cheese

⅓   cup milk

1   slightly beaten egg

1   fresh jalapeño chile pepper, seeded and finely chopped* (optional)

1 In a large skillet cook ground beef, onion, and garlic until meat is brown and onion is tender. Drain off fat.

2 In a 3½- or 4-quart slow cooker combine enchilada sauce, drained corn, and undrained green chile peppers. Stir in meat mixture. Cover and cook on low-heat setting for 6 to 8 hours or on high-heat setting for 3 to 4 hours.

3 In a medium bowl stir together corn muffin mix, ½ cup of the cheese, the milk, egg, and, if desired, jalapeño chile pepper, stirring just until combined.

4 If using low-heat setting, turn to high-heat setting. Stir meat mixture. Drop batter by tablespoons onto meat mixture to make 8 dumplings. Cover and cook for 50 minutes more (do not lift cover). Sprinkle remaining ½ cup cheese over dumplings. Remove liner from slow cooker, if possible, or turn off slow cooker. Let stand, uncovered, for 20 minutes before serving.

Per serving: 474 cal., 24 g total fat (9 g sat. fat), 113 mg chol., 805 mg sodium, 35 g carbo., 1 g fiber, 30 g pro.

***NOTE:** Because chile peppers contain volatile oils that can burn your skin and eyes, avoid direct contact with them as much as possible. When working with chile peppers, wear plastic or rubber gloves. If your bare hands do touch the peppers, wash your hands and nails well with soap and warm water.

For a top-notch taco salad, serve this zesty three bean-and-beef combo over torn mixed greens.

BEEF & BEAN MEDLEY

1	pound ground beef
1	large onion, chopped
6	slices bacon, crisp-cooked, drained, and crumbled
2	16-ounce cans baked beans
1	15-ounce can butter beans, rinsed and drained
1	15-ounce can red kidney beans, rinsed and drained
1	cup ketchup
3	tablespoons vinegar
2	tablespoons packed brown sugar
⅛	teaspoon black pepper
1	8- to 10-ounce bag corn chips or tortilla chips
2	cups shredded cheddar cheese (8 ounces)
½	cup sliced green onions

1 In a large skillet cook ground beef and onion until beef is brown. Drain off fat.

2 Transfer beef mixture to a 3½- or 4-quart slow cooker. Add bacon, baked beans, butter beans, kidney beans, ketchup, vinegar, brown sugar, and pepper. Stir ketchup mixture into beef mixture in slow cooker.

3 Cover and cook on low-heat setting for 4 to 6 hours or on high-heat setting for 2 to 3 hours.

4 Serve over or with corn or tortilla chips. Sprinkle with shredded cheese and green onions.

Per serving: 520 cal., 24 g total fat (9 g sat. fat), 64 mg chol., 1,311 mg sodium, 54 g carbo., 9 g fiber, 28 g pro.

PREP:
25 minutes

COOK:
Low 4 hours, High 2 hours

MAKES:
10 to 12 servings

SLOW COOKER:
3½- or 4-quart

These standout "loose-meat" sandwiches get their firepower from a Scotch bonnet chile pepper and ground black pepper.

HOT & SPICY SLOPPY JOES

PREP:
25 minutes

COOK:
Low 8 hours, High 4 hours

MAKES:
12 to 14 sandwiches

SLOW COOKER:
5- to 6-quart

2	pounds ground beef
4	medium onions, cut into strips
4	medium green sweet peppers, cut into strips
2	medium red sweet peppers, cut into strips
1	cup ketchup
¼	cup cider vinegar
1	fresh Scotch bonnet chile pepper, seeded and finely chopped,* or ¼ teaspoon cayenne pepper
1	tablespoon chili powder
½	teaspoon salt
½	teaspoon black pepper
12	to 14 hoagie rolls or hot dog buns, split and toasted

1 In a very large skillet cook ground beef and onions until meat is brown and onions are tender. Drain off fat.

2 In a 5- to 6-quart slow cooker combine ground beef mixture, sweet pepper strips, ketchup, vinegar, chile pepper or cayenne pepper, chili powder, salt, and black pepper.

3 Cover and cook on low-heat setting for 8 to 10 hours or on high-heat setting for 4 to 5 hours. Serve in rolls or buns.

Per sandwich: 592 cal., 18 g total fat (6 g sat. fat), 48 mg chol., 1,051 mg sodium, 83 g carbo., 6 g fiber, 27 g pro.

*NOTE: Because chile peppers contain volatile oils that can burn your skin and eyes, avoid direct contact with them as much as possible. When working with chile peppers, wear plastic or rubber gloves. If your bare hands do touch the peppers, wash your hands and nails well with soap and warm water.

If your family likes extra spicy spaghetti sauce, make this recipe with hot-style Italian sausage and the 1/4 teaspoon crushed red pepper.

OLIVE-SPAGHETTI SAUCE

1	pound lean ground beef
1	pound bulk Italian sausage
1	large onion, chopped
2	cloves garlic, minced
1	28-ounce can diced tomatoes, undrained
1	6-ounce can tomato paste
1	4½-ounce can (drained weight) sliced mushrooms, drained
½	cup dry red wine or beef broth
½	cup chopped green sweet pepper
½	cup sliced ripe or pimiento-stuffed green olives
2	teaspoons Worcestershire sauce
½	teaspoon sugar
⅛	to ¼ teaspoon crushed red pepper
2	bay leaves
1	pound spaghetti, cooked and drained
	Grated Parmesan cheese (optional)

PREP:
20 minutes

COOK:
Low 7 hours, High 3½ hours

MAKES:
8 to 10 servings

SLOW COOKER:
3½- to 5-quart

1 In a large skillet cook ground beef, sausage, onion, and garlic until meat is brown and onion is tender; drain off fat.

2 In a 3½- to 5-quart slow cooker combine meat mixture, undrained tomatoes, tomato paste, drained mushrooms, wine, sweet pepper, olives, Worcestershire sauce, sugar, crushed red pepper, and bay leaves. Cover and cook on low-heat setting for 7 to 9 hours or on high-heat setting for 3½ to 4½ hours.

3 Discard bay leaves. If necessary, skim fat from sauce. Serve sauce over spaghetti. If desired, pass Parmesan cheese.

Per serving: 582 cal., 25 g total fat (9 g sat. fat), 79 mg chol., 774 mg sodium, 56 g carbo., 4 g fiber, 28 g pro.

All-time favorite sloppy joes take an Italian spin in this slow-cooked version. Serve them with coleslaw or pasta salad on the side.

SLOPPY GUISEPPES

PREP:
30 minutes

COOK:
Low 6 hours, High 3 hours

BAKE:
13 minutes

OVEN:
450°F

MAKES:
10 sandwiches

SLOW COOKER:
3¹⁄₂- or 4-quart

1   pound bulk hot Italian sausage

1   pound lean ground beef

1   large onion, chopped

3   cloves garlic, minced

2   cups purchased tomato-basil pasta sauce

1   6-ounce can tomato paste

1   4-ounce can (drained weight) sliced mushrooms, drained

2   tablespoons balsamic vinegar

10   hoagie rolls, split

1   12-ounce jar roasted red sweet peppers, cut into thin strips

1¹⁄₂   cups shredded mozzarella cheese (6 ounces)

1 In a very large skillet cook sausage, ground beef, onion, and garlic until meat is brown. Drain off fat.

2 In a 3¹⁄₂- or 4-quart slow cooker combine pasta sauce, tomato paste, drained mushrooms, and balsamic vinegar. Stir in meat mixture. Cover and cook on low-heat setting for 6 hours or on high-heat setting for 3 hours.

3 Preheat oven to 450°F. Skim fat from top of meat mixture in slow cooker. Hollow out the bottoms of the hoagie rolls, leaving a ¹⁄₂-inch-thick shell. Place roll bottoms, cut sides up, on a large baking sheet. Place roll tops, cut sides up, on another large baking sheet. Bake one baking sheet at a time for 5 to 7 minutes or until rolls are toasted.

4 Divide meat mixture among hollowed out roll bottoms. Top with roasted red peppers and mozzarella cheese. Bake for 3 to 4 minutes more or until cheese is melted. Top with roll tops.

Per sandwich: 712 cal., 27 g total fat (10 g sat. fat), 73 mg chol., 1,271 mg sodium, 84 g carbo., 6 g fiber, 32 g pro.

FOR 5- TO 6-QUART SLOW COOKER:

Use 1¹⁄₂ pounds bulk hot Italian sausage, 1¹⁄₂ pounds lean ground beef, 2 large onions, and 5 cloves garlic. In a very large skillet cook meat, half at a time, until meat is brown, adding onion and garlic to skillet with the second half of meat. Drain off fat. Continue with step 2, except use one 26- to 28-ounce jar tomato-basil pasta sauce, two 6-ounce cans tomato paste, two 4-ounce cans drained sliced mushrooms, 3 tablespoons balsamic vinegar, 15 hoagie rolls, two 12-ounce jars roasted red sweet peppers, and 2¹⁄₂ cups shredded mozzarella cheese. Makes 15 sandwiches.

Per sandwich: 754 cal., 31 g total fat (11 g sat. fat), 78 mg chol., 1,384 mg sodium, 87 g carbo., 6 g fiber, 33 g pro.

If there are any of these beef-and-pork meatballs leftover, reheat them to serve in hoagie buns for a sensational sandwich. If you like, sprinkle on some shredded mozzarella cheese instead of the Parmesan cheese.

HOMESTYLE ITALIAN MEATBALLS

2	eggs
1/3	cup soft bread crumbs
1/4	cup finely snipped fresh parsley
1/4	cup grated Parmesan cheese
1/4	cup finely chopped onion
1	teaspoon salt
1	clove garlic, minced
1/2	teaspoon crushed red pepper
1	pound ground beef
8	ounces lean ground pork
1	tablespoon olive oil
1	26- to 28-ounce jar marinara pasta sauce
1/2	cup water
	Hot cooked pasta
	Grated Parmesan cheese (optional)

PREP:
30 minutes

COOK:
Low 5 hours, High 2 1/2 hours

MAKES:
6 servings

SLOW COOKER:
3 1/2- or 4-quart

1 In a large bowl beat eggs with a fork. Stir in bread crumbs, parsley, the 1/4 cup Parmesan cheese, the onion, salt, garlic, and crushed red pepper. Add ground beef and ground pork; mix just until combined. Using a scant 1/4 cup mixture per meatball, form mixture into 18 meatballs.

2 In a very large skillet heat oil over medium heat. Brown meatballs in hot oil. Drain off fat. Transfer meatballs to a 3 1/2- or 4-quart slow cooker. Pour marinara sauce and the water over meatballs.

3 Cover and cook on low-heat setting for 5 to 6 hours or on high-heat setting for 2 1/2 to 3 hours.

4 Serve meatballs and sauce over hot cooked pasta. If desired, sprinkle with additional Parmesan cheese.

Per serving: 526 cal., 19 g total fat (6 g sat. fat), 139 mg chol., 1,099 mg sodium, 56 g carbo., 4 g fiber, 31 g pro.

There's no need to dirty a dish. Serve the meat mixture right from the slow cooker.

CHILAQUILES

PREP:
25 minutes

COOK:
Low 4 hours

STAND:
30 minutes

MAKES:
6 to 8 servings

SLOW COOKER:
3½- or 4-quart

FOR A 5- TO 6-QUART SLOW COOKER:
Double all ingredients, except use 3 cloves garlic. Makes 12 to 14 servings.

12	ounces ground beef
12	ounces ground lean pork
1	medium onion, chopped
2	cloves garlic, minced
1	15-ounce can chili beans in chili gravy, undrained
1	10-ounce can enchilada sauce
1	2¼-ounce can sliced pitted ripe olives, drained
½	cup lower-sodium beef broth
1	4.5- to 4.8-ounce package tostada shells, broken, or 4 cups tortilla chips
2	cups shredded Monterey Jack cheese (8 ounces)
	Sour cream, snipped fresh cilantro, purchased salsa, broken tostada shells, and/or tortilla chips (optional)

1 In a large skillet cook ground beef, ground pork, onion, and garlic until meat is brown and onion is tender. Drain off fat.

2 In a 3½- or 4-quart slow cooker combine undrained beans, enchilada sauce, drained olives, and beef broth. Add meat mixture, the package of broken tostada shells, and the cheese. Stir just to combine. Cover and cook on low-heat setting for 4 to 5 hours.

3 Remove liner from slow cooker, if possible, or turn off slow cooker. Let stand, uncovered, for 30 minutes before serving. Serve mixture directly from slow cooker. If desired, garnish each serving with sour cream, cilantro, and salsa and serve with additional broken tostada shells or tortilla chips.

Per serving: 500 cal., 28 g total fat (12 g sat. fat), 96 mg chol., 817 mg sodium, 30 g carbo., 5 g fiber, 32 g pro.

Let's hear it for frozen meatballs. They make this recipe super simple. For a variation, try plain frozen meatballs instead of the Italian-style version.

CREAMY MEATBALLS & VEGETABLES

1   16-ounce package frozen cooked Italian-style meatballs (32), thawed

1   20-ounce package refrigerated red-skinned potato wedges*

1   16-ounce package loose-pack frozen stir-fry vegetables (any combination)

2   10¾-ounce cans condensed cream of mushroom or cream of onion soup

1   cup water

⅛   teaspoon black pepper

½   cup dairy sour cream

PREP:
15 minutes

COOK:
Low 5 hours, High 2½ hours

MAKES:
6 servings

SLOW COOKER:
4- to 5-quart

1 In a 4- to 5-quart slow cooker combine thawed meatballs, potato wedges, and vegetables. In a medium bowl combine mushroom or onion soup, the water, and pepper. Pour over meatball mixture in slow cooker. Cover and cook on low-heat setting for 5 to 7 hours or on high-heat setting for 2½ to 3½ hours.

2 Carefully remove ¼ cup of the cooking liquid from slow cooker. In a small bowl stir the ¼ cup hot cooking liquid into the sour cream. Stir sour cream mixture into mixture in slow cooker.

Per serving: 433 cal., 29 g total fat (12 g sat. fat), 38 mg chol., 1,439 mg sodium, 30 g carbo., 7 g fiber, 15 g pro.

*NOTE: If you prefer, you can substitute 1½ pounds red skinned potatoes, cut into wedges, for the refrigerated potatoes. Precook them in boiling lightly salted water for 6 to 7 minutes or until almost tender.

Have this robust sandwich filling ready in your slow cooker for a quick meal after a busy day.

SLOW-SIMMERED PORK SANDWICHES

PREP:
25 minutes

COOK:
Low 8 hours, High 4 hours; plus 30 minutes on High

MAKES:
10 sandwiches

SLOW COOKER:
3½- or 4-quart

1	2½- to 3-pound pork sirloin roast or boneless pork shoulder roast
	Salt
	Black pepper
½	cup water
3	tablespoons cider vinegar
2	tablespoons Worcestershire sauce
1	teaspoon ground cumin or chili powder
1	recipe Homemade BBQ Sauce or 3½ cups bottled barbecue sauce
10	kaiser rolls or hamburger buns, split

1 Trim fat from meat. If necessary, cut meat to fit in a 3½- or 4-quart slow cooker. Season meat with salt and pepper. In a small bowl stir together the water, cider vinegar, Worcestershire sauce, and cumin or chili powder. Pour over meat in slow cooker.

2 Cover and cook on low-heat setting for 8 to 10 hours or on high-heat setting for 4 to 5 hours.

3 Remove meat from cooker; discard cooking liquid. Using 2 forks, shred meat and return it to slow cooker. Stir in 2 cups of the Homemade BBQ Sauce or bottled barbecue sauce. If using low-heat setting, turn to high-heat setting. Cover and cook for 30 to 45 minutes or until heated through. Serve meat mixture in rolls. Pass remaining Homemade BBQ Sauce or bottled barbecue sauce.

HOMEMADE BBQ SAUCE: In a medium saucepan combine 2½ cups ketchup; 1 cup finely chopped onion; ¼ cup packed dark brown sugar; 3 tablespoons cider vinegar; 3 tablespoons bottled Pickapeppa Sauce or Worcestershire sauce; 3 cloves garlic, minced; and ¼ teaspoon bottled hot pepper sauce. Bring mixture to boiling; reduce heat. Cover and simmer for 15 minutes, stirring occasionally. Use the sauce immediately or let it cool slightly, then transfer to a storage container. Cover and chill for up to 3 days. Makes 3½ cups.

Per sandwich: 426 cal., 9 g total fat (3 g sat. fat), 71 mg chol., 1,143 mg sodium, 55 g carbo., 2 g fiber, 31 g pro.

Teamed with apples, parsnips, sweet potatoes, and onion, this ready-when-you-are pork shoulder is reminiscent of the home-style pot roasts of Pennsylvania Dutch country.

PENNSYLVANIA POT ROAST

1	2½- to 3-pound boneless pork shoulder roast
1	tablespoon cooking oil
6	small parsnips, peeled and quartered
2	small sweet potatoes, peeled and quartered
1	small onion, sliced
1	cup beef broth
½	cup apple juice or apple cider
1	teaspoon dried basil, crushed
1	teaspoon dried marjoram, crushed
½	teaspoon salt
¼	teaspoon black pepper
2	small cooking apples, cored and cut into wedges
½	cup cold water
¼	cup all-purpose flour
	Salt
	Black pepper

PREP:
30 minutes

COOK:
Low 6½ hours plus 30 minutes, High 3 hours plus 30 minutes

MAKES:
6 servings

SLOW COOKER:
4½- to 6-quart

1 Trim fat from meat. In a large skillet heat oil over medium-high heat. Brown meat in hot oil, turning to brown on all sides. In a 4½- to 6-quart slow cooker combine parsnips, sweet potatoes, and onion. Place meat on vegetables. In a medium bowl combine beef broth, apple juice or cider, basil, marjoram, the ½ teaspoon salt, and the ¼ teaspoon pepper. Pour over meat.

2 Cover and cook on low-heat setting for 6½ to 8½ hours or on high-heat setting for 3 to 4 hours. Add apple wedges. Cover and cook for 30 minutes more. Remove meat, vegetables, and apples to a serving platter; cover and keep warm.

3 For gravy, skim fat from cooking liquid; strain liquid through a fine-mesh sieve. Measure 1¾ cups of the cooking liquid; pour into a medium saucepan. In a small bowl stir the cold water into flour; stir into cooking liquid in saucepan. Cook and stir until thickened and bubbly. Cook and stir for 1 minute more. Season to taste with additional salt and additional pepper. Pass gravy with meat.

Per serving: 485 cal., 16 g total fat (5 g sat. fat), 126 mg chol., 492 mg sodium, 45 g carbo., 8 g fiber, 40 g pro.

For a hearty Tex-Mex meal, serve these onion-topped shredded pork sandwiches with sides of refried beans and Spanish rice.

MEXICAN-STYLE POT ROAST SANDWICHES

PREP:
30 minutes

COOK:
Low 10 hours, High 5 hours

MAKES:
8 servings

SLOW COOKER:
3½- or 4-quart

1	3- to 3½-pound boneless pork shoulder roast
4	cloves garlic, thinly sliced
1½	cups vinegar
1	cup fresh cilantro leaves
1	medium onion, cut into wedges
¼	cup water
1	teaspoon dried oregano, crushed
1	teaspoon ground cumin
½	teaspoon salt
¼	teaspoon black pepper
1	tablespoon cooking oil
2	medium red onions, thinly sliced
¼	cup lime juice
8	hoagie buns or kaiser rolls, split and toasted

1 Trim fat from meat. With a sharp knife, make slits evenly on all sides of the meat. Insert garlic slices into slits. Place meat in a 3½- or 4-quart slow cooker.

2 In a blender combine vinegar, cilantro, onion wedges, the water, oregano, cumin, salt, and pepper. Cover and blend until smooth. Pour over meat in slow cooker.

3 Cover and cook on low-heat setting for 10 to 12 hours or on high-heat setting for 5 to 6 hours.

4 Just before serving, in a large skillet heat oil over medium heat. Cook red onions in hot oil about 15 minutes or until tender. Carefully add lime juice to skillet. Cook and stir for 3 to 5 minutes or until lime juice is evaporated.

5 Meanwhile, using a slotted spoon, remove meat from slow cooker and place on cutting board. Shred meat by pulling two forks through it in opposite directions; discard any fat. Transfer shredded meat to a large bowl. Add 1 cup of the cooking liquid remaining in slow cooker, tossing to coat.

6 Divide shredded meat among toasted bun or roll bottoms. If desired, drizzle with additional cooking liquid. Top with cooked red onions and bun or roll tops.

Per serving: 540 cal., 15 g total fat (4 g sat. fat), 110 mg chol., 793 mg sodium, 57 g carbo., 3 g fiber, 42 g pro.

This harvest meal features tender pork shoulder and sausage seasoned with tarragon and fennel, plus a generous helping of fluffy mashed sweet potatoes.

PORK & APRICOTS WITH SWEET POTATOES

2½	pounds sweet potatoes, peeled and cut into 1½-inch chunks
1	3½- to 4-pound boneless pork shoulder roast
1½	teaspoons fennel seeds, crushed
1	teaspoon dried tarragon, crushed
3	cloves garlic, minced
1½	teaspoons salt
1	teaspoon freshly ground black pepper
2	tablespoons cooking oil
12	to 16 ounces kielbasa or other smoked sausage links, halved lengthwise and cut into 2-inch-long pieces
1	14-ounce can chicken broth
½	cup apricot nectar
½	cup dried apricots
	Chicken broth
¼	cup apricot nectar
4	teaspoons cornstarch

PREP:
35 minutes

COOK:
Low 6½ hours plus 30 minutes, High 3 hours plus 30 minutes

MAKES:
8 servings

SLOW COOKER:
6-quart

1 Place sweet potatoes in the bottom of a 6-quart slow cooker. Trim fat from pork roast. In a small bowl combine fennel seeds, tarragon, garlic, salt, and pepper. Sprinkle fennel seeds mixture evenly over pork roast; rub in with your fingers. In a 12-inch skillet heat oil over medium-high heat. Brown pork roast on all sides in hot oil. Drain off fat. Place pork roast on sweet potatoes in slow cooker. Add sausage to slow cooker. Pour the can of broth and the ½ cup apricot nectar over all.

2 Cover and cook on low-heat setting for 6½ to 8½ hours or on high-heat setting for 3 to 4 hours. Add dried apricots. Cover; cook for 30 minutes more.

3 Using a slotted spoon, transfer pork, sausage, and apricots to serving platter. Using a slotted spoon, transfer sweet potato chunks to a large bowl; mash with a potato masher.

4 Strain cooking liquid into a glass measuring cup. Skim fat from cooking liquid. Reserve 2 cups of the cooking liquid (if necessary add additional broth to measure 2 cups total liquid). In a small bowl whisk together the ¼ cup apricot nectar and the cornstarch. In a medium saucepan combine reserved cooking liquid and the cornstarch mixture. Cook and stir over medium heat until thickened and bubbly; cook for 2 minutes more. Serve with pork, sausage, and mashed sweet potatoes.

Per serving: 565 cal., 28 g total fat (11 g sat. fat), 159 mg chol., 1,161 mg sodium, 29 g carbo., 4 g fiber, 47 g pro.

Both root beer and root beer concentrate intensify the color and pleasant sweetness of these hearty sandwiches. Look for the concentrate in the spice section of your supermarket.

SWEET PORK SANDWICHES

PREP:
15 minutes

COOK:
Low 8 hours, High 4 hours

MAKES:
8 to 10 sandwiches

SLOW COOKER:
3½- to 5-quart

1   2½- to 3-pound boneless pork shoulder roast

½   teaspoon salt

½   teaspoon black pepper

2   medium onions, cut into thin wedges

3   12-ounce bottles or cans root beer
     (do not use diet root beer)

1   cup bottled chili sauce

¼   teaspoon root beer concentrate (optional)
     Several dashes bottled hot pepper sauce (optional)

8   to 10 hamburger buns, split (and toasted, if desired)
     Lettuce leaves (optional)
     Tomato slices (optional)

1 Trim fat from meat. If necessary, cut meat to fit in a 3½- to 5-quart slow cooker. Sprinkle meat with salt and pepper. Place meat in slow cooker. Add onions and one bottle or can of the root beer.

2 Cover and cook on low-heat setting for 8 to 10 hours or on high-heat setting for 4 to 5 hours.

3 Meanwhile, for sauce, in a medium saucepan combine the remaining 2 bottles or cans of root beer and the chili sauce. Bring to boiling; reduce heat. Boil gently, uncovered, for 30 to 35 minutes or until desired consistency, stirring occasionally. If desired, stir in root beer concentrate and hot pepper sauce.

4 Transfer meat to a large bowl. Using a slotted spoon, remove onions from cooking liquid and place in bowl with meat. Discard cooking liquid. Using 2 forks, gently shred the meat.

5 To serve, if desired, line bun bottoms with lettuce leaves and tomato slices. Spoon shredded meat and onions onto bun bottoms; spoon on sauce. Top with bun tops.

Per sandwich: 399 cal., 10 g total fat (3 g sat. fat), 92 mg chol., 884 mg sodium, 42 g carbo., 3 g fiber, 33 g pro.

Having a meal ready when you come in the door after a busy day is a welcome relief. This variation uses lentils instead of the traditional beans. If you like, substitute beef bottom round for the pork.

PORK & LENTIL CASSOULET

12	ounces boneless pork shoulder roast
1	tablespoon cooking oil
1	large onion, cut into wedges
2	cloves garlic, minced
2½	cups water
1	14½-ounce can diced tomatoes, undrained
4	medium carrots and/or parsnips, cut into ½-inch-thick slices (2 cups)
2	stalks celery, thinly sliced
¾	cup dry brown or yellow lentils
1½	teaspoons dried rosemary, crushed
1	teaspoon instant beef bouillon granules
¼	teaspoon salt
¼	teaspoon black pepper

PREP:
20 minutes

COOK:
Low 9 hours, High 4½ hours

MAKES:
4 servings

SLOW COOKER:
3½- or 4-quart

1 Trim fat from meat; cut meat into ¾-inch cubes. In a large nonstick skillet heat oil over medium-high heat. Cook meat, onion, and garlic in hot oil until meat is browned. Transfer mixture to a 3½- or 4-quart slow cooker; add the water, undrained tomatoes, carrots and/or parsnips, celery, lentils, rosemary, bouillon granules, salt, and pepper.

2 Cover and cook on low-heat setting for 9 to 10 hours or on high-heat setting for 4½ to 5 hours. Season to taste with additional salt and pepper.

Per serving: 345 cal., 9 g total fat (2 g sat. fat), 55 mg chol., 640 mg sodium, 37 g carbo., 14 g fiber, 29 g pro.

A creamy lime dressing provides a cooling counterpoint to gutsy jerk-seasoned pork.

JERK PORK WRAPS WITH LIME MAYO

PREP:
30 minutes

COOK:
Low 8 hours, High 4 hours

MAKES:
6 to 8 wraps

SLOW COOKER:
3¹/₂- or 4-quart

1   1¹/₂- to 2-pound boneless pork shoulder roast
1   tablespoon Jamaican jerk seasoning
¹/₄   teaspoon dried thyme, crushed
1   cup water
1   tablespoon lime juice
6   to 8 10-inch flour tortillas
6   to 8 lettuce leaves (optional)
1   medium red or green sweet pepper, chopped
1   medium mango, peeled, seeded, and chopped,
    or 1 cup chopped pineapple
1   recipe Lime Mayo

1 Trim fat from meat. Sprinkle jerk seasoning evenly over meat; rub in with your fingers. Place meat in a 3¹/₂- or 4-quart slow cooker. Sprinkle with thyme. Pour the water over meat. Cover and cook on low-heat setting for 8 to 10 hours or on high-heat setting for 4 to 5 hours.

2 Remove meat from slow cooker; discard cooking liquid. Using 2 forks, shred meat; discard any fat. Place meat in a medium bowl. Stir lime juice into meat.

3 If desired, line tortillas with lettuce leaves. Divide meat mixture among tortillas, placing meat in center of each tortilla. Top with sweet pepper and mango or pineapple. Spoon Lime Mayo onto meat on tortillas. Fold up one side of each tortilla; fold in side edges. Roll up to serve.

LIME MAYO: In a small bowl stir together ¹/₂ cup light or regular mayonnaise, ¹/₄ cup finely chopped red onion, ¹/₄ teaspoon finely shredded lime peel, 1 tablespoon lime juice, and 1 clove garlic, minced. Cover and store in refrigerator until ready to serve or for up to 1 week.

Per wrap: 314 cal., 13 g total fat (3 g sat. fat), 48 mg chol., 503 mg sodium, 33 g carbo., 2 g fiber, 16 g pro.

Five-spice powder often blends cloves, fennel seeds, star anise, cinnamon, and peppercorns. You can make it at home with the recipe below or pick some up in the spice aisle of larger supermarkets.

FIVE-SPICE PORK SANDWICHES AU JUS

1   2½-pound boneless pork shoulder roast

1   cup apple juice or apple cider

2   tablespoons soy sauce

2   tablespoons hoisin sauce

1½ teaspoons Homemade Five-Spice Powder
    or purchased five-spice powder

8   kaiser rolls, split and toasted

2   cups shredded napa cabbage

1 Trim fat from meat. If necessary, cut meat to fit into a 3½- or 4-quart slow cooker. Place meat in slow cooker. For sauce, in a small bowl combine apple juice or cider, soy sauce, hoisin sauce, and five-spice powder. Pour over meat. Cover and cook on low-heat setting for 5½ to 6½ hours or on high-heat setting for 3 hours.

2 Transfer meat to a cutting board. Using 2 forks, shred the meat. Skim fat from cooking juices. Divide cooking juices among 8 small bowls. Serve meat on toasted rolls with shredded cabbage. Serve with cooking juices.

HOMEMADE FIVE-SPICE POWDER: In a blender combine 3 tablespoons ground cinnamon, 6 star anise or 2 teaspoons anise seeds, 1½ teaspoons fennel seeds, 1½ teaspoons whole Szechwan peppercorns or whole black peppercorns, and ¾ teaspoon ground cloves. Cover and blend to a fine powder. Store in a tightly covered container. Makes about ⅓ cup.

Per sandwich: 401 cal., 12 g total fat (4 g sat. fat), 94 mg chol., 702 mg sodium, 36 g carbo., 2 g fiber, 34 g pro.

PREP:
25 minutes

COOK:
Low 5½ hours, High 3 hours

MAKES:
8 sandwiches

SLOW COOKER:
3½- or 4-quart

Pork shoulder roast takes on a tropical flavor when rubbed with Jamaican jerk seasoning and simmered with pineapple and green chile peppers.

CARIBBEAN PORK POT ROAST

PREP:
20 minutes

COOK:
Low 8 hours, High 4 hours

MAKES:
8 to 10 servings

SLOW COOKER:
4- to 5-quart

1   3½- to 4-pound boneless pork shoulder roast

2   teaspoons salt-free Jamaican jerk seasoning

½   teaspoon salt

2   tablespoons cooking oil

1   20-ounce can pineapple tidbits (juice pack)

2   4-ounce cans diced green chile peppers, undrained

2   tablespoons quick-cooking tapioca

1   tablespoon packed brown sugar

6   to 7½ cups hot cooked rice

1 Trim fat from meat. Sprinkle Jamaican jerk seasoning and salt evenly over meat; rub in with your fingers. In a large skillet heat oil over medium-high heat. Brown meat in hot oil, turning to brown on all sides. Drain off fat.

2 Place meat in a 4- to 5-quart slow cooker. Drain pineapple, reserving ½ cup of the juice. In a medium bowl combine pineapple, the reserved juice, undrained chile peppers, tapioca, and brown sugar. Pour over meat in slow cooker.

3 Cover and cook on low-heat setting for 8 to 10 hours or on high-heat setting for 4 to 5 hours.

4 Transfer meat to a serving platter. Skim fat from pineapple mixture. Serve meat and pineapple mixture over rice.

Per serving: 547 cal., 18 g total fat (5 g sat. fat), 132 mg chol., 378 mg sodium, 52 g carbo., 1 g fiber, 43 g pro.

For a truly German meal, serve this well-seasoned pork roast and tangy gravy with Bavarian-style sauerkraut, dark rye bread, and a mug of cold beer.

BAVARIAN PORK ROAST

1	1½- to 2-pound boneless pork shoulder roast
2	teaspoons caraway seeds
1	teaspoon dried marjoram, crushed
¾	teaspoon salt
½	teaspoon black pepper
1	tablespoon olive oil or cooking oil
½	cup water
1	tablespoon white wine vinegar
1	8-ounce carton dairy sour cream
4	teaspoons cornstarch

1 Trim fat from meat. If necessary, cut meat to fit into a 3½- or 4-quart slow cooker. In a small bowl combine caraway seeds, marjoram, salt, and pepper. Rub caraway seed mixture over meat.

2 In a large skillet heat oil over medium-high heat. Brown meat on all sides in hot oil. Drain off fat. Place meat in slow cooker. Add the water to skillet; bring to a gentle boil over medium heat, stirring to loosen brown bits in bottom of skillet. Pour skillet juices and vinegar over meat in slow cooker.

3 Cover and cook on low-heat setting for 7 to 8 hours or on high-heat setting for 3½ to 4 hours. Transfer meat to a serving platter. Cover meat with foil and keep warm.

4 For gravy, skim fat from cooking juices; measure 1¼ cups juices (add water, if necessary). Pour cooking juices into a saucepan; bring to boiling. In a small bowl combine sour cream and cornstarch. Stir into cooking juices. Cook and stir over medium heat until thickened and bubbly. Cook and stir for 2 minutes more. Serve meat with gravy.

Per serving: 277 cal., 18 g total fat (8 g sat. fat), 92 mg chol., 398 mg sodium, 4 g carbo., 0 g fiber, 24 g pro.

PREP:
20 minutes

COOK:
Low 7 hours, High 3½ hours

MAKES:
6 servings

SLOW COOKER:
3½- or 4-quart

With a bouquet garni, removing the seasonings from dishes like this slow-simmered pork is a cinch—there's no fishing around for individual pieces. Just use a slotted spoon to remove the pouch of seasonings from the cooking liquid in one motion. A coffee filter makes a handy substitute for cheesecloth.

CARNITAS

PREP:
10 minutes

COOK:
Low 10 hours, High 4½ hours

MAKES:
6 servings

SLOW COOKER:
3½- or 4-quart

FOR 5- TO 6-QUART SLOW COOKER:
Use 4 pounds boneless pork shoulder roast, 2 tablespoons whole black peppercorns, 4 teaspoons cumin seeds, 8 cloves garlic, 2 teaspoons dried oregano, 6 bay leaves, three 14-ounce cans chicken broth, 4 teaspoons finely shredded lime peel, ¼ cup lime juice, and 24 flour tortillas. Makes 12 servings.

Per serving: 397 cal., 14 g total fat (4 g sat. fat), 99 mg chol., 785 mg sodium, 30 g carbo., 1 g fiber, 34 g pro.

1   2-pound boneless pork shoulder roast
    Salt
    Black pepper
1   tablespoon whole black peppercorns
2   teaspoons cumin seeds
4   cloves garlic, minced
1   teaspoon dried oregano, crushed
3   bay leaves
2   14-ounce cans chicken broth
2   teaspoons finely shredded lime peel
2   tablespoons lime juice
12 7- to 8-inch flour tortillas
    Dairy sour cream
    Purchased salsa

1 Trim fat from meat. Cut meat into 2-inch pieces. Sprinkle meat generously with salt and pepper. Place in a 3½- or 4-quart slow cooker.

2 To make a bouquet garni, cut a 6-inch square from a double thickness of 100%-cotton cheesecloth. Place peppercorns, cumin seeds, garlic, oregano, and bay leaves in center of cheesecloth square. Bring up corners of cheesecloth and tie closed with clean 100%-cotton string. Add to slow cooker.

3 Add broth. Cover and cook on low-heat setting for 10 to 12 hours or on high-heat setting for 4½ to 5 hours.

4 Using a slotted spoon, remove meat from slow cooker. Discard bouquet garni and cooking liquid. Coarsely shred meat by pulling two forks through it in opposite directions; discard any fat. Sprinkle meat with lime peel and lime juice; toss to mix. Serve with tortillas, sour cream, and salsa.

Per serving: 396 cal., 14 g total fat (4 g sat. fat), 99 mg chol., 942 mg sodium, 31 g carbo., 1 g fiber, 34 g pro.

This coriander- and cumin-seasoned pork is great served on toasted buns. For a change of pace use it in tacos.

SHREDDED SAVORY PORK

1	2-pound boneless pork blade roast
2	large onions, quartered
3	fresh jalapeño chile peppers, cut up*
1	cup water
8	cloves garlic, minced
2	teaspoons ground coriander
2	teaspoons ground cumin
2	teaspoons dried oregano, crushed
½	teaspoon salt
½	teaspoon black pepper

PREP:
20 minutes
COOK:
Low 8 hours, High 4 hours
MAKES:
8 to 10 servings
SLOW COOKER:
3½- or 4-quart

1 Trim fat from meat. If necessary, cut meat to fit in a 3½- or 4-quart slow cooker. In the slow cooker combine onions and chile peppers. Top with meat. In a small bowl combine the water, garlic, coriander, cumin, oregano, salt, and black pepper. Pour over meat.

2 Cover and cook on low-heat setting for 8 to 9 hours or on high-heat setting for 4 to 4½ hours.

3 Using a slotted spoon, remove meat reserving cooking liquid in slow cooker. When cool enough to handle, shred the meat by pulling two forks through it in opposite directions. Add enough of the cooking liquid to the shredded meat to moisten. Discard remaining cooking liquid.

Per serving: 202 cal., 9 g total fat (3 g sat. fat), 77 mg chol., 229 mg sodium, 6 g carbo., 1 g fiber, 23 g pro.

*NOTE: Because chile peppers contain volatile oils that can burn your skin and eyes, avoid direct contact with them as much as possible. When working with chile peppers, wear plastic or rubber gloves. If your bare hands do touch the peppers, wash your hands and nails well with soap and warm water.

MAKE-AHEAD TIP: Place shredded meat in a freezer container. Cover and freeze for up to 6 months. Thaw overnight in refrigerator before using.

Choucroute garnie (pronounced shoo-KROOT gar-NEE) means "garnished sauerkraut" in French.
The dish traditionally features sauerkraut topped with meats, such as sausage and pork, and potatoes.

CHOUCROUTE GARNIE

PREP:
20 minutes

COOK:
Low 9 hours, High 4½ hours

MAKES:
4 servings

SLOW COOKER:
3½- to 4½-quart

**FOR 5- OR 6-QUART
SLOW COOKER:**
Use 3 small cooking apples,
3 cooked knockwurst, 3 medium
potatoes, 3 medium carrots,
¾ cup chopped onion, 2 bay
leaves, 3 medium smoked
pork loin chops or 12 ounces
cooked ham slice, one 27-ounce
can sauerkraut, ¾ cup water,
¾ cup dry white wine or
apple juice, 1½ teaspoons
instant chicken bouillon
granules, ⅛ teaspoon ground
cloves, and ¼ teaspoon black
pepper. Makes 6 servings.

Per serving: 380 cal., 21 g total fat
(8 g sat. fat), 58 mg chol., 1,923 mg
sodium, 28 g carbo., 4 g fiber, 18 g pro.

2	small cooking apples
2	cooked knockwurst
2	medium potatoes, quartered
2	medium carrots, cut into ½-inch pieces
½	cup chopped onion
1	bay leaf
2	medium smoked pork loin chops, cut ¾ inch thick, or 8 ounces cooked ham slice, cut into pieces
1	14-ounce can sauerkraut, drained
½	cup water
½	cup dry white wine or apple juice
1	teaspoon instant chicken bouillon granules
⅛	teaspoon ground cloves
⅛	teaspoon black pepper

1 Core apples and cut into quarters. Score all sides of knockwurst in a diamond pattern by making shallow diagonal cuts at 1-inch intervals. In a 3½- to 4½-quart slow cooker layer potatoes, carrots, onion, bay leaf, pork chops or ham, sauerkraut, apples, and knockwurst. In a small bowl combine the water, wine or apple juice, bouillon granules, cloves, and pepper; add to slow cooker.

2 Cover and cook on low-heat setting for 9 to 10 hours or on high-heat setting for 4½ to 5 hours. Discard bay leaf.

Per serving: 380 cal., 21 g total fat (8 g sat. fat), 58 mg chol., 1,753 mg sodium, 28 g carbo., 4 g fiber, 18 g pro.

Beer, vinegar, and German-style mustard infuse these chops with a wonderful tang that's typical of old-style German cooking.

GERMAN PORK CHOPS WITH SPAETZLE

2	large carrots, thinly sliced
1	large onion, cut into thin wedges
2	tablespoons quick-cooking tapioca
6	pork rib chops, cut ¾ inch thick
	Salt
	Black pepper
1	cup chicken broth
½	cup beer or chicken broth
¼	cup German-style or coarse-grain brown mustard
2	tablespoons cider vinegar
1	teaspoon caraway seeds
½	teaspoon salt
½	teaspoon dried thyme, crushed
½	teaspoon dried leaf sage, crushed
1	10½-ounce package spaetzle mix
½	cup dairy sour cream
	Snipped fresh parsley (optional)

PREP:
30 minutes

COOK:
Low 5 hours, High 2½ hours

MAKES:
6 servings

SLOW COOKER:
4- to 5-quart

1 Place carrots and onion in a 4- to 5-quart slow cooker. Sprinkle with tapioca. Sprinkle chops with salt and pepper. Place in the slow cooker. In a medium bowl combine broth, beer, mustard, vinegar, caraway seeds, salt, thyme, and sage. Pour over all. Cover; cook on low-heat setting for 5 to 5½ hours or on high-heat setting for 2½ hours.

2 To serve, prepare spaetzle mix according to package directions.

3 Using a slotted spoon, transfer chops and vegetables to a serving platter. In a small bowl stir ½ cup of the hot cooking liquid into the sour cream. Stir sour cream mixture into remaining cooking liquid in slow cooker.

4 Serve chops with spaetzle and sauce. If desired, sprinkle with parsley.

Per serving: 534 cal., 15 g total fat (5 g sat. fat), 138 mg chol., 1,184 mg sodium, 46 g carbo., 3 g fiber, 47 g pro.

Taking the time to brown the pork chops gives them a rich, appetizing brown color that will last through hours of simmering.

PORK CHOPS WITH HERB-TOMATO SAUCE

PREP:
20 minutes

COOK:
Low 7 hours, High 3½ hours

MAKES:
4 servings

SLOW COOKER:
3½- or 4-quart

4   pork rib chops (with bone), cut ¾ inch thick (about 1¾ pounds)

    Nonstick cooking spray

1   small onion, chopped

2   teaspoons quick-cooking tapioca, crushed*

3   cloves garlic, minced

1   teaspoon dried Italian seasoning, crushed

½   teaspoon black pepper

½   teaspoon Worcestershire sauce

¼   teaspoon salt

¼   teaspoon crushed red pepper

2   14½-ounce cans stewed tomatoes, undrained

1 Trim fat from chops. Coat an unheated 12-inch skillet with nonstick cooking spray. Preheat over medium-high heat. Brown chops in hot skillet, turning to brown evenly. Set aside.

2 In a 3½- or 4-quart slow cooker combine onion, tapioca, garlic, Italian seasoning, black pepper, Worcestershire sauce, salt, and crushed red pepper. Add chops. Pour undrained tomatoes over chops.

3 Cover and cook on low-heat setting for 7 to 8 hours or on high-heat setting for 3½ to 4 hours.

4 To serve, transfer chops to a serving platter. Using a slotted spoon, spoon tomatoes over chops. If desired, pour some of the cooking liquid over chops and tomatoes.

Per serving: 241 cal., 6 g total fat (2 g sat. fat), 62 mg chol., 287 mg sodium, 19 g carbo., 4 g fiber, 27 g pro.

*****NOTE:** Crush tapioca with a mortar and pestle or in a spice grinder.

The trio of fennel, Italian seasoning, and balsamic vinegar lends authentic Italian flavor to these meaty chops.

ITALIAN PORK CHOPS

6	pork rib chops (with bone), cut ¾ inch thick (about 3 pounds)
1	large fennel bulb, cut into thin wedges
1	medium onion, chopped
1	teaspoon dried Italian seasoning, crushed
2	cloves garlic, minced
	Salt
	Black pepper
2	14½-ounce cans diced tomatoes with basil, garlic, and oregano, undrained
2	tablespoons balsamic vinegar
1	large zucchini, cut into 1-inch pieces
2	tablespoons cornstarch
2	tablespoons cold water
	Hot cooked orzo
2	tablespoons pine nuts or slivered almonds, toasted

PREP:
25 minutes

COOK:
Low 7 hours, High 3½ hours

MAKES:
6 servings

SLOW COOKER:
5- to 6-quart

1 Trim fat from chops. In a 5- to 6-quart slow cooker combine fennel and onion. Place chops on top of vegetables in slow cooker; sprinkle with Italian seasoning, garlic, salt, and pepper. Pour undrained tomatoes and balsamic vinegar over chops. Top with zucchini pieces.

2 Cover and cook on low-heat setting for 7 to 8 hours or on high-heat setting for 3½ to 4 hours.

3 Using a slotted spoon, transfer chops and vegetables to a serving platter; cover and keep warm. In a medium saucepan stir together cornstarch and the cold water; stir in cooking juices. Cook and stir over medium heat until thickened and bubbly; cook and stir for 2 minutes more. Serve over chops and vegetables. Serve with orzo. Sprinkle with nuts.

Per serving: 396 cal., 10 g total fat (3 g sat. fat), 71 mg chol., 879 mg sodium, 41 g carbo., 3 g fiber, 36 g pro.

Six cloves may seem like a lot of garlic, but slow simmering mellows the cloves for a mild flavor.

GARLIC-SMOTHERED PORK CHOPS

PREP:
25 minutes

COOK:
Low 5 hours, High 2½ hours

MAKES:
4 servings

SLOW COOKER:
3½- or 4-quart

**FOR 5- TO 6-QUART
SLOW COOKER:**
Use 6 pork rib chops (about
3 pounds), 2 pounds Yukon
gold potatoes, 1 pound parsnips
(about 3 medium), 8 cloves
garlic, one 14-ounce can chicken
broth, 3 tablespoons butter,
½ cup half-and-half or light
cream, and 2 tablespoons
parsley (optional). Leave soup
and dip mix amount the same.
Makes 6 servings.

Per serving: 462 cal., 16 g total fat
(8 g sat. fat), 94 mg chol., 924 mg
sodium, 45 g carbo., 6 g fiber, 34 g pro.

4	pork rib chops (with bone), cut ¾ inch thick (about 2 pounds)
½	of a 2.4-ounce package garlic and herb soup and dip mix (1 envelope)
1	pound Yukon gold potatoes, peeled if desired and cut into 1-inch chunks
12	ounces parsnips, peeled and cut into 1-inch chunks (about 2 medium)
6	cloves garlic, peeled
1¼	cups chicken broth
2	tablespoons butter
⅓	cup half-and-half or light cream
	Salt
	Black pepper
1	tablespoon snipped fresh parsley (optional)

1 Trim fat from chops. Place chops on a tray or large plate. Sprinkle all sides of chops evenly with dry soup mix; rub in with your fingers. Set aside (the mix will moisten as the chops stand).

2 In a 3½- or 4-quart slow cooker combine potatoes, parsnips, garlic, and broth. Place chops on top of vegetables in slow cooker. Cover and cook on low-heat setting for 5 to 6 hours or on high-heat setting for 2½ to 3 hours.

3 Transfer chops to a serving platter; cover and keep warm. Drain vegetables, reserving cooking juices. Mash vegetables with a potato masher. Add butter. Stir in half-and-half and, if necessary, some of the reserved cooking juices to make mixture light and fluffy. Season vegetable mixture to taste with salt and pepper. Discard remaining cooking liquid. If desired, sprinkle vegetable mixture with parsley. Serve with chops.

Per serving: 440 cal., 16 g total fat (8 g sat. fat), 94 mg chol., 1,224 mg sodium, 41 g carbo., 5 g fiber, 33 g pro.

You'll find fresh or canned tomatillos in large supermarkets or Mexican food stores.

TOMATILLO BRAISED PORK RIBS

1¼   teaspoons ground cumin

1   teaspoon salt

½   teaspoon black pepper

2   pounds boneless pork country-style ribs

2   medium onions, cut into thin wedges

1   large red sweet pepper, cut into thin bite-size strips

1   fresh jalapeño chile pepper, seeded and finely chopped*

3   cloves garlic, minced

¼   cup water

12   ounces fresh tomatillos, husked and chopped (2½ cups), or one 11- to 13-ounce can tomatillos, rinsed, drained, and cut up

    Hot cooked rice (optional)

    Snipped fresh cilantro (optional)

1 In a small bowl combine cumin, salt, and black pepper. Sprinkle cumin mixture evenly over ribs; rub in with your fingers. Place ribs in a 3½- or 4-quart slow cooker. Add onions, sweet pepper, chile pepper, and garlic to slow cooker. Pour the water over all. Cover and cook on low-heat setting for 10 to 11 hours or on high-heat setting for 5 to 6 hours.

2 If using low-heat setting, turn to high-heat setting. Stir in tomatillos. Cover and cook for 30 minutes more. Using a slotted spoon, transfer ribs and vegetables to a serving platter. Discard cooking liquid. If desired, serve with hot cooked rice and sprinkle with cilantro.

Per serving: 270 cal., 12 g total fat (4 g sat. fat), 96 mg chol., 492 mg sodium, 8 g carbo., 1 g fiber, 30 g pro.

*NOTE: Because chile peppers contain volatile oils that can burn your skin and eyes, avoid direct contact with them as much as possible. When working with chile peppers, wear plastic or rubber gloves. If your bare hands do touch the peppers, wash your hands and nails well with soap and warm water.

PREP:
25 minutes

COOK:
Low 10 hours, High 5 hours; plus 30 minutes on High

MAKES:
6 servings

SLOW COOKER:
3½- or 4-quart

FOR 5- TO 6-QUART SLOW COOKER:
Use 2 teaspoons ground cumin, 1½ teaspoons salt, ¾ teaspoon black pepper, 3 pounds boneless pork country-style ribs, 3 medium onions, 3 medium red sweet peppers, 2 jalapeño chile peppers, 4 cloves garlic, and 1½ pounds fresh tomatillos or two 11- to 13-ounce cans tomatillos. Makes 8 servings.

Per serving: 313 cal., 14 g total fat (5 g sat. fat), 108 mg chol., 554 mg sodium, 11 g carbo., 2 g fiber, 34 g pro.

Quick browning in a skillet seals in natural juices, adding flavor and aroma to the country-style ribs.

RIBS WITH APPLES & SAUERKRAUT

PREP:
25 minutes

COOK:
*Low 7 hours, High 3½ hours;
plus 30 minutes on High*

MAKES:
4 to 6 servings

SLOW COOKER:
4- to 5-quart

1	tablespoon cooking oil
2½	to 3 pounds pork country-style ribs
3	medium potatoes, cut into ½-inch-thick slices
3	medium carrots, cut into ¼-inch-thick slices
1	medium onion, halved and thinly sliced
1	14-ounce can sauerkraut, rinsed and drained
1	teaspoon caraway seeds or fennel seeds
⅛	teaspoon ground cloves
1½	cups apple juice or apple cider
1	medium cooking apple, cored and cut into thin wedges

1 In a large skillet heat oil over medium-high heat. Brown ribs in hot oil, turning to brown evenly on all sides. In a 4- to 5-quart slow cooker combine potatoes, carrots, onion, and sauerkraut. Sprinkle vegetables with caraway seeds and cloves. Top with browned ribs. Pour apple juice over all.

2 Cover and cook on low-heat setting for 7 to 8 hours or on high-heat setting for 3½ to 4 hours.

3 If using low-heat setting, turn to high-heat setting. Add apple wedges. Cover and cook for 30 minutes more.

4 Serve ribs, vegetables, and apples in shallow bowls with cooking juices spooned over all.

Per serving: 467 cal., 16 g total fat (5 g sat. fat), 101 mg chol., 805 mg sodium, 45 g carbo., 7 g fiber, 35 g pro.

Lime juice, green olives, jalapeño pepper, and allspice lend these tender, meaty ribs plenty of Caribbean flavor.

CUBAN COUNTRY-STYLE PORK RIBS

1	14½-ounce can diced tomatoes, drained
1	medium carrot, chopped
1	medium onion, chopped
½	cup pitted green olives, sliced
½	cup dry white wine
⅓	cup raisins
1	tablespoon lime juice
1	fresh jalapeño chile pepper, seeded and finely chopped*
2	cloves garlic, minced
½	teaspoon ground allspice
2	pounds boneless pork country-style ribs
	Snipped fresh cilantro
3	cups hot cooked rice

PREP:
25 minutes

COOK:
Low 8 hours, High 4 hours

MAKES:
6 servings

SLOW COOKER:
3½- to 4½-quart

1 In a 3½- to 4½-quart slow cooker combine drained tomatoes, carrot, onion, green olives, white wine, raisins, lime juice, chile pepper, garlic, and allspice. Add ribs; spoon some of the vegetable mixture over ribs.

2 Cover and cook on low-heat setting for 8 to 9 hours or on high-heat setting for 4 to 4½ hours.

3 Using a slotted spoon, transfer ribs and vegetables to a serving platter; reserve cooking liquid in slow cooker. Sprinkle ribs and vegetable mixture with cilantro. Serve with hot cooked rice. Drizzle with some of the reserved cooking liquid to moisten.

Per serving: 415 cal., 14 g total fat (4 g sat. fat), 96 mg chol., 795 mg sodium, 35 g carbo., 1 g fiber, 32 g pro.

*NOTE: Because chile peppers contain volatile oils that can burn your skin and eyes, avoid direct contact with them as much as possible. When working with chile peppers, wear plastic or rubber gloves. If your bare hands do touch the peppers, wash your hands and nails well with soap and warm water.

FOR 5- TO 6-QUART SLOW COOKER:
Use 2 cans drained diced tomatoes, 2 carrots, 2 onions, ¾ cup olives, ½ cup raisins, and 3 to 3½ pounds boneless pork country-style ribs. (Do not increase wine, lime juice, jalapeño chile pepper, garlic, or allspice.) Serve with 4 cups hot cooked rice. Makes 8 servings.

Per serving: 458 cal., 15 g total fat (5 g sat. fat), 108 mg chol., 826 mg sodium, 38 g carbo., 2 g fiber, 36 g pro.

Convenient chili sauce, apricot preserves, and canned chipotle chile peppers make this fiery barbecue sauce easy to stir together.

APRICOT CHIPOTLE PORK RIBS

PREP:
10 minutes

BROIL:
10 minutes

COOK:
Low 6 hours, High 3 hours

MAKES:
6 servings

SLOW COOKER:
4- to 5-quart

3	pounds pork loin back ribs
	Salt
	Black pepper
½	cup bottled chili sauce
½	cup apricot preserves
2	tablespoons packed brown sugar
1	to 2 canned chipotle chile peppers in adobo sauce, chopped*

1 Preheat broiler. Cut ribs into 2- or 3-rib portions. Sprinkle lightly with salt and black pepper. Place ribs on the rack of an unheated broiler pan. Broil ribs 5 to 6 inches from the heat about 10 minutes or until browned, turning once. Transfer ribs to a 4- to 5-quart slow cooker.

2 In a small bowl combine chili sauce, apricot preserves, brown sugar, and chipotle peppers. Pour over ribs in slow cooker. Cover and cook on low-heat setting for 6 to 7 hours or on high-heat setting for 3 to 3½ hours.

3 Remove ribs to a serving platter. Transfer sauce to a small bowl; skim fat from sauce. Pass sauce with ribs.

Per serving: 314 cal., 11 g total fat (4 g sat. fat), 81 mg chol., 472 mg sodium, 27 g carbo., 2 g fiber, 25 g pro.

*NOTE: Because chile peppers contain volatile oils that can burn your skin and eyes, avoid direct contact with them as much as possible. When working with chile peppers, wear plastic or rubber gloves. If your bare hands do touch the peppers, wash your hands and nails well with soap and warm water.

Two-rib pieces cook evenly while simmering in the pineapple-soy sauce mixture and are easier to serve.

KOREAN-STYLE PORK RIBS

3   pounds pork baby back ribs

Salt

Black pepper

1   12-ounce jar pineapple preserves

½   cup unsweetened pineapple juice

2   tablespoons grated fresh ginger
or 2 teaspoons ground ginger

2   tablespoons soy sauce

3   cloves garlic, minced

1 Preheat broiler. Cut ribs into two-rib portions. Season ribs with salt and pepper. Place ribs on the unheated rack of a broiler pan. Broil 6 inches from the heat about 10 minutes or until brown, turning once. Transfer ribs to a 4- to 5-quart slow cooker.

2 In a medium bowl combine pineapple preserves, pineapple juice, ginger, soy sauce, and garlic. Pour sauce over ribs. Cover and cook on low-heat setting for 6 to 7 hours or on high-heat setting for 3 to 3½ hours.

3 Transfer ribs to a serving platter. Skim fat from cooking liquid. Drizzle some of the cooking liquid over ribs before serving.

Per serving: 816 cal., 54 g total fat (20 g sat. fat), 184 mg chol., 544 mg sodium, 43 g carbo., 1 g fiber, 38 g pro.

PREP:
10 minutes

BROIL:
10 minutes

COOK:
Low 6 hours, High 3 hours

MAKES:
6 servings

SLOW COOKER:
4- to 5-quart

Broil the ribs for a few minutes before adding them to the slow cooker to give them a rich, brown color.

BLACKBERRY-GLAZED PORK RIBS

PREP:
20 minutes

BROIL:
10 minutes

COOK:
Low 6 hours, High 3 hours

MAKES:
4 servings

SLOW COOKER:
3¹/₂- or 4-quart

Nonstick cooking spray

2 pounds pork baby back ribs

2 tablespoons herbes de Provence

¹/₂ teaspoon salt

¹/₄ teaspoon black pepper

1 10-ounce jar blackberry spreadable fruit

2 tablespoons Dijon-style mustard

1 tablespoon red wine vinegar

1 tablespoon blackberry-flavored brandy (optional)

1 Preheat broiler. Coat a 3¹/₂- or 4-quart slow cooker with nonstick cooking spray; set aside. Cut ribs into 2- to 3-rib portions. In a small bowl combine herbes de Provence, salt, and pepper. Sprinkle evenly over both sides of ribs; rub in with your fingers. Place ribs on the unheated rack of a broiler pan. Broil 6 inches from the heat about 10 minutes or until browned, turning once. Transfer ribs to prepared slow cooker.

2 In a medium bowl combine spreadable fruit, mustard, vinegar, and, if desired, brandy. Pour over ribs. Cover and cook on low-heat setting for 6 to 7 hours or on high-heat setting for 3 to 3¹/₂ hours.

3 To serve, transfer ribs to a serving platter. Pour cooking liquid into a small bowl. Skim off fat. Serve cooking liquid with ribs.

Per serving: 800 cal., 53 g total fat (20 g sat. fat), 184 mg chol., 641 mg sodium, 45 g carbo., 1 g fiber, 39 g pro.

Reminiscent of mu shu pork, this roll-up features tender pork simmered with cabbage, shiitake mushrooms, and a soy sauce-and-ginger cooking sauce.

ASIAN PORK & CABBAGE ROLL-UPS

2	pounds boneless pork shoulder
4	cups coarsely chopped cabbage
1	cup chicken broth
1½	cups sliced fresh shiitake mushrooms
2	tablespoons soy sauce
1	tablespoon dry sherry
1	tablespoon grated fresh ginger or 1 teaspoon ground ginger
2	cloves garlic, minced
½	teaspoon toasted sesame oil
¼	teaspoon crushed red pepper
12	7- to 8-inch flour tortillas
½	cup hoisin sauce and/or plum sauce
½	cup sliced green onions

1 Trim fat from meat. Cut meat into 1-inch pieces. In a 4- to 5-quart slow cooker combine meat, cabbage, broth, mushrooms, soy sauce, sherry, ginger, garlic, sesame oil, and crushed red pepper. Cover and cook on low-heat setting for 7 to 8 hours or on high-heat setting for 3½ to 4 hours.

2 Spread flour tortillas with hoisin or plum sauce. Using a slotted spoon, remove meat, cabbage, and mushrooms from slow cooker; discard cooking juices. Divide meat, cabbage, and mushrooms among tortillas. Sprinkle with sliced green onions. Roll up tortillas.

Per serving: 455 cal., 15 g total fat (4 g sat. fat), 98 mg chol., 1,115 mg sodium, 40 g carbo., 3 g fiber, 37 g pro.

PREP:
30 minutes

COOK:
Low 7 hours, High 3½ hours

MAKES:
6 servings

SLOW COOKER:
4- to 5-quart

Serve these fruity meatballs with mashed potatoes and steamed vegetables for a complete meal.

SWEET & SASSY MEATBALLS

PREP:
30 minutes

COOK:
Low 5 hours, High 2½ hours

MAKES:
8 to 10 servings

SLOW COOKER:
3½- or 4-quart

8   slices bacon

2   slightly beaten eggs

½   cup fine dry bread crumbs

½   cup finely chopped onion

3   cloves garlic, minced

¼   teaspoon salt

2   pounds lean ground pork

½   of a 16-ounce can or one 8-ounce can
     jellied cranberry sauce (1 cup)

1   cup bottled barbecue sauce

1 In a 12-inch skillet cook bacon until crisp. Drain on paper towels; crumble bacon and set aside. Drain off all but 1 tablespoon of the bacon drippings; set skillet aside.

2 For meatballs, in a large bowl combine crumbled bacon, eggs, bread crumbs, onion, garlic, and salt. Add ground pork; mix well. Shape into 36 meatballs (each about 1½-inch diameter).

3 Brown meatballs, half at a time, in reserved bacon drippings. Drain meatballs on paper towels. Transfer meatballs to a 3½- or 4-quart slow cooker.

4 In a medium bowl combine cranberry sauce and barbecue sauce. Pour over meatballs in slow cooker. Cover and cook on low-heat setting for 5 to 6 hours or on high-heat setting for 2½ to 3 hours.

Per serving: 308 cal., 15 g total fat (6 g sat. fat), 116 mg chol., 756 mg sodium, 20 g carbo., 1 g fiber, 20 g pro.

Bring a taste of the bayou to your dinner table with this slow-simmering version of a Cajun classic.

RED BEANS & RICE

1 cup dry small red beans or red kidney beans

2 cooked smoked pork hocks

12 ounces cooked andouille sausage or cooked smoked sausage links, cut in ½-inch pieces

3 cups reduced-sodium chicken broth

1 medium red sweet pepper, chopped

2 stalks celery, chopped

1 medium onion, chopped

3 cloves garlic, minced

2 tablespoons tomato paste

1 tablespoon Cajun seasoning

Several drops bottled hot pepper sauce

1⅓ cups instant white rice

PREP:
20 minutes

STAND:
1 hour

COOK:
Low 9 hours, High 4½ hours; plus 30 minutes on High

MAKES:
6 to 8 servings

SLOW COOKER:
4- to 5-quart

1 Rinse beans. In a large saucepan combine beans and 6 cups water. Bring to boiling; reduce heat. Simmer, uncovered, for 10 minutes. Remove from heat. Cover and let stand for 1 hour. Drain and rinse beans.

2 In a 4- to 5-quart slow cooker combine beans, pork hocks, sausage, broth, sweet pepper, celery, onion, garlic, tomato paste, Cajun seasoning, and bottled hot pepper sauce. Cover and cook on low-heat setting for 9 to 11 hours or on high-heat setting for 4½ to 5½ hours.

3 Remove pork hocks. When cool enough to handle, cut meat off bones; cut meat into bite-size pieces. Discard bones. Stir meat and uncooked instant rice into bean mixture in slow cooker. If using low-heat setting, turn to high-heat setting. Cover and cook for 30 minutes more.

Per serving: 336 cal., 7 g total fat (2 g sat. fat), 59 mg chol., 1,013 mg sodium, 44 g carbo., 6 g fiber, 26 g pro.

Roasted sweet peppers infuse these tender chops with a smoky, slightly sweet flavor.

MEDITERRANEAN LAMB CHOPS

PREP:
20 minutes

COOK:
Low 5 hours, High 2½ hours

MAKES:
6 servings

SLOW COOKER:
4- to 5-quart

6   lamb loin chops, cut 1½ inches thick

1   26- to 28-ounce jar garlic and onion pasta sauce

1   19-ounce can white kidney beans (cannellini beans), drained

1   cup red onion cut into thin wedges

½   cup pitted kalamata olives, halved

½   cup bottled roasted red sweet peppers, cut into strips

2   tablespoons balsamic vinegar

2   teaspoons snipped fresh rosemary

Hot cooked orzo or rice

1 Trim fat from chops. Arrange chops on the bottom of a 4- to 5-quart slow cooker. In a medium bowl combine pasta sauce, beans, red onion, olives, roasted peppers, balsamic vinegar, and rosemary. Pour over chops in slow cooker.

2 Cover and cook on low-heat setting for 5 to 6 hours or on high-heat setting for 2½ to 3 hours.

3 Serve chops and sauce over hot cooked orzo or rice.

Per serving: 358 cal., 12 g total fat (4 g sat. fat), 70 mg chol., 829 mg sodium, 36 g carbo., 8 g fiber, 30 g pro.

You'll find diced tomatoes with green chile peppers along with the other canned tomato products or in the Mexican-food section of the supermarket.

SAUCY LAMB SHANKS

1	14½-ounce can diced tomatoes and green chile peppers, undrained
1	cup beef broth
1	large onion, chopped
3	cloves garlic, minced
½	cup golden raisins
½	cup dry red wine
3	tablespoons quick-cooking tapioca
2	tablespoons honey
2	teaspoons ground cumin
½	teaspoon salt
½	teaspoon cayenne pepper
¼	teaspoon ground cinnamon
4	meaty lamb shanks* (about 4 pounds)
	Hot cooked rice
	Snipped fresh cilantro

1 In a 5- to 6-quart slow cooker combine undrained tomatoes and green chile peppers, broth, onion, garlic, raisins, wine, tapioca, honey, cumin, salt, cayenne pepper, and cinnamon. Add lamb shanks to slow cooker, turning to coat.

2 Cover and cook on low-heat setting for 10 to 11 hours or on high-heat setting for 5 to 5½ hours.

3 Remove lamb shanks from slow cooker; keep warm. Skim fat from sauce in slow cooker. Serve lamb shanks and sauce with hot cooked rice. Sprinkle with snipped cilantro.

Per serving: 417 cal., 5 g total fat (2 g sat. fat), 127 mg chol., 971 mg sodium, 43 g carbo., 4 g fiber, 43 g pro.

*NOTE: Ask the butcher to halve the lamb shanks crosswise to make them fit more easily into the slow cooker.

PREP:
20 minutes

COOK:
Low 10 hours, High 5 hours

MAKES:
4 servings

SLOW COOKER:
5- to 6-quart

This meaty fire-roasted tomato sauce owes its zesty kick to crushed red pepper. If you like milder foods, use only ¼ teaspoon crushed red pepper rather than the ½ teaspoon called for in the recipe.

PASTA WITH LAMB

PREP:
20 minutes

COOK:
*Low 8 hours plus 5 minutes,
High 4½ hours plus 5 minutes*

MAKES:
8 servings

SLOW COOKER:
3½- or 4-quart

**FOR 5- TO 6-QUART
SLOW COOKER:**
Use 1½ pounds lean boneless lamb, three 14½-ounce cans diced tomatoes, 1 cup tomato paste, 1½ cups shredded carrot, 1 large onion, ½ cup dry white wine, 5 cloves garlic, 1½ teaspoons salt, 1½ teaspoons dried rosemary, 1½ teaspoons dried oregano, ¾ teaspoon crushed red pepper, and 1½ cups frozen peas. Makes 12 servings.

Per serving: 355 cal., 3 g total fat (1 g sat. fat), 36 mg chol., 602 mg sodium, 57 g carbo., 4 g fiber, 22 g pro.

1   pound lean boneless lamb
2   14½-ounce cans fire-roasted diced tomatoes or regular diced tomatoes, undrained
1   6-ounce can tomato paste
1   cup shredded carrots
1   medium onion, chopped
⅓   cup dry white wine
3   cloves garlic, minced
1   teaspoon salt
1   teaspoon dried rosemary, crushed
1   teaspoon dried oregano, crushed
½   teaspoon crushed red pepper
1   cup loose-pack frozen peas
    Hot cooked linguine
    Finely shredded Parmesan cheese

1 Trim fat from lamb. Cut lamb into ¾-inch pieces. In a 3½- or 4-quart slow cooker combine lamb, undrained tomatoes, tomato paste, carrots, onion, wine, garlic, salt, rosemary, oregano, and crushed red pepper.

2 Cover and cook on low-heat setting for 8 to 9 hours or on high-heat setting for 4½ to 5 hours.

3 Stir in frozen peas. Cover and cook for 5 minutes more. Serve sauce over hot cooked linguine; sprinkle with Parmesan cheese.

Per serving: 353 cal., 3 g total fat (1 g sat. fat), 36 mg chol., 601 mg sodium, 57 g carbo., 4 g fiber, 22 g pro.

Chutney is a condiment often used in Indian cooking. It's made of chopped fresh fruit (mango is a classic), vegetables, and spices, and often is enlivened by hot peppers, fresh ginger, and/or vinegar. Look for it in the gourmet section or the condiment aisle of your supermarket.

CHUTNEY-SAUCED LAMB

1	tablespoon cooking oil
1½	pounds lean lamb stew meat cut into 1-inch pieces
1	20-ounce can pineapple chunks, drained
2	cups loose-pack frozen small whole onions
1	9-ounce jar fruit chutney
½	cup mixed dried fruit bits
1	tablespoon quick-cooking tapioca
1	tablespoon balsamic vinegar
1	teaspoon finely shredded lemon peel
3	cups hot cooked couscous or rice

1 In a large skillet heat oil over medium-high heat. Brown meat, half at a time, in hot oil. Drain off fat.

2 Transfer meat to a 3½- or 4-quart slow cooker. Stir in pineapple chunks, onions, chutney, dried fruit bits, tapioca, balsamic vinegar, and lemon peel.

3 Cover and cook on low-heat setting for 6 to 8 hours or on high-heat setting for 3 to 4 hours. Serve meat mixture with hot cooked couscous or rice.

Per serving: 413 cal., 6 g total fat (2 g sat. fat), 72 mg chol., 118 mg sodium, 63 g carbo., 4 g fiber, 27 g pro.

PREP:
20 minutes

COOK:
Low 6 hours, High 3 hours

MAKES:
6 servings

SLOW COOKER:
3½- or 4-quart

If you'd rather, use ground beef, pork, or turkey instead of the lamb in this lively bean medley.

LAMB-SAUSAGE CASSOULET

PREP:
20 minutes

COOK:
Low 5 hours, High 2½ hours

MAKES:
6 servings

SLOW COOKER:
4- to 5-quart

1	pound lean ground lamb
¾	cup chopped onion
1	pound cooked smoked Polish sausage, cut into ½-inch-thick slices
3	15-ounce cans Great Northern beans, rinsed and drained
1	8-ounce can tomato sauce
¾	cup chicken broth
¼	cup dry white wine or chicken broth
2	tablespoons quick-cooking tapioca
2	bay leaves
1	clove garlic, minced
½	teaspoon dried thyme, crushed
1	tablespoon snipped fresh parsley

1 In a large skillet cook ground lamb and onion until lamb is browned and onion is tender; drain well.

2 In a 4- to 5-quart slow cooker combine lamb mixture, sausage slices, beans, tomato sauce, broth, wine, tapioca, bay leaves, garlic, and thyme. Cover and cook on low-heat setting for 5 to 6 hours or on high-heat setting for 2½ to 3 hours.

3 Discard bay leaves. Sprinkle lamb-bean mixture with parsley.

Per serving: 745 cal., 35 g total fat (13 g sat. fat), 102 mg chol., 1,480 mg sodium, 57 g carbo., 12 g fiber, 47 g pro.

POULTRY

3

For a satisfying meal, serve these moist, tender hens with mashed potatoes and cooked broccoli or asparagus spears.

CHERRY-SAUCED CORNISH HENS

PREP:
20 minutes

COOK:
Low 5 hours

MAKES:
4 servings

SLOW COOKER:
5- to 6-quart

2	1½-pound Cornish game hens, thawed and halved
½	cup seedless raspberry preserves
¼	cup bottled chili sauce
2	tablespoons balsamic vinegar
1	tablespoon cornstarch
1	tablespoon cold water
¼	cup snipped dried tart cherries

1 Place hens, skin sides up, in a 5- to 6-quart slow cooker. In a small bowl combine raspberry preserves, chili sauce, and balsamic vinegar; spoon over hens.

2 Cover and cook on low-heat setting for 5 to 5½ hours.

3 Transfer hens to a serving platter. Strain cooking juices, reserving 1⅓ cups of the juices. In a small saucepan combine cornstarch and the cold water; stir in reserved cooking juices and dried cherries. Cook and stir until thickened and bubbly; cook and stir for 2 minutes more. Serve sauce over hens.

Per serving: 568 cal., 27 g total fat (7 g sat. fat), 208 mg chol., 318 mg sodium, 41 g carbo., 2 g fiber, 36 g pro.

This spicy sauce, traditionally made with chiles and chocolate, is a treat for the taste buds. For a more traditional garnish, sprinkle with toasted pepitas (pumpkin seeds) instead of the almonds.

MOLE WITH CHICKEN & RICE

1	14½-ounce can diced tomatoes, undrained
1	medium onion, chopped
¼	cup slivered almonds, toasted
3	cloves garlic, quartered
2	canned jalapeño chile peppers, drained
3	tablespoons unsweetened cocoa powder
3	tablespoons raisins
1	tablespoon sesame seeds
1	teaspoon sugar
¼	teaspoon salt
¼	teaspoon ground cinnamon
⅛	teaspoon ground nutmeg
⅛	teaspoon ground coriander
2	tablespoons quick-cooking tapioca
1	2½- to 3-pound broiler-fryer chicken, cut up and skinned
2	tablespoons slivered almonds, toasted
2	to 3 cups hot cooked rice

1 For mole sauce, in a blender or food processor combine undrained tomatoes, onion, the ¼ cup almonds, the garlic, jalapeño chile peppers, cocoa powder, raisins, sesame seeds, sugar, salt, cinnamon, nutmeg, and coriander. Cover and blend or process until tomato mixture is a coarse puree.

2 Place tapioca in a 3½- or 4-quart slow cooker. Add chicken; pour mole sauce over. Cover and cook on low-heat setting for 9 to 11 hours or on high-heat setting for 4½ to 5½ hours.

3 Transfer chicken to a serving platter. Stir sauce; pour sauce over chicken. Sprinkle with the 2 tablespoons almonds. Serve with hot cooked rice.

Per serving: 448 cal., 23 g total fat (5 g sat. fat), 99 mg chol., 586 mg sodium, 24 g carbo., 4 g fiber, 36 g pro.

PREP:
25 minutes

COOK:
Low 9 hours, High 4½ hours

MAKES:
4 to 6 servings

SLOW COOKER:
3½- or 4-quart

Serve a tossed salad and crusty Italian bread with this creamy chicken and you have a first-rate meal that requires little work.

DRIED TOMATO CHICKEN ALFREDO

PREP:
15 minutes

COOK:
Low 5½ hours plus 30 minutes, High 3 hours plus 30 minutes

MAKES:
4 servings

SLOW COOKER:
3½- or 4-quart

1	medium onion, halved and thinly sliced
2½	pounds meaty chicken pieces (breast halves, thighs, and/or drumsticks), skinned
	Salt
	Black pepper
½	cup dried tomatoes (not oil-packed), cut into strips or chopped
1	4-ounce can (drained weight) sliced mushrooms, drained
1	16-ounce jar light Parmesan Alfredo pasta sauce
1	9-ounce package frozen artichoke hearts, thawed and drained
	Hot cooked pasta
1	ounce Parmesan cheese, shaved

1 Place onion in a 3½- or 4-quart slow cooker; top with chicken. Sprinkle chicken lightly with salt and pepper. Top chicken with dried tomatoes and drained mushrooms; pour Alfredo sauce over mixture in slow cooker.

2 Cover and cook on low-heat setting for 5½ to 6 hours or on high-heat setting for 3 hours.

3 Add artichoke hearts to slow cooker; cover and cook for 30 minutes more. Serve chicken, vegetables, and sauce over hot cooked pasta. Top with shaved Parmesan.

Per serving: 576 cal., 23 g total fat (11 g sat. fat), 167 mg chol., 1,419 mg sodium, 38 g carbo., 7 g fiber, 50 g pro.

Lemonade concentrate takes the edge off the Dijon-style mustard in this chicken-and-potato duo.

TANGY CHICKEN & NEW POTATOES

1½	pounds tiny new potatoes, quartered
1	small onion, cut into wedges
1	tablespoon quick-cooking tapioca
3	pounds meaty chicken pieces (breast halves, thighs, and drumsticks), skinned
½	teaspoon salt
¼	teaspoon black pepper
¼	cup frozen lemonade concentrate, thawed
3	tablespoons Dijon-style mustard
1	teaspoon finely shredded lemon peel
1	6-ounce jar marinated artichoke hearts, undrained

PREP:
20 minutes

COOK:
Low 7 hours, High 3½ hours

MAKES:
4 to 6 servings

SLOW COOKER:
6- to 7-quart

1 In a 6- to 7-quart slow cooker combine potatoes and onion; sprinkle with tapioca. Arrange chicken over vegetables. Sprinkle with salt and pepper.

2 In a small bowl combine lemonade concentrate, mustard, and lemon peel; pour over chicken.

3 Cover and cook on low-heat setting for 7 to 8 hours or on high-heat setting for 3½ to 4 hours.

4 Divide chicken among 4 to 6 shallow bowls. Stir undrained artichoke hearts into vegetable mixture in slow cooker. Spoon vegetable mixture over chicken.

Per serving: 509 cal., 14 g total fat (3 g sat. fat), 138 mg chol., 829 mg sodium, 47 g carbo., 3 g fiber, 51 g pro.

Cinnamon, cloves, golden raisins, and dried apricots add a spicy-sweet twist to this saucy chicken dish.

MOROCCAN CHICKEN

PREP:
20 minutes

COOK:
Low 6 hours, High 3 hours

MAKES:
4 servings

SLOW COOKER:
3½- or 4-quart

2½	pounds meaty chicken pieces (breast halves, thighs, and drumsticks), skinned
½	teaspoon salt
½	teaspoon black pepper
¼	teaspoon ground cinnamon
⅛	teaspoon ground cloves or allspice
1	14½-ounce can diced tomatoes with onions and garlic, undrained
½	cup golden raisins
½	cup dried apricots, snipped
1	tablespoon quick-cooking tapioca
2	cups hot cooked couscous

1 Place chicken in a 3½- or 4-quart slow cooker. In a small bowl combine salt, pepper, cinnamon, and cloves or allspice; sprinkle over chicken. In a medium bowl combine undrained tomatoes, raisins, apricots, and tapioca; pour over chicken.

2 Cover and cook on low-heat setting for 6 to 7 hours or on high-heat setting for 3 to 3½ hours.

3 To serve, divide couscous among four dinner plates; top with chicken. Skim off fat from tomato mixture in slow cooker. Spoon tomato mixture over chicken and couscous.

Per serving: 474 cal., 10 g total fat (3 g sat. fat), 115 mg chol., 900 mg sodium, 54 g carbo., 4 g fiber, 43 g pro.

If you have large chicken breast halves that are more than 12 ounces each, cut them in half so they will cook through in the slow cooker.

CHICKEN IN ALE

4	medium potatoes, peeled and thinly sliced
3	leeks, thinly sliced
1	medium onion, cut into thin wedges
1	teaspoon salt
¼	teaspoon black pepper
2½	pounds meaty chicken pieces (breast halves, thighs, and drumsticks), skinned
½	cup ale or nonalcoholic beer
½	cup chicken broth
2	tablespoons brown mustard
1	tablespoon packed brown sugar
1	tablespoon quick-cooking tapioca
½	teaspoon dried thyme, crushed

1 In a 5- to 6-quart slow cooker combine potatoes, leeks, and onion; sprinkle with half of the salt and pepper. Arrange chicken pieces on top of vegetables; sprinkle with remaining salt and pepper. In a medium bowl combine ale, broth, mustard, brown sugar, tapioca, and thyme; pour over chicken.

2 Cover and cook on low-heat setting for 6 to 7 hours or on high-heat setting for 3 to 3½ hours.

Per serving: 403 cal., 10 g total fat (3 g sat. fat), 115 mg chol., 923 mg sodium, 34 g carbo., 3 g fiber, 41 g pro.

PREP:
30 minutes

COOK:
Low 6 hours, High 3 hours

MAKES:
4 servings

SLOW COOKER:
5- to 6-quart

Purchased Alfredo sauce makes this classic dish a weeknight keeper.

ALFREDO CHICKEN

PREP:
20 minutes

COOK:
Low 5½ hours plus 30 minutes,
High 2½ hours plus 30 minutes

MAKES:
6 servings

SLOW COOKER:
3½- or 4-quart

3   pounds meaty chicken pieces
    (breast halves, thighs, and drumsticks), skinned

Salt

Black pepper

1   16-ounce jar light Parmesan Alfredo pasta sauce

1   9-ounce package frozen Italian green beans, thawed

3   cups hot cooked whole wheat pasta

    Finely shredded Parmesan cheese (optional)

1 Place chicken pieces in a 3½- or 4-quart slow cooker. Sprinkle lightly with salt and pepper. Pour pasta sauce over chicken.

2 Cover and cook on low-heat setting for 5½ to 6½ hours or on high-heat setting for 2½ to 3 hours. Add green beans. Cover and cook for 30 minutes more.

3 Using a slotted spoon, remove chicken and green beans to a serving platter. Stir cooked pasta into sauce in slow cooker; serve with the chicken and green beans. If desired, sprinkle with Parmesan cheese.

Per serving: 392 cal., 15 g total fat (7 g sat. fat), 123 mg chol., 680 mg sodium, 26 g carbo., 3 g fiber, 36 g pro.

Chicken, hominy, and tomatoes with green chile peppers star in this Southwestern-style favorite.

POSOLE

2 14½- to 15½-ounce cans golden hominy, drained

2 14-ounce cans reduced-sodium chicken broth

2 10-ounce cans diced tomatoes and green chile peppers,* undrained

1 medium onion, finely chopped

2 cloves garlic, minced

1 teaspoon dried oregano, crushed

½ teaspoon salt

½ teaspoon ground cumin

   Dash bottled hot pepper sauce

1 pound skinless, boneless chicken breast halves and/or thighs, cut into 1-inch pieces

   Snipped fresh cilantro (optional)

   Lime wedges (optional)

   Dairy sour cream (optional)

1 In a 4½- or 5-quart slow cooker combine hominy, broth, undrained tomatoes and chile peppers, onion, garlic, oregano, salt, cumin, and hot pepper sauce. Stir in chicken.

2 Cover and cook on low-heat setting for 5 to 6 hours or on high-heat setting for 2½ to 3 hours. If desired, serve with cilantro, lime wedges, and sour cream.

Per serving: 192 cal., 2 g total fat (0 g sat. fat), 44 mg chol., 1,187 mg sodium, 20 g carbo., 4 g fiber, 22 g pro.

*NOTE: For a less spicy recipe, substitute one 14½-ounce can diced tomatoes for one of the cans of diced tomatoes and green chile peppers.

PREP:
20 minutes

COOK:
Low 5 hours, High 2½ hours

MAKES:
6 servings

SLOW COOKER:
4½- or 5-quart

If you love blue cheese, this dish will become addictive. For added crunch, top with toasted walnuts.

CREAMY BLUE CHEESE CHICKEN

PREP:
30 minutes

COOK:
Low 5 hours, High 2½ hours

MAKES:
8 servings

SLOW COOKER:
5- to 6-quart

8   bone-in chicken breast halves, skinned

½   teaspoon salt

¼   teaspoon black pepper

¾   cup chicken broth

⅓   cup finely crumbled blue cheese

⅔   cup half-and-half or light cream

2   teaspoons cornstarch

2   tablespoons finely chopped walnuts, toasted

    Finely crumbled blue cheese (optional)

1 Place chicken in a 5- to 6-quart slow cooker. Sprinkle with salt and pepper. Pour broth over chicken; sprinkle with the ⅓ cup blue cheese.

2 Cover and cook on low-heat setting for 5 hours or on high-heat setting for 2½ hours.

3 Transfer chicken to a serving platter; discard cooking liquid. Cover chicken with foil to keep warm.

4 For sauce, in a small saucepan combine half-and-half and cornstarch. Cook and stir over medium heat until thickened and bubbly. Cook and stir for 2 minutes more. Spoon sauce over chicken. Sprinkle with nuts and, if desired, additional blue cheese.

Per serving: 222 cal., 7 g total fat (3 g sat. fat), 93 mg chol., 398 mg sodium, 2 g carbo., 0 g fiber, 35 g pro.

Garam masala is a blend of ground spices that's often used in Indian cooking. Look for it in the seasoning section of larger supermarkets or at food specialty shops.

TANDOORI CHICKEN & VEGETABLES

3	carrots, thinly sliced
1	onion, halved and thinly sliced
1½	teaspoons garam masala
½	teaspoon garlic salt
¼	teaspoon ground ginger
¼	teaspoon ground turmeric
6	large skinless, boneless chicken breast halves or 2¼ to 2½ pounds skinless, boneless chicken thighs
1	14½-ounce can diced tomatoes with basil, oregano, and garlic, undrained
	Hot cooked rice

1 In a 4- to 5-quart slow cooker combine carrots and onion; set aside.

2 In a small bowl combine garam masala, garlic salt, ginger, and turmeric. Sprinkle mixture evenly over chicken. Place chicken on top of vegetables in slow cooker. Pour undrained tomatoes over chicken.

3 Cover and cook on low-heat setting for 4 to 5 hours or on high-heat setting for 2 to 2½ hours.

4 Serve chicken and vegetables with hot cooked rice. Spoon cooking liquid over chicken and rice to moisten.

Per serving: 343 cal., 3 g total fat (1 g sat. fat), 99 mg chol., 549 mg sodium, 33 g carbo., 2 g fiber, 43 g pro.

PREP:
20 minutes

COOK:
Low 4 hours, High 2 hours

MAKES:
6 servings

SLOW COOKER:
4- to 5-quart

Look for sweet smoked paprika at food specialty shops or in the seasoning aisle of larger supermarkets.

CHICKEN WITH SMOKY PAPRIKA SAUCE

PREP:
25 minutes

COOK:
Low 5 hours, High 2½ hours

MAKES:
6 servings

SLOW COOKER:
4- to 5-quart

1   6-ounce jar (drained weight) sliced mushrooms, drained

2   small onions, cut into very thin wedges

1   small fennel bulb, very thinly sliced

6   small bone-in chicken breast halves (about 3 pounds total), skinned if desired

½   teaspoon salt

⅛   teaspoon black pepper

1   10-ounce container refrigerated Alfredo pasta sauce

1½   teaspoons sweet smoked paprika

6   ounces dried angel hair pasta, cooked according to package directions and drained

1   3-ounce package cream cheese, cubed and softened

2   tablespoons sliced almonds, toasted

1 In a 4- to 5-quart slow cooker combine drained mushrooms, onions, and fennel. Arrange chicken on top of vegetables; sprinkle with salt and pepper. In a small bowl stir together Alfredo pasta sauce and paprika; spoon over chicken.

2 Cover and cook on low-heat setting for 5 to 6 hours or on high-heat setting for 2½ to 3 hours.

3 Remove chicken from slow cooker. Stir cooked pasta and cream cheese into mixture in slow cooker; transfer to a serving platter. Arrange chicken on top of pasta mixture; sprinkle with almonds.

Per serving: 464 cal., 24 g total fat (4 g sat. fat), 112 mg chol., 605 mg sodium, 29 g carbo., 3 g fiber, 38 g pro.

Thanks to your slow cooker, you can enjoy this Tex-Mex restaurant fare at home whenever you like.

TOMATILLO & PEPPERED CHICKEN FAJITAS

1	11- to 13-ounce can tomatillos, drained and coarsely chopped
1	large red onion, halved and thinly sliced
2	large green, red, and/or yellow sweet peppers, cut into bite-size strips
2	fresh jalapeño chile peppers, seeded and sliced*
2	tablespoons lime juice
1	tablespoon packed brown sugar
1	teaspoon ground cumin
½	teaspoon salt
¼	teaspoon cayenne pepper
1	pound skinless, boneless chicken breast halves or thighs, cut into bite-size strips
2	cups shredded lettuce
½	cup finely shredded carrot
⅓	cup thinly sliced green onions
⅓	cup snipped fresh cilantro
8	7- to 8-inch flour tortillas, warmed**
¾	cup crumbled queso fresco or shredded Monterey Jack cheese (3 ounces)

PREP:
30 minutes

COOK:
Low 5½ hours, High 3 hours

MAKES:
4 servings

SLOW COOKER:
3½- or 4-quart

1 In a 3½- or 4-quart slow cooker combine tomatillos, red onion, sweet peppers, chile peppers, lime juice, brown sugar, cumin, salt, and cayenne pepper. Stir in chicken strips.

2 Cover and cook on low-heat setting for 5½ to 6 hours or on high-heat setting for 3 hours.

3 Using a slotted spoon, transfer chicken mixture to a serving bowl. In a medium bowl combine lettuce, carrot, green onions, and cilantro. Serve chicken mixture on tortillas; top with lettuce mixture and cheese.

Per serving: 439 cal., 9 g total fat (3 g sat. fat), 73 mg chol., 1,247 mg sodium, 54 g carbo., 6 g fiber, 35 g pro.

***NOTE:** Because chile peppers contain volatile oils that can burn your skin and eyes, avoid direct contact with them as much as possible. When working with chile peppers, wear plastic or rubber gloves. If your bare hands do touch the peppers, wash your hands and nails well with soap and warm water.

****NOTE:** To warm tortillas, preheat oven to 350°F. Wrap tortillas tightly in foil. Heat in the oven about 10 minutes or until heated through.

Fine angel hair pasta is the right texture for soaking up the creamy cheese-and-herb-flavored sauce.

CHICKEN WITH GREEN BEANS & GARLIC

PREP:
15 minutes

COOK:
Low 4 hours, High 2 hours

MAKES:
6 servings

SLOW COOKER:
4- to 5-quart

1   16-ounce package frozen French-style green beans, thawed

1   large onion, finely chopped

½   cup bottled roasted red sweet peppers, chopped

6   skinless, boneless chicken breast halves (about 2 pounds total)

1   10¾-ounce can condensed cream of chicken with herbs soup

½   cup grated Parmesan cheese

8   large cloves garlic, peeled and thinly sliced

½   teaspoon salt

¼   teaspoon black pepper

    Hot cooked angel hair pasta

1 In a 4- to 5-quart slow cooker combine green beans, onion, and roasted red peppers. Arrange chicken breast halves on top. In a medium bowl combine cream of chicken with herbs soup, ¼ cup of the Parmesan cheese, the garlic, salt, and black pepper. Pour over chicken.

2 Cover and cook on low-heat setting for 4 to 5 hours or on high-heat setting for 2 to 2½ hours.

3 Serve chicken and green bean mixture over hot cooked pasta. Sprinkle with the remaining ¼ cup Parmesan cheese.

Per serving: 490 cal., 7 g total fat (2 g sat. fat), 98 mg chol., 759 mg sodium, 57 g carbo., 4 g fiber, 48 g pro.

If using the bacon garnish, be sure to sprinkle it on just before serving so it stays nice and crispy.

JALAPEÑO CHICKEN BREASTS

6	bone-in chicken breast halves, skinned
1	tablespoon chili powder
	Salt
½	cup chicken broth
2	tablespoons lemon juice
⅓	cup bottled pickled jalapeño chile pepper slices, drained
1	tablespoon cornstarch
1	tablespoon cold water
1	8-ounce package cream cheese, softened and cut into cubes
2	slices bacon, crisp-cooked, drained, and crumbled (optional)

1 Sprinkle chicken with chili powder and salt. Arrange chicken, bone sides down, in a 4½- to 6-quart slow cooker. Pour broth and lemon juice around chicken in slow cooker. Top with jalapeño chile pepper slices.

2 Cover and cook on low-heat setting for 5 to 6 hours or on high-heat setting for 2½ to 3 hours.

3 Transfer chicken and jalapeño peppers to a serving platter, reserving cooking liquid in slow cooker. Cover chicken with foil to keep warm.

4 If using low-heat setting, turn to high-heat setting. For sauce, in a small bowl combine cornstarch and the cold water; stir into cooking liquid in slow cooker. Add cream cheese; whisk until combined. Cover and cook about 15 minutes more or until thickened. If desired, sprinkle chicken with bacon. Serve sauce with chicken.

Per serving: 290 cal., 15 g total fat (9 g sat. fat), 114 mg chol., 498 mg sodium, 5 g carbo., 1 g fiber, 32 g pro.

PREP:
15 minutes

COOK:
Low 5 hours, High 2½ hours; plus 15 minutes on High

MAKES:
6 servings

SLOW COOKER:
4½- to 6-quart

Apples, raisins, cherries, and chutney add irresistible fruit flavor to this East Indian-style dish.

CREAMY CURRIED CHICKEN

PREP:
25 minutes

COOK:
Low 4 hours

MAKES:
6 servings

SLOW COOKER:
4- to 5-quart

1½ to 2 teaspoons curry powder

¼ teaspoon salt

⅛ to ¼ teaspoon cayenne pepper

6 skinless, boneless chicken breast halves (2 pounds)

3 medium cooking apples
(such as Granny Smith or Rome Beauty),
cored and cut into eighths

½ cup golden raisins

¼ cup snipped tart dried cherries

1 10¾-ounce can condensed cream of potato soup

½ cup mango chutney, snipped
Hot cooked rice

¼ cup chopped peanuts

1 In a small bowl combine curry powder, salt, and cayenne pepper. Sprinkle half of the mixture evenly over chicken breast halves.

2 Place chicken breast halves in a 4- to 5-quart slow cooker. Top with apples, raisins, and dried cherries. In a medium bowl stir together cream of potato soup, chutney, and remaining curry powder mixture. Pour over chicken and fruit.

3 Cover and cook on low-heat setting for 4 hours.

4 Serve over hot cooked rice. Sprinkle individual servings with peanuts.

Per serving: 481 cal., 7 g total fat (2 g sat. fat), 92 mg chol., 618 mg sodium, 63 g carbo., 5 g fiber, 41 g pro.

Don't skimp on the rice. The sweet and savory chicken mixture deserves a generous ³/₄ cup hot cooked rice for each serving rather than the standard ¹/₂ cup.

TROPICAL CHICKEN

3	pounds bone-in chicken thighs and/or drumsticks, skinned
½	teaspoon lemon-pepper seasoning
1	15¼-ounce can pineapple chunks (juice pack), undrained
1	cup mango nectar or apricot nectar
2	tablespoons quick-cooking tapioca
2	tablespoons soy sauce
	Hot cooked rice
¼	cup flaked coconut, toasted (optional)

1 Sprinkle chicken with lemon-pepper seasoning. Place chicken in a 3½- or 4-quart slow cooker. In a medium bowl combine undrained pineapple, nectar, tapioca, and soy sauce; pour over chicken.

2 Cover and cook on low-heat setting for 7 to 8 hours or on high-heat setting for 3½ to 4 hours.

3 Using a slotted spoon, transfer chicken to a serving platter. Skim fat from pineapple mixture in slow cooker. Serve chicken and pineapple mixture with hot cooked rice. If desired, pass coconut.

Per serving: 508 cal., 8 g total fat (2 g sat. fat), 161 mg chol., 736 mg sodium, 64 g carbo., 1 g fiber, 43 g pro.

PREP:
15 minutes

COOK:
Low 7 hours, High 3½ hours

MAKES:
4 servings

SLOW COOKER:
3½- or 4-quart

FOR 5- TO 6-QUART SLOW COOKER: Use 4½ pounds chicken thighs and/or drumsticks, ¾ teaspoon lemon-pepper seasoning, one 20-ounce can pineapple chunks, 1⅓ cups mango nectar or apricot nectar, 3 tablespoons quick-cooking tapioca, and 3 tablespoons soy sauce. Serve over hot cooked rice. If desired, pass ⅓ cup toasted coconut. Makes 6 servings

Per serving: 480 cal., 8 g total fat (2 g sat. fat), 161 mg chol., 733 mg sodium, 57 g carbo., 1 g fiber, 43 g pro.

Three kinds of beans team up with chicken, onion, and bacon for mouthwatering results.

ONE-POT WINTER DINNER

PREP:
20 minutes

COOK:
Low 7 hours, High 3½ hours

MAKES:
8 servings

SLOW COOKER:
5- to 6-quart

1 pound skinless, boneless chicken thighs,
   cut into ½-inch pieces

2 31-ounce cans pork and beans in tomato sauce

1 15- to 16-ounce can butter beans, rinsed and drained

1 15- to 16-ounce can dark red kidney beans,
   rinsed and drained

1 cup finely chopped onion

1 cup ketchup

¼ cup packed brown sugar

¼ cup cider vinegar

¼ teaspoon black pepper

6 slices bacon, crisp-cooked and crumbled

1 In a 5- to 6-quart slow cooker combine chicken, pork and beans, butter beans, kidney beans, onion, ketchup, brown sugar, vinegar, and pepper.

2 Cover and cook on low-heat setting for 7 to 8 hours or on high-heat setting for 3½ to 4 hours.

3 Stir in bacon before serving.

Per serving: 458 cal., 7 g total fat (2 g sat. fat), 67 mg chol., 1,758 mg sodium, 74 g carbo., 14 g fiber, 32 g pro.

This colorful chicken-and-veggie combination owes its rich, full flavor to a tantalizing mix of ginger, lemon juice, and hoisin sauce.

LEMONY ASIAN CHICKEN

1	tablespoon cooking oil
1½	pounds skinless, boneless chicken thighs, cut into 1-inch pieces
5	medium carrots, coarsely chopped
1	large onion, cut into thin wedges
1	tablespoon quick-cooking tapioca
½	teaspoon ground ginger
¼	teaspoon black pepper
½	cup bottled hoisin sauce
⅓	cup water
2	tablespoons lemon juice
1	medium red, green, or yellow sweet pepper, cut into thin strips
1	6-ounce package frozen pea pods
	Hot cooked rice
	Chopped peanuts (optional)

1 In a large skillet heat oil over medium-high heat. Brown chicken, half at a time, in hot oil, turning to brown evenly. In a 3½- or 4-quart slow cooker combine carrots and onion. Sprinkle with tapioca. Arrange chicken over vegetables. Sprinkle chicken with ginger and black pepper. In a small bowl combine hoisin sauce, the water, and lemon juice; pour over chicken.

2 Cover and cook on low-heat setting for 4 to 4½ hours or on high-heat setting for 2 to 2¼ hours.

3 If using low-heat setting, turn to high-heat setting. Add sweet pepper. Cover and cook for 30 minutes more.

4 To serve, stir frozen pea pods into chicken mixture. Serve over hot cooked rice. If desired, sprinkle individual servings with peanuts.

Per serving: 359 cal., 8 g total fat (2 g sat. fat), 91 mg chol., 391 mg sodium, 41 g carbo., 3 g fiber, 27 g pro.

PREP:
25 minutes

COOK:
Low 4 hours, High 2 hours; plus 30 minutes on High

MAKES:
6 servings

SLOW COOKER:
3½- or 4-quart

There's no need to peel potatoes for this European-style dish. The cream of potato soup contributes plenty of potato flavor.

GERMAN-STYLE CHICKEN THIGHS

PREP:
15 minutes

COOK:
Low 7 hours, High 3½ hours

MAKES:
4 servings

SLOW COOKER:
4- to 6-quart

1   14-ounce can sauerkraut, rinsed and drained

1   10¾-ounce can condensed cream of potato soup

¼   cup water

1   tablespoon Worcestershire sauce

1   teaspoon dried thyme, crushed

¼   teaspoon black pepper

3   to 3½ pounds bone-in chicken thighs, skinned

    Hot cooked spaetzle or wide noodles

    Snipped fresh parsley (optional)

1 In a 4- to 6-quart slow cooker combine sauerkraut, potato soup, the water, Worcestershire sauce, thyme, and pepper. Add chicken; stir to coat chicken.

2 Cover and cook on low-heat setting for 7 to 8 hours or on high-heat setting for 3½ to 4 hours.

3 Serve chicken and sauce over hot cooked spaetzle. If desired, sprinkle individual servings with parsley.

Per serving: 422 cal., 10 g total fat (3 g sat. fat), 193 mg chol., 1,385 mg sodium, 34 g carbo., 4 g fiber, 44 g pro.

If you like your chicken extra hot, add three jalapeño peppers instead of two.

CARIBBEAN CHICKEN THIGHS

2 teaspoons Jamaican jerk seasoning

1 teaspoon salt

2½ to 3 pounds skinless, boneless chicken thighs

1 7-ounce package tropical blend mixed dried fruit bits

2 medium red, yellow, and/or green sweet peppers, seeded and coarsely chopped

2 medium fresh jalapeño chile peppers, halved, seeded, and thinly sliced*

⅓ cup frozen orange juice concentrate, thawed

2 tablespoons cider vinegar

2 tablespoons water

2 teaspoons quick-cooking tapioca

2 cloves garlic, minced

Hot cooked rice or couscous

PREP:
20 minutes

COOK:
Low 7 hours, High 3½ hours

MAKES:
6 servings

SLOW COOKER:
3½- or 4-quart

1 In a small bowl combine jerk seasoning and salt; sprinkle evenly onto chicken thighs. Place chicken thighs in a 3½- or 4-quart slow cooker. Top with fruit bits, sweet peppers, and chile peppers. In a small bowl combine orange juice concentrate, vinegar, the water, tapioca, and garlic; pour over chicken and fruit.

2 Cover and cook on low-heat setting for 7 to 8 hours or on high-heat setting for 3½ to 4 hours.

3 Serve chicken mixture over hot cooked rice or couscous.

Per serving: 496 cal., 9 g total fat (3 g sat. fat), 151 mg chol., 660 mg sodium, 59 g carbo., 3 g fiber, 41 g pro.

*NOTE: Because chile peppers contain volatile oils that can burn your skin and eyes, avoid direct contact with them as much as possible. When working with chile peppers, wear plastic or rubber gloves. If your bare hands do touch the peppers, wash your hands and nails well with soap and warm water.

Artichokes, garlic, Italian seasoning, and seasoned salt give this saucy chicken plenty of old-world flavor.

CHICKEN WITH CHUNKY TOMATO SAUCE

PREP:
20 minutes

COOK:
Low 6 hours, High 3 hours

MAKES:
6 servings

SLOW COOKER:
3½- to 5-quart

½ of a 28-ounce can Italian-style whole peeled tomatoes in puree (1⅔ cups)

2 small onions, cut into thin wedges

1 tablespoon quick-cooking tapioca

2 cloves garlic, minced

2 teaspoons dried Italian seasoning, crushed

½ teaspoon seasoned salt

¼ teaspoon black pepper

1¼ pounds skinless, boneless chicken thighs

1 9-ounce package frozen artichoke hearts, thawed

6 ounces dried penne pasta, cooked according to package directions and drained

¼ cup finely shredded Parmesan cheese (1 ounce)

1 In a 3½- to 5-quart slow cooker combine tomatoes in puree, onions, tapioca, and garlic; stir gently to break up tomatoes slightly. In a small bowl combine Italian seasoning, seasoned salt, and pepper; sprinkle half of the seasoning mixture over the tomato mixture.

2 Arrange chicken thighs on tomato mixture; sprinkle with remaining seasoning mixture. Place artichoke hearts on top of chicken.

3 Cover and cook on low-heat setting for 6 to 7 hours or on high-heat setting for 3 to 3½ hours.

4 Using a slotted spoon, transfer chicken to a serving platter. Spoon sauce over hot cooked pasta; toss to coat. Sprinkle with Parmesan cheese. Serve chicken with pasta mixture.

Per serving: 293 cal., 6 g total fat (2 g sat. fat), 78 mg chol., 288 mg sodium, 33 g carbo., 5 g fiber, 26 g pro.

You'll love the pleasant sweetness and tang from the pineapple chunks.

TANGY PINEAPPLE CHICKEN

1   tablespoon cooking oil

2   pounds skinless, boneless chicken thighs, cut into 1-inch-wide strips

1   20-ounce can pineapple tidbits (juice pack), drained

1   large red sweet pepper, chopped

½   cup bottled barbecue sauce

¼   cup bottled clear Italian salad dressing

2   teaspoons dried oregano, crushed

1 In a large skillet heat oil over medium heat. Cook chicken, half at a time, in hot oil until brown. Drain off fat.

2 Place chicken in a 3½- or 4-quart slow cooker. Top with pineapple and sweet pepper. In a small bowl combine barbecue sauce, Italian salad dressing, and oregano. Pour over mixture in slow cooker.

3 Cover and cook on low-heat setting for 5 to 6 hours or on high-heat setting for 2½ to 3 hours.

Per serving: 314 cal., 12 g total fat (2 g sat. fat), 121 mg chol., 436 mg sodium, 20 g carbo., 2 g fiber, 31 g pro.

PREP:
30 minutes

COOK:
Low 5 hours, High 2½ hours

MAKES:
6 servings

SLOW COOKER:
3½- or 4-quart

Chicken, eggplant, and olives are common in both Greek and Italian cuisines, so either the Greek or Italian seasoning is a delightful choice for this fresh-tasting dish.

MEDITERRANEAN CHICKEN THIGHS

PREP:
20 minutes

COOK:
Low 5 hours, High 2½ hours

MAKES:
6 servings

SLOW COOKER:
4- to 5-quart

½   of a medium eggplant, peeled and cubed (8 ounces)

1   medium onion, cut into wedges

¼   cup pitted ripe olives, halved

2   cloves garlic, minced

3   pounds bone-in chicken thighs, skinned

2   teaspoons finely shredded lemon peel

1   teaspoon dried Greek seasoning or Italian seasoning, crushed

⅛   teaspoon salt

¼   teaspoon black pepper

⅓   cup chicken broth

2   medium plum tomatoes, coarsely chopped

½   cup shredded Parmesan cheese (2 ounces)

1 In a 4- to 5-quart slow cooker combine eggplant, onion, olives, and garlic. Arrange chicken over eggplant mixture. Sprinkle chicken with lemon peel, Greek seasoning, salt, and pepper. Pour broth over all.

2 Cover and cook on low-heat setting for 5 to 6 hours or on high-heat setting for 2½ to 3 hours.

3 Using a slotted spoon, transfer chicken and eggplant mixture to a serving platter. Discard cooking liquid. Sprinkle chicken with tomatoes and cheese.

Per serving: 206 cal., 7 g total fat (2 g sat. fat), 112 mg chol., 368 mg sodium, 5 g carbo., 2 g fiber, 29 g pro.

For Asian flair, serve the chicken over aromatic jasmine or basmati rice instead of plain rice.

SESAME GINGER CHICKEN

Nonstick cooking spray

1 16-ounce package frozen cut green beans, thawed

1 15-ounce can (drained weight) straw mushrooms, drained, or two 8-ounce cans (drained weight) mushrooms stems and pieces, drained

3 pounds skinless, boneless chicken thighs or skinless, boneless chicken breast halves

½ cup ginger preserves or apricot preserves

¼ cup cider vinegar

2 tablespoons quick-cooking tapioca

2 tablespoons hoisin sauce or oyster sauce

2 teaspoons toasted sesame oil

⅛ teaspoon cayenne pepper

¼ cup sliced almonds, toasted

1 tablespoon sesame seeds, toasted

Hot cooked rice

PREP:
15 minutes

COOK:
Low 6 hours, High 3 hours

MAKES:
8 to 10 servings

SLOW COOKER:
5- to 6-quart

1 Lightly coat a 5- to 6-quart slow cooker with nonstick cooking spray. In the prepared slow cooker combine beans and drained mushrooms. Arrange chicken over vegetables. In a small bowl combine preserves, vinegar, tapioca, hoisin sauce, sesame oil, and cayenne pepper; pour over chicken.

2 Cover and cook on low-heat setting for 6 hours or on high-heat setting for 3 hours.

3 In a small bowl combine almonds and sesame seeds. Spoon chicken mixture over hot cooked rice; sprinkle with almond mixture.

Per serving: 461 cal., 13 g total fat (2 g sat. fat), 141 mg chol., 613 mg sodium, 47 g carbo., 4 g fiber, 39 g pro.

Navy beans, meaty chicken pieces, and Polish sausage add up to one flavorful, comforting meal.

CHICKEN CASSOULET

PREP:
25 minutes

STAND:
1 hour

COOK:
Low 9 hours, High 4½ hours

MAKES:
6 servings

SLOW COOKER:
3½- or 4-quart

1	cup dry navy beans
3	pounds bone-in chicken thighs and drumsticks
8	ounces cooked Polish sausage
1	cup tomato juice
1	tablespoon Worcestershire sauce
1	teaspoon instant beef or chicken bouillon granules
½	teaspoon dried basil, crushed
½	teaspoon dried oregano, crushed
½	teaspoon paprika
½	cup chopped carrot
½	cup chopped celery
½	cup chopped onion

1 Rinse beans; place in a medium saucepan. Add enough water to cover beans by 2 inches. Bring to boiling; reduce heat. Simmer, uncovered, for 10 minutes. Remove from heat. Cover; let stand for 1 hour. Drain and rinse beans.

2 Skin chicken pieces; set aside. Halve sausage lengthwise and cut into 1-inch pieces. In a medium bowl combine drained beans, tomato juice, Worcestershire sauce, bouillon granules, basil, oregano, and paprika.

3 In a 3½- or 4-quart slow cooker combine carrot, celery, and onion. Arrange chicken pieces and sausage over vegetables. Pour bean mixture over chicken and sausage.

4 Cover and cook on low-heat setting for 9 to 11 hours or on high-heat setting for 4½ to 5½ hours.

Per serving: 412 cal., 16 g total fat (5 g sat. fat), 130 mg chol., 728 mg sodium, 26 g carbo., 9 g fiber, 39 g pro.

Saffron, the traditional seasoning for this Spanish dish, goes a long way. Just a dash adds appealing yellow color and a bittersweet note to this chicken-and-seafood classic.

PAELLA

2	medium carrots, cut into ½-inch pieces
1	large onion, coarsely chopped
1	bay leaf
3	pounds bone-in chicken thighs and drumsticks, skinned
1	cup cubed cooked ham (5 ounces)
1	14½-ounce can stewed tomatoes, undrained, cut up
½	of a 6-ounce can tomato paste (⅓ cup)
2	teaspoons instant chicken bouillon granules
2	cloves garlic, minced
¼	teaspoon black pepper
1	pound fresh or thawed frozen shrimp in shells, peeled and deveined
1	cup loose-pack frozen peas
2	cups water
1	cup long grain rice
¼	teaspoon salt
	Dash ground saffron or ⅛ teaspoon ground turmeric

1 In a 3½- to 5-quart slow cooker combine carrots, onion, and bay leaf. Arrange chicken pieces and ham over vegetables. In a medium bowl combine undrained tomatoes, tomato paste, bouillon granules, garlic, and pepper; pour over mixture in slow cooker.

2 Cover and cook on low-heat setting for 8 to 9 hours or on high-heat setting for 4 to 4½ hours.

3 If using low-heat setting, turn to high-heat setting. Stir shrimp and peas into mixture in slow cooker. Cook about 20 minutes more or until shrimp are opaque.

4 Meanwhile, in a medium saucepan combine the water, uncooked rice, salt, and saffron or turmeric. Bring to boiling; reduce heat. Cover and simmer for 15 minutes. Remove from heat. Let stand, covered, for 10 minutes. Fluff rice with a fork.

5 To serve, discard bay leaf. Using a slotted spoon, transfer chicken mixture to a serving platter, reserving cooking liquid in slow cooker. Serve chicken mixture with hot cooked rice. Drizzle with enough of the reserved cooking liquid to moisten.

Per serving: 445 cal., 9 g total fat (2 g sat. fat), 202 mg chol., 1,056 mg sodium, 42 g carbo., 4 g fiber, 47 g pro.

PREP:
30 minutes

COOK:
Low 8 hours, High 4 hours; plus 20 minutes on High

STAND:
10 minutes

MAKES:
6 servings

SLOW COOKER:
3½- to 5-quart

These tropical drumsticks, with an innovative blend of lemonade concentrate and hoisin sauce, are all but impossible to resist.

LEMON-HOISIN CHICKEN DRUMSTICKS

PREP:
25 minutes

COOK:
Low 6 hours, High 3 hours

MAKES:
6 servings

SLOW COOKER:
3½- or 4-quart

4 pounds chicken drumsticks, skinned

½ teaspoon five-spice powder*

¼ teaspoon salt

⅛ teaspoon cayenne pepper

⅓ cup frozen lemonade concentrate, thawed

¼ cup hoisin sauce

¼ cup rice vinegar or cider vinegar

2 tablespoons cornstarch

2 tablespoons cold water

⅓ cup thinly sliced green onions

1 tablespoon sesame seeds, toasted

1 Place chicken in a 3½- or 4-quart slow cooker. In a small bowl combine five-spice powder, salt, and cayenne pepper; sprinkle over chicken. In a medium bowl combine lemonade concentrate, hoisin sauce, and vinegar; pour over chicken.

2 Cover and cook on low-heat setting for 6 to 7 hours or on high-heat setting for 3 to 3½ hours.

3 Using a slotted spoon, transfer chicken to a serving platter; cover and keep warm. Strain cooking juices in slow cooker; skim off fat. Transfer 1½ cups of the cooking juices to a small saucepan. In a small bowl combine cornstarch and the cold water; add to saucepan along with green onions. Cook and stir until thickened and bubbly; cook and stir for 2 minutes more. Spoon over chicken; sprinkle with sesame seeds.

Per serving: 272 cal., 7 g total fat (2 g sat. fat), 130 mg chol., 355 mg sodium, 14 g carbo., 0 g fiber, 36 g pro.

*NOTE: You can use Homemade Five-Spice Powder (see recipe on page 73) or purchased five-spice powder.

Because it's made with frozen stir-fry vegetables and bottled plum sauce, this Asian-style chicken goes together without a lot of prep time.

CHICKEN WITH SWEET-SOUR PLUM SAUCE

3	pounds chicken drumsticks, skinned
½	teaspoon salt
½	teaspoon garlic-pepper seasoning
1	16-ounce package frozen (yellow, green, and red) peppers and onion stir-fry vegetables, thawed
½	cup bottled plum sauce
¼	cup rice vinegar or cider vinegar
3	tablespoons soy sauce
2	tablespoons quick-cooking tapioca
½	teaspoon ground ginger
	Hot cooked rice
	Sliced green onions (optional)

1 Place chicken in a 5- to 6-quart slow cooker. Sprinkle with salt and garlic-pepper seasoning. Top with thawed stir-fry vegetables. In a small bowl combine plum sauce, vinegar, soy sauce, tapioca, and ginger; spoon over vegetables and chicken in slow cooker.

2 Cover and cook on low-heat setting for 6 to 8 hours or on high-heat setting for 3½ to 4 hours.

3 Serve over hot cooked rice. If desired, sprinkle with green onions.

Per serving: 338 cal., 4 g total fat (1 g sat. fat), 98 mg chol., 892 mg sodium, 40 g carbo., 1 g fiber, 31 g pro.

PREP:
20 minutes

COOK:
Low 6 hours, High 3½ hours

MAKES:
6 servings

SLOW COOKER:
5- to 6-quart

This homey hash uses frozen hash browns for the traditional potatoes, but substitutes ground chicken or turkey for leftover cooked meat and includes a rich topping of Swiss cheese.

CHICKEN HASH

PREP:
20 minutes

COOK:
Low 4½ hours, High 2½ hours

MAKES:
4 or 5 servings

SLOW COOKER:
3½- or 4-quart

Nonstick cooking spray

6 cups loose-pack frozen diced hash brown potatoes, thawed

1 pound ground chicken or turkey

1 large onion, finely chopped

½ cup snipped fresh parsley

1 12-ounce can evaporated milk

2 tablespoons Worcestershire sauce for chicken

1 tablespoon yellow mustard

¾ teaspoon salt

¼ teaspoon black pepper

½ cup shredded Swiss cheese (2 ounces)

1 Lightly coat a 3½- or 4-quart slow cooker with nonstick cooking spray. In prepared slow cooker stir together potatoes, ground chicken, onion, and parsley. In a medium bowl whisk together evaporated milk, Worcestershire sauce, mustard, salt, and pepper; stir into potato mixture.

2 Cover and cook on low-heat setting for 4½ to 5 hours or on high-heat setting for 2½ hours.

3 Spoon off fat. Sprinkle chicken mixture with cheese before serving.

Per serving: 617 cal., 22 g total fat (7 g sat. fat), 38 mg chol., 845 mg sodium, 72 g carbo., 5 g fiber, 37 g pro.

Raisins lend sweetness to these Tex-Mex-seasoned wraps.

CHICKEN PICADILLO WRAPS

2	pounds uncooked ground chicken or turkey
2	large onions, finely chopped
1	14½-ounce can diced tomatoes, undrained
½	cup golden raisins
¼	cup thinly sliced pimiento-stuffed green olives
¼	cup tomato paste
2	tablespoons chopped canned jalapeño peppers*
1	tablespoon packed brown sugar
½	teaspoon salt
½	teaspoon ground cumin
½	teaspoon ground cinnamon
16	8- to 10-inch flour tortillas, warmed**
½	cup slivered almonds, toasted
	Shredded lettuce (optional)
	Dairy sour cream (optional)

1 In a 12-inch nonstick skillet cook ground chicken and onions over medium heat until chicken is no longer pink and onion is tender. Drain off fat.

2 In a 3½- or 4-quart slow cooker combine chicken mixture, undrained tomatoes, raisins, olives, tomato paste, jalapeño peppers, brown sugar, salt, cumin, and cinnamon.

3 Cover and cook on low-heat setting for 5 to 6 hours or on high-heat setting for 2½ to 3 hours.

4 Divide picadillo mixture among warm tortillas; sprinkle with almonds. If desired, add lettuce and sour cream. Roll up tortillas.

Per serving: 475 cal., 19 g total fat (2 g sat. fat), 0 mg chol., 631 mg sodium, 49 g carbo., 4 g fiber, 27 g pro.

***NOTE:** Because chile peppers contain volatile oils that can burn your skin and eyes, avoid direct contact with them as much as possible. When working with chile peppers, wear plastic or rubber gloves. If your bare hands do touch the peppers, wash your hands and nails well with soap and warm water.

****NOTE:** To warm tortillas, preheat oven to 350°F. Wrap tortillas tightly in foil. Heat in the oven about 10 minutes or until heated through.

PREP:
15 minutes

COOK:
Low 5 hours, High 2½ hours

OVEN:
350°F

MAKES:
8 servings

SLOW COOKER:
3½- or 4-quart

FOR 5- TO 6-QUART SLOW COOKER:
Double all ingredients and brown chicken and onions half at a time. Makes 16 servings.

There's enough gravy to spoon over the turkey and, if you like, mashed potatoes as well.

WINE-SAUCED TURKEY

PREP:
15 minutes

COOK:
Low 9 hours, High 4½ hours

MAKES:
6 to 8 servings

SLOW COOKER:
3½- to 6-quart

¾ cup dry white wine

½ cup chopped onion

1 clove garlic, minced

1 bay leaf

1 3½- to 4-pound frozen boneless turkey roast, thawed

1 teaspoon dried rosemary, crushed

¼ teaspoon black pepper

⅓ cup half-and-half, light cream, or milk

2 tablespoons cornstarch

1 In a 3½- to 6-quart slow cooker combine white wine, onion, garlic, and bay leaf. If turkey is wrapped in netting, remove netting and discard. If gravy packet is present, remove and refrigerate for another use. In a small bowl combine rosemary and pepper. Sprinkle rosemary mixture evenly over turkey; rub in with your fingers. Place turkey in slow cooker.

2 Cover and cook on low-heat setting for 9 to 10 hours or on high-heat setting for 4½ to 5 hours.

3 Transfer turkey to a serving platter. Cover and keep warm. For gravy, strain cooking juices; discard solids. Skim fat from cooking juices. Measure 1⅓ cups cooking juices into a small saucepan. In a small bowl combine half-and-half and cornstarch; stir into cooking juices in saucepan. Cook and stir until thickened and bubbly. Cook and stir for 2 minutes more.

4 Slice turkey. Spoon some of the gravy over turkey. Pass remaining gravy with turkey.

Per serving: 365 cal., 9 g total fat (3 g sat. fat), 176 mg chol., 193 mg sodium, 5 g carbo., 0 g fiber, 58 g pro.

To quick-thaw the beans, place them in a colander and rinse them under running water for a minute or two.

TURKEY & MUSHROOMS WITH COUSCOUS

1   9-ounce package frozen cut green beans, thawed

1   4-ounce can (drained weight) sliced mushrooms, undrained

1   small onion, finely chopped

1   clove garlic, minced

¼   teaspoon black pepper

1½   pounds turkey breast tenderloins or skinless, boneless chicken breasts

1   10¾-ounce can condensed golden mushroom soup

½   of an 8-ounce tub cream cheese spread with chive and onion or garden vegetables

¾   cup quick-cooking couscous

PREP:
10 minutes

COOK:
Low 5 hours, High 2½ hours

STAND:
5 minutes

MAKES:
4 servings

SLOW COOKER:
3½- or 4-quart

1 In a 3½- or 4-quart slow cooker combine green beans, undrained mushrooms, onion, garlic, and pepper. Place turkey on green bean mixture. In a small bowl stir together golden mushroom soup and cream cheese spread. Pour over turkey.

2 Cover and cook on low-heat setting for 5 to 6 hours or on high-heat setting for 2½ hours.

3 Using a slotted spoon, transfer turkey to a serving platter; cover and keep warm. Remove liner from slow cooker, if possible, or turn off slow cooker. Stir uncooked couscous into mixture in slow cooker. Cover and let stand for 5 minutes. Serve couscous mixture with cooked turkey.

Per serving: 509 cal., 14 g total fat (8 g sat. fat), 132 mg chol., 877 mg sodium, 43 g carbo., 5 g fiber, 48 g pro.

With this super simple recipe, you can enjoy turkey and stuffing without the hassle.

TURKEY WITH CORN BREAD STUFFING

PREP:
20 minutes

COOK:
Low 3½ hours

STAND:
10 minutes

MAKES:
8 servings

SLOW COOKER:
4- to 5-quart

1 8-ounce package corn bread stuffing mix (4 cups)

1 cup honey-roasted peanuts, coarsely chopped

½ cup finely chopped celery

1 10¾-ounce can condensed cream of celery soup

½ cup apricot preserves

¼ cup butter, melted

2 1½-pound boneless turkey breast portions

  Nonstick cooking spray

1 tablespoon soy sauce

1 In a large bowl combine stuffing mix, peanuts, and celery; stir in cream of celery soup, ¼ cup of the preserves, and the melted butter.

2 At 1½-inch intervals, cut slits crosswise in each turkey breast portion, cutting three-quarters of the way through turkey breast. Spoon some of the stuffing mixture into each slit.

3 Lightly coat a 4- to 5-quart slow cooker with nonstick cooking spray. Spoon remaining stuffing mixture into the prepared slow cooker. Add turkey, stuffed sides up.

4 Cover and cook on low-heat setting for 3½ to 4½ hours or until an instant-read thermometer inserted into center of turkey registers 170°F.

5 In a small bowl combine remaining ¼ cup apricot preserves and the soy sauce; spoon over turkey. Let stand for 10 minutes before slicing to serve.

Per serving: 521 cal., 16 g total fat (6 g sat. fat), 129 mg chol., 874 mg sodium, 43 g carbo., 2 g fiber, 48 g pro.

Squirt additional lemon juice on this tasty salad to add extra pizzazz.

TURKEY WITH HOT TABBOULEH SALAD

Nonstick cooking spray or a disposable slow-cooker liner

1½	cups bulgur
¾	cup sliced green onions
1½	to 1¾ pounds turkey breast tenderloins, cut into 1-inch-thick slices (about 2 tenderloins)
2	teaspoons lemon-pepper seasoning
½	teaspoon garlic salt
¼	teaspoon black pepper
¾	cup chicken broth
¼	cup olive oil
¼	cup lemon juice
1	small cucumber, chopped
1	small tomato, chopped
½	cup snipped fresh parsley
¼	cup snipped fresh mint
	Lemon wedges (optional)

PREP:
15 minutes

COOK:
Low 3 hours, High 1½ hours

MAKES:
6 servings

SLOW COOKER:
3½- or 4-quart

1 Lightly coat a 3½- or 4-quart slow cooker with nonstick cooking spray or line with slow-cooker liner. In the prepared cooker combine bulgur and green onions. In a large bowl toss turkey slices with lemon-pepper seasoning, garlic salt, and pepper; add to slow cooker. Add broth, olive oil, and lemon juice.

2 Cover and cook on low-heat setting for 3 to 4 hours or on high-heat setting for 1½ to 2 hours.

3 Stir in cucumber, tomato, parsley, and mint. If desired, serve with lemon wedges.

Per serving: 347 cal., 10 g total fat (2 g sat. fat), 75 mg chol., 620 mg sodium, 32 g carbo., 8 g fiber, 33 g pro.

Refrigerated biscuits are the secret to the easy dumplings for this family-pleaser.

TURKEY & DUMPLINGS

PREP:
15 minutes

COOK:
Low 6 hours, High 3 hours;
plus 45 minutes on High

STAND:
15 minutes

MAKES:
5 or 6 servings

SLOW COOKER:
4- to 5-quart

1½	cups thinly sliced carrot
1½	cups thinly sliced celery
2	small onions, cut into very thin wedges
1½	pounds turkey breast tenderloin, cut into ¾-inch cubes
1	14-ounce can reduced-sodium chicken broth
1	10¾-ounce can condensed cream of chicken soup
2	teaspoons dried leaf sage, crushed
¼	teaspoon black pepper
¼	cup all-purpose flour
1	6-ounce package (5) refrigerated biscuits, cut into quarters

1 In a 4- to 5-quart slow cooker combine carrot, celery, and onions; stir in turkey. Set aside ½ cup of the broth. In a medium bowl combine remaining broth, the cream of chicken soup, sage, and pepper; stir into mixture in slow cooker.

2 Cover and cook on low-heat setting for 6 to 7 hours or on high-heat setting for 3 to 3½ hours.

3 If using low-heat setting, turn to high-heat setting. In a small bowl whisk together reserved ½ cup broth and the flour; stir into mixture in slow cooker. Arrange quartered biscuits on top of mixture in slow cooker. Cover and cook for 45 minutes more.

4 Remove liner from slow cooker, if possible, or turn off slow cooker. Let stand, covered, for 15 minutes before serving.

Per serving: 359 cal., 8 g total fat (2 g sat. fat), 95 mg chol., 1,070 mg sodium, 30 g carbo., 3 g fiber, 39 g pro.

Use small turkey thighs or halve larger ones for this fruited dish sweetened with maple syrup.

TURKEY WITH MAPLE-SAUCED SWEETS

1	pound sweet potatoes, peeled and cut into 2-inch chunks
1	small onion, halved lengthwise and thinly sliced
1/3	cup dried apricots, quartered
1/2	teaspoon salt
1/4	teaspoon black pepper
1/4	teaspoon ground ginger
1 1/2	to 2 pounds small turkey thighs (about 4)
2	tablespoons water
2	tablespoons maple-flavored syrup
1	tablespoon butter, melted
2	teaspoons quick-cooking tapioca
1	teaspoon dry mustard
1/4	cup chopped pecans, toasted (optional)

1 In a 3½- or 4-quart slow cooker combine sweet potatoes, onion, and dried apricots. In a small bowl combine salt, pepper, and ginger; sprinkle half of the salt mixture over sweet potato mixture in slow cooker.

2 Remove skin from turkey thighs; arrange thighs on sweet potato mixture. Sprinkle with remaining salt mixture. In a small bowl combine the water, maple-flavored syrup, butter, tapioca, and dry mustard; pour over turkey thighs.

3 Cover and cook on low-heat setting for 6 to 8 hours or on high-heat setting for 3½ to 4 hours.

4 Using tongs or a slotted spoon, transfer turkey and sweet potatoes to a serving dish. Spoon some of the cooking liquid over turkey and sweet potatoes. If desired, sprinkle with pecans.

Per serving: 300 cal., 8 g total fat (4 g sat. fat), 73 mg chol., 444 mg sodium, 33 g carbo., 3 g fiber, 23 g pro.

PREP:
30 minutes
COOK:
Low 6 hours, High 3½ hours
MAKES:
4 servings
SLOW COOKER:
3½- or 4-quart

FOR 5- TO 6-QUART SLOW COOKER:
Use 2 pounds sweet potatoes, 1 medium onion, ¾ cup dried apricots, 1 teaspoon salt, ½ teaspoon black pepper, ½ teaspoon ground ginger, 3 pounds small turkey thighs (about 6), ¼ cup water, ¼ cup maple-flavored syrup, 2 tablespoons butter, 1 tablespoon quick-cooking tapioca, 2 teaspoons dry mustard, and ½ cup chopped pecans (optional). Makes 6 servings.

Per serving: 401 cal., 11 g total fat (5 g sat. fat), 97 mg chol., 592 mg sodium, 45 g carbo., 5 g fiber, 31 g pro.

When you're shopping for leeks, avoid those that are more than 1½ inches in diameter. Larger leeks are older and tougher.

LEEK & ONION-SAUCED TURKEY

PREP:
30 minutes

COOK:
Low 6 hours, High 3 hours

MAKES:
6 servings

SLOW COOKER:
5- to 6-quart

6   small turkey thighs (4 to 5 pounds)

1   teaspoon poultry seasoning

¼   teaspoon black pepper

6   medium carrots, halved lengthwise and cut in half crosswise

5   medium leeks, thinly sliced

1   cup thinly sliced celery

¼   cup quick-cooking tapioca, crushed

2   10½-ounce cans condensed French onion soup

Snipped fresh flat-leaf parsley

Mashed potatoes

1 Remove skin from turkey thighs. In a small bowl combine poultry seasoning and pepper. Sprinkle evenly over turkey thighs; rub in with your fingers.

2 In a 5- to 6-quart slow cooker combine carrots, leeks, and celery. Sprinkle with tapioca. Arrange turkey thighs over vegetables; pour French onion soup over all.

3 Cover and cook on low-heat setting for 6 to 7 hours or on high-heat setting for 3 to 3½ hours.

4 Transfer turkey thighs to a serving platter. Using a slotted spoon, remove vegetables from slow cooker; place on top of turkey. Sprinkle with parsley. Serve with mashed potatoes and some of the cooking liquid.

Per serving: 536 cal., 16 g total fat (5 g sat. fat), 137 mg chol., 1,394 mg sodium, 52 g carbo., 6 g fiber, 45 g pro.

To keep the meat mixture from sticking to your hands, wet them with cold water before shaping the meatballs.

TURKEY & RICE BALLS IN MARINARA SAUCE

1	beaten egg
½	cup finely chopped onion
1	teaspoon salt
1	teaspoon dried Italian seasoning, crushed
¼	teaspoon black pepper
⅔	cup long grain rice
1½	pounds uncooked ground turkey
2	tablespoons cooking oil
1	medium onion, cut into thin wedges
2	medium zucchini, halved lengthwise and sliced
1	medium yellow summer squash, halved lengthwise and sliced
1	15-ounce container refrigerated marinara sauce
1	8-ounce can tomato sauce
1	tablespoon quick-cooking tapioca
¼	cup grated Parmesan cheese
¼	cup slivered fresh basil (optional)

PREP:
45 minutes

COOK:
Low 6 hours, High 3 hours

MAKES:
6 servings

SLOW COOKER:
4- to 6-quart

1 In a large bowl combine egg, onion, salt, Italian seasoning, and pepper. Add uncooked rice and turkey; mix well. Shape into twenty-four meatballs.

2 In an extra-large skillet heat oil over medium heat. Add meatballs; cook about 10 minutes or until browned, turning occasionally.

3 Meanwhile, place onion wedges in a 4- to 6-quart slow cooker. Transfer browned meatballs to slow cooker. Top with zucchini and yellow summer squash. In a medium bowl combine marinara sauce, tomato sauce, and tapioca; spoon over vegetables.

4 Cover and cook on low-heat setting for 6 to 7 hours or on high-heat setting for 3 to 3½ hours.

5 Serve topped with Parmesan cheese. If desired, sprinkle with basil.

Per serving: 389 cal., 17 g total fat (4 g sat. fat), 128 mg chol., 972 mg sodium, 31 g carbo., 2 g fiber, 27 g pro.

Bottled turkey gravy seasoned with Dijon mustard and thyme is the foundation for this delightful sausage, veggie, and apple combo.

TURKEY SAUSAGE & APPLES

PREP:
20 minutes

COOK:
Low 4 hours, High 2 hours; plus 1 hour on High

MAKES:
6 servings

SLOW COOKER:
4- to 5-quart

1½ pounds cooked smoked turkey sausage

2 medium green, yellow, and/or red sweet peppers, cut into 1½-inch pieces

1 medium onion, cut into thin wedges

1 12-ounce jar turkey gravy

2 tablespoons Dijon-style mustard

¾ teaspoon dried thyme, crushed

¼ teaspoon black pepper

3 medium cooking apples (such as Rome Beauty or Granny Smith), cored and cut into quarters

Hot cooked noodles

1 Cut turkey sausage diagonally into ½-inch-thick slices. Place turkey sausage in a 4- to 5-quart slow cooker. Add sweet peppers and onion. In a small bowl combine gravy, mustard, thyme, and black pepper; spoon over sausage mixture.

2 Cover and cook on low-heat setting for 4 to 6 hours or on high-heat setting for 2 to 3 hours.

3 If using low-heat setting, turn to high-heat setting. Stir in apples. Cover and cook for 1 hour more. Serve over hot cooked noodles.

Per serving: 459 cal., 13 g total fat (3 g sat. fat), 129 mg chol., 1,497 mg sodium, 57 g carbo., 4 g fiber, 28 g pro.

Baked bean combos are always popular. This version has smoked turkey sausage added to the medley of beans to give it main-dish status.

FOUR-BEAN & SAUSAGE DINNER

1	pound cooked smoked turkey sausage, halved lengthwise and cut into ½-inch-thick pieces
1	15-ounce can red kidney beans, rinsed and drained
1	15-ounce can black beans, rinsed and drained
1	15-ounce can Great Northern beans, rinsed and drained
1	15-ounce can butter beans, rinsed and drained
1	8-ounce can tomato sauce
1	medium green sweet pepper, chopped
½	cup chopped onion
½	cup ketchup
¼	cup packed brown sugar
2	teaspoons Worcestershire sauce
1	teaspoon dry mustard
½	teaspoon bottled hot pepper sauce

1 In a 3½- or 4-quart slow cooker combine sausage, kidney beans, black beans, Great Northern beans, butter beans, tomato sauce, sweet pepper, onion, ketchup, brown sugar, Worcestershire sauce, dry mustard, and hot pepper sauce.

2 Cover and cook on low-heat setting for 8 to 10 hours or on high-heat setting for 4 to 5 hours.

Per serving: 324 cal., 5 g total fat (1 g sat. fat), 38 mg chol., 1,243 mg sodium, 50 g carbo., 11 g fiber, 24 g pro.

PREP:
15 minutes

COOK:
Low 8 hours, High 4 hours

MAKES:
8 servings

SLOW COOKER:
3½- or 4-quart

To shorten the prep time, use thawed frozen Italian-style cooked turkey meatballs instead of making meatballs from scratch.

TURKEY SAUSAGE SUBS

PREP:
25 minutes

BAKE:
20 minutes

COOK:
Low 3½ hours, High 2 hours

OVEN:
350°F

MAKES:
6 servings

SLOW COOKER:
4- to 5-quart

1   egg

1   25-ounce jar mushroom and ripe olive pasta sauce

⅓   cup roasted garlic-flavored fine dry bread crumbs

½   teaspoon salt

¼   teaspoon cayenne pepper

1½ pounds uncooked sweet Italian turkey sausage links, casings removed

1   large onion, cut into thin wedges

2   large green, yellow, and/or orange sweet peppers, cut into thin strips

6   hoagie buns, split and toasted

¾   cup shredded mozzarella cheese (3 ounces)

1 Preheat oven to 350°F. For meatballs, in a large bowl beat egg with a fork. Stir in ¼ cup of the pasta sauce, the bread crumbs, salt, and cayenne pepper. Add turkey sausage; mix well. Using wet hands, shape mixture into 24 meatballs. In a 15×10×1-inch baking pan arrange meatballs in a single layer. Bake for 20 to 25 minutes or until cooked through (165°F).*

2 In a 4- to 5-quart slow cooker combine onion, sweet peppers, and remaining pasta sauce. Gently stir in meatballs. Cover and cook on low-heat setting for 3½ to 4 hours or on high-heat setting for 2 to 2½ hours.

3 To serve, place meatballs on bottoms of buns. Top with sauce and cheese. Add tops of buns.

Per serving: 747 cal., 25 g total fat (7 g sat. fat), 117 mg chol., 2,266 mg sodium, 94 g carbo., 7 g fiber, 39 g pro.

*NOTE: The internal color of a meatball is not a reliable doneness indicator. A turkey meatball cooked to 165°F is safe, regardless of color. To measure the doneness of a meatball, insert an instant-read thermometer into the center of the meatball.

MEATLESS MAIN DISHES

4

Looking for ways to use zucchini and yellow summer squash? Try this no-fuss pasta.

CREAMY PASTA & VEGETABLES

PREP:
20 minutes

COOK:
Low 5 hours, High 2½ hours

MAKES:
10 servings

SLOW COOKER:
3½- or 4-quart

2   26- to 32-ounce jars tomato-basil pasta sauce
     or your favorite purchased pasta sauce

1   medium zucchini, halved lengthwise and cut into
     ½-inch-thick slices

1   medium yellow summer squash, halved lengthwise
     and cut into ½-inch-thick slices

1   medium onion, chopped

¼   cup dry white wine

½   of an 8-ounce package cream cheese, cubed
     Hot cooked mafalda or other pasta
     Finely shredded Parmesan cheese

1 In a 3½- or 4-quart slow cooker stir together pasta sauce, zucchini, yellow summer squash, onion, and wine. Cover and cook on low-heat setting for 5 to 7 hours or on high-heat setting for 2½ to 3½ hours.

2 Stir in cream cheese until melted. Serve over hot cooked pasta. Top individual servings with Parmesan cheese.

Per serving: 460 cal., 15 g total fat (8 g sat. fat), 36 mg chol., 1,067 mg sodium, 56 g carbo., 4 g fiber, 24 g pro.

Be sure to rinse the leeks thoroughly to remove the grit trapped between layers.

PUMPKIN-SAUCED RAVIOLI

1	20-ounce package frozen cheese-filled ravioli or tortellini
3	medium leeks, halved lengthwise and sliced (about 1 cup)
2	14-ounce cans vegetable broth
1	15-ounce can pumpkin
¼	cup water
2	tablespoons packed brown sugar
½	teaspoon ground ginger
¼	teaspoon salt
¼	teaspoon black pepper
¾	cup finely shredded Parmesan cheese (3 ounces)
¾	cup chopped walnuts, toasted

1 In a 3½- or 4-quart slow cooker stir together ravioli or tortellini, leeks, broth, pumpkin, the water, brown sugar, ginger, salt, and pepper.

2 Cover and cook on low-heat setting for 4 hours or on high-heat setting for 2 hours.

3 Top individual servings with Parmesan cheese and walnuts. Serve immediately.

Per serving: 379 cal., 15 g total fat (4 g sat. fat), 36 mg chol., 1,030 mg sodium, 50 g carbo., 4 g fiber, 15 g pro.

PREP:
20 minutes
COOK:
Low 4 hours, High 2 hours
MAKES:
6 servings
SLOW COOKER:
3½- or 4-quart

Italian blend cheeses are sold in several combinations. Try various brands until you find the one you like best.

MEDITERRANEAN PASTA, BEANS & CHEESE

PREP:
15 minutes

COOK:
Low 5 hours

MAKES:
6 to 8 servings

SLOW COOKER:
3½- or 4-quart

Disposable slow-cooker liner

1 19-ounce can white kidney beans (cannellini beans), rinsed and drained

1 15-ounce jar cheese dip

1 14½-ounce can diced tomatoes with basil, garlic, and oregano, undrained

1 8-ounce package shredded Italian blend cheeses (2 cups)

1 medium red or green sweet pepper, chopped

1 cup chopped onion

⅔ cup water

12 ounces dried penne pasta

1 2¼-ounce can sliced pitted ripe olives, drained

1 Place slow-cooker liner in a 3½- or 4-quart slow cooker. In a large bowl stir together beans, cheese dip, undrained tomatoes, shredded cheese, sweet pepper, onion, and the water. Transfer to lined slow cooker.

2 Cover and cook on low-heat setting for 5 to 5½ hours.

3 Before serving, cook pasta according to package directions; drain. Carefully spoon bean mixture into a very large bowl; stir in olives and pasta.

Per serving: 629 cal., 29 g total fat (15 g sat. fat), 91 mg chol., 1,880 mg sodium, 73 g carbo., 7 g fiber, 30 g pro.

The mix of white kidney beans and soybeans provides lots of protein for this one-dish meal.

MEATLESS SHEPHERD'S PIE

2   19-ounce cans white kidney beans (cannellini beans), rinsed and drained

1   12-ounce package frozen green soybeans (edamame)

3   carrots, peeled and sliced

1   large onion, cut into wedges

1   14½-ounce can diced tomatoes, drained

1   12-ounce jar mushroom gravy

2   cloves garlic, minced

1   24-ounce package refrigerated mashed potatoes

1   cup shredded cheddar cheese (4 ounces)

1 In a 5- to 6-quart slow cooker stir together white kidney beans, soybeans, carrots, onion, tomatoes, gravy, and garlic.

2 Cover and cook on low-heat setting for 10 to 12 hours or on high-heat setting for 5 to 6 hours.

3 If using low-heat setting, turn to high-heat setting. Spoon mashed potatoes on top of bean mixture. Sprinkle with cheese. Cover and cook about 30 minutes more or until potatoes are heated through.

Per serving: 320 cal., 9 g total fat (3 g sat. fat), 15 mg chol., 805 mg sodium, 47 g carbo., 13 g fiber, 20 g pro.

PREP:
25 minutes

COOK:
Low 10 hours, High 5 hours; plus 30 minutes on High

MAKES:
8 servings

SLOW COOKER:
5- to 6-quart

If your supermarket doesn't carry vegetarian chili beans, look for them in health or organic food stores.

CHILI BEANS & POTATOES

PREP:
15 minutes

COOK:
Low 8 hours, High 4 hours

MAKES:
8 servings

SLOW COOKER:
4- to 5-quart

2   pounds tiny new potatoes, quartered

2   15- to 16-ounce cans vegetarian chili beans, undrained

1   10-ounce package frozen whole kernel corn

1   to 2 chipotle chile peppers in adobo sauce, drained and finely chopped*

½   cup vegetable broth or chicken broth

Shredded cheddar cheese

Dairy sour cream

1 In a 4- to 5-quart slow cooker combine the potatoes, undrained beans, corn, chipotle peppers, and broth.

2 Cover and cook on low-heat setting for 8 to 9 hours or on high-heat setting for 4 to 4½ hours. Garnish individual servings with cheese and sour cream.

Per serving: 463 cal., 6 g total fat (3 g sat. fat), 13 mg chol., 537 mg sodium, 44 g carbo., 7 g fiber, 11 g pro.

*NOTE: Because chile peppers contain volatile oils that can burn your skin and eyes, avoid direct contact with them as much as possible. When working with chile peppers, wear plastic or rubber gloves. If your bare hands do touch the peppers, wash your hands and nails well with soap and warm water.

Curry is an Indian or Far Eastern dish that features foods seasoned with curry powder—a blend of up to 20 ground spices, herbs, and seeds.

VEGETABLE CURRY

4	medium carrots, sliced
2	medium potatoes, cut into ½-inch cubes
1	15-ounce can garbanzo beans (chickpeas), rinsed and drained
8	ounces fresh green beans, cut into 1-inch pieces
1	cup coarsely chopped onion
3	cloves garlic, minced
2	tablespoons quick-cooking tapioca
2	teaspoons curry powder
1	teaspoon ground coriander
¼	to ½ teaspoon crushed red pepper
¼	teaspoon salt
⅛	teaspoon ground cinnamon
1	14-ounce can vegetable broth or chicken broth
1	14½-ounce can diced tomatoes, undrained
	Hot cooked rice

PREP:
20 minutes

COOK:
Low 7 hours, High 3½ hours

STAND:
5 minutes

MAKES:
4 servings

SLOW COOKER:
3½- to 5-quart

1 In a 3½- to 5-quart slow cooker combine carrots, potatoes, garbanzo beans, green beans, onion, garlic, tapioca, curry powder, coriander, crushed red pepper, salt, and cinnamon. Pour broth over all.

2 Cover and cook on low-heat setting for 7 to 9 hours or on high-heat setting for 3½ to 4½ hours.

3 Stir in undrained tomatoes. Let stand, covered, for 5 minutes. Serve with hot cooked rice.

Per serving: 407 cal., 3 g total fat (0 g sat. fat), 0 mg chol., 1,068 mg sodium, 87 g carbo., 12 g fiber, 13 g pro.

Chutney lends sweetness and a touch of heat while the almonds add crunch to this hearty apple-and-bean medley.

CURRIED BEANS

PREP:
20 minutes

STAND:
1 hour

COOK:
Low 8 hours, High 4 hours; plus 15 minutes on High

MAKES:
6 servings

SLOW COOKER:
3½- or 4-quart

FOR 5- TO 6-QUART SLOW COOKER:
Use 1½ pounds dry red kidney beans, two 14-ounce cans vegetable broth, 1½ cups water, 2 medium onions, two 4-ounce cans (drained weight) mushrooms, 1 cup golden raisins, 2 tablespoons curry powder, ¼ teaspoon black pepper, and 3 medium apples. Makes 10 servings.

Per serving: 317 cal., 1 g total fat (0 g sat. fat), 0 mg chol., 418 mg sodium, 64 g carbo., 20 g fiber, 18 g pro.

1   pound dry red kidney beans (3½ cups)

1   14-ounce can vegetable broth

¾   cup water

1   medium onion, cut into thin wedges

1   4-ounce can (drained weight) sliced mushrooms, drained

½   cup golden raisins

1   tablespoon curry powder

¼   teaspoon black pepper

1   large red and/or green apple, peeled if desired, cored, and sliced

    Hot cooked couscous (optional)

    Bottled chutney (optional)

    Chopped almonds, toasted (optional)

1 Rinse beans; place in a large saucepan. Add enough water to cover beans by 2 inches. Bring to boiling; reduce heat. Simmer, uncovered, for 10 minutes. Remove from heat. Cover and let stand for 1 hour. Drain and rinse beans.

2 In a 3½- or 4-quart slow cooker stir together beans, broth, the water, onion, drained mushrooms, raisins, curry powder, and pepper.

3 Cover and cook on low-heat setting for 8 to 9 hours or on high-heat setting for 4 to 5 hours.

4 If desired, mash beans slightly. Stir in apple. If using low-heat setting, turn to high-heat setting. Cover and cook for 15 minutes more. If desired, serve over couscous and top with chutney. If desired, sprinkle with almonds.

Per serving: 325 cal., 1 g total fat (0 g sat. fat), 0 mg chol., 350 mg sodium, 64 g carbo., 21 g fiber, 20 g pro.

Raisins and mixed dried fruit bits lend subtle sweetness to this bean-and-couscous combo.

FRUITED COUSCOUS & BEANS

2   15-ounce cans Great Northern or pinto beans, rinsed and drained

1   large onion, finely chopped

1   cup golden raisins

1   cup mixed dried fruit bits

2   teaspoons grated fresh ginger

¾   teaspoon salt

¼   teaspoon crushed red pepper

1   14-ounce can vegetable broth or chicken broth

1¾   cups unsweetened pineapple juice

1   10-ounce package quick-cooking couscous

1   tablespoon olive oil

½   cup sliced almonds, toasted

Sliced green onions (optional)

PREP:
20 minutes

COOK:
Low 6 hours, High 3 hours

STAND:
5 minutes

MAKES:
6 servings

SLOW COOKER:
3½- or 4-quart

1 In a 3½- or 4-quart slow cooker combine beans, onion, raisins, dried fruit bits, ginger, salt, and crushed red pepper. Pour broth and pineapple juice over bean mixture in slow cooker.

2 Cover and cook on low-heat setting for 6 to 7 hours or on high-heat setting for 3 to 3½ hours.

3 Stir in couscous and oil. Remove liner from slow cooker, if possible, or turn off slow cooker. Cover and let stand for 5 to 10 minutes or until couscous is tender. Fluff with a fork. Sprinkle individual servings with almonds and, if desired, green onions.

Per serving: 623 cal., 9 g total fat (1 g sat. fat), 0 mg chol., 596 mg sodium, 120 g carbo., 14 g fiber, 22 g pro.

This bayou blockbuster simmers tomato, zucchini, and garbanzo beans into a Cajun-style stew.

VEGETABLE MEDLEY WITH COUSCOUS

PREP:
20 minutes

COOK:
Low 8 hours, High 4 hours

MAKES:
4 servings

SLOW COOKER:
3½- or 4-quart

2   medium zucchini, halved lengthwise and sliced

1   15-ounce can garbanzo beans (chickpeas), rinsed and drained

2   medium carrots, chopped

1   small onion, thinly sliced

1   teaspoon sugar

2   cloves garlic, minced

½   teaspoon salt

½   teaspoon Cajun seasoning

Dash cayenne pepper

2   14½-ounce cans diced tomatoes, undrained

1   cup water

2   cups hot cooked couscous or brown rice

1 In 3½- or 4-quart slow cooker combine zucchini, beans, carrots, onion, sugar, garlic, salt, Cajun seasoning, and cayenne pepper. Stir in undrained tomatoes and the water.

2 Cover and cook on low-heat setting for 8 to 10 hours or on high-heat setting for 4 to 5 hours. Serve vegetable mixture over hot cooked couscous.

Per serving: 304 cal., 2 g total fat (0 g sat. fat), 0 mg chol., 1,001 mg sodium, 61 g carbo., 9 g fiber, 11 g pro.

Beef or chicken broth also will work well in this meatless south-of-the-border entrée.

PINTO BEAN & COUSCOUS TOSTADAS

1½	cups dry pinto beans
2	cups water
1	14-ounce can vegetable broth
1	cup chopped carrots
¼	teaspoon salt
¼	teaspoon crushed red pepper
1	cup purchased salsa
1	cup quick-cooking couscous
8	tostada shells
	Shredded cheddar cheese
	Dairy sour cream, shredded lettuce, and/or purchased salsa (optional)

PREP:
25 minutes

STAND:
1 hour plus 5 minutes

COOK:
Low 8 hours, High 4 hours

MAKES:
8 servings

SLOW COOKER:
3½- or 4-quart

1 Rinse beans; place in a large saucepan. Add enough water to cover beans by 2 inches. Bring to boiling; reduce heat. Simmer, uncovered, for 10 minutes. Remove from heat. Cover and let stand for 1 hour. Drain and rinse beans.

2 In a 3½- or 4-quart slow cooker stir together beans, the 2 cups water, broth, carrots, salt, and crushed red pepper.

3 Cover and cook on low-heat setting for 8 to 10 hours or on high-heat setting for 4 to 5 hours.

4 Stir in the 1 cup salsa and the uncooked couscous. Remove liner from slow cooker, if possible, or turn off slow cooker. Cover and let stand for 5 minutes. Serve bean-couscous mixture on tostada shells; top with cheese. If desired, serve with sour cream, lettuce, and/or additional salsa.

Per serving: 304 cal., 6 g total fat (2 g sat. fat), 9 mg chol., 477 mg sodium, 49 g carbo., 8 g fiber, 13 g pro.

Sprinkle crumbled tortilla chips on top of each serving of these creamy beans for a little crunch.

CHEESY GREEN CHILES & BEANS

PREP:
15 minutes

COOK:
Low 6 hours, High 3 hours

MAKES:
8 servings

SLOW COOKER:
3½- to 5-quart

3   15- to 16-ounce cans pinto beans, rinsed and drained

1   14½-ounce can stewed tomatoes, undrained, cut up

1   cup purchased salsa

2   4-ounce cans diced green chile peppers

1   teaspoon ground cumin

1   teaspoon dried oregano, crushed

1   8-ounce package cream cheese, cubed

4   cups hot cooked rice

1   cup shredded Colby and Monterey Jack cheese (4 ounces)

1 In a 3½- to 5-quart slow cooker stir together beans, undrained tomatoes, salsa, chile peppers, cumin, and oregano.

2 Cover and cook on low-heat setting for 6 to 8 hours or on high-heat setting for 3 to 4 hours. Add cream cheese, stirring until melted. Serve over rice and top with cheese.

Per serving: 428 cal., 16 g total fat (9 g sat. fat), 44 mg chol., 959 mg sodium, 55 g carbo., 9 g fiber, 18 g pro.

For extra color, use one green sweet pepper and one yellow or red sweet pepper.

RED BEANS CREOLE

3½ cups dry red beans (1½ pounds)

5 cups water

3 cups chopped onion

2 4-ounce cans (drained weight) sliced mushrooms, drained

6 cloves garlic, minced

2 tablespoons Creole seasoning

1 14½-ounce can diced tomatoes with basil, garlic, and oregano, undrained

2 cups instant brown rice

2 medium green sweet peppers, cut into strips

Bottled hot pepper sauce (optional)

1 Rinse beans; place in a large saucepan. Add enough water to cover beans by 2 inches. Bring to boiling; reduce heat. Simmer, uncovered, for 10 minutes. Remove from heat. Cover and let stand for 1 hour. Drain and rinse beans.

2 In a 3½- or 4-quart slow cooker combine beans, the 5 cups water, the onion, drained mushrooms, garlic, and Creole seasoning.

3 Cover and cook on low-heat setting for 11 to 13 hours or on high-heat setting for 5½ to 6½ hours.

4 If using low-heat setting, turn to high-heat setting. Stir in undrained tomatoes, uncooked rice, and sweet pepper. Cover and cook for 30 minutes more. If desired, pass bottled hot pepper sauce.

Per serving: 415 cal., 2 g total fat (0 g sat. fat), 0 mg chol., 541 mg sodium, 81 g carbo., 16 g fiber, 23 g pro.

PREP:
25 minutes

STAND:
1 hour

COOK:
Low 11 hours, High 5½ hours; plus 30 minutes on High

MAKES:
4 or 5 servings

SLOW COOKER:
3½- or 4-quart

A tasty and convenient ingredient to have on hand, wild rice mix makes this entrée extra easy.

WILD RICE WITH PINTO BEANS

PREP:
15 minutes

COOK:
Low 7 hours, High 3½ hours

MAKES:
6 servings

SLOW COOKER:
3½- or 4-quart

2   15-ounce cans pinto beans, rinsed and drained

1   14½-ounce can diced tomatoes with onion
    and garlic, undrained

1   6-ounce package long grain and wild rice mix

1   medium onion, chopped

1   stalk celery, sliced

¼   teaspoon black pepper

2   14-ounce cans vegetable broth

1 In a 3½- or 4-quart slow cooker combine beans, undrained tomatoes, rice mix and seasoning packet, onion, celery, and pepper. Pour broth over all.

2 Cover and cook on low-heat setting for 7 to 8 hours or on high-heat setting for 3½ to 4 hours.

Per serving: 245 cal., 2 g total fat (0 g sat. fat), 0 mg chol., 1,683 mg sodium, 51 g carbo., 8 g fiber, 11 g pro.

Be sure to select sweet peppers that have flat bottoms so they won't tip over during cooking.

RICE-STUFFED PEPPERS

4	medium red, green, and/or yellow sweet peppers
1	cup cooked converted rice
1½	cups frozen green soybeans (edamame)
½	cup shredded carrot
¼	cup bottled stir-fry sauce
½	cup water
1	tablespoon sesame seeds, toasted

1 Cut tops from sweet peppers and set aside. Remove membranes and seeds from sweet peppers. Chop enough of the tops of the sweet peppers to equal ⅓ cup. In a medium bowl stir together the chopped sweet pepper, rice, soybeans, carrot, and stir-fry sauce. Spoon mixture into sweet peppers.

2 Pour the water into a 4- to 5-quart slow cooker. Place sweet peppers, filled sides up, in slow cooker.

3 Cover and cook on low-heat setting for 5 to 6 hours or on high-heat setting for 2½ to 3 hours.

4 Transfer sweet peppers to serving platter. Sprinkle with sesame seeds.

Per serving: 184 cal., 3 g total fat (0 g sat. fat), 1 mg chol., 385 mg sodium, 30 g carbo., 8 g fiber, 10 g pro.

PREP:
25 minutes

COOK:
Low 5 hours, High 2½ hours

MAKES:
4 servings

SLOW COOKER:
4- to 5-quart

Flecks of colorful zucchini, sweet peppers, and tomatoes dress up the rice in this cheesy dish.

BROWN RICE PRIMAVERA

PREP:
25 minutes

COOK:
High 2 hours plus 30 minutes

MAKES:
6 servings

SLOW COOKER:
5- to 6-quart

1 medium eggplant, peeled if desired and cubed

2 medium zucchini, halved lengthwise and cut into ½-inch pieces

1 medium onion, cut into thin wedges

1 14-ounce can vegetable broth

2 medium red and/or yellow sweet peppers, cut into thin, bite-size strips

1 14½-ounce can diced tomatoes with basil, garlic, and oregano, drained

1 cup instant brown rice

8 ounces feta cheese, crumbled (2 cups)

1 In a 5- to 6-quart slow cooker stir together eggplant, zucchini, onion, and broth. Cover and cook on high-heat setting for 2 to 2½ hours.

2 Stir in sweet peppers, drained tomatoes, and uncooked rice. Cover and cook for 30 minutes more. Sprinkle individual servings with feta cheese.

Per serving: 212 cal., 9 g total fat (6 g sat. fat), 34 mg chol., 1,045 mg sodium, 26 g carbo., 5 g fiber, 9 g pro.

Toss a crisp, green lettuce salad to go along with this double-cheese rice main dish.

WALNUT-CHEESE RISOTTO

	Nonstick cooking spray
1½	cups converted rice (do not substitute long grain rice)
2	14-ounce cans vegetable broth
1½	cups milk
2	cups shredded carrot
1	10¾-ounce can condensed cream of mushroom soup
1	medium onion, chopped
1	teaspoon finely shredded lemon peel
¼	teaspoon black pepper
6	ounces process Swiss cheese, torn
1	cup finely shredded Asiago cheese (4 ounces)
1	cup loose-pack frozen peas
¾	cup chopped walnuts, toasted

1 Coat a 4- to 5-quart slow cooker with cooking spray. Add rice, broth, milk, carrot, cream of mushroom soup, onion, lemon peel, and pepper to prepared cooker; stir lightly to combine. Cover and cook on low-heat setting for 5 to 5½ hours.

2 Stir in Swiss cheese, Asiago cheese, peas, and walnuts. Remove liner from cooker, if possible, or turn off cooker. Let stand, covered, for 15 minutes before serving.

Per serving: 428 cal., 21 g total fat (9 g sat. fat), 38 mg chol., 1,163 mg sodium, 43 g carbo., 3 g fiber, 17 g pro.

PREP:
20 minutes

COOK:
Low 5 hours

STAND:
15 minutes

MAKES:
8 servings

SLOW COOKER:
4- to 5-quart

Gruyère cheese, similar to Swiss cheese, boasts a full, well-rounded, nutty flavor.

MUSHROOMS & SWEET POTATOES ON RICE

PREP:
25 minutes

COOK:
Low 5 hours, High 2½ hours

MAKES:
6 servings

SLOW COOKER:
4- to 6-quart

4	medium sweet potatoes (about 2 pounds), peeled and cut into 1-inch cubes
8	ounces assorted fresh mushrooms (such as button, stemmed shiitake, or cremini), quartered
2	medium onions, cut into wedges
1	12-ounce jar mushroom gravy
½	cup vegetable broth
1	tablespoon quick-cooking tapioca
1	teaspoon dried thyme, crushed
¼	teaspoon salt
¼	teaspoon black pepper
	Hot cooked brown rice
1½	cups shredded Gruyère or Swiss cheese (6 ounces)

1 In a 4- to 6-quart slow cooker stir together sweet potatoes, mushrooms, onions, gravy, broth, tapioca, thyme, salt, and pepper.

2 Cover and cook on low-heat setting for 5 to 6 hours or on high-heat setting for 2½ to 3 hours.

3 Serve over rice. Sprinkle individual servings with cheese.

Per serving: 413 cal., 12 g total fat (6 g sat. fat), 31 mg chol., 695 mg sodium, 62 g carbo., 7 g fiber, 16 g pro.

Three kinds of grains make this dish wholesome, filling, and infinitely interesting.

MULTI-GRAIN PILAF

²⁄₃	cup wheat berries
½	cup regular barley
½	cup wild rice (not quick-cooking)
2	14-ounce cans vegetable broth or chicken broth
2	cups frozen green soybeans (edamame) or baby lima beans
1	medium red sweet pepper, chopped
1	medium onion, finely chopped
1	tablespoon butter or margarine
¾	teaspoon dried sage, crushed
½	teaspoon salt
¼	teaspoon coarsely ground black pepper
4	cloves garlic, minced
	Grated Parmesan cheese (optional)

PREP:
25 minutes

COOK:
Low 6 hours, High 3 hours

MAKES:
6 servings

SLOW COOKER:
3½- or 4-quart

1 Rinse and drain wheat berries, barley, and wild rice. In a 3½- or 4-quart slow cooker combine wheat berries, barley, wild rice, broth, soybeans or lima beans, sweet pepper, onion, butter, sage, salt, black pepper, and garlic.

2 Cover and cook on low-heat setting for 6 to 8 hours or on high-heat setting for 3 to 4 hours. Stir before serving. If desired, sprinkle individual servings with Parmesan cheese.

Per serving: 342 cal., 9 g total fat (2 g sat. fat), 5 mg chol., 814 mg sodium, 50 g carbo., 10 g fiber, 20 g pro.

Be sure to use firm tofu for this dish because it cuts into even strips that will hold their shape as you stir them into the vegetables and rice.

MEXICAN TOFU WITH VEGETABLES & RICE

PREP:
25 minutes

COOK:
Low 7 hours, High 3 hours; plus 15 minutes on High

MAKES:
6 servings

SLOW COOKER:
3½- or 4-quart

FOR 5- TO 6-QUART COOKER:

Use 1 medium head cauliflower, cut into florets (6 cups); 2 large red sweet peppers, cut in bite-size strips (2 cups); 2 large green sweet peppers, cut in bite-size strips (2 cups); 2½ cups packaged, purchased baby carrots; one 10-ounce package frozen whole kernel corn; one 16-ounce jar corn and black bean salsa; one 14-ounce can vegetable broth; 2½ cups instant brown rice; and one 16-ounce package firm tofu.* Makes 10 servings.

Per serving: 187 cal., 3 g total fat (0 g sat. fat), 0 mg chol., 515 mg sodium, 33 g carbo., 5 g fiber, 10 g pro.

4	cups cauliflower florets
3	cups bite-size strips red and/or green sweet peppers
2	cups packaged, peeled baby carrots, halved lengthwise
1½	cups loose-pack frozen whole kernel corn
½	of a 16-ounce jar black bean and corn salsa or salsa with cilantro (about 1 cup)
1	cup vegetable broth
1½	cups instant brown rice
½	of a 16-ounce package extra-firm tub-style tofu (fresh bean curd),* drained and cut into bite-size strips
	Shredded Mexican cheese blend or shredded Monterey Jack cheese with jalapeño chile peppers (optional)

1 In a 3½- or 4-quart slow cooker stir together cauliflower, sweet peppers, carrots, corn, salsa, and broth.

2 Cover and cook on low-heat setting for 7 to 8 hours or on high-heat setting for 3 to 4 hours.

3 If using low-heat setting, turn to high-heat setting. Stir in uncooked rice. Cover and cook for 15 minutes more. Stir in tofu just before serving. If desired, sprinkle with cheese.

Per serving: 198 cal., 3 g total fat (0 g sat. fat), 0 mg chol., 473 mg sodium, 37 g carbo., 6 g fiber, 10 g pro.

***NOTE:** Do not use silken-style tofu.

Mild tofu soaks up the enchanting blend of peanut sauce, soy sauce, fresh ginger, and toasted sesame oil in this easy Asian-inspired dish.

SESAME VEGETABLES & TOFU

1	16-ounce package frozen (yellow, green, and red) peppers and onion stir-fry vegetables
1	10-ounce package frozen cut green beans
1	8-ounce can sliced bamboo shoots, drained
1	cup vegetable broth
1	4½-ounce can (drained weight) sliced mushrooms, drained
¼	cup bottled peanut sauce
2	tablespoons soy sauce
1	tablespoon grated fresh ginger
2	teaspoons toasted sesame oil
2	cups broccoli florets
4	ounces banh pho (Vietnamese wide rice noodles)
8	ounces refrigerated, water-packed firm tofu (fresh bean curd), drained and cut into bite-size strips
½	cup peanuts, coarsely chopped

PREP:
25 minutes

COOK:
Low 3½ hours; plus 30 minutes on High

MAKES:
6 to 8 servings

SLOW COOKER:
4- to 5-quart

1 In a 4- to 5-quart slow cooker stir together frozen stir-fry vegetables, frozen green beans, bamboo shoots, broth, drained mushrooms, peanut sauce, soy sauce, ginger, and sesame oil.

2 Cover and cook on low-heat setting for 3½ to 4½ hours.

3 Turn slow cooker to high-heat setting. Stir in broccoli. Cover and cook for 30 minutes more.

4 Meanwhile, cook banh pho according to package directions; drain. Just before serving, stir noodles and tofu into vegetable mixture in slow cooker. Sprinkle individual servings with peanuts.

Per serving: 277 cal., 11 g total fat (2 g sat. fat), 0 mg chol., 735 mg sodium, 34 g carbo., 6 g fiber, 11 g pro.

Penne and rigatoni are delicious with chunky tomato-based sauces like this one.

PASTA WITH LENTIL SAUCE

PREP:
15 minutes

COOK:
Low 12 hours, High 6 hours

MAKES:
8 servings

SLOW COOKER:
4½- or 5-quart

1   26- to 32-ounce jar meatless tomato-based pasta sauce

1   14-ounce can vegetable broth

½   cup water

1   cup dry brown or yellow lentils, rinsed and drained

1   cup chopped onion

1   cup chopped carrot

1   cup chopped celery

¼   teaspoon crushed red pepper

    Hot cooked pasta

    Finely shredded Parmesan cheese (optional)

1 In a 4½- or 5-quart slow cooker stir together pasta sauce, broth, and the water. Stir in lentils, onion, carrot, celery, and crushed red pepper.

2 Cover and cook on low-heat setting for 12 to 14 hours or on high-heat setting for 6 to 7 hours.

3 Serve sauce over hot-cooked pasta. If desired, pass Parmesan cheese.

Per serving: 404 cal., 4 g total fat (1 g sat. fat), 0 mg chol., 667 mg sodium, 75 g carbo., 12 g fiber, 16 g pro.

Traditional moussaka is a layered eggplant and meat casserole. This meatless slow cooker adaptation mixes many of the same flavors with cubes of eggplant, lentils, and potatoes.

LENTIL "MOUSSAKA"

¾ cup dry brown or yellow lentils, rinsed and drained

2 medium potatoes, cut into ½-inch cubes

1 cup vegetable broth

2 cloves garlic, minced

½ teaspoon salt

¼ teaspoon ground cinnamon

¼ teaspoon black pepper

1 medium eggplant, cubed

3 medium carrots, thinly sliced

1 14½-ounce can diced tomatoes with basil, garlic, and oregano, undrained

1 8-ounce package cream cheese, softened

2 eggs, slightly beaten

1 In a 3½- or 4-quart slow cooker stir together lentils, potatoes, broth, garlic, salt, cinnamon, and pepper. Top with eggplant and carrots.

2 Cover and cook on low-heat setting for 6 hours or on high-heat setting for 3 hours.

3 Stir in undrained tomatoes. In a medium bowl combine cream cheese and eggs; beat with an electric mixer on low speed until combined. Dollop cream cheese mixture over lentil mixture in slow cooker. If using low-heat setting, turn to high-heat setting. Cover and cook for 30 minutes more.

Per serving: 333 cal., 15 g total fat (9 g sat. fat), 112 mg chol., 868 mg sodium, 36 g carbo., 11 g fiber, 15 g pro.

PREP:
20 minutes

COOK:
Low 6 hours, High 3 hours; plus 30 minutes on High

MAKES:
6 servings

SLOW COOKER:
3½- or 4-quart

FOR 5- TO 6-QUART SLOW COOKER:
Use 1¼ cups brown or yellow lentils, 4 medium potatoes, one 14-ounce can vegetable broth, 3 cloves garlic, ½ teaspoon ground cinnamon, 1 large eggplant, 4 medium carrots, and two 14½-ounce cans diced tomatoes with basil, garlic, and oregano. Do not change amounts of salt, pepper, cream cheese, and eggs. Makes 8 servings.

Per serving: 347 cal., 12 g total fat (7 g sat. fat), 84 mg chol., 1,002 mg sodium, 47 g carbo., 14 g fiber, 16 g pro.

If your motto is "The hotter the better," serve these meatless tacos with hot-style salsa and Monterey Jack cheese with jalapeños instead of cheddar cheese.

LENTIL-BULGUR TACOS

PREP:
20 minutes

COOK:
Low 4 hours, High 2 hours; plus 30 minutes on High

OVEN:
350°F

MAKES:
12 servings

SLOW COOKER:
3½- or 4-quart

1	14-ounce can vegetable broth
1½	cups dry brown or yellow lentils, rinsed and drained
1	6-ounce can tomato paste
2	carrots, chopped
1	onion, chopped
2	cloves garlic, minced
1	1.25-ounce package taco seasoning mix
2½	cups water
½	cup bulgur
24	corn tortillas, warmed*
	Purchased salsa, shredded lettuce, shredded cheddar cheese, and/or dairy sour cream (optional)

1 In a 3½- or 4-quart slow cooker stir together broth, lentils, tomato paste, carrots, onion, garlic, and taco seasoning mix. Stir in the water.

2 Cover and cook on low-heat setting for 4 to 6 hours or on high-heat setting for 2 to 3 hours.

3 If using low-heat setting, turn to high-heat setting. Stir in uncooked bulgur. Cover and cook for 30 minutes more.

4 Divide lentil mixture among corn tortillas. If desired, top with salsa, lettuce, cheese, and/or sour cream.

Per serving: 245 cal., 2 g total fat (0 g sat. fat), 0 mg chol., 449 mg sodium, 48 g carbo., 12 g fiber, 11 g pro.

*NOTE: To warm tortillas, preheat oven to 350°F. Wrap tortillas tightly in foil. Heat in the oven about 10 minutes or until heated through.

An appetizing main dish, this savory gratin also is terrific as a side dish for twelve.

BARLEY & SQUASH GRATIN

1	2-pound butternut squash, peeled, halved, seeded, and cubed (about 5 cups)
1	10-ounce package frozen chopped spinach, thawed and well drained
1	medium onion, cut into wedges
1	cup regular barley
1	14-ounce can vegetable broth
½	cup water
3	cloves garlic, minced
¾	teaspoon salt
¼	teaspoon black pepper
½	cup shredded Parmesan cheese (2 ounces)

1 In a 3½- or 4-quart slow cooker stir together squash, spinach, onion, barley, broth, the water, garlic, salt, and pepper.

2 Cover and cook on low-heat setting for 6 to 7 hours or on high-heat setting for 3 to 3½ hours.

3 Remove liner from slow cooker, if possible, or turn off slow cooker. Sprinkle with Parmesan cheese. Let stand, covered, for 10 minutes before serving.

Per serving: 196 cal., 3 g total fat (1 g sat. fat), 5 mg chol., 737 mg sodium, 36 g carbo., 8 g fiber, 9 g pro.

PREP:
15 minutes

COOK:
Low 6 hours, High 3 hours

STAND:
10 minutes

MAKES:
6 servings

SLOW COOKER:
3½- or 4-quart

Tubes of refrigerated cooked polenta usually are sold in the produce section of the supermarket. Choose the flavor that appeals to you.

POLENTA & VEGETABLE RAGOUT

PREP:
20 minutes

COOK:
Low 8 hours plus 15 minutes, High 4 hours plus 15 minutes

MAKES:
5 servings

SLOW COOKER:
5- to 6-quart

1   26- to 32-ounce jar meatless tomato-based pasta sauce

1   medium eggplant, peeled and cubed (about 1 pound)

1   medium zucchini, halved lengthwise and cut into ½-inch-thick slices

1   medium onion, chopped

8   ounces fresh mushrooms, quartered

1   cup vegetable broth

¼   cup dry red wine (optional)

1   16-ounce tube refrigerated cooked polenta, cut into 1-inch cubes

⅓   cup grated or finely shredded Parmesan cheese

1 In a 5- to 6-quart slow cooker stir together pasta sauce, eggplant, zucchini, onion, mushrooms, broth, and, if desired, wine.

2 Cover and cook on low-heat setting for 8 to 10 hours or on high-heat setting for 4 to 5 hours.

3 Stir in polenta cubes. Cover and cook for 15 minutes more. Sprinkle individual servings with Parmesan cheese.

Per serving: 296 cal., 7 g total fat (2 g sat. fat), 5 mg chol., 1,341 mg sodium, 49 g carbo., 10 g fiber, 10 g pro.

SOUPS & STEWS

Ask any BLT lover—bacon and tomatoes are a match made in food heaven. Here the duo works its magic on a rib-sticking stew.

BACON BEEF STEW

PREP:
30 minutes

COOK:
Low 9 hours, High 4½ hours

MAKES:
6 main-dish servings

SLOW COOKER:
3½- or 4-quart

6   slices bacon, cut into 1-inch pieces

1½   pounds boneless beef sirloin steak, cut 1 inch thick

2   medium potatoes, peeled and cut into ¾-inch pieces

2   cups packaged peeled baby carrots

1½   cups loose-pack frozen small whole onions

1   14½-ounce can diced tomatoes with basil, oregano, and garlic, undrained

1   12-ounce jar brown gravy

1 In a large skillet cook bacon over medium heat until crisp. Drain bacon on paper towels, reserving 1 tablespoon drippings in skillet. Wrap bacon and chill until ready to serve. Trim fat from beef. Cut beef into 1-inch pieces. In the same skillet brown beef, half at a time, in hot drippings. Drain off fat. Set aside.

2 In a 3½- or 4-quart slow cooker combine potatoes, carrots, and frozen onions. Add beef. In a medium bowl combine undrained tomatoes and gravy; stir into beef mixture in slow cooker.

3 Cover and cook on low-heat setting for 9 to 10 hours or on high-heat setting for 4½ to 5 hours. Sprinkle individual servings with bacon.

Per serving: 326 cal., 12 g total fat (4 g sat. fat), 77 mg chol., 883 mg sodium, 26 g carbo., 4 g fiber, 30 g pro.

It's easy to feed a houseful of fans with this great-tasting recipe. Prepare your choice of toppers and simmer the lively meat-and-bean combo ahead of time. Come serving time, set out the toppers, the lime slices, and a stack of bowls.

GAME DAY CHILI

2 pounds boneless beef round steak or boneless pork shoulder roast

2 large onions, chopped

2 large yellow, red, and/or green sweet peppers, chopped

2 15-ounce cans chili beans with chili gravy

2 14½-ounce cans Mexican-style stewed tomatoes, undrained, cut up

1 15-ounce can kidney beans or pinto beans, rinsed and drained

1 cup beer or beef broth

1 to 2 tablespoons chopped canned chipotle chile peppers in adobo sauce*

2 teaspoons garlic salt

2 teaspoons ground cumin

1 teaspoon dried oregano, crushed

1 recipe Cilantro Sour Cream, Cheese 'n' Nuts, Avocado-Tomato Salsa, Crunchy Corn Topper, and/or Hotter-than-Heck Topper (optional)

Lime slices (optional)

1 Trim fat from meat. Cut meat into ½-inch cubes. In a 5½- or 6-quart slow cooker combine meat, onions, sweet peppers, undrained chili beans with chili gravy, undrained tomatoes, kidney beans, beer, chipotle chile peppers, garlic salt, cumin, and oregano.

2 Cover and cook on low-heat setting for 10 to 12 hours or on high-heat setting for 5 to 6 hours. Spoon off fat. Serve with desired toppers and, if desired, lime slices.

Per serving: 294 cal., 5 g total fat (1 g sat. fat), 52 mg chol., 823 mg sodium, 32 g carbo., 8 g fiber, 29 g pro.

*NOTE: Because chile peppers contain volatile oils that can burn your skin and eyes, avoid direct contact with them as much as possible. When working with chile peppers, wear plastic or rubber gloves. If your bare hands do touch the peppers, wash your hands and nails well with soap and warm water.

PREP:
25 minutes

COOK:
Low 10 hours, High 5 hours

MAKES:
10 to 12 main-dish servings

SLOW COOKER:
5½- or 6-quart

CILANTRO SOUR CREAM:
In a small bowl combine one 8-ounce carton dairy sour cream and ¼ cup snipped fresh cilantro.

CHEESE 'N' NUTS: In a small bowl combine 1 cup shredded cheddar cheese, Monterey Jack cheese, or Mexican cheese blend (4 ounces) and ½ cup finely chopped walnuts, toasted.

AVOCADO-TOMATO SALSA:
In a medium bowl combine 1 ripe yet firm avocado, peeled, pitted, and chopped; 1 cup yellow and/or red cherry tomatoes, quartered; 1 tablespoon lemon juice or lime juice; and 1 fresh jalapeño chile pepper, seeded and chopped.*

CRUNCHY CORN TOPPER:
In a medium bowl combine 1 cup corn chips, slightly crushed, and 1 cup dried corn.

HOTTER-THAN-HECK TOPPER: In a small bowl combine ½ cup sliced pickled jalapeño chile peppers; ½ cup chopped, peeled jicama; and ¼ cup snipped fresh cilantro.

If you like chili with plenty of kick, use two chile peppers. For a chili kids will enjoy, leave the chile peppers out altogether.

DOUBLE-BEAN CHILI

PREP:
25 minutes

COOK:
Low 9 hours, High 4½ hours; plus 30 minutes on High

MAKES:
6 main-dish servings

SLOW COOKER:
3½- or 4-quart

1	pound boneless beef top round steak
2	14½-ounce cans diced tomatoes, undrained
1	14-ounce can beef broth
1	large onion, chopped
1	or 2 fresh jalapeño or serrano chile peppers, seeded and finely chopped*
2	cloves garlic, minced
4	teaspoons chili powder
1	tablespoon packed brown sugar
1½	teaspoons dried oregano, crushed
½	teaspoon ground cumin
¼	teaspoon black pepper
1	15-ounce can pinto beans, rinsed and drained
1	15-ounce can black beans, rinsed and drained
	Lime wedges (optional)
	Dairy sour cream (optional)
	Fresh cilantro or parsley leaves (optional)
	Tortilla chips (optional)

1 Trim fat from meat. Cut meat into 1-inch pieces. In a 3½- or 4-quart slow cooker combine meat, undrained tomatoes, broth, onion, chile peppers, garlic, chili powder, brown sugar, oregano, cumin, and black pepper.

2 Cover and cook on low-heat setting for 9 to 11 hours or on high-heat setting for 4½ to 5½ hours.

3 If using low-heat setting, turn to high-heat setting. Stir in pinto beans and black beans. Cover and cook for 30 minutes more. If desired, serve individual servings with lime wedges and sour cream and garnish with cilantro or parsley and tortilla chips.

Per serving: 280 cal., 5 g total fat (1 g sat. fat), 42 mg chol., 931 mg sodium, 35 g carbo., 9 g fiber, 28 g pro.

***NOTE:** Because chile peppers contain volatile oils that can burn your skin and eyes, avoid direct contact with them as much as possible. When working with chile peppers, wear plastic or rubber gloves. If your bare hands do touch the peppers, wash your hands and nails well with soap and warm water.

For authentic old-world flavor be sure to use Hungarian paprika and include the caraway seeds.

GOULASH STEW

2	pounds boneless beef top round roast
3	medium carrots, chopped
2	medium potatoes, peeled and chopped
1½	cups chopped onion
1	tablespoon paprika
2	cloves garlic, minced
½	teaspoon dried marjoram, crushed
¼	teaspoon caraway seeds, crushed (optional)
¼	teaspoon black pepper
1	bay leaf
2	14-ounce cans chicken broth
2	14½-ounce cans diced tomatoes, undrained
3	tablespoons tomato paste
½	cup dairy sour cream

1 Trim fat from meat. Cut meat into ½-inch cubes. In a 4- to 5-quart slow cooker combine meat, carrots, potatoes, onion, paprika, garlic, marjoram, caraway seeds (if desired), pepper, and bay leaf. Pour broth over all.

2 Cover and cook on low-heat setting for 8 to 10 hours or on high-heat setting for 4 to 5 hours.

3 In a small bowl combine undrained tomatoes and tomato paste; add to slow cooker and stir to combine. If using low-heat setting, turn to high-heat setting. Cook for 30 minutes more. Discard bay leaf. Top individual servings with sour cream.

Per serving: 330 cal., 7 g total fat (3 g sat. fat), 94 mg chol., 873 mg sodium, 26 g carbo., 4 g fiber, 39 g pro.

PREP:
25 minutes

COOK:
Low 8 hours, High 4 hours; plus 30 minutes on High

MAKES:
6 to 8 main-dish servings

SLOW COOKER:
4- to 5-quart

Start this quick-to-assemble recipe before you head out for a busy Saturday at the game or running errands, and supper will be ready and waiting when you return.

BUSY-DAY BEEF-VEGETABLE SOUP

PREP:
20 minutes

COOK:
Low 8 hours, High 4 hours

MAKES:
4 main-dish servings

SLOW COOKER:
3½- or 4-quart

1   pound boneless beef chuck roast

3   medium carrots, cut into ½-inch-thick slices

2   small potatoes, peeled if desired and cut into ½-inch cubes

1   medium onion, chopped

½   teaspoon salt

½   teaspoon dried thyme, crushed

1   bay leaf

2   14½-ounce cans diced tomatoes, undrained

1   cup water

½   cup loose-pack frozen peas

     Fresh parsley sprigs (optional)

1 Trim fat from meat. Cut meat into bite-size pieces. In a 3½- or 4-quart slow cooker combine meat, carrots, potatoes, and onion. Sprinkle with salt and thyme. Add bay leaf. Pour undrained tomatoes and the water over all.

2 Cover and cook on low-heat setting for 8 to 10 hours or on high-heat setting for 4 to 5 hours.

3 Discard bay leaf. Stir in frozen peas. If desired, garnish with parsley.

Per serving: 269 cal., 4 g total fat (1 g sat. fat), 67 mg chol., 746 mg sodium, 29 g carbo., 4 g fiber, 28 g pro.

Unlike most beef-and-potato stews, this version is creamy and shows stew in a new light. Thanks to some cream and a dose of crushed dried thyme, this hearty dish is smooth and has a delicious herbal undertone.

CREAMY BEEF & POTATO STEW

12	ounces boneless beef chuck
1	16-ounce package frozen cut green beans
1	5- to 5½-ounce package dry au gratin potato mix
½	teaspoon dried thyme, crushed
3	cups water
1½	cups half-and-half or light cream
	Finely shredded Parmesan cheese

1 Trim fat from meat. Cut meat into ¾-inch pieces. In a 3½- or 4-quart slow cooker combine meat, frozen green beans, dry potato mix (including contents of sauce packet), and thyme. Pour the water over all.

2 Cover and cook on low-heat setting for 7 to 8 hours or on high-heat setting for 3½ to 4 hours.

3 If using high-heat setting, turn to low-heat setting. Stir in half-and-half. Cover and cook for 15 minutes more to heat through. Sprinkle individual servings with Parmesan cheese.

Per serving: 388 cal., 16 g total fat (9 g sat. fat), 86 mg chol., 907 mg sodium, 39 g carbo., 5 g fiber, 27 g pro.

PREP:
10 minutes

COOK:
Low 7 hours, High 3½ hours; plus 15 minutes on Low

MAKES:
4 main-dish servings

SLOW COOKER:
3½- or 4-quart

You'll want to serve this wonderful stew with crusty Italian bread so you can soak up every drop.

BEEF STEW WITH RED WINE GRAVY

PREP:
30 minutes

COOK:
Low 12 hours, High 6 hours

MAKES:
6 main-dish servings

SLOW COOKER:
4¹⁄₂- to 6-quart

2   pounds boneless beef chuck roast

¼   cup all-purpose flour

2   teaspoons dried Italian seasoning, crushed

1   teaspoon salt

½   teaspoon black pepper

2   tablespoons olive oil

2   large onions, cut into thin wedges

8   ounces parsnips, peeled, quartered lengthwise, and halved

8   ounces carrots, quartered lengthwise and halved

8   ounces Jerusalem artichokes, peeled and coarsely chopped

1   cup dry red wine or beef broth

½   cup beef broth

¼   cup tomato paste

      Chopped tomatoes, golden raisins, and/or red wine vinegar or balsamic vinegar (optional)

1 Trim fat from meat. Cut meat into 1-inch cubes. In a large resealable plastic bag combine flour, Italian seasoning, salt, and pepper. Add meat cubes, a few at a time, shaking to coat meat cubes. In a 12-inch skillet heat 1 tablespoon of the oil over medium-high heat. Brown half of the meat in hot oil, turning to brown evenly. Remove meat from skillet. Brown remaining meat in remaining 1 tablespoon oil. Drain off fat.

2 Meanwhile, in a 4¹⁄₂- to 6-quart slow cooker combine onions, parsnips, carrots, and Jerusalem artichokes. Add meat to slow cooker. Pour wine and broth over all.

3 Cover and cook on low-heat setting for 12 to 14 hours or on high-heat setting for 6 to 7 hours. Stir in tomato paste. If desired, sprinkle individual servings with tomatoes, raisins, and/or vinegar.

Per serving: 356 cal., 9 g total fat (2 g sat. fat), 90 mg chol., 601 mg sodium, 26 g carbo., 4 g fiber, 35 g pro.

Pork stew meat or boneless lamb are equally as good as beef in this colorful stew. The cooking times are the same for all types of meat.

OLD-FASHIONED BEEF STEW

2	tablespoons all-purpose flour
12	ounces beef stew meat cut into ¾-inch cubes
2	tablespoons cooking oil
1	medium onion, cut into thin wedges
3	cups cubed potatoes (about 3 medium)
1½	cups loose-pack frozen cut green beans
1	cup loose-pack frozen whole kernel corn
2	medium carrots, sliced
2	cups vegetable juice
1	cup water
1	tablespoon Worcestershire sauce
1½	teaspoons instant beef bouillon granules
1	teaspoon dried oregano, crushed
½	teaspoon dried marjoram, crushed
¼	teaspoon black pepper
1	bay leaf

PREP:
20 minutes

COOK:
Low 10 hours, High 5 hours

MAKES:
5 main-dish servings

SLOW COOKER:
3½- or 4-quart

1 Place flour in a resealable plastic bag. Add meat cubes, a few at a time, shaking to coat meat cubes. In a large saucepan brown meat in hot oil. Drain off fat.

2 In a 3½- or 4-quart slow cooker layer browned meat, onion, potatoes, green beans, corn, and carrots. In a medium bowl combine vegetable juice, the water, Worcestershire sauce, bouillon granules, oregano, marjoram, pepper, and bay leaf. Pour over beef and vegetables in slow cooker.

3 Cover and cook on low-heat setting for 10 to 12 hours or on high-heat setting for 5 to 6 hours. Discard bay leaf.

Per serving: 331 cal., 13 g total fat (4 g sat. fat), 43 mg chol., 744 mg sodium, 36 g carbo., 6 g fiber, 18 g pro.

Instant coffee crystals and a trio of spices—cumin, ginger, and allspice—create a rich, brown color and a piquant flavor in this meaty vegetable soup.

ZESTY BEEF SOUP

PREP:
30 minutes

COOK:
Low 8 hours, High 4 hours

MAKES:
6 main-dish servings

SLOW COOKER:
3½- or 4-quart

2	tablespoons all-purpose flour
1	pound beef stew meat cut into 1-inch pieces
2	tablespoons cooking oil
12	ounces tiny new potatoes, halved or quartered
4	medium carrots, cut into ½-inch pieces
1	large onion, chopped
1	14½-ounce can diced tomatoes with chili spices, undrained
1	14-ounce can beef broth
2	tablespoons packed brown sugar
1	tablespoon Worcestershire sauce
1	tablespoon cider vinegar
1½	teaspoons instant coffee crystals
1	teaspoon ground cumin
½	teaspoon ground ginger
¼	teaspoon ground allspice

1 Place flour in a large resealable plastic bag. Add meat pieces a few at a time, shaking to coat meat pieces. In a large skillet heat 1 tablespoon of the oil over medium-high heat. Brown half of the meat in hot oil, turning to brown evenly. Remove meat from skillet. Brown remaining meat in remaining 1 tablespoon oil. Drain off fat.

2 In a 3½- or 4-quart slow cooker combine potatoes, carrots, and onion. Add meat.

3 In a large bowl stir together undrained tomatoes, broth, brown sugar, Worcestershire sauce, vinegar, coffee crystals, cumin, ginger, and allspice. Pour over meat and vegetables.

4 Cover and cook on low-heat setting for 8 to 10 hours or on high-heat setting for 4 to 5 hours.

Per serving: 257 cal., 8 g total fat (2 g sat. fat), 45 mg chol., 663 mg sodium, 27 g carbo., 3 g fiber, 19 g pro.

Cooking for hours in a slow cooker makes the beef or pork fork-tender. Serve biscuits and a mixed green salad to accompany the stew.

HOMESTYLE BEEF STEW

2	tablespoons all-purpose flour
1	pound beef or pork stew meat cut into 1-inch pieces
2	tablespoons cooking oil
2	cups cubed, peeled potatoes
4	medium carrots, sliced
2	stalks celery, sliced
1	medium onion, chopped
2	teaspoons instant beef bouillon granules
2	cloves garlic, minced
1	teaspoon dried basil, crushed
½	teaspoon dried thyme, crushed
2½	cups vegetable juice

1 Place flour in a large resealable plastic bag. Add meat pieces a few at a time, shaking to coat meat pieces. In a large skillet heat 1 tablespoon of the oil over medium-high heat. Brown half of the meat in hot oil, turning to brown evenly. Remove meat from skillet. Brown remaining meat in remaining 1 tablespoon oil. Drain off fat.

2 Meanwhile, in a 3½- or 4-quart slow cooker layer potatoes, carrots, celery, and onion. Sprinkle with bouillon granules, garlic, basil, and thyme; add meat. Pour vegetable juice over meat.

3 Cover and cook on low-heat setting for 7 to 9 hours or on high-heat setting for 3½ to 4½ hours.

Per serving: 485 cal., 28 g total fat (9 g sat. fat), 77 mg chol., 978 mg sodium, 34 g carbo., 5 g fiber, 25 g pro.

PREP:
35 minutes

COOK:
Low 7 hours, High 3½ hours

MAKES:
4 main-dish servings

SLOW COOKER:
3½- or 4-quart

Canned beets and tomatoes as well as convenient coleslaw mix make this full-bodied meal-in-a-bowl super easy.

BEEF & BEET SOUP

PREP:
20 minutes

COOK:
Low 9 hours, High 4½ hours; plus 30 minutes on High

MAKES:
8 to 10 main-dish servings

SLOW COOKER:
5- to 6-quart

2½ pounds beef stew meat cut into ¾- to 1-inch cubes

2 14½-ounce cans diced beets, undrained

2 14-ounce cans beef broth

1 14½-ounce can diced tomatoes, undrained

1½ cups water

1½ cups chopped onion

½ teaspoon dried dill

¼ teaspoon black pepper

4 cups packaged shredded cabbage with carrot (coleslaw mix)

½ cup dairy sour cream

1 In a 5- to 6-quart slow cooker combine meat, undrained beets, broth, undrained tomatoes, the water, onion, dill, and pepper.

2 Cover and cook on low-heat setting for 9 to 11 hours or on high-heat setting for 4½ to 5½ hours.

3 If using low-heat setting, turn to high-heat setting. Stir in coleslaw mix. Cover and cook for 30 minutes more. Top individual servings with sour cream.

Per serving: 270 cal., 8 g total fat (3 g sat. fat), 89 mg chol., 806 mg sodium, 15 g carbo., 3 g fiber, 33 g pro.

Make your own beef stew meat by cutting beef chuck or shoulder roast into 1-inch pieces.

HEARTY BEEF STEW WITH GREEN BEANS

1   pound beef stew meat cut into 1-inch pieces

1   pound small red potatoes, quartered (about 2 cups)

4   medium carrots, cut into ½-inch pieces

1   10¾-ounce can condensed cream of mushroom or cream of celery soup

½   cup dry red wine or water

½   cup water

1   envelope regular onion soup mix

½   teaspoon dried marjoram or thyme, crushed

1   9-ounce package frozen cut green beans, thawed

1 In a 3½- or 4-quart slow cooker combine meat, potatoes, and carrots.

2 In a bowl combine mushroom or celery soup, wine, the water, dry onion soup mix, and marjoram or thyme. Pour soup mixture over meat mixture in slow cooker.

3 Cover and cook on low-heat setting for 8 to 10 hours or on high-heat setting for 4 to 5 hours.

4 Stir in thawed green beans. Cover and cook for 10 minutes more.

Per serving: 358 cal., 9 g total fat (3 g sat. fat), 70 mg chol., 1,345 mg sodium, 36 g carbo., 6 g fiber, 28 g pro.

PREP:
20 minutes

COOK:
Low 8 hours plus 10 minutes, High 4 hours plus 10 minutes

MAKES:
4 main-dish servings

SLOW COOKER:
3½- or 4-quart

If you have leftovers, create another meal by spooning this zesty chili over baked potatoes.

MEXICAN CHILI

PREP:
25 minutes

COOK:
Low 8 hours, High 4 hours

MAKES:
8 to 10 main-dish servings

SLOW COOKER:
4- to 6-quart

1 pound lean ground beef

3 14½-ounce cans Mexican-style stewed tomatoes, undrained, cut up

2 15½-ounce cans red kidney beans, rinsed and drained

2 stalks celery, chopped

1 large onion, finely chopped

1 cup water

1 6-ounce can tomato paste

1 4-ounce can diced green chile peppers, undrained

2 cloves garlic, minced

4 teaspoons chili powder

1 teaspoon ground cumin

1 cup shredded cheddar cheese (4 ounces)

½ cup dairy sour cream

Fresh cilantro sprigs (optional)

1 In a large skillet cook ground beef until brown. Drain off fat.

2 Meanwhile, in a 4- to 6-quart slow cooker combine undrained tomatoes, beans, celery, onion, the water, tomato paste, undrained chile peppers, garlic, chili powder, and cumin. Stir in cooked ground beef.

3 Cover and cook on low-heat setting for 8 to 10 hours or on high-heat setting for 4 to 5 hours. Serve with shredded cheddar cheese and sour cream. If desired, garnish with cilantro.

Per serving: 340 cal., 13 g total fat (7 g sat. fat), 56 mg chol., 695 mg sodium, 34 g carbo., 9 g fiber, 25 g pro.

This easy soup, full of beef and beans, is sure to become a popular choice at your dinner table, especially if you top each serving with a generous dollop of sour cream and a few tortilla chips.

BEEFY TACO SOUP

1 pound lean cooked beef

1 15½-ounce can black-eyed peas

1 15-ounce can black beans

1 15-ounce can chili beans with chili gravy

1 15-ounce can garbanzo beans (chickpeas)

1 14½-ounce can Mexican-style stewed tomatoes, undrained

1 11-ounce can whole kernel corn with sweet peppers

1 1¼-ounce package taco seasoning mix

Dairy sour cream (optional)

Tortilla chips (optional)

1 In a large skillet cook ground beef until brown; drain off fat.

2 Transfer meat to a 3½- to 6-quart slow cooker. Stir in undrained black-eyed peas, undrained black beans, undrained chili beans, undrained garbanzo beans, undrained tomatoes, undrained corn, and taco seasoning mix.

3 Cover and cook on low-heat setting for 6 to 8 hours or on high-heat setting for 3 to 4 hours. If desired, top individual servings with sour cream and tortilla chips.

Per serving: 392 cal., 13 g total fat (4 g sat. fat), 41 mg chol., 1,294 mg sodium, 49 g carbo., 12 g fiber, 24 g pro.

PREP:
15 minutes

COOK:
Low 6 hours, High 3 hours

MAKES:
8 main-dish servings

SLOW COOKER:
3½- to 6-quart

This recipe makes a whole mess of chili and freezes well. If you like spicy chili, add more cayenne.

GIDDYUP CHILI

PREP:
20 minutes

COOK:
Low 8 hours, High 4 hours

MAKES:
10 main-dish servings

SLOW COOKER:
5- to 6-quart

2   pounds ground beef

2   cups chopped onion

¾   cup chopped green or red sweet pepper

3   cloves garlic, minced

2   14-ounce cans chicken broth

2   15-ounce cans dark red kidney beans, rinsed and drained

1   15-ounce can Great Northern beans, rinsed and drained

1   14½-ounce can diced tomatoes, undrained

1   6-ounce can tomato paste

1   tablespoon yellow mustard

2   teaspoons chili powder

1   teaspoon ground cumin

½   teaspoon salt

¼   teaspoon black pepper

¼   to ½ teaspoon cayenne pepper
     Shredded cheddar cheese

1 In a very large skillet cook ground beef, onion, sweet pepper, and garlic until meat is brown. Drain off fat.

2 In a 5- to 6-quart slow cooker combine meat mixture, broth, kidney beans, Great Northern beans, undrained tomatoes, tomato paste, mustard, chili powder, cumin, salt, black pepper, and cayenne pepper.

3 Cover and cook on low-heat setting for 8 to 10 hours or on high-heat setting for 4 to 5 hours.

4 Top individual servings with cheese.

Per serving: 411 cal., 17 g total fat (8 g sat. fat), 75 mg chol., 827 mg sodium, 34 g carbo., 9 g fiber, 33 g pro.

The exotic flavor of this hearty stew comes from allspice, the berries of the pimiento tree. Allspice, available whole or ground, tastes like a mix of cinnamon, nutmeg, and cloves— hence its name.

ALLSPICE MEATBALL STEW

2   16-ounce packages frozen cooked Italian-style meatballs, thawed

1   14-ounce can beef broth

1   cup sliced carrots

2   teaspoons Worcestershire sauce

½   to ¾ teaspoon ground allspice

½   teaspoon ground cinnamon

1   16-ounce package frozen cut green beans

2   14½-ounce cans stewed tomatoes, undrained, cut up

1 In a 3½- or 4-quart slow cooker combine thawed meatballs, broth, carrots, Worcestershire sauce, allspice, and cinnamon. Top with frozen green beans (do not stir).

2 Cover and cook on low-heat setting for 7 to 8 hours or on high-heat setting for 3½ to 4 hours.

3 If using low-heat setting, turn to high-heat setting. Stir in undrained tomatoes. Cover and cook for 30 minutes more.

Per serving: 406 cal., 26 g total fat (12 g sat. fat), 73 mg chol., 1,225 mg sodium, 20 g carbo., 7 g fiber, 21 g pro.

PREP:
15 minutes

COOK:
Low 7 hours, High 3½ hours; plus 30 minutes on High

MAKES:
8 main-dish servings

SLOW COOKER:
3½- or 4-quart

If you could capture the flavor of autumn in a food, this is what it would taste like: hearty, spicy, and earthy. With big chunks of sweet potatoes, this stew even offers the colors of the season.

HEARTY PORK-BEER STEW

PREP:
35 minutes

COOK:
Low 7 hours, High 3½ hours

MAKES:
8 main-dish servings

SLOW COOKER:
5- to 6-quart

1   pound boneless pork shoulder roast

Nonstick cooking spray

2   large sweet potatoes, peeled and cut into 1-inch cubes

3   medium parsnips, peeled and cut into ¾-inch-thick slices

2   small green apples, cut into wedges

1   medium onion, cut into thin wedges

3   cups vegetable broth or chicken broth

1   tablespoon packed brown sugar

1   tablespoon Dijon-style mustard

1½ teaspoons dried thyme, crushed

2   cloves garlic, minced

½   teaspoon crushed red pepper

1   12-ounce can (1½ cups) beer or 1½ cups vegetable broth or chicken broth

4   large plum tomatoes, cut up

1 Trim fat from meat. Cut meat into ¾-inch pieces. Lightly coat an unheated large skillet with nonstick cooking spray. Preheat over medium-high heat. Add meat; cook and stir until meat is brown. Set aside.

2 In a 5- to 6-quart slow cooker combine sweet potatoes, parsnips, apples, and onion. Add meat. In a medium bowl whisk together broth, brown sugar, mustard, thyme, garlic, and crushed red pepper. Pour over meat along with the beer.

3 Cover and cook on low-heat setting for 7 to 8 hours or on high-heat setting for 3½ to 4 hours. Stir in tomatoes.

Per serving: 209 cal., 4 g total fat (1 g sat. fat), 37 mg chol., 471 mg sodium, 27 g carbo., 5 g fiber, 14 g pro.

This pork stew is served with cheesy cornmeal dumplings. For a fuller flavor, use sharp cheddar.

PORK STEW WITH CORNMEAL DUMPLINGS

1   pound boneless pork shoulder roast

1   28-ounce can diced tomatoes, undrained

4   medium carrots, cut into ½-inch pieces

2   medium potatoes, peeled and cubed

1   12-ounce can (1½ cups) beer or 1½ cups
     apple juice or apple cider

¼   cup quick-cooking tapioca

1   tablespoon Worcestershire sauce

1   teaspoon dried thyme, crushed

2   cloves garlic, minced

½   teaspoon salt

½   cup all-purpose flour

½   cup shredded cheddar cheese (2 ounces)

⅓   cup yellow cornmeal

1   teaspoon baking powder

⅛   teaspoon salt

1   beaten egg

2   tablespoons milk

2   tablespoons cooking oil

2   tablespoons shredded cheddar cheese

1 Trim fat from meat. Cut meat into 1-inch cubes. In a 4- to 5-quart slow cooker combine meat, undrained tomatoes, carrots, potatoes, beer, tapioca, Worcestershire sauce, thyme, garlic, the ½ teaspoon salt, and ¼ teaspoon *black pepper.*

2 Cover and cook on low-heat setting for 9 to 11 hours or on high-heat setting for 4 to 5 hours.

3 For dumplings, in a medium bowl stir together flour, the ½ cup cheddar cheese, the cornmeal, baking powder, the ⅛ teaspoon salt, and a dash *black pepper.* In a small bowl combine beaten egg, milk, and oil. Add to flour mixture; stir with a fork just until combined.

4 If using low-heat setting, turn to high-heat setting. Stir stew; drop dumplings by tablespoonfuls onto stew into 6 mounds. Cover and cook for 50 minutes more (do not lift cover). Sprinkle dumplings with the 2 tablespoons cheddar cheese.

Per serving: 417 cal., 16 g total fat (6 g sat. fat), 100 mg chol., 707 mg sodium, 40 g carbo., 3 g fiber, 23 g pro.

PREP:
25 minutes

COOK:
*Low 9 hours, High 4 hours;
plus 50 minutes on High*

MAKES:
6 main-dish servings

SLOW COOKER:
4- to 5-quart

Here's a delicious way to use pork shoulder—one of the best bargains at the meat counter. Often this cut is on special, so take advantage of its value and flavor.

PORK & SWEET POTATO STEW

PREP:
25 minutes

COOK:
Low 6 hours, High 3 hours

MAKES:
6 to 8 main-dish servings

SLOW COOKER:
4- to 5-quart

2   pounds boneless pork shoulder roast

1   tablespoon cooking oil

2   pounds sweet potatoes, peeled and cut into 1-inch pieces

1   large onion, coarsely chopped

⅓   cup dried apples, coarsely chopped

1   tablespoon quick-cooking tapioca

1   clove garlic, minced

½   teaspoon dried sage, crushed

¼   teaspoon ground cardamom

¼   teaspoon black pepper

2   cups chicken broth

1   cup apple juice or apple cider

1 Trim fat from meat. Cut meat into 1-inch cubes. In a large skillet heat oil over medium-high heat. Brown meat, half at a time, in hot oil. Drain off fat.

2 In a 4- to 5-quart slow cooker stir together meat, sweet potatoes, onion, dried apples, tapioca, garlic, sage, cardamom, and pepper. Add broth and apple juice or cider and stir to combine.

3 Cover and cook on low-heat setting for 6 to 8 hours or on high-heat setting for 3 to 4 hours.

Per serving: 377 cal., 11 g total fat (3 g sat. fat), 99 mg chol., 507 mg sodium, 35 g carbo., 4 g fiber, 32 g pro.

Select firm tomatillos with tight-fitting, dry husks. Avoid shriveled or bruised ones.

CHILI VERDE

1½   pounds boneless pork shoulder roast

1   tablespoon olive oil

12   ounces fresh tomatillos, husked and chopped,
or two 11- to 13-ounce cans tomatillos, drained
and coarsely chopped

1   15½-ounce can Great Northern beans or one
16-ounce can navy beans, rinsed and drained

1   medium onion, chopped

1   4-ounce can diced green chile peppers, undrained

2   cloves garlic, minced

¾   teaspoon ground cumin

½   teaspoon salt

1   14-ounce can chicken broth

1   cup chopped fresh spinach

2   teaspoons lime juice
Snipped fresh cilantro (optional)
Dairy sour cream (optional)

1 Trim fat from meat. Cut meat into ¾-inch pieces. In a large skillet heat olive oil over medium-high heat. Brown meat, half at a time, in hot oil. Drain off fat.

2 In a 3½- or 4-quart slow cooker combine meat, tomatillos, beans, onion, undrained chile peppers, garlic, cumin, and salt. Pour broth over all.

3 Cover and cook on low-heat setting for 6 to 7 hours or on high-heat setting for 3½ to 4 hours.

4 Stir in spinach and lime juice. If desired, top individual servings with cilantro and sour cream.

Per serving: 300 cal., 11 g total fat (3 g sat. fat), 76 mg chol., 606 mg sodium, 21 g carbo., 4 g fiber, 29 g pro.

PREP:
25 minutes

COOK:
Low 6 hours, High 3½ hours

MAKES:
6 main-dish servings

SLOW COOKER:
3½- or 4-quart

FOR 5- TO 6-QUART SLOW COOKER:
Increase to 2 pounds pork and brown in an extra-large skillet. Use 1¼ pounds fresh tomatillos or three 11- to 13-ounce cans tomatillos, two 15½-ounce cans Great Northern beans, ¾ cup chopped onion, 3 cloves garlic, 1 teaspoon ground cumin, two 14-ounce cans chicken broth, 2 cups chopped fresh spinach, and 1 tablespoon lime juice. (Do not change the amounts of olive oil, green chile peppers, and salt.) Makes 8 main-dish servings.

Per serving: 348 cal., 11 g total fat (3 g sat. fat), 77 mg chol., 680 mg sodium, 30 g carbo., 6 g fiber, 32 g pro.

Versatile pork pairs with golden squash in this sage-scented stew. Serve over noodles or rice and set out sliced pears with pecans for dessert.

PORK & WINTER SQUASH STEW

PREP:
25 minutes

COOK:
Low 6 hours, High 3 hours

MAKES:
6 main-dish servings

SLOW COOKER:
3½- or 4-quart

2½   pounds boneless pork shoulder roast

      Nonstick spray coating

1½   pounds winter squash (such as butternut), peeled, seeded, and cut into 1½- to 2-inch pieces

2   tablespoons quick-cooking tapioca

1   teaspoon ground sage

1   10½-ounce can condensed French onion soup

½   cup water

3   cups hot cooked noodles or rice

1 Trim fat from meat. Cut meat in 1-inch cubes. Lightly coat an unheated large skillet with nonstick cooking spray. Preheat over medium heat. In hot skillet cook meat, half at a time, until brown. Drain off fat.

2 Place squash in a 3½- or 4-quart slow cooker. Sprinkle with tapioca and sage. Add meat. Pour French onion soup and the water over all.

3 Cover and cook on low-heat setting for 6 to 8 hours or on high-heat setting for 3 to 4 hours. Serve over hot cooked noodles or rice.

Per serving: 449 cal., 13 g total fat (4 g sat. fat), 150 mg chol., 520 mg sodium, 39 g carbo., 4 g fiber, 43 g pro.

Serve this meat-filled chili at an after-the-game open-house or for a bowl-watching party. Set out an assortment of the toppers so guests can personalize their bowls of chili.

HEARTY PORK CHILI

1½	pounds boneless pork shoulder roast
2	15-ounce cans black, kidney, and/or garbanzo beans (chickpeas), drained and rinsed
2	14½-ounce cans diced tomatoes with onions and garlic, undrained
1	10-ounce can chopped tomatoes and green chile peppers, undrained
1½	cups chopped celery
1	cup chopped green sweet pepper
3	cloves garlic, minced
1	tablespoon chili powder
1	teaspoon ground cumin
1	teaspoon dried oregano, crushed
2	cups vegetable juice or tomato juice
	Toppers (such as shredded Mexican-blend cheese or cheddar cheese, dairy sour cream, thinly sliced green onion, snipped fresh cilantro, thinly sliced jalapeño chile peppers,* and/or sliced pitted ripe olives) (optional)

1 Trim fat from meat. Cut meat into 1-inch cubes. In a 5- to 6-quart slow cooker combine meat, beans, undrained tomatoes, celery, sweet pepper, garlic, chili powder, cumin, and oregano. Stir in vegetable juice.

2 Cover and cook on low-heat setting for 8 to 10 hours or on high-heat setting for 4 to 5 hours. If desired, serve with toppers.

Per serving: 251 cal., 6 g total fat (2 g sat. fat), 55 mg chol., 1,126 mg sodium, 28 g carbo., 8 g fiber, 27 g pro.

*NOTE: Because chile peppers contain volatile oils that can burn your skin and eyes, avoid direct contact with them as much as possible. When working with chile peppers, wear plastic or rubber gloves. If your bare hands do touch the peppers, wash your hands and nails well with soap and warm water.

PREP:
30 minutes

COOK:
Low 8 hours, High 4 hours

MAKES:
8 main-dish servings

SLOW COOKER:
5- to 6-quart

The Peruvian Rub adds spicy flavor as well as just-right heat to this intriguing stew.

ANDES PORK STEW

PREP:
30 minutes

COOK:
Low 7 hours, High 3½ hours

MAKES:
6 main-dish servings

SLOW COOKER:
3½- to 5-quart

1¼ pounds lean boneless pork

1 recipe Peruvian Rub

   Nonstick cooking spray

1 14-ounce can beef, chicken, or vegetable broth

1 12-ounce can light beer (1½ cups)

1 medium sweet potato (about 8 ounces), peeled and cut into chunks

2 medium carrots, coarsely chopped

8 ounces pearl onions, peeled, or 1 small white onion, cut into bite-size pieces

1 small turnip or rutabaga (about 6 ounces), cut into bite-size pieces

2 stalks celery, cut into ½-inch-thick slices

2 tablespoons packed brown sugar

1 15-ounce can hominy, rinsed and drained

2 tablespoons snipped fresh cilantro

4 teaspoons lemon juice

1 Trim fat from meat. Cut meat into 1-inch cubes. Place Peruvian Rub in a resealable plastic bag. Add meat cubes, a few at a time, shaking to coat meat cubes. Coat an unheated large nonstick skillet with nonstick cooking spray. Preheat over medium heat. Brown meat, half at a time, in hot skillet. Transfer meat to a 3½- to 5-quart slow cooker. Add broth, beer, sweet potato, carrots, pearl onions, turnip or rutabaga, celery, and brown sugar. Stir until combined.

2 Cover and cook on low-heat setting for 7 to 8 hours or on high-heat setting for 3½ to 4 hours. Stir in hominy, cilantro, and lemon juice.

PERUVIAN RUB: In a small bowl combine 2 cloves garlic, minced; 1 teaspoon ground cumin; ¾ teaspoon salt; ¾ teaspoon dried oregano, crushed; ½ teaspoon ground ginger; ¼ teaspoon cayenne pepper; ¼ teaspoon dried thyme, crushed; and ¼ teaspoon ground allspice.

Per serving: 273 cal., 6 g total fat (2 g sat. fat), 52 mg chol., 738 mg sodium, 26 g carbo., 4 g fiber, 24 g pro.

Cabbage, cumin, and hot pepper sauce take traditional split pea soup to new flavor heights.

DUTCH SPLIT PEA SOUP WITH PORK

1	tablespoon cooking oil
1	pound pork stew meat cut into 1-inch cubes
1	cup chopped cooked ham (5 ounces)
1	medium carrot, sliced
1	medium onion, sliced
1½	cups dry split peas, rinsed and drained
½	teaspoon dried sage, crushed
½	teaspoon dried thyme, crushed
¼	teaspoon ground cumin
2	bay leaves
	Several dashes bottled hot pepper sauce
3	14-ounce cans chicken broth
2	cups coarsely chopped cabbage
	Snipped fresh chives (optional)

PREP:
25 minutes

COOK:
*Low 8 hours plus 30 minutes,
High 4 hours plus 30 minutes*

MAKES:
6 main-dish servings

SLOW COOKER:
3½- or 4-quart

1 In an extra-large skillet heat oil over medium-high heat. Brown meat in hot oil. Drain off fat.

2 In a 3½- or 4-quart slow cooker combine browned meat, ham, carrot, onion, split peas, sage, thyme, cumin, bay leaves, and bottled hot pepper sauce. Pour broth over all.

3 Cover and cook on low-heat setting for 8 to 9 hours or on high-heat setting for 4 to 4½ hours.

4 Add cabbage; cover and cook 30 to 60 minutes more or until cabbage is tender. Discard bay leaves. If desired, sprinkle individual servings with chives.

Per serving: 362 cal., 10 g total fat (3 g sat. fat), 65 mg chol., 1,170 mg sodium, 35 g carbo., 14 g fiber, 32 g pro.

If your supermarket doesn't routinely carry smoked pork hocks, plan ahead and ask the butcher to order some for you.

CURRIED SPLIT PEA SOUP

PREP:
25 minutes

COOK:
Low 9 hours, High 4½ hours

MAKES:
6 main-dish servings

SLOW COOKER:
5- to 6-quart

1	pound dry split peas, rinsed and drained
1	pound smoked pork hocks or meaty ham bone
1½	cups cubed cooked ham (about 8 ounces)
1½	cups chopped celery
1	cup chopped onion
1	cup chopped carrot
3	to 4 teaspoons curry powder
1	tablespoon dried marjoram, crushed
2	bay leaves
¼	teaspoon black pepper
6	cups water

1 In a 5- to 6-quart slow cooker combine split peas, pork hocks, ham, celery, onion, carrot, curry powder, marjoram, bay leaves, and pepper. Stir in the water.

2 Cover and cook on low-heat setting for 9 to 11 hours or on high-heat setting for 4½ to 5½ hours.

3 Discard bay leaves. Remove pork hocks. When pork hocks are cool enough to handle, remove meat from bones; discard bones. Coarsely chop meat. Return meat to soup.

Per serving: 379 cal., 6 g total fat (2 g sat. fat), 32 mg chol., 788 mg sodium, 54 g carbo., 22 g fiber, 29 g pro.

To round out a meal featuring this hearty soup, serve popovers and a tossed salad.

HAM & LENTIL SOUP

1	cup dry brown or yellow lentils
4	cups water
1	medium onion, chopped
1	cup chopped celery
1	cup sliced carrots
2	teaspoons instant chicken bouillon granules
2	cloves garlic, minced
½	teaspoon salt
½	teaspoon finely shredded lemon peel
⅛	to ¼ teaspoon cayenne pepper
2	cups torn fresh spinach leaves
1	cup cubed cooked ham (5 ounces)

1 Rinse and drain lentils. In a 3½- or 4-quart slow cooker combine lentils, the water, onion, celery, carrots, bouillon granules, garlic, salt, lemon peel, and cayenne pepper.

2 Cover and cook on low-heat setting for 7 to 8 hours or on high-heat setting for 3½ to 4 hours.

3 Stir in spinach and ham. Serve immediately.

Per serving: 251 cal., 4 g total fat (1 g sat. fat), 19 mg chol., 1,238 mg sodium, 36 g carbo., 17 g fiber, 20 g pro.

PREP:
20 minutes

COOK:
Low 7 hours, High 3½ hours

MAKES:
4 main-dish servings

SLOW COOKER:
3½- or 4-quart

Bake some corn muffins to go with this zesty meal-in-a-bowl.

WHITE BEAN-GARLIC SOUP

PREP:
15 minutes

COOK:
Low 4 hours, High 2 hours

MAKES:
8 main-dish servings

SLOW COOKER:
5- to 6-quart

3   15- to 16-ounce cans navy beans, rinsed and drained

2   14½-ounce cans stewed tomatoes, undrained, cut up

2   14-ounce cans chicken broth with roasted garlic
     or regular chicken broth

2   cups cubed cooked ham (about 10 ounces)

1   10¾-ounce can condensed cream of potato soup

4   cloves garlic, minced

1   teaspoon dried rosemary, crushed

1 In a 5- to 6-quart slow cooker combine beans, undrained tomatoes, broth, ham, cream of potato soup, garlic, and rosemary.

2 Cover and cook on low-heat setting for 4 to 5 hours or on high-heat setting for 2 to 2½ hours.

Per serving: 333 cal., 6 g total fat (2 g sat. fat), 24 mg chol., 2,059 mg sodium, 51 g carbo., 10 g fiber, 21 g pro.

Ten minutes of boiling on the range top gives the black-eyed peas a head start on the rest of the soup ingredients and ensures they'll be tender at serving time.

HAM & BLACK-EYED PEA SOUP

4	cups water
12	ounces dry black-eyed peas (2 cups)
2	14-ounce cans reduced-sodium chicken broth
1	cup ham cut into ½-inch pieces (5 ounces)
4	medium carrots, cut into ½-inch-thick slices
2	stalks celery, sliced
¼	cup dried minced onion
1	teaspoon dried sage, crushed
1	teaspoon dried thyme, crushed
¼	teaspoon cayenne pepper
1½	cups water
1	tablespoon lemon juice

1 In a 3-quart saucepan combine the 4 cups water and black-eyed peas; bring to boiling. Boil, uncovered, for 10 minutes. Drain and rinse.

2 In a 4- to 5-quart slow cooker combine broth, ham, carrots, celery, dried minced onion, sage, thyme, and cayenne pepper. Stir in the 1½ cups water. Stir in black-eyed peas.

3 Cover and cook on low-heat setting for 9 to 11 hours or on high-heat setting for 4½ to 5½ hours.

4 Stir in lemon juice.

Per serving: 131 cal., 2 g total fat (1 g sat. fat), 13 mg chol., 654 mg sodium, 20 g carbo., 5 g fiber, 8 g pro.

PREP:
30 minutes

COOK:
Low 9 hours, High 4½ hours

MAKES:
6 main-dish servings

SLOW COOKER:
4- to 5-quart

Longtime old-country favorites—sausage, potatoes, and sauerkraut—are stars in this soup.

SAUSAGE-SAUERKRAUT SOUP

PREP:
30 minutes

COOK:
Low 10 hours, High 5 hours

MAKES:
6 main-dish servings

SLOW COOKER:
4- to 5-quart

4 cups chicken broth

1 14- to 16-ounce can sauerkraut, rinsed and drained

12 ounces cooked Polish sausage, chopped

1 10¾-ounce can condensed cream of mushroom soup

8 ounces fresh mushrooms, sliced

2 medium carrots, chopped

2 medium stalks celery, chopped

1 medium potato, cut into small cubes

1 medium onion, chopped

2 tablespoons vinegar

2 teaspoons dried dill

½ teaspoon black pepper

2 slices bacon, crisp-cooked, drained, and crumbled (optional)

1 In a 4- to 5-quart slow cooker stir together broth, sauerkraut, Polish sausage, cream of mushroom soup, mushrooms, carrots, celery, potato, onion, vinegar, dill, and pepper.

2 Cover and cook on low-heat setting for 10 to 12 hours or on high-heat setting for 5 to 6 hours.

3 If necessary, skim off fat before serving. If desired, sprinkle individual servings with bacon.

Per serving: 295 cal., 20 g total fat (7 g sat. fat), 43 mg chol., 1,960 mg sodium, 18 g carbo., 4 g fiber, 12 g pro.

This lively soup boasts six seasonings plus Italian sausage. Vary the spiciness by choosing either sweet or hot sausage.

"IT'S ITALIAN" SAUSAGE SOUP

1	pound Italian sausage (casings removed if present)
1	large onion, chopped
1	clove garlic, minced
2	medium carrots, chopped
1	stalk celery, chopped
1	14½-ounce can diced tomatoes, undrained
1	8-ounce can tomato sauce
1	teaspoon dried oregano, crushed
½	teaspoon dried rosemary, crushed
½	teaspoon dried basil, crushed
¼	teaspoon dried thyme, crushed
¼	teaspoon fennel seeds, crushed
1	bay leaf
3	14-ounce cans chicken broth
½	cup dried orzo pasta or finely broken cappellini pasta
	Finely shredded Parmesan cheese (optional)

1 In a large skillet combine Italian sausage, onion, and garlic. Cook over medium heat until sausage is brown. Drain off fat.

2 In a 4½- to 6-quart slow cooker combine carrots and celery. Place sausage mixture on top of vegetables in slow cooker. In a medium bowl combine undrained tomatoes, tomato sauce, oregano, rosemary, basil, thyme, fennel seeds, and bay leaf. Pour over sausage mixture. Pour broth over all.

3 Cover and cook on low-heat setting for 8 to 10 hours or on high-heat setting for 4 to 5 hours.

4 If using low-heat setting, turn to high-heat setting. Add pasta; cover and cook for 20 minutes more. Discard bay leaf. If desired, serve with Parmesan cheese.

Per serving: 250 cal., 13 g total fat (5 g sat. fat), 38 mg chol., 923 mg sodium, 17 g carbo., 2 g fiber, 12 g pro.

PREP:
25 minutes

COOK:
Low 8 hours, High 4 hours; plus 20 minutes on High

MAKES:
8 main-dish servings

SLOW COOKER:
4½- to 6-quart

Tender lamb dressed up with flavorful spices, dried apricots, and dates adds up to a hearty meal with great taste. Serve it with couscous, a semolina product that's a staple in North African cuisine.

MOROCCAN LAMB & FRUIT STEW

PREP:
30 minutes

COOK:
Low 7 hours, High 3½ hours; plus 30 minutes on High

MAKES:
6 main-dish servings

SLOW COOKER:
3½- or 4-quart

2	pounds boneless leg of lamb or beef bottom round roast
½	to 1 teaspoon crushed red pepper
¾	teaspoon ground turmeric
¾	teaspoon ground ginger
¾	teaspoon ground cinnamon
½	teaspoon salt
2	tablespoons olive oil or cooking oil
2	large onions, chopped
3	cloves garlic, minced
1	14-ounce can beef broth
2	tablespoons cold water
1	tablespoon cornstarch
1	cup pitted dates
1	cup dried apricots, halved
	Hot cooked couscous or rice
¼	cup slivered almonds, toasted

1 Trim fat from meat. Cut meat into 1- to 1½-inch pieces. In a shallow bowl combine crushed red pepper, turmeric, ginger, cinnamon, and salt. Sprinkle red pepper mixture evenly over meat. In a large skillet heat oil over medium-high heat. Brown meat, one-third at a time, in the hot oil.

2 Transfer meat to a 3½- or 4-quart slow cooker. Add onions and garlic; stir to combine. Pour broth over all.

3 Cover and cook on low-heat setting for 7 to 9 hours or on high-heat setting for 3½ to 4½ hours.

4 Skim fat from cooking juices. In a small bowl combine cold water and cornstarch; stir into mixture in slow cooker. Add dates and dried apricots; stir to combine. If using low-heat setting, turn to high-heat setting. Cover and cook about 30 minutes more or until mixture is slightly thickened and bubbly.

5 Serve stew over hot cooked couscous. Sprinkle with almonds.

Per serving: 508 cal., 13 g total fat (2 g sat. fat), 95 mg chol., 541 mg sodium, 63 g carbo., 7 g fiber, 38 g pro.

Team this lamb-and-bean combo with slices of foccacia or garlic bread.

ITALIAN LAMB SOUP

1	pound boneless lamb shoulder
2	14-ounce cans beef broth
1	15-ounce or 19-ounce can white kidney beans (cannellini beans), rinsed and drained
1	14½-ounce can diced tomatoes, undrained
1	medium onion, chopped
½	cup dry red wine
3	tablespoons tomato paste
3	cloves garlic, minced
1	teaspoon dried Italian seasoning, crushed
¼	teaspoon salt
2	cups kale or fresh spinach, chopped

1 Trim fat from meat. Cut meat into 1-inch pieces. In a 3½- or 4-quart slow cooker combine meat, broth, white kidney beans, undrained tomatoes, onion, wine, tomato paste, garlic, Italian seasoning, and salt.

2 Cover and cook on low-heat setting for 9 to 11 hours or on high-heat setting for 4½ to 5½ hours.

3 If using kale and if using low-heat setting, turn to high-heat setting. Stir in kale. Cover and cook for 30 minutes more. If using spinach, stir in just before serving.

Per serving: 202 cal., 4 g total fat (1 g sat. fat), 48 mg chol., 879 mg sodium, 19 g carbo., 4 g fiber, 22 g pro.

PREP:
20 minutes

COOK:
Low 9 hours, High 4½ hours;
plus 30 minutes on High (if using kale)

MAKES:
6 main-dish servings

SLOW COOKER:
3½- or 4-quart

Mango chutney weaves its velvety sweet-sour flavor throughout this thick, brown stew.

NORTH AFRICAN LAMB STEW

PREP:
20 minutes

COOK:
Low 8 hours, High 4 hours

MAKES:
6 main-dish servings

SLOW COOKER:
3½- or 4-quart

2¾   pounds boneless lamb shoulder
     Nonstick cooking spray
3   medium carrots, thinly sliced
2   stalks celery, sliced
2   cups water
1   9-ounce jar (¾ cup) mango chutney
2   tablespoons quick-cooking tapioca
2   to 3 cups hot cooked couscous

1 Trim fat from meat. Cut meat into ¾- to 1-inch **pieces.** Lightly coat an unheated 12-inch skillet with nonstick cooking spray. Preheat over medium heat. Cook meat in hot skillet until light brown. Drain off fat.

2 In a 3½- or 4-quart slow cooker combine carrots and celery. Add meat. In a medium bowl combine the water, chutney, and tapioca; pour over meat and vegetables in slow cooker.

3 Cover and cook on low-heat setting for 8 to 10 hours or on high-heat setting for 4 to 5 hours. Serve over hot cooked couscous.

Per serving: 404 cal., 9 g total fat (3 g sat. fat), 131 mg chol., 282 mg sodium, 35 g carbo., 3 g fiber, 45 g pro.

If you prefer, make this first-rate stew with boneless lean beef instead of lamb.

HEARTY LAMB STEW

6	cups water
2	cups dry navy beans
1	pound lean boneless lamb
1	tablespoon cooking oil
1	cup chopped carrot
1	cup chopped peeled parsnip
½	cup chopped onion
2	cloves garlic, minced
½	teaspoon salt
½	teaspoon dried rosemary, crushed
½	teaspoon dried thyme, crushed
¼	teaspoon dried sage, crushed
⅛	teaspoon black pepper
2	14-ounce cans chicken broth
2	cups chopped fresh spinach

PREP:
30 minutes

STAND:
1 hour

COOK:
Low 7 hours, High 3½ hours

MAKES:
6 main-dish servings

SLOW COOKER:
3½- or 4-quart

1 Rinse beans. In a large saucepan combine the water and beans. Bring to boiling; reduce heat. Simmer, uncovered, for 10 minutes. Remove from heat. Cover and let stand for 1 hour. Drain and rinse beans.

2 Trim fat from meat. Cut meat into ¾-inch pieces. In a large skillet heat oil over medium-high heat. Brown meat, half at a time, in hot oil. Drain off fat.

3 In a 3½- or 4-quart slow cooker combine drained beans, lamb, carrot, parsnip, onion, garlic, salt, rosemary, thyme, sage, and pepper. Pour broth over all.

4 Cover and cook on low-heat setting for 7 to 8 hours or on high-heat setting for 3½ to 4 hours.

5 Stir in spinach.

Per serving: 382 cal., 7 g total fat (1 g sat. fat), 50 mg chol., 799 mg sodium, 49 g carbo., 18 g fiber, 32 g pro.

This no-tend recipe is an updated version of traditional Scottish lamb-and-barley soup.

SCOTCH BROTH

PREP:
20 minutes

COOK:
Low 6 hours, High 3 hours

MAKES:
6 main-dish servings

SLOW COOKER:
4- to 5-quart

1   pound lean boneless lamb

1   tablespoon cooking oil (optional)

1   cup dry yellow split peas

2   stalks celery, chopped

2   medium carrots, chopped

1   large onion, chopped

½   cup regular barley (not quick-cooking)

2   32-ounce cartons (8 cups) chicken broth

1   teaspoon dried leaf sage, crushed

1 Trim fat from meat. Cut meat into ½-inch pieces. If desired, in a large skillet heat oil over medium-high heat; brown meat in hot oil. Drain off fat.

2 In a 4- to 5-quart slow cooker combine meat, split peas, celery, carrots, onion, and barley. Stir in broth and sage.

3 Cover and cook on low-heat setting for 6 to 8 hours or on high-heat setting for 3 to 4 hours.

Per serving: 245 cal., 5 g total fat (1 g sat. fat), 46 mg chol., 1,017 mg sodium, 28 g carbo., 6 g fiber, 24 g pro.

For an exceptional meal, serve this intriguing stew with hot cooked jasmine rice and pita bread.

INDIAN LAMB STEW

2   pounds lean boneless lamb

1   tablespoon cooking oil

2   cups chopped potatoes

2   medium carrots, chopped

1   medium onion, chopped

½   cup dried plums, coarsely snipped

½   teaspoon finely shredded lemon peel

1   tablespoon lemon juice

3   cloves garlic, minced

1½   teaspoons curry powder

½   teaspoon ground ginger

¼   teaspoon salt

¼   teaspoon ground cinnamon

2   14-ounce cans chicken broth

1   cup loose-pack frozen peas

    Snipped fresh mint

1 Trim fat from meat. Cut into ¾- to 1-inch pieces. In a large skillet heat oil over medium-high heat. Brown lamb, half at a time, in hot oil. Drain off fat.

2 In a 4- to 5-quart slow cooker combine lamb, potatoes, carrots, onion, dried plums, lemon peel, lemon juice, garlic, curry powder, ginger, salt, and cinnamon. Pour broth over all.

3 Cover and cook on low-heat setting for 10 to 12 hours or on high-heat setting for 5 to 6 hours.

4 Remove liner from slow cooker, if possible, or turn slow cooker off. Stir in frozen peas; let stand for 5 minutes before serving. Sprinkle individual servings with mint.

Per serving: 315 cal., 8 g total fat (2 g sat. fat), 97 mg chol., 764 mg sodium, 26 g carbo., 4 g fiber, 35 g pro.

PREP:
20 minutes

COOK:
Low 10 hours, High 5 hours

STAND:
5 minutes

MAKES:
6 main-dish servings

SLOW COOKER:
4- to 5-quart

Barley is a good choice for a slow-cooker stew because it retains its shape and chewy texture during the long cooking.

LAMB & BARLEY STEW WITH MINT

PREP:
20 minutes

COOK:
Low 8 hours, High 4 hours

MAKES:
4 to 6 main-dish servings

SLOW COOKER:
3½- or 4-quart

1½ pounds lean boneless lamb

2½ cups chicken broth

1 14½-ounce can diced tomatoes, undrained

1 medium onion, chopped

½ cup regular barley (not quick-cooking)

¼ cup dry white wine (optional)

4 cloves garlic, minced

2 tablespoons snipped fresh dill or
  1½ teaspoons dried dill

½ teaspoon salt

¼ teaspoon black pepper

1 7-ounce jar roasted red sweet peppers,
  drained and thinly sliced

¼ cup snipped fresh mint

1 Trim fat from meat. Cut meat into 1-inch cubes. In a 3½- or 4-quart slow cooker combine meat, broth, undrained tomatoes, onion, barley, wine (if desired), garlic, dried dill (if using), salt, and black pepper.

2 Cover and cook on low-heat setting for 8 to 10 hours or on high-heat setting for 4 to 5 hours.

3 To serve, stir in the fresh dill (if using), roasted peppers, and mint.

Per serving: 370 cal., 10 g total fat (3 g sat. fat), 113 mg chol., 1,216 mg sodium, 28 g carbo., 7 g fiber, 41 g pro.

The easiest way to crush tapioca is to use a mortar and pestle, or place the tapioca between layers of waxed paper and crush it with a rolling pin.

IRISH STEW

1	pound lean boneless lamb
2	tablespoons cooking oil
2	medium turnips, peeled and cut into ½-inch pieces
3	medium carrots, cut into ½-inch pieces
2	medium potatoes, peeled and cut into ½-inch pieces
2	medium onions, cut into thin wedges
¼	cup quick-cooking tapioca, crushed
½	teaspoon salt
¼	teaspoon black pepper
¼	teaspoon dried thyme, crushed
2	14-ounce cans beef broth

1 Trim fat from meat. Cut into 1-inch pieces. In a large skillet heat oil over medium-high heat. Brown meat, half at a time, in hot oil. Drain well.

2 In a 3½- or 4-quart slow cooker combine turnips, carrots, potatoes, onions, tapioca, salt, pepper, and thyme. Stir in meat and broth.

3 Cover and cook on low-heat setting for 10 to 11 hours or on high-heat setting for 5 to 5½ hours.

Per serving: 234 cal., 8 g total fat (2 g sat. fat), 49 mg chol., 784 mg sodium, 21 g carbo., 3 g fiber, 19 g pro.

PREP:
25 minutes

COOK:
Low 10 hours, High 5 hours

MAKES:
6 main-dish servings

SLOW COOKER:
3½- or 4-quart

This comforting one-dish meal gets its appealing golden color from carrots, winter squash, apricots, orange peel, and orange juice.

FRUITED SOUTHWESTERN LAMB STEW

PREP:
30 minutes

COOK:
Low 10 hours, High 5 hours

MAKES:
6 to 8 main-dish servings

SLOW COOKER:
4- to 5-quart

1	tablespoon cooking oil
1½	pounds lamb stew meat cut into 1-inch pieces
2	cups winter squash peeled and cut into 1-inch pieces
2	medium carrots, sliced
1	medium onion, chopped
½	cup dried apricots, snipped
1	teaspoon finely shredded orange peel
¼	cup orange juice
2	teaspoons ground cumin
2	teaspoons ground ancho chile pepper
½	teaspoon ground cinnamon
½	teaspoon salt
¼	teaspoon black pepper
2	14-ounce cans chicken broth
	Toasted pumpkin seeds (optional)

1 In a large skillet heat oil over medium-high heat. Brown meat, half at a time, in hot oil. Drain off fat.

2 In a 4- to 5-quart slow cooker combine meat, winter squash, carrots, onion, dried apricots, orange peel, orange juice, cumin, ancho chile pepper, cinnamon, salt, and pepper. Pour broth over all.

3 Cover and cook on low-heat setting for 10 to 12 hours or on high-heat setting for 5 to 6 hours.

4 If desired, sprinkle individual servings with toasted pumpkin seeds.

Per serving: 233 cal., 7 g total fat (2 g sat. fat), 75 mg chol., 823 mg sodium, 16 g carbo., 3 g fiber, 25 g pro.

If you prefer, substitute skinless, boneless thighs for the chicken breast halves.

CHICKEN-PASTA SOUP

1	tablespoon olive oil or cooking oil
1½	pounds skinless, boneless chicken breast halves, cut into 1-inch pieces
2	stalks celery, chopped
2	medium carrots, chopped
1	large onion, chopped
1	teaspoon dried basil, crushed
¼	teaspoon black pepper
3	14-ounce cans chicken broth
1½	cups dried rotini pasta

1 In a 10-inch skillet heat oil over medium-high heat. Cook chicken, half at a time, in hot oil about 2 minutes or until browned (chicken will not be cooked through).

2 In a 3½- or 4-quart slow cooker combine celery, carrots, and onion. Arrange chicken over vegetables. Sprinkle with basil and pepper. Pour chicken broth over all.

3 Cover and cook on high-heat setting* for 4½ to 5½ hours. Stir in uncooked pasta; cook about 30 minutes more or until tender.

Per serving: 248 cal., 4 g total fat (1 g sat. fat), 68 mg chol., 879 mg sodium, 20 g carbo., 2 g fiber, 30 g pro.

***NOTE:** Cook this soup only on the high-heat setting. Our Test Kitchen does not recommend the low-heat setting because the pasta does not cook as well, even if the slow cooker is turned to high when the pasta is added.

PREP:
20 minutes

COOK:
High 4½ hours plus 30 minutes

MAKES:
6 main-dish servings

SLOW COOKER:
3½- or 4-quart

Stirring in the spinach just before serving gives this home-style soup a fresh-from-the-garden accent.

CHICKEN & GARBANZO BEAN SOUP

PREP:
20 minutes

COOK:
Low 8 hours, High 4 hours

MAKES:
6 main-dish servings

SLOW COOKER:
4- to 5-quart

1	tablespoon olive oil
1	pound skinless, boneless chicken breast halves or thighs, cut into bite-size pieces
2	14-ounce cans chicken broth
1	15-ounce can garbanzo beans (chickpeas), drained
2½	cups sliced carrots
1	cup sliced celery
1	large onion, cut into thin wedges
½	cup water
1	teaspoon dried marjoram, crushed
1	teaspoon dried thyme, crushed
½	teaspoon black pepper
¼	teaspoon salt
1	cup shredded fresh spinach or escarole

1 In a large skillet heat olive oil over medium-high heat. Brown chicken in hot oil until no longer pink. Drain off fat.

2 In a 4- to 5-quart slow cooker combine chicken, broth, beans, carrots, celery, onion, the water, marjoram, thyme, pepper, and salt.

3 Cover and cook on low-heat setting for 8 to 10 hours or on high-heat setting for 4 to 5 hours.

4 Stir in spinach or escarole.

Per serving: 201 cal., 5 g total fat (1 g sat. fat), 45 mg chol., 992 mg sodium, 20 g carbo., 5 g fiber, 23 g pro.

Taco seasoning mix provides great south-of-the-border flavor and eliminates the need to measure lots of herbs and spices.

MEXICAN CHICKEN CHOWDER

1½	pounds skinless, boneless chicken thighs, cut into bite-size pieces
1	14-ounce can reduced-sodium chicken broth
1	11-ounce can whole kernel corn with sweet peppers
1	10¾-ounce can condensed cream of potato soup or one 10¾-ounce can reduced-fat and reduced-sodium condensed cream of chicken soup
1	cup water
½	cup finely chopped onion
½	cup chopped celery
1	4-ounce can diced green chile peppers, undrained
½	of a 1¼-ounce package taco seasoning mix (about 2 tablespoons)
1	8-ounce carton dairy sour cream
½	cup shredded cheddar cheese (2 ounces)
2	tablespoons snipped fresh cilantro
	Tortilla chips (optional)

1 In a 3½- or 4-quart slow cooker combine chicken, broth, corn, cream of potato soup, the water, onion, celery, undrained chile peppers, and taco seasoning mix.

2 Cover and cook on low-heat setting for 6 to 7 hours or on high-heat setting for 3 to 3½ hours.

3 Stir 1 cup of the hot mixture into sour cream. Stir sour cream mixture into mixture in slow cooker. Remove liner from slow cooker, if possible, or turn off slow cooker. Cover and let stand for 5 minutes. Sprinkle individual servings with cheddar cheese and cilantro. If desired, serve with tortilla chips.

Per serving: 349 cal., 18 g total fat (9 g sat. fat), 121 mg chol., 1,189 mg sodium, 16 g carbo., 2 g fiber, 30 g pro.

PREP:
25 minutes

COOK:
Low 6 hours, High 3 hours

STAND:
5 minutes

MAKES:
6 main-dish servings

SLOW COOKER:
3½- or 4-quart

Although chicken soup is comforting when you're under the weather, don't wait until you're sick to enjoy this version. Its delightful blend of herbs makes it terrific any time.

HERBED CHICKEN NOODLE SOUP

PREP:
25 minutes

COOK:
Low 6 hours, High 3 hours; plus 1 hour on High

MAKES:
6 main-dish servings

SLOW COOKER:
3½- or 4-quart

1   pound boneless, skinless chicken thighs, cut into 1-inch pieces

1   10¾-ounce can condensed cream of chicken soup

2   stalks celery, thinly sliced

2   medium carrots, thinly sliced

1   medium onion, chopped

1   4½-ounce can (drained weight) sliced mushrooms, drained

1   clove garlic, minced

½   teaspoon dried sage, crushed

½   teaspoon dried thyme, crushed

¼   teaspoon dried rosemary, crushed

⅛   teaspoon black pepper

2   14-ounce cans chicken broth

½   of a 16-ounce package frozen homestyle egg noodles (about 3 cups)

1 In a 3½- or 4-quart slow cooker combine chicken, cream of chicken soup, celery, carrots, onion, drained mushrooms, garlic, sage, thyme, rosemary, and pepper. Pour broth over all.

2 Cover and cook on low-heat setting for 6 to 7 hours or on high-heat setting for 3 to 3½ hours.

3 If using low-heat setting, turn to high-heat setting. Stir in frozen noodles. Cover and cook for 1 hour more.

Per serving: 241 cal., 8 g total fat (2 g sat. fat), 103 mg chol., 1,115 mg sodium, 22 g carbo., 2 g fiber, 20 g pro.

A spoonful of sour cream and a sprinkling of avocado and tortilla chips on each serving helps tame this lively Tex-Mex medley.

CHICKEN TORTILLA SOUP

1½	pounds skinless, boneless chicken thighs, cut into 1-inch pieces
2	14-ounce cans chicken broth
1	10-ounce can diced tomatoes and green chiles, undrained
1	cup loose-pack frozen whole kernel corn
1	medium red sweet pepper, chopped
2	cloves garlic, minced
1	teaspoon ground cumin
2	tablespoons snipped fresh cilantro
1	tablespoon lime juice
	Tortilla chips with lime or regular tortilla chips, broken (optional)
	Chopped avocado (optional)
	Dairy sour cream (optional)

1 In a 3½- or 4-quart slow cooker combine chicken, broth, undrained tomatoes and green chiles, frozen corn, sweet pepper, garlic, and cumin.

2 Cover and cook on low-heat setting for 6 to 7 hours or on high-heat setting for 3 to 3½ hours.

3 Stir in cilantro and lime juice. Serve with broken tortilla chips, chopped avocado, and sour cream.

Per serving: 188 cal., 5 g total fat (1 g sat. fat), 92 mg chol., 854 mg sodium, 10 g carbo., 1 g fiber, 25 g pro.

PREP:
15 minutes

COOK:
Low 6 hours, High 3 hours

MAKES:
6 main-dish servings

SLOW COOKER:
3½- or 4-quart

Reminiscent of chicken pot pie, this satisfying soup is bound to become a favorite with your family.

COCK-A-LEEKY SOUP

PREP:
35 minutes

COOK:
Low 6 hours, High 3 hours

MAKES:
6 main-dish servings

SLOW COOKER:
3¹⁄₂- or 4-quart

1   tablespoon olive oil

2   pounds boneless, skinless chicken thighs, cut into 1-inch pieces

6   medium leeks, thinly sliced (2 cups)

1   medium carrot, coarsely shredded

1   medium onion, cut into thin wedges

½   teaspoon dried thyme, crushed

½   teaspoon dried marjoram, crushed

¼   teaspoon salt

2   14-ounce cans chicken broth

1   10¾-ounce can condensed cream of onion soup

1   cup milk

1 In a large skillet heat olive oil over medium-high heat. Brown chicken, half at a time, in hot oil. Drain off fat.

2 In a 3½- or 4-quart slow cooker combine chicken, leeks, carrot, onion, thyme, marjoram, and salt. Stir in broth and cream of onion soup.

3 Cover and cook on low-heat setting for 6 to 7 hours or on high-heat setting for 3 to 3½ hours.

4 Skim off fat. Stir milk into chicken mixture in slow cooker.

Per serving: 307 cal., 12 g total fat (3 g sat. fat), 130 mg chol., 1,119 mg sodium, 14 g carbo., 1 g fiber, 34 g pro.

Leeks and carrots add a fresh-from-the-garden note to the chewy barley and tender chicken.

CHICKEN, BARLEY & LEEK STEW

1	tablespoon olive oil
1	pound skinless, boneless chicken thighs, cut into 1-inch pieces
1	49-ounce can chicken broth
1	cup regular barley (not quick-cooking)
3	medium leeks, halved lengthwise and sliced
2	medium carrots, thinly sliced
1½	teaspoons dried basil or Italian seasoning, crushed
¼	teaspoon cracked black pepper
	Salt
	Cracked black pepper
	Slivered fresh basil or snipped fresh parsley (optional)

1 In a large skillet heat olive oil over medium-high heat. Cook chicken in hot oil until browned, turning to brown evenly.

2 In a 4- to 5-quart slow cooker combine chicken, broth, barley, leeks, carrots, basil, and the ¼ teaspoon cracked black pepper.

3 Cover and cook on low-heat setting for 4 to 5 hours or on high-heat setting for 2 to 2½ hours or until barley is tender. Season to taste with salt and additional cracked black pepper. If desired, garnish with basil or parsley.

Per serving: 253 cal., 7 g total fat (1 g sat. fat), 63 mg chol., 1,027 mg sodium, 27 g carbo., 3 g fiber, 21 g pro.

PREP:
20 minutes

COOK:
Low 4 hours, High 2 hours

MAKES:
6 main-dish servings

SLOW COOKER:
4- to 5-quart

You'll love the way this soup hits so many flavor buttons—a little heat from the spices, a bit of sweetness from the coconut milk, and some nuttiness from the peanuts. Together the flavors work distinct charm on the vibrant, colorful veggies.

CURRIED CHICKEN SOUP

PREP:
25 minutes

COOK:
Low 5 hours, High 2½ hours; plus 15 minutes on High

MAKES:
8 main-dish servings

SLOW COOKER:
3½- or 4-quart

1½ to 2 pounds skinless, boneless chicken thighs, cut into 1-inch pieces

2 14-ounce cans chicken broth

3 cups cauliflower florets (1 small head)

3 stalks celery, sliced

1 medium red or yellow sweet pepper, chopped

1 small onion, chopped

2 cloves garlic, minced

1 tablespoon curry powder

½ teaspoon salt

½ teaspoon ground cumin

¼ teaspoon crushed red pepper

1 13½-ounce can unsweetened light coconut milk

2 medium zucchini or yellow summer squash, halved lengthwise and sliced (2½ cups)

Chopped peanuts (optional)

1 In a 3½- or 4-quart slow cooker combine chicken, broth, cauliflower, celery, sweet pepper, onion, garlic, curry powder, salt, cumin, and crushed red pepper.

2 Cover and cook on low-heat setting for 5 hours or on high-heat setting for 2½ hours.

3 If using low-heat setting, turn to high-heat setting. Stir in coconut milk and zucchini. Cover and cook for 15 to 30 minutes more or until zucchini is tender. If desired, sprinkle individual servings with peanuts.

Per serving: 226 cal., 13 g total fat (9 g sat. fat), 69 mg chol., 654 mg sodium, 8 g carbo., 2 g fiber, 20 g pro.

Add a bit of savory contrast by sprinkling herb-seasoned croutons onto each serving.

CHICKEN FLORENTINE SOUP

1	tablespoon olive oil
2	pounds skinless, boneless chicken thighs, cut into 1-inch pieces
2	14-ounce cans chicken broth
2	14½-ounce cans diced tomatoes with basil, oregano, and garlic, undrained
1	15- to 19-ounce can white kidney beans (cannellini beans), rinsed and drained
½	teaspoon finely shredded lemon peel
2	tablespoons lemon juice
2	cloves garlic, minced
1	teaspoon dried Italian seasoning, crushed
¼	teaspoon salt
1½	cups chopped zucchini
2	cups chopped fresh spinach

PREP:
20 minutes

COOK:
Low 5 hours, High 2½ hours; plus 15 minutes on High

MAKES:
8 main-dish servings

SLOW COOKER:
5- to 6-quart

1 In a large skillet heat olive oil over medium-high heat. Brown chicken, half at a time, in hot oil. Drain off fat.

2 In a 5- to 6-quart slow cooker combine chicken, broth, undrained tomatoes, beans, lemon peel, lemon juice, garlic, Italian seasoning, and salt.

3 Cover and cook on low-heat setting for 5 to 6 hours or on high-heat setting for 2½ to 3 hours.

4 If using low-heat setting, turn to high-heat setting. Stir in zucchini. Cover and cook about 15 minutes more or until zucchini is tender. Stir in spinach.

Per serving: 240 cal., 7 g total fat (1 g sat. fat), 92 mg chol., 1,168 mg sodium, 18 g carbo., 3 g fiber, 28 g pro.

Canned coconut milk is available in the baking aisle of the supermarket.

MULLIGATAWNY

PREP:
25 minutes

COOK:
Low 6 hours, High 3 hours;
plus 15 minutes on High

MAKES:
6 main-dish servings

SLOW COOKER:
3½- or 4-quart

1	tablespoon olive oil
1	pound boneless, skinless chicken thighs, cut into 1-inch pieces
2	cups chopped potato
1	medium Granny Smith apple, peeled and coarsely chopped
1	large onion, chopped
2	medium carrots, sliced
1	teaspoon finely shredded lime peel
1	tablespoon lime juice
1½	teaspoons curry powder
¼	teaspoon salt
2	14-ounce cans chicken broth
½	cup purchased unsweetened coconut milk
½	cup instant white rice

1 In a large skillet heat olive oil over medium-high heat. Brown chicken, half at a time, in hot oil. Drain off fat.

2 In a 3½- or 4-quart slow cooker combine chicken, potato, apple, onion, carrots, lime peel, lime juice, curry powder, and salt. Pour broth over all.

3 Cover and cook on low-heat setting for 6 to 7 hours or on high-heat setting for 3 to 3½ hours.

4 If using low-heat setting, turn to high-heat setting. Stir in coconut milk and uncooked rice. Cover and cook about 15 minutes or until rice is tender.

Per serving: 250 cal., 10 g total fat (4 g sat. fat), 62 mg chol., 701 mg sodium, 22 g carbo., 2 g fiber, 18 g pro.

Olives give an unusual flair and grand flavor to this Spanish-inspired chicken stew.

SPANISH CHICKEN STEW

1¼	pounds skinless, boneless chicken thighs, cut into 1½-inch pieces
12	ounces red-skinned potatoes, cut into ½-inch-thick wedges
1	medium onion, thinly sliced
2	cloves garlic, minced
½	teaspoon dried thyme, crushed
¼	teaspoon salt
¼	teaspoon black pepper
1	14½-ounce can diced tomatoes, undrained
1	cup chicken broth
1	medium red sweet pepper, cut into ¼-inch-wide strips
⅓	cup small pimiento-stuffed olives, cut up

1 In a 3½- or 4-quart slow cooker combine chicken, potatoes, onion, garlic, thyme, salt, and black pepper. Add undrained tomatoes and broth.

2 Cover and cook on low-heat setting for 7 to 8 hours or on high-heat setting for 3½ to 4 hours.

3 If using low-heat setting, turn to high-heat setting. Stir in sweet pepper and olives. Cover and cook for 30 minutes more.

Per serving: 288 cal., 7 g total fat (2 g sat. fat), 118 mg chol., 856 mg sodium, 24 g carbo., 4 g fiber, 31 g pro.

PREP:
30 minutes

COOK:
Low 7 Hours, High 3½ hours; plus 30 minutes on High

MAKES:
4 main-dish servings

SLOW COOKER:
3½- or 4-quart

One taste lets you in on the surprise—this mild but richly flavored chili contains chicken and white beans.

WHITE SURPRISE CHILI

PREP:
25 minutes

STAND:
1 hour

COOK:
Low 12 hours, High 6 hours

MAKES:
10 main-dish servings

SLOW COOKER:
5- to 6-quart

6	cups water
1	pound dry Great Northern beans
6	cups chicken broth
1	large onion, chopped
2	cloves garlic, minced
2	4-ounce cans diced green chile peppers, undrained
1	tablespoon dried oregano, crushed
1	tablespoon ground cumin
½	teaspoon salt
½	teaspoon black pepper
½	teaspoon cayenne pepper
6	cups chopped cooked chicken
	Shredded Monterey Jack cheese (optional)
	Sliced green onions (optional)

1 Rinse beans. In a 5- to 6-quart Dutch oven combine the water and beans. Bring to boiling; reduce heat. Simmer, uncovered, for 10 minutes. Remove from heat. Cover and let stand for 1 hour. Drain and rinse beans.

2 In a 5- to 6-quart slow cooker combine drained beans, broth, onion, garlic, undrained green chile peppers, oregano, cumin, salt, black pepper, and cayenne pepper. Stir in cooked chicken.

3 Cover and cook on low-heat setting for 12 to 14 hours or on high-heat setting for 6 to 7 hours. If desired, sprinkle individual servings with cheese and green onions.

Per serving: 340 cal., 7 g total fat (2 g sat. fat), 76 mg chol., 865 mg sodium, 32 g carbo., 10 g fiber, 35 g pro.

Here's a tasty soup that's brimming with tender noodles and vegetables. Add a few drops of teriyaki or soy sauce for another layer of flavor.

ASIAN CHICKEN NOODLE SOUP

6	cups water
2	3-ounce packages chicken-flavored ramen noodles
1	teaspoon grated fresh ginger
2	cups chopped cooked chicken (10 ounces)
1	16-ounce package frozen broccoli stir-fry vegetables
¼	cup sliced green onions
	Crushed red pepper
	Teriyaki sauce or soy sauce

1 In a 3½- to 4½-quart slow cooker combine the water, seasoning packets from the ramen noodles (set noodles aside), and ginger. Stir in cooked chicken and frozen vegetables.

2 Cover and cook on low-heat setting for 5 to 6 hours or on high-heat setting for 2½ to 3 hours.

3 If using low-heat setting, turn to high-heat setting. Stir in the ramen noodles. Cover and cook for 10 to 15 minutes more or just until noodles are tender. Stir in green onions. Sprinkle individual servings with crushed red pepper and serve with teriyaki sauce.

Per serving: 249 cal., 9 g total fat (1 g sat. fat), 42 mg chol., 818 mg sodium, 23 g carbo., 2 g fiber, 19 g pro.

PREP:
15 minutes

COOK:
Low 5 hours, High 2½ hours; plus 10 minutes on High

MAKES:
6 main-dish servings

SLOW COOKER:
3½- to 4½-quart

Dress up individual servings of this full-flavored soup with spoonfuls of sour cream on top and tortilla chips on the side.

MEXICAN TURKEY-VEGETABLE SOUP

PREP:
35 minutes

COOK:
Low 7 hours, High 3½ hours

MAKES:
4 main-dish servings

SLOW COOKER:
3½- or 4-quart

1	tablespoon olive oil
2	1-pound turkey thighs, skinned, boned, and cut into ¾-inch pieces
1	cup loose-pack frozen whole kernel corn
1	medium onion, chopped
2	stalks celery, sliced
1	medium carrot, sliced
1	small red sweet pepper, chopped
2	tablespoons tomato paste
½	teaspoon finely shredded lime peel
1	tablespoon lime juice
2	cloves garlic, minced
1½	teaspoons ground ancho chile pepper*
1	teaspoon ground cumin*
¼	teaspoon salt
2	14-ounce cans chicken broth
1	tablespoon snipped fresh cilantro

FOR A 5- TO 6-QUART SLOW COOKER:
Use three 1-pound turkey thighs, 2 cups loose-pack frozen whole kernel corn, 1 large onion, 3 stalks celery, 2 medium carrots, 1 large red sweet pepper, 3 tablespoons tomato paste, 1 teaspoon finely shredded lime peel, 2 tablespoons lime juice, 3 cloves garlic, 2 teaspoons ground ancho chile pepper,* 1½ teaspoons ground cumin,* ½ teaspoon salt, three 14-ounce cans chicken broth, and 2 tablespoons snipped fresh cilantro. Makes 6 or 7 main-dish servings.

Per serving: 319 cal., 10 g total fat (3 g sat. fat), 102 mg chol., 1,149 mg sodium, 25 g carbo., 4 g fiber, 34 g pro.

① In a large skillet heat olive oil over medium-high heat. Brown turkey, half at a time, in hot oil. Drain off fat.

② In a 3½- or 4-quart slow cooker combine corn, onion, celery, carrot, sweet pepper, tomato paste, lime peel, lime juice, garlic, ancho chile pepper, cumin, and salt. Arrange turkey over corn mixture; pour broth over.

③ Cover and cook on low-heat setting for 7 to 8 hours or on high-heat setting for 3½ to 4 hours. Stir in cilantro.

Per serving: 299 cal., 11 g total fat (3 g sat. fat), 102 mg chol., 1,097 mg sodium, 18 g carbo., 3 g fiber, 33 g pro

***NOTE:** If desired, omit the ground ancho chile pepper and the cumin and add 1 tablespoon chili powder for the 3½- to 4-quart slow cooker or 4½ teaspoons chili powder for the 5- to 6-quart slow cooker.

Cod, orange roughy, halibut, and haddock are all excellent fish choices for this creamy chowder.

CREAMY FISH & POTATO STEW

1½   pounds potatoes, peeled and chopped (4 cups)

2   medium carrots, sliced

1   medium onion, chopped

2   tablespoons tomato paste

½   teaspoon dried thyme, crushed

¼   teaspoon salt

¼   teaspoon black pepper

1   bay leaf

2   14-ounce cans chicken broth

1   12-ounce can tomato juice

1½   pounds fresh or frozen firm white fish

½   cup half-and-half or light cream

1   tablespoon snipped flat-leaf parsley

PREP:
15 minutes

COOK:
*Low 6 hours, High 3 hours;
plus 15 minutes on High*

MAKES:
6 main-dish servings

SLOW COOKER:
3½- or 4-quart

1 In a 3½- or 4-quart slow cooker combine potatoes, carrots, onion, tomato paste, thyme, salt, pepper, and bay leaf. Pour broth and tomato juice over all.

2 Cover and cook on low-heat setting for 6 to 8 hours or on high-heat setting for 3 to 4 hours. Discard bay leaf.

3 Thaw fish, if frozen. Cut fish into 1-inch pieces.

4 Mash potato mixture in slow cooker slightly with a potato masher. If using low-heat setting, turn to high-heat setting. Stir fish and half-and-half into potato mixture in slow cooker. Cover and cook about 15 minutes or until fish flakes easily when tested with a fork. Stir in parsley.

Per serving: 291 cal., 9 g total fat (2 g sat. fat), 74 mg chol., 869 mg sodium, 26 g carbo., 3 g fiber, 26 g pro.

Ginger, jerk seasoning, lime, and garlic turn simple white fish into a tropical delight.

CARIBBEAN FISH STEW

PREP:
30 minutes

COOK:
*Low 6 hours, High 3 hours;
plus 15 minutes on High*

MAKES:
6 main-dish servings

SLOW COOKER:
4- to 5-quart

2   pounds sweet potatoes, peeled and coarsely chopped

1   large red sweet pepper, chopped

1   medium onion, chopped

1   tablespoon grated fresh ginger

½   teaspoon finely shredded lime peel

1   tablespoon lime juice

1   teaspoon Jamaican jerk seasoning

2   cloves garlic, minced

2   14-ounce cans chicken broth

1   14½-ounce can diced tomatoes, undrained

1   pound fresh or frozen firm white fish

2   tablespoons snipped fresh cilantro

1 In a 4- to 5-quart slow cooker combine sweet potatoes, sweet pepper, onion, ginger, lime peel, lime juice, jerk seasoning, and garlic. Pour broth and undrained tomatoes over all.

2 Cover and cook on low-heat setting for 6 to 8 hours or on high-heat setting for 3 to 4 hours.

3 Thaw fish, if frozen. Cut into 1-inch pieces.

4 If using low-heat setting, turn to high-heat setting. Stir in fish. Cover and cook about 15 minutes more or until fish flakes easily when tested with a fork. Sprinkle individual servings with cilantro.

Per serving: 232 cal., 5 g total fat (1 g sat. fat), 45 mg chol., 792 mg sodium, 29 g carbo., 4 g fiber, 17 g pro.

Because this sensational soup serves a crowd, it's ideal for toting to potlucks, church suppers, or family get-togethers.

FISH CHOWDER

3	pounds fresh or frozen fish fillets (such as cod, haddock, or orange roughy)
2	pounds potatoes, peeled and chopped
3	large onions, chopped
¾	cup chopped celery
2	tablespoons butter or margarine
3	bay leaves
1	tablespoon salt
¾	teaspoon dried dill
¾	teaspoon black pepper
3	cups water
¾	cup dry vermouth, dry white wine, or water
3	cups whipping cream, half-and-half, or light cream
⅓	cup snipped fresh parsley

1 Thaw fish, if frozen. Rinse fish; pat dry with paper towels. Cut fish into 2-inch pieces; cover and chill.

2 In a 5- to 6-quart slow cooker combine potatoes, onions, celery, butter, bay leaves, salt, dill, and pepper. Stir in the water and vermouth.

3 Cover and cook on low-heat setting for 7 hours or on high-heat setting for 3½ hours.

4 If using low-heat setting, turn to high-heat setting. Place fish on top of vegetable mixture in slow cooker. Cover and cook for 30 to 45 minutes more or until fish flakes easily when tested with a fork. Discard bay leaves. Using a fork, break fish into bite-size pieces. Stir in cream and parsley.

Per serving: 396 cal., 25 g total fat (15 g sat. fat), 136 mg chol., 680 mg sodium, 17 g carbo., 2 g fiber, 23 g pro.

PREP:
35 minutes

COOK:
Low 7 hours, High 3½ hours; plus 30 minutes on High

MAKES:
12 main-dish servings

SLOW COOKER:
5- to 6-quart

Easy is right! The dry scalloped potato mix makes this wonderful dill-infused salmon chowder as simple as can be.

EASY POTATO & SALMON CHOWDER

PREP:
15 minutes

COOK:
Low 6 hours, High 3 hours; plus 20 minutes on High

MAKES:
8 main-dish servings

SLOW COOKER:
3¹/₂- or 4-quart

2	14-ounce cans chicken broth
1¹/₂	cups loose-pack frozen whole kernel corn
3	medium carrots, thinly sliced
1¹/₂	cups water
1	medium onion, chopped
1	4.9-ounce package dry scalloped potato mix
2	teaspoons dried dill
2	cups half-and-half or light cream
¹/₂	cup all-purpose flour
2	6-ounce cans skinless, boneless salmon, drained

1 In a 3¹/₂- or 4-quart slow cooker combine broth, corn, carrots, the water, onion, dry potato mix (including contents of seasoning packet), and dill.

2 Cover and cook on low-heat setting for 6 to 8 hours or on high-heat setting for 3 to 4 hours.

3 If using low-heat setting, turn to high-heat setting. In a medium bowl whisk together half-and-half and flour. Gradually stir into vegetable mixture in slow cooker. Gently stir in salmon. Cover and cook for 20 to 30 minutes more or until thickened.

Per serving: 269 cal., 10 g total fat (5 g sat. fat), 45 mg chol., 827 mg sodium, 32 g carbo., 2 g fiber, 14 g pro.

Old Bay seafood seasoning originated in the Chesapeake Bay area. You'll find it with the herbs and spices at the supermarket.

SHRIMP BISQUE

3	medium carrots, chopped
1	large potato, peeled and chopped
2	stalks celery, chopped
1	large onion, chopped
2	tablespoons tomato paste
1	teaspoon dried thyme, crushed
½	teaspoon Old Bay seasoning
¼	teaspoon salt
2	14-ounce cans chicken broth
1	14½-ounce can diced tomatoes, undrained
12	ounces fresh or frozen medium shrimp
⅔	cup half-and-half or light cream
	Crisp-cooked bacon, crumbled

PREP:
25 minutes

COOK:
*Low 6 hours, High 3 hours;
plus 45 minutes on High*

MAKES:
6 main-dish servings

SLOW COOKER:
3½- or 4-quart

1 In a 3½- or 4-quart slow cooker combine carrots, potato, celery, onion, tomato paste, thyme, Old Bay seasoning, and salt. Stir in broth and undrained tomatoes.

2 Cover and cook on low-heat setting for 6 to 8 hours or on high-heat setting for 3 to 4 hours. Cool slightly.

3 Thaw shrimp, if frozen. Peel and devein shrimp; halve shrimp lengthwise. Rinse shrimp; pat dry with paper towels. Transfer one-quarter of the soup mixture to a blender or food processor. Cover and blend or process until smooth. Repeat with remaining soup mixture, one-quarter at a time, until all of the soup is blended.

4 If using low-heat setting, turn to high-heat setting. Return pureed soup to slow cooker. Stir in shrimp and half-and-half. Cover and cook about 45 minutes more or until shrimp is opaque. Sprinkle individual servings with bacon.

Per serving: 185 cal., 6 g total fat (3 g sat. fat), 80 mg chol., 988 mg sodium, 18 g carbo., 2 g fiber, 13 g pro.

Andouille sausage is a smoked sausage often used in Cajun cooking. This shrimp dish combines andouille with Cajun seasoning for plenty of zing.

CAJUN SHRIMP SOUP

PREP:
30 minutes

COOK:
Low 6 hours, High 3 hours; plus 5 minutes on High

MAKES:
4 main-dish servings

SLOW COOKER:
3½- or 4-quart

8 ounces andouille sausage or other cooked smoked sausage, halved lengthwise and cut into ½-inch-thick slices

2 14½-ounce cans diced tomatoes, undrained

1 medium sweet red pepper, chopped

1 medium onion, finely chopped

1 stalk celery, sliced

1 teaspoon Cajun seasoning

2 cloves garlic, minced

¼ teaspoon bottled hot pepper sauce

1 bay leaf

2 14-ounce cans chicken broth

12 ounces medium fresh or frozen shrimp

¾ cup instant white rice

1 tablespoon snipped fresh parsley

1 In a 3½- or 4-quart slow cooker combine sausage, undrained tomatoes, sweet pepper, onion, celery, Cajun seasoning, garlic, bottled hot pepper sauce, and bay leaf. Pour broth over all.

2 Cover and cook on low-heat setting for 6 to 8 hours or on high-heat setting for 3 to 4 hours.

3 Thaw shrimp, if frozen. Peel and devein shrimp. Rinse shrimp; pat dry with paper towels.

4 If using low-heat setting, turn to high-heat setting. Stir shrimp and uncooked rice into mixture in slow cooker. Cover and cook for 5 to 10 minutes more or until shrimp is opaque. Discard bay leaf. Stir in parsley.

Per serving: 294 cal., 4 g total fat (1 g sat. fat), 146 mg chol., 1,698 mg sodium, 33 g carbo., 2 g fiber, 28 g pro.

Take the chill off a cold, blustery day with this creamy golden chowder accented with bits of red sweet pepper and bacon.

CORN & CLAM CHOWDER

2	6½-ounce cans chopped clams
1	8-ounce bottle clam juice
2	cups water
2	15-ounce cans cream-style corn
1	10¾-ounce can condensed cream of onion or cream of celery soup
1	10-ounce package frozen whole kernel corn
1	medium onion, chopped
½	cup chopped red sweet pepper
1	small fresh jalapeño chile pepper, seeded and finely chopped*
½	cup half-and-half or light cream
2	slices bacon, crisp-cooked, drained, and crumbled

1 Drain clams, reserving juice. Cover and chill clams. In a 4- to 5-quart slow cooker combine reserved clam juice, bottled clam juice, the water, cream-style corn, cream of onion soup, frozen corn, onion, sweet pepper, and chile pepper.

2 Cover and cook on low-heat setting for 6 to 7 hours or on high-heat setting for 3 to 3½ hours.

3 If using low-heat setting, turn to high-heat setting. Stir in clams, half-and-half, and bacon. Cover and cook for 10 minutes more.

Per serving: 234 cal., 6 g total fat (2 g sat. fat), 37 mg chol., 706 mg sodium, 35 g carbo., 3 g fiber, 15 g pro.

***NOTE:** Because chile peppers contain volatile oils that can burn your skin and eyes, avoid direct contact with them as much as possible. When working with chile peppers, wear plastic or rubber gloves. If your bare hands do touch the peppers, wash your hands and nails well with soap and warm water.

PREP:
15 minutes

COOK:
Low 6 hours, High 3 hours; plus 10 minutes on High

MAKES:
8 main-dish servings

SLOW COOKER:
4- to 5-quart

This creamy clam soup with bacon and half-and-half is slightly smoky and extra rich.

POTATO-CLAM CHOWDER

PREP:
20 minutes

COOK:
*Low 6 hours, High 3 hours;
plus 30 minutes on High*

MAKES:
6 main-dish servings

SLOW COOKER:
3½- or 4-quart

3 slices bacon, cut up, or 4 ounces salt pork, diced

2 6½-ounce cans minced clams

3 medium potatoes (1 pound), peeled and cut into bite-size pieces (3 cups)

1 cup chopped onion

1 cup coarsely shredded carrot

1 10¾-ounce can condensed cream of mushroom soup

¼ teaspoon black pepper

3 cups half-and-half or light cream

1 In a skillet cook bacon or salt pork until crisp; drain off fat. Drain clams, reserving liquid; add enough water to clam liquid to measure 1¾ cups total liquid. Cover clams; chill.

2 In a 3½- or 4-quart slow cooker combine reserved clam liquid, potatoes, onion, and carrot. Stir in cream of mushroom soup and pepper. Add bacon or salt pork.

3 Cover and cook on low-heat setting for 6 to 7 hours or on high-heat setting for 3 to 4 hours.

4 If using low-heat setting, turn to high-heat setting. Stir in clams and half-and-half. Cover and cook for 30 minutes more.

Per serving: 339 cal., 19 g total fat (10 g sat. fat), 76 mg chol., 558 mg sodium, 26 g carbo., 2 g fiber, 17 g pro.

Your taste buds will dance among the sweet, spicy, and savory flavors in this truly unique soup. Apples, raisins, and apple pie spice enhance the olives, tomatoes, and chili.

PICADILLO SOUP

2   15-ounce cans chili without beans

1   14½-ounce can Mexican-style stewed tomatoes, undrained

2   cups water

2   large cooking apples, peeled, cored, and coarsely chopped (2¼ cups)

½   cup golden raisins

½   teaspoon apple pie spice or pumpkin pie spice

    Sliced pitted ripe olives

1 In a 3½- or 4-quart slow cooker combine chili, undrained tomatoes, the water, apples, raisins, and spice.

2 Cover and cook on low-heat setting for 7 to 8 hours or on high-heat setting for 3½ to 4 hours. Top individual servings with olives.

Per serving: 377 cal., 22 g total fat (10 g sat. fat), 37 mg chol., 1,040 mg sodium, 31 g carbo., 3 g fiber, 16 g pro.

PREP:
15 minutes

COOK:
Low 7 hours, High 3½ hours

MAKES:
6 main-dish servings

SLOW COOKER:
3½- or 4-quart

The easy dumplings are the only last-minute preparations. For the rest of the meal, serve a packaged salad and dressing, fresh pineapple, and cookies.

SOUTHWESTERN BEAN STEW

PREP:
30 minutes

COOK:
*Low 8 hours, High 4 hours;
plus 30 minutes on High*

MAKES:
4 main-dish servings

SLOW COOKER:
3½- or 4-quart

1   15-ounce can red kidney beans, rinsed and drained

1   15-ounce can black beans, pinto beans, or
    Great Northern beans, rinsed and drained

1   14½-ounce can Mexican-style stewed tomatoes,
    undrained, cut up

1   14-ounce can vegetable broth or chicken broth

1   10-ounce package frozen whole kernel corn

2   medium carrots, thinly sliced

1   large onion, chopped

½   cup water

1   4-ounce can diced green chile peppers, undrained

2   to 3 teaspoons chili powder

2   cloves garlic, minced

⅓   cup all-purpose flour

¼   cup yellow cornmeal

1   teaspoon baking powder

    Dash salt

    Dash black pepper

1   beaten egg white

2   tablespoons milk

1   tablespoon cooking oil

1 In a 3½- or 4-quart slow cooker combine kidney beans, black beans, undrained tomatoes, broth, corn, carrots, onion, the water, undrained chile peppers, chili powder, and garlic.

2 Cover and cook on low-heat setting for 8 to 10 hours or on high-heat setting for 4 to 5 hours.

3 For dumplings, in a medium bowl stir together flour, cornmeal, baking powder, salt, and black pepper. In a small bowl combine egg white, milk, and oil. Add egg white mixture to flour mixture; stir with a fork just until combined.

4 If using low-heat setting, turn to high-heat setting. Drop the dumpling mixture by rounded teaspoonfuls to make eight mounds on top of stew. Cover and cook for 30 minutes more (do not lift cover).

Per serving: 396 cal., 6 g total fat (1 g sat. fat), 1 mg chol., 1,406 mg sodium, 78 g carbo., 15 g fiber, 22 g pro.

Taste this robust chili and you'll agree that three beans are better than one. Each type has a distinctive flavor and texture, making every spoonful of this meatless meal-in-a-bowl an adventure.

BEAN MEDLEY CHILI

1	15-ounce can black beans, rinsed and drained
1	15-ounce can dark red kidney beans, rinsed and drained
1	15-ounce can garbanzo beans (chickpeas), rinsed and drained
2	large onions, chopped
1	large red sweet pepper, chopped
1	large green sweet pepper, chopped
3	tablespoons chili powder
12	cloves garlic, minced
1	canned chipotle chile pepper in adobo sauce, finely chopped*
1	teaspoon ground cumin
¼	teaspoon salt
2	14½-ounce cans diced tomatoes, undrained
1	14-ounce can chicken broth
¼	cup snipped fresh cilantro
	Hot cooked white or brown rice (optional)

1 In a 4- to 5-quart slow cooker combine black beans, kidney beans, garbanzo beans, onions, red sweet pepper, green sweet pepper, chili powder, garlic, chipotle chile pepper, cumin, and salt. Add undrained tomatoes and broth.

2 Cover and cook on low-heat setting for 8 to 10 hours or on high-heat setting for 4 to 5 hours. Stir in cilantro. If desired, serve bean mixture with hot cooked rice.

Per serving: 226 cal., 2 g total fat (0 g sat. fat), 1 mg chol., 1,081 mg sodium, 46 g carbo., 12 g fiber, 12 g pro.

*NOTE: Because chile peppers contain volatile oils that can burn your skin and eyes, avoid direct contact with them as much as possible. When working with chile peppers, wear plastic or rubber gloves. If your bare hands do touch the peppers, wash your hands and nails well with soap and warm water.

PREP:
25 minutes

COOK:
Low 8 hours, High 4 hours

MAKES:
8 main-dish servings

SLOW COOKER:
4- to 5-quart

Minestrone is Italian for "big soup" and this one is big indeed. It's full of tomatoes, beans, onion, carrot, barley, spinach, and zucchini.

CHUNKY MINESTRONE

PREP:
20 minutes

COOK:
Low 8 hours, High 4 hours; plus 30 minutes on High

MAKES:
8 main-dish servings

SLOW COOKER:
4- to 5-quart

2   14-ounce cans vegetable broth

2   14½-ounce cans diced tomatoes, undrained

1   15- to 16-ounce can navy beans or one 15- to 19-ounce can white kidney beans (cannellini beans), rinsed and drained

1½ cups chopped onion

¾ cup water

1   large carrot, halved lengthwise and thinly sliced (about ¾ cup)

½ cup regular barley

1   teaspoon dried Italian seasoning, crushed

2   cloves garlic, minced

¼ teaspoon black pepper

4   cups shredded fresh spinach

1   medium zucchini, quartered lengthwise and sliced (about 1½ cups)

Salt (optional)

Black pepper (optional)

Grated Parmesan cheese

1 In a 4- to 5-quart slow cooker combine broth, undrained tomatoes, beans, onion, the water, carrot, barley, Italian seasoning, garlic, and the ¼ teaspoon pepper.

2 Cover and cook on low-heat setting for 8 to 10 hours or on high-heat setting for 4 to 5 hours.

3 If using low-heat setting, turn to high-heat setting. Stir in spinach and zucchini. Cover and cook for 30 minutes more. If desired, season with salt and additional pepper. Sprinkle individual servings with Parmesan cheese.

Per serving: 174 cal., 1 g total fat (1 g sat. fat), 2 mg chol., 877 mg sodium, 32 g carbo., 7 g fiber, 8 g pro.

Kick the flavor of this soup up a notch with a sprinkling of cilantro and a squirt of lime juice.

SOUTHWESTERN PINTO BEAN SOUP

2	cups dry pinto beans
5	cups cold water
2	14-ounce cans chicken broth
½	cup water
1	large onion, chopped
3	cloves garlic, minced
1	teaspoon ground cumin
¼	teaspoon cayenne pepper
1	14½-ounce can fire-roasted diced tomatoes, undrained
	Shredded Monterey Jack cheese
	Snipped fresh cilantro
	Lime wedges

PREP:
15 minutes

STAND:
1 hour

COOK:
Low 8 hours plus 30 minutes, High 4 hours plus 30 minutes

MAKES:
6 main-dish servings

SLOW COOKER:
3½- or 4-quart

1 Rinse dry beans. In a Dutch oven combine beans and the 5 cups cold water. Bring to boiling; reduce heat. Simmer, uncovered, for 10 minutes. Remove from heat. Cover and let stand for 1 hour. Drain and rinse beans.

2 In a 3½- or 4-quart slow cooker combine beans, broth, the ½ cup water, the onion, garlic, cumin, and cayenne pepper.

3 Cover and cook on low-heat setting for 8 to 10 hours or on high-heat setting for 4 to 5 hours.

4 Stir in undrained tomatoes; cover and cook for 30 minutes more. If desired, partially mash mixture with a potato masher, leaving soup chunky. Top individual servings with cheese and cilantro. Serve with lime wedges.

Per serving: 309 cal., 5 g total fat (3 g sat. fat), 14 mg chol., 772 mg sodium, 46 g carbo., 10 g fiber, 18 g pro.

If you think all-vegetable chili tends to be bland, try this one. Tomatoes with green chile peppers punch up the flavor.

TWO-BEAN CHILI

PREP:
15 minutes

COOK:
Low 9 hours, High 4½ hours

MAKES:
8 main-dish servings

SLOW COOKER:
4- or 4½-quart

2   15-ounce cans garbanzo beans (chickpeas),
     rinsed and drained

2   15-ounce cans red kidney beans, rinsed and drained

2   14-ounce cans beef broth

2   11-ounce cans whole kernel corn with sweet peppers,
     drained

1   10-ounce can diced tomatoes and green chile peppers,
     undrained

1   large onion, chopped

4   teaspoons chili powder

2   cloves garlic, minced

¼   teaspoon black pepper

¼   teaspoon crushed red pepper (optional)

     Dairy sour cream (optional)

     Corn chips (optional)

1 In a 4- or 4½-quart slow cooker combine garbanzo beans, kidney beans, broth, corn, undrained tomatoes and green chile peppers, onion, chili powder, garlic, black pepper, and, if desired, crushed red pepper.

2 Cover and cook on low-heat setting for 9 to 10 hours or on high-heat setting for 4½ to 5 hours. If desired, top individual servings with sour cream. If desired, serve with corn chips.

Per serving: 267 cal., 2 g total fat (0 g sat. fat), 1 mg chol., 1,294 mg sodium, 53 g carbo., 14 g fiber, 16 g pro.

A takeoff on the French classic, cassoulet, this stew features a trio of beans simmered with leeks, carrots, celery, and turnips.

VEGETABLE STEW WITH PARMESAN TOAST

2	14-ounce cans vegetable broth
1	15- to 16-ounce can navy beans, rinsed and drained
1	15- to 16-ounce can white kidney beans (cannellini beans), rinsed and drained
1	15- to 16-ounce can butter beans, rinsed and drained
4	medium leeks, sliced
4	medium carrots, peeled and cut into ½-inch-thick slices
4	stalks celery, sliced
2	medium turnips, peeled and diced
4	cloves garlic, minced
2	teaspoons dried Italian seasoning, crushed
2	bay leaves
½	to 1 teaspoon cracked black pepper
¼	teaspoon salt
16	slices baguette-style French bread
1	tablespoon olive oil
½	cup finely shredded Parmesan cheese (2 ounces)
1	14½-ounce can fire-roasted diced tomatoes or diced tomatoes, drained

PREP:
35 minutes

COOK:
Low 10 hours, High 5 hours

BAKE:
7 minutes

OVEN:
400°F

MAKES:
8 main-dish servings

SLOW COOKER:
5- to 6-quart

1 In a 5- to 6-quart slow cooker stir together broth, navy beans, white kidney beans, butter beans, leeks, carrots, celery, turnips, garlic, Italian seasoning, bay leaves, pepper, and salt.

2 Cover and cook on low-heat setting for 10 to 11 hours or on high-heat setting for 5 to 5½ hours.

3 For Parmesan toast, preheat oven to 400°F. Brush baguette slices with olive oil; sprinkle with Parmesan cheese. Place on a baking sheet and bake about 7 minutes or until lightly toasted and cheese is melted.

4 Discard bay leaves. Stir drained tomatoes into bean mixture in slow cooker. Serve stew in shallow bowls with Parmesan toast.

Per serving: 288 cal., 4 g total fat (1 g sat. fat), 4 mg chol., 1,409 mg sodium, 50 g carbo., 10 g fiber, 15 g pro.

This soup tickles the taste buds with the robust elements of southwestern cuisine—jalapeño chile pepper, black beans, cilantro, and chili powder.

VEGGIE SOUTHWEST SOUP

PREP:
30 minutes

COOK:
Low 7 hours, High 3½ hours

MAKES:
8 main-dish servings

SLOW COOKER:
5- to 6-quart

4   14½-ounce cans stewed tomatoes, undrained, cut-up

2   15-ounce cans black beans, rinsed and drained

2   cups water

1   15¼-ounce can whole kernel corn, drained

2   large green sweet peppers, chopped

1   fresh jalapeño chile pepper, seeded and finely chopped*

1   teaspoon dried cilantro, crushed

1   teaspoon garlic powder

1   teaspoon black pepper

1   teaspoon dried basil, crushed

½   teaspoon chili powder

1 In a 5- to 6-quart slow cooker combine undrained tomatoes, beans, the water, corn, sweet peppers, chile pepper, cilantro, garlic powder, black pepper, basil, and chili powder.

2 Cover and cook on low-heat setting for 7 to 8 hours or on high-heat setting for 3½ to 4 hours.

Per serving: 192 cal., 2 g total fat (0 g sat. fat), 0 mg chol., 715 mg sodium, 39 g carbo., 8 g fiber, 10 g pro.

*NOTE: Because chile peppers contain volatile oils that can burn your skin and eyes, avoid direct contact with them as much as possible. When working with chile peppers, wear plastic or rubber gloves. If your bare hands do touch the peppers, wash your hands and nails well with soap and warm water.

Sharp cheddar and American cheese team up to make this creamy pleaser extra rich.

BROCCOLI CHEESE SOUP

6   cups chopped broccoli stems and florets

8   ounces potatoes (2 small), peeled and chopped

1   medium onion, chopped

2   cloves garlic, minced

1/8 teaspoon cayenne pepper

3   14-ounce cans reduced-sodium chicken broth

8   ounces process American cheese, cut into 1/2-inch cubes

1/2 cup shredded sharp cheddar cheese (2 ounces)

1   cup half-and-half or light cream

1 In a 3 1/2- or 4-quart slow cooker combine broccoli, potatoes, onion, garlic, and cayenne pepper. Pour broth over all.

2 Cover and cook on low-heat setting for 5 to 6 hours or on high-heat setting for 2 1/2 to 3 hours.

3 Add American cheese and cheddar cheese, stirring until melted; stir in half-and-half.

Per serving: 310 cal., 20 g total fat (13 g sat. fat), 62 mg chol., 1,150 mg sodium, 16 g carbo., 3 g fiber, 18 g pro.

PREP:
25 minutes

COOK:
Low 5 hours, High 2 1/2 hours

MAKES:
6 main-dish servings

SLOW COOKER:
3 1/2- or 4-quart

With two types of cheese, this sophisticated soup is full of body. For a milder flavor, substitute regular beer for the ale.

CHEDDAR ALE SOUP

PREP:
25 minutes

COOK:
Low 8 hours, High 4 hours

MAKES:
6 main-dish servings

SLOW COOKER:
3½- or 4-quart

1½	pounds potatoes, chopped
4	medium carrots, chopped
1	medium onion, chopped
1	stalk celery, chopped
2	cloves garlic, minced
2	teaspoons Dijon-style mustard
½	teaspoon dried thyme, crushed
⅛	to ¼ teaspoon cayenne pepper
2	14-ounce cans chicken broth
1	cup ale
1½	cups shredded cheddar cheese (6 ounces)
1	3-ounce package cream cheese, cut up

1 In a 3½- or 4-quart slow cooker combine potatoes, carrots, onion, celery, garlic, mustard, thyme, and cayenne pepper. Pour broth and ale over all.

2 Cover and cook on low-heat setting for 8 to 9 hours or on high-heat setting for 4 to 4½ hours.

3 Add cheddar cheese and cream cheese; stir until melted.

Per serving: 300 cal., 15 g total fat (9 g sat. fat), 47 mg chol., 830 mg sodium, 28 g carbo., 3 g fiber, 12 g pro.

Even kids will eat their veggies when they're cloaked in a creamy, cheesy bowlful of soup.
Serve it with fresh fruit and corn bread.

CHEESY VEGETABLE SOUP

3   medium potatoes, peeled and chopped (3 cups)

4   carrots, chopped

1   16-ounce package frozen whole kernel corn

1   large onion, chopped

2   cups water

1   10¾-ounce can condensed cream of chicken soup

1   teaspoon dried thyme, crushed

¼   teaspoon black pepper

8   ounces American cheese, cubed

1 In a 3½- or 4-quart slow cooker combine potatoes, carrots, frozen corn, and onion. Stir in the water, cream of chicken soup, thyme, and pepper.

2 Cover and cook on low-heat setting for 8 to 9 hours or on high-heat setting for 4 to 4½ hours.

3 Stir cheese into hot soup until melted.

Per serving: 349 cal., 16 g total fat (8 g sat. fat), 40 mg chol., 968 mg sodium, 41 g carbo., 5 g fiber, 14 g pro.

PREP:
20 minutes

COOK:
Low 8 hours, High 4 hours

MAKES:
6 to 8 main-dish servings

SLOW COOKER:
3½- or 4-quart

There's nothing fancy or surprising about this soup. It's tried and true, and kids of all ages love it.

CHEESY POTATO SOUP

PREP:
20 minutes

COOK:
*Low 8 hours plus 1 hour,
High 4 hours plus 30 minutes*

MAKES:
6 main-dish servings

SLOW COOKER:
3½- or 4-quart

6	medium potatoes, peeled and chopped (6 cups)
2½	cups water
1	medium onion, chopped
2	teaspoons instant chicken bouillon granules
¼	teaspoon black pepper
1½	cups shredded American cheese (6 ounces)
1	12-ounce can (1½ cups) evaporated milk

1 In a 3½- or 4-quart slow cooker combine potatoes, the water, onion, bouillon granules, and pepper.

2 Cover and cook on low-heat setting for 8 to 9 hours or on high-heat setting for 4 to 4½ hours.

3 Stir American cheese and evaporated milk into potato mixture in slow cooker. Cover and cook on low-heat setting for 1 hour more or on high-heat setting for 30 minutes more. If desired, mash potatoes slightly.

Per serving: 308 cal., 13 g total fat (8 g sat. fat), 43 mg chol., 765 mg sodium, 35 g carbo., 3 g fiber, 14 g pro.

Grated fresh ginger, curry powder, and a jalapeño chile pepper deftly season this hearty, meatless soup.

CURRIED LENTIL SOUP

2 medium sweet potatoes (about 1 pound), peeled and coarsely chopped

1 cup dry brown or yellow lentils, rinsed and drained

1 medium onion, chopped

1 medium fresh jalapeño chile pepper, seeded and finely chopped*

3 cloves garlic, minced

3 14-ounce cans vegetable broth or chicken broth

1 14½-ounce can diced tomatoes, undrained

1 tablespoon curry powder

1 teaspoon grated fresh ginger

Plain yogurt or dairy sour cream (optional)

1 In a 4- to 5-quart slow cooker combine sweet potatoes, lentils, onion, jalapeño chile pepper, and garlic. Add broth, undrained tomatoes, curry powder, and ginger.

2 Cover and cook on low-heat setting for 8 to 10 hours or on high-heat setting for 4 to 5 hours. If desired, top individual servings with yogurt or sour cream.

Per serving: 316 cal., 2 g total fat (0 g sat. fat), 0 mg chol., 1,425 mg sodium, 60 g carbo., 18 g fiber, 18 g pro.

***NOTE:** Because chile peppers contain volatile oils that can burn your skin and eyes, avoid direct contact with them as much as possible. When working with chile peppers, wear plastic or rubber gloves. If your bare hands do touch the peppers, wash your hands and nails well with soap and warm water.

PREP:
20 minutes

COOK:
Low 8 hours, High 4 hours

MAKES:
4 to 6 main-dish servings

SLOW COOKER:
4- to 5-quart

"Provençal" means this stew is typical of the cooking of the Provence region of France. The area's cuisine often features tomatoes and garlic.

PROVENÇAL VEGETABLE STEW

PREP:
30 minutes

COOK:
Low 8 hours, High 4 hours

BAKE:
6 minutes

OVEN:
400°F

MAKES:
4 main-dish servings

SLOW COOKER:
3½- or 4-quart

2	baby eggplants or 1 very small eggplant (about 8 ounces)
1	large zucchini, quartered lengthwise and cut into ½-inch-thick slices
1	large yellow summer squash, quartered lengthwise and cut into ½-inch-thick slices
1	15- to 19-ounce can white kidney beans (cannellini beans) or Great Northern beans, rinsed and drained
1	large tomato, chopped
4	cloves garlic, minced
¼	teaspoon dried rosemary or thyme, crushed
¼	teaspoon black pepper
1	tablespoon snipped fresh basil or 1 teaspoon dried basil, crushed
1½	cups tomato juice
1	tablespoon white or regular balsamic vinegar
4	½-inch-thick slices baguette-style French bread
2	teaspoons olive oil
3	tablespoons finely shredded Romano or Parmesan cheese

1 If desired, peel eggplant. Cut eggplant into ¾-inch pieces (you should have about 3 cups).

2 In a 3½- or 4-quart slow cooker combine eggplant, zucchini, yellow summer squash, white kidney beans, tomato, garlic, rosemary, pepper, and dried basil (if using). Stir in tomato juice.

3 Cover and cook on low-heat setting for 8 to 10 hours or on high-heat setting for 4 to 5 hours. Stir in fresh basil (if using) and balsamic vinegar.

4 Meanwhile, for croutons, preheat oven to 400°F. Lightly brush bread slices with oil. Sprinkle with 1 tablespoon of the Romano cheese. Place bread slices on baking sheet. Bake for 6 to 8 minutes or until toasted.

5 To serve, ladle vegetable mixture into bowls. Top with croutons and sprinkle with remaining 2 tablespoons Romano cheese.

Per serving: 220 cal., 5 g total fat (1 g sat. fat), 3 mg chol., 630 mg sodium, 40 g carbo., 9 g fiber, 12 g pro.

Pair this full-flavored soup with your family's favorite sandwich for a complete meal.

BARLEY-VEGETABLE SOUP

4	cups tomato juice
2½	cups chopped zucchini
2	14-ounce cans chicken broth
1½	cups coarsely chopped yellow and/or red sweet peppers
1	large onion, chopped
½	cup regular barley (not quick-cooking)
¼	teaspoon salt
¼	teaspoon black pepper
3	cloves garlic, minced

1 In a 3½- to 5-quart slow cooker combine tomato juice, zucchini, chicken broth, sweet peppers, onion, barley, salt, black pepper, and garlic.

2 Cover and cook on low-heat setting for 8 to 9 hours or on high-heat setting for 4 to 4½ hours.

Per serving: 88 cal., 1 g total fat (0 g sat. fat), 1 mg chol., 803 mg sodium, 19 g carbo., 3 g fiber, 3 g pro.

PREP:
20 minutes

COOK:
Low 8 hours, High 4 hours

MAKES:
8 side-dish servings

SLOW COOKER:
3½- to 5-quart

Full-flavored cousins of the white mushroom, cremini give this soup a deep, rich woodsy flavor.

MUSHROOM-BARLEY SOUP

PREP:
20 minutes

COOK:
Low 6 hours, High 3 hours

MAKES:
8 side-dish servings

SLOW COOKER:
4- to 5-quart

12 ounces cremini or button mushrooms, sliced (about 4 cups)

⅔ cup regular barley

2 medium carrots, sliced

1 large onion, chopped

2 cloves garlic, minced

1 teaspoon dried thyme, crushed

¼ teaspoon black pepper

3 14-ounce cans beef broth

1 14½-ounce can diced tomatoes, undrained

2 cups shredded fresh spinach

1 In a 4- to 5-quart slow cooker combine mushrooms, barley, carrots, onion, garlic, thyme, and pepper. Stir in broth and undrained tomatoes.

2 Cover and cook on low-heat setting for 6 to 7 hours or on high-heat setting for 3 to 3½ hours.

3 Stir in spinach before serving.

Per serving: 96 cal., 1 g total fat (0 g sat. fat), 0 mg chol., 655 mg sodium, 17 g carbo., 3 g fiber, 5 g pro.

*Beets, apples, and potatoes combine with delectable results in this creative ginger-
and curry-seasoned side dish.*

CURRIED APPLE BEET SOUP

2   pounds beets, peeled and chopped
2   medium cooking apples, chopped
1   cup chopped round red potatoes
1   medium onion, chopped
1   tablespoon curry powder
½   teaspoon ground ginger
2   cloves garlic, minced
¼   teaspoon salt
2   14-ounce cans chicken broth
1   cup apple juice or apple cider
1   8-ounce carton dairy sour cream
     Crisp-cooked and crumbled bacon
     Dairy sour cream (optional)

1 In a 4- to 5-quart slow cooker combine beets, apples, potatoes, onion, curry powder, ginger, garlic, and salt. Pour broth and apple juice over all.

2 Cover and cook on low-heat setting for 7 to 8 hours or on high-heat setting for 3½ to 4 hours.

3 In a small bowl stir together the 8-ounce carton sour cream and about 1 cup of the hot cooking liquid. Stir sour cream mixture into mixture in slow cooker. Top individual servings with crisp-cooked bacon. If desired, serve with additional sour cream.

Per serving: 142 cal., 7 g total fat (4 g sat. fat), 15 mg chol., 528 mg sodium, 17 g carbo., 3 g fiber, 4 g pro.

PREP:
25 minutes

COOK:
Low 7 hours, High 3½ hours

MAKES:
10 side-dish servings

SLOW COOKER:
4- to 5-quart

Cubes of firm tofu will hold together better than softer versions as they simmer in this soup.

HOT & SOUR SOUP

PREP:
20 minutes

COOK:
Low 6 hours, High 3 hours;
plus 30 minutes on High

MAKES:
8 side-dish servings

SLOW COOKER:
3½- or 4-quart

4	cups chicken broth
1	cup bias-sliced carrots
1	8-ounce can bamboo shoots, drained
1	8-ounce can sliced water chestnuts, drained
1	4-ounce can (drained weight) sliced mushrooms, drained
3	tablespoons rice vinegar or white vinegar
1	tablespoon soy sauce
1	teaspoon sugar
¼	teaspoon crushed red pepper
2	tablespoons cornstarch
2	tablespoons cold water
8	ounces frozen peeled and deveined uncooked shrimp
4	ounces refrigerated water-packed firm tofu, drained and cubed
2	tablespoons snipped fresh parsley or cilantro

1 In a 3½- or 4-quart slow cooker combine broth, carrots, drained bamboo shoots, drained water chestnuts, drained mushrooms, vinegar, soy sauce, sugar, and crushed red pepper.

2 Cover and cook on low-heat setting for 6 to 8 hours or on high-heat setting for 3 to 4 hours.

3 If using low-heat setting, turn to high-heat setting. In a small bowl stir together cornstarch and cold water; stir into broth mixture in slow cooker. Add frozen shrimp and tofu. Cover and cook for 30 minutes more. Sprinkle with parsley.

Per serving: 80 cal., 1 g total fat (0 g sat. fat), 44 mg chol., 718 mg sodium, 9 g carbo., 1 g fiber, 7 g pro.

This lively chowder uses the "three sisters" of Native American cooking: corn, beans, and squash.

THREE SISTERS CORN CHOWDER

3 large red-skinned potatoes, peeled if desired and cut into ½-inch cubes (about 1½ pounds)

1½ cups loose-pack frozen whole kernel corn

1 cup loose-pack frozen baby lima beans

1 medium onion, chopped

½ cup chopped fresh Anaheim or poblano chile pepper* or green sweet pepper

½ cup chopped red sweet pepper

1 4-ounce can diced green chile peppers, drained

3 cloves garlic, minced

½ teaspoon salt

2 14-ounce cans vegetable broth or chicken broth

1 14¾-ounce can cream-style corn

1 small zucchini, halved lengthwise and sliced

1 cup whipping cream

1 In a 4- to 6-quart slow cooker combine potatoes, frozen corn, frozen lima beans, onion, fresh chile pepper, red sweet pepper, canned chile peppers, garlic, and salt. Pour broth over all.

2 Cover and cook on low-heat setting for 8 to 9 hours or on high-heat setting for 4 to 4½ hours.

3 If using low-heat setting, turn cooker to high-heat setting. Stir in cream-style corn and zucchini. Cover and cook for 30 minutes more. Stir in whipping cream.

Per serving: 383 cal., 17 g total fat (9 g sat. fat), 55 mg chol., 1,073 mg sodium, 54 g carbo., 6 g fiber, 10 g pro.

*NOTE: Because chile peppers contain volatile oils that can burn your skin and eyes, avoid direct contact with them as much as possible. When working with chile peppers, wear plastic or rubber gloves. If your bare hands do touch the peppers, wash your hands and nails well with soap and warm water.

PREP:
25 minutes

COOK:
Low 8 hours, High 4 hours; plus 30 minutes on High

MAKES:
6 to 8 side-dish servings

SLOW COOKER:
4- to 6-quart

Fit this classic into your schedule by cooking it for as little as 2½ hours or as long as 10 hours.

FRENCH ONION SOUP

PREP:
30 minutes

COOK:
Low 5 hours, High 2½ hours

BROIL:
2 minutes

MAKES:
8 side-dish servings

SLOW COOKER:
3½- or 4-quart

3	tablespoons butter or margarine
4	to 6 onions, thinly sliced (4 to 6 cups)
1	clove garlic, minced
4½	cups beef broth
1½	teaspoons Worcestershire sauce
⅛	teaspoon black pepper
8	1-inch-thick slices French bread
1	cup shredded Swiss or Gruyère cheese (4 ounces)

1 In a large skillet melt butter over medium-low heat. Add onions and garlic; cover and cook about 20 minutes or until tender, stirring occasionally. Transfer onion mixture to a 3½- or 4-quart slow cooker. Add broth, Worcestershire sauce, and pepper.

2 Cover and cook on low-heat setting for 5 to 10 hours or on high-heat setting for 2½ to 3 hours.

3 Before serving soup, toast bread slices. Preheat broiler. Arrange bread slices on a baking sheet and sprinkle with cheese. Broil 3 to 4 inches from heat for 2 to 3 minutes or until cheese is lightly browned and bubbly.

4 Ladle soup into bowls; top with toast slices.

Per serving: 255 cal., 10 g total fat (6 g sat. fat), 24 mg chol., 876 mg sodium, 31 g carbo., 2 g fiber, 10 g pro.

FOR 5- OR 6-QUART SLOW COOKER:
Use ¼ cup butter or margarine; 6 to 8 thinly sliced onions (6 to 8 cups); 1 clove garlic, minced; 6 cups beef broth; 2 teaspoons Worcestershire sauce; ⅛ teaspoon black pepper; 12 slices 1-inch-thick French bread; and 1½ cups shredded Swiss or Gruyère cheese (6 ounces). Prepare as above, except use a very large skillet to cook onions and garlic. Makes 12 side-dish servings.

Per serving: 250 cal., 10 g total fat (5 g sat. fat), 23 mg chol., 816 mg sodium, 31 g carbo., 2 g fiber, 10 g pro.

The classic potato-and-leek soup is traditionally served chilled but, as this recipe proves, it's also great warm.

WARM VICHYSSOISE

2½	pounds Yukon gold potatoes, peeled and cut into 1-inch pieces
2	14-ounce cans chicken broth
2	cups sliced leeks (about 6 leeks)
1	medium onion, chopped
½	cup water
¼	teaspoon salt
¼	teaspoon ground white pepper
¾	cup half-and-half or milk
	Half-and-half or milk (optional)
1	tablespoon snipped fresh chives

1 In a 3½- or 4-quart slow cooker combine potatoes, broth, leeks, onion, the water, salt, and white pepper.

2 Cover and cook on low-heat setting for 8 to 9 hours or on high-heat setting for 4 to 4½ hours. Stir in ¾ cup half-and-half or milk. Cool slightly.

3 Transfer about one-third of the soup mixture to a blender or food processor. Cover and blend or process until smooth. Transfer to a large serving bowl. Repeat with remaining soup mixture until all of the soup is blended.

4 If desired, thin with additional half-and-half or milk. Serve immediately. Sprinkle individual servings with chives.

Per serving: 138 cal., 3 g total fat (2 g sat. fat), 9 mg chol., 490 mg sodium, 25 g carbo., 2 g fiber, 4 g pro.

PREP:
30 minutes

COOK:
Low 8 hours, High 4 hours

MAKES:
8 side-dish servings

SLOW COOKER:
3½- or 4-quart

Caraway seeds and a horseradish-sour cream topping add distinctive flavor to this fabulous cabbage concoction.

CABBAGE & POTATO SOUP

PREP:
30 minutes

COOK:
Low 6 hours, High 3 hours

MAKES:
6 to 8 side-dish servings

SLOW COOKER:
3½- or 4-quart

1	small head green cabbage, chopped
1½	cups chopped round red potatoes
1	cup thin bite-size carrot strips
1	medium onion, cut into thin wedges
3	tablespoons quick-cooking tapioca
2	tablespoons dry sherry (optional)
1	tablespoon lemon juice
¼	teaspoon caraway seeds
¼	teaspoon salt
¼	teaspoon black pepper
3	14-ounce cans chicken broth
½	cup half-and-half or light cream
½	cup dairy sour cream
2	tablespoons prepared horseradish

1 In a 3½- or 4-quart slow cooker combine cabbage, potatoes, carrots, onion, tapioca, sherry (if desired), lemon juice, caraway seeds, salt, and pepper. Pour broth over all.

2 Cover and cook on low-heat setting for 6 to 7 hours or on high-heat setting for 3 to 3½ hours. Stir half-and-half into mixture in slow cooker.

3 In a small bowl combine sour cream and horseradish. Serve soup with sour cream mixture.

Per serving: 152 cal., 6 g total fat (4 g sat. fat), 17 mg chol., 951 mg sodium, 21 g carbo., 3 g fiber, 4 g pro.

Maple syrup complements the naturally sweet potatoes, while bacon gives them a salty, savory edge.

NEW ENGLAND SWEET POTATO SOUP

2½ to 3 pounds sweet potatoes, peeled and cut into 1-inch pieces

1 medium onion, chopped

¼ cup maple-flavored syrup

1 clove garlic, minced

½ teaspoon dried sage, crushed

¼ teaspoon salt

⅛ teaspoon black pepper

2 14-ounce cans chicken broth

1 cup water

½ cup half-and-half or light cream

5 slices bacon, crisp-cooked and crumbled

PREP:
25 minutes

COOK:
Low 6 hours, High 3 hours

MAKES:
10 side-dish servings

SLOW COOKER:
3½- or 4-quart

1 In a 3½- or 4-quart slow cooker combine sweet potatoes, onion, maple-flavored syrup, garlic, sage, salt, and pepper. Pour broth and the water over all.

2 Cover and cook on low-heat setting for 6 to 8 hours or on high-heat setting for 3 to 4 hours.

3 Using a potato masher, mash the soup until desired consistency.* Whisk in half-and-half until well mixed. Top individual servings with crumbled bacon.

Per serving: 137 cal., 3 g total fat (1 g sat. fat), 10 mg chol., 517 mg sodium, 24 g carbo., 3 g fiber, 4 g pro.

*NOTE: For a smoother texture, use an immersion blender to puree the soup.

This easy-to-fix soup goes together in almost no time because the pumpkin pie mix already includes seasonings—so there's no need to measure them.

PUMPKIN BISQUE

PREP:
10 minutes

COOK:
Low 4 hours, High 2 hours

MAKES:
10 side-dish servings

SLOW COOKER:
3½- or 4-quart

1	30-ounce can pumpkin pie mix
1	15-ounce can pumpkin
2	14-ounce cans chicken broth
½	cup water
¼	teaspoon salt
¼	teaspoon black pepper
1	cup half-and-half or light cream
	Dairy sour cream (optional)

1 In a 3½- or 4-quart slow cooker combine pumpkin pie mix, pumpkin, broth, the water, salt, and pepper.

2 Cover and cook on low-heat setting for 4 to 5 hours or on high-heat setting for 2 to 2½ hours. Stir in half-and-half. If desired, top individual servings with sour cream.

Per serving: 144 cal., 4 g total fat (2 g sat. fat), 9 mg chol., 578 mg sodium, 27 g carbo., 8 g fiber, 3 g pro.

The bounty here is fresh veggies—tomatoes and your choice of carrots, celery, sweet peppers, fennel, and/or onion. A classic grilled cheese sandwich is the perfect accompaniment.

GARDEN BOUNTY TOMATO SOUP

2 pounds plum tomatoes, chopped

2 cups finely chopped fresh vegetables
(such as carrots, celery, sweet peppers, fennel, and/or onion)

2 14-ounce cans beef broth

1 6-ounce can tomato paste

1 to 2 teaspoons sugar

1 In a 3¹/₂- or 4-quart slow cooker combine tomatoes, desired fresh vegetables, broth, tomato paste, and sugar.

2 Cover and cook on low-heat setting for 6 to 8 hours or on high-heat setting for 3 to 4 hours.

Per serving: 58 cal., 0 g total fat (0 g sat. fat), 0 mg chol., 407 mg sodium, 11 g carbo., 3 g fiber, 3 g pro.

PREP:
25 minutes

COOK:
Low 6 hours, High 3 hours

MAKES:
8 to 10 side-dish servings

SLOW COOKER:
3¹/₂- or 4-quart

The splash of cream added before serving helps round out the flavor of this curry-flavored soup.

WINTER SQUASH BISQUE

PREP:
15 minutes

COOK:
Low 5 hours, High 2½ hours

MAKES:
6 side-dish servings

SLOW COOKER:
3½- or 4-quart

2   12-ounce packages frozen cooked winter squash, thawed

2   14-ounce cans chicken broth or vegetable broth

3   medium cooking apples, peeled, cored, and chopped

2   teaspoons curry powder

½   cup whipping cream

      Dry-roasted, shelled sunflower seeds (optional)

1 Place squash in a 3½- or 4-quart slow cooker. Stir broth into squash; stir in chopped apples and curry powder.

2 Cover and cook on low-heat setting for 5 to 7 hours or on high-heat setting for 2½ to 3½ hours.

3 Before serving, stir in whipping cream. If desired, sprinkle individual servings with sunflower seeds.

Per serving: 193 cal., 9 g total fat (5 g sat. fat), 27 mg chol., 561 mg sodium, 28 g carbo., 4 g fiber, 4 g pro.

At your next dinner party, serve this sophisticated blend of winter squash, potato, and corn as the first course.

GOLDEN SQUASH BOWL

1½	pounds butternut squash, peeled, seeded, and cut into 1-inch pieces
1	large potato, peeled and cut into 1-inch pieces
1	8¼- or 8½-ounce can cream-style corn
1	cup loose-pack frozen whole kernel corn
1	medium onion, chopped
1	clove garlic, minced
½	teaspoon dried leaf sage, crushed
¼	teaspoon salt
⅛	teaspoon black pepper
2	14-ounce cans chicken broth
½	cup dairy sour cream
3	slices bacon, crisp-cooked and crumbled

1 In a 3½- or 4-quart slow cooker combine squash, potato, cream-style corn, frozen corn, onion, garlic, sage, salt, and pepper. Pour broth over all.

2 Cover and cook on low-heat setting for 7 to 8 hours or on high-heat setting for 3½ to 4 hours.

3 In a small bowl combine sour cream and about ½ cup of hot cooking liquid from the slow cooker. Stir into mixture in slow cooker. Cool slightly.

4 Transfer about one-third of the mixture to a blender or food processor. Cover and blend or process until smooth. Transfer to a large serving bowl. Repeat with remaining soup until all of the soup is blended. Sprinkle individual servings with bacon.

Per serving: 130 cal., 4 g total fat (2 g sat. fat), 10 mg chol., 633 mg sodium, 21 g carbo., 2 g fiber, 4 g pro.

PREP:
25 minutes

COOK:
Low 7 hours, High 3½ hours

MAKES:
8 side-dish servings

SLOW COOKER:
3½- or 4-quart

If you have an immersion blender, use it to puree the soup mixture in the slow cooker instead of transferring it to a blender or food processor.

CURRIED WINTER VEGETABLE SOUP

PREP:
30 minutes

COOK:
Low 6 hours, High 3 hours

MAKES:
8 to 10 side-dish servings

SLOW COOKER:
3½- or 4-quart

4	cups chopped, peeled celeriac (2 pounds)
3	cups chopped, peeled butternut squash (1 pound)
2	14-ounce cans chicken broth
1	medium onion, chopped
2	tablespoons dry sherry
1	tablespoon grated fresh ginger
2	teaspoons curry powder
2	cloves garlic, minced
½	cup whipping cream
¼	cup sliced green onions

1 In a 3½- or 4-quart slow cooker combine celeriac, butternut squash, broth, onion, sherry, ginger, curry powder, and garlic.

2 Cover and cook on low-heat setting for 6 to 8 hours or on high-heat setting for 3 to 4 hours. Stir in whipping cream. Cool slightly.

3 Transfer half of the soup mixture to a blender or food processor. Cover and blend or process until smooth. Transfer to a large serving bowl. Repeat with remaining soup mixture. Sprinkle individual servings with green onions.

Per serving: 119 cal., 6 g total fat (4 g sat. fat), 22 mg chol., 484 mg sodium, 14 g carbo., 2 g fiber, 3 g pro.

Serve this elegant butternut squash soup as an appetizer. Or team it with turkey or ham sandwiches for a light meal.

THAI WINTER SQUASH SOUP

2	pounds butternut squash, peeled and cut into ¾-inch pieces
2	cups thinly sliced bok choy
1	medium onion, cut into thin wedges
1	medium fresh jalapeño chile pepper, seeded and finely chopped*
½	teaspoon finely shredded lime peel
2	tablespoons lime juice
1	teaspoon ground ginger
3	cloves garlic, minced
½	teaspoon salt
2	14-ounce cans vegetable broth
1	cup unsweetened coconut milk
1	tablespoon snipped fresh cilantro
1	tablespoon snipped fresh basil

PREP:
30 minutes

COOK:
Low 7 hours, High 3½ hours

MAKES:
8 side-dish servings

SLOW COOKER:
3½- or 4-quart

1 In a 3½- or 4-quart slow cooker combine squash, bok choy, onion, chile pepper, lime peel, lime juice, ginger, garlic, and salt. Pour broth over all.

2 Cover and cook on low-heat setting for 7 to 8 hours or on high-heat setting for 3½ to 4 hours.

3 Stir in coconut milk, cilantro, and basil.

Per serving: 99 cal., 6 g total fat (5 g sat. fat), 0 mg chol., 557 mg sodium, 12 g carbo., 2 g fiber, 2 g pro.

*NOTE: Because chile peppers contain volatile oils that can burn your skin and eyes, avoid direct contact with them as much as possible. When working with chile peppers, wear plastic or rubber gloves. If your bare hands do touch the peppers, wash your hands and nails well with soap and warm water.

Tart Granny Smith apples are a tasty choice for this creamy soup that's seasoned with an intriguing blend of ginger, cinnamon, cloves, and curry powder.

BUTTERNUT APPLE SOUP

PREP:
25 minutes

COOK:
Low 8 hours, High 4 hours

MAKES:
8 side-dish servings

SLOW COOKER:
4- to 5-quart

1   2-pound butternut squash, peeled, halved, seeded, and cut into 1-inch pieces

2   medium cooking apples, peeled and coarsely chopped

1   large onion, chopped

1   teaspoon ground ginger

1   teaspoon curry powder

¼   teaspoon salt

¼   teaspoon ground cinnamon

⅛   teaspoon ground cloves

2   14-ounce cans chicken broth

1   cup apple juice or apple cider

½   cup half-and-half or light cream

    Dairy sour cream (optional)

    Green and/or red apple slices (optional)

1 In a 4- to 5-quart slow cooker combine squash, apples, onion, ginger, curry powder, salt, cinnamon, and cloves. Pour broth and apple juice over all.

2 Cover and cook on low-heat setting for 8 to 9 hours or on high-heat setting for 4 to 4½ hours. Cool slightly.

3 Transfer one-third of the soup to a blender. Cover and blend until smooth. Transfer to a large serving bowl. Repeat with remaining soup until all of the soup is blended. Stir half-and-half into blended soup. If desired, top individual servings with sour cream and apple slices.

Per serving: 96 cal., 2 g total fat (1 g sat. fat), 7 mg chol., 481 mg sodium, 19 g carbo., 3 g fiber, 2 g pro.

LIGHT MAIN DISHES

6

Horseradish is the star in this saucy beef roast. If you prefer even more heat, increase the horseradish to two tablespoons.

SPICY BEEF ROAST

PREP:
20 minutes

COOK:
Low 10 hours, High 5 hours

MAKES:
10 servings

SLOW COOKER:
3½- to 4½-quart

1	3½- to 4-pound boneless beef chuck pot roast
	Salt
	Black pepper
2	tablespoons cooking oil (optional)
½	cup water
1	tablespoon Worcestershire sauce
1	tablespoon tomato paste
2	cloves garlic, minced
	Several dashes bottled hot pepper sauce
1	tablespoon cornstarch
1	tablespoon cold water
1	tablespoon prepared horseradish
½	teaspoon salt

1 Trim fat from meat. If necessary, cut meat to fit in a 3½- to 4½-quart slow cooker. Sprinkle meat with salt and pepper. If desired, in a large skillet heat oil over medium heat; brown meat in hot oil, turning to brown evenly. Drain off fat. Place meat in slow cooker. In a small bowl combine the ½ cup water, the Worcestershire sauce, tomato paste, garlic, and hot pepper sauce. Pour over meat in cooker.

2 Cover and cook on low-heat setting for 10 to 12 hours or on high-heat setting for 5 to 6 hours.

3 Transfer meat to a serving platter, reserving cooking juices. Cover meat with foil to keep warm.

4 For gravy, strain cooking juices and skim off fat. Transfer strained cooking juices to a medium saucepan. In a small bowl combine cornstarch and the 1 tablespoon cold water; stir into liquid in saucepan. Cook and stir over medium heat until thickened and bubbly. Cook and stir for 2 minutes more. Stir in horseradish and the ½ teaspoon salt. Serve gravy with meat.

Per serving: 203 cal., 6 g total fat (2 g sat. fat), 94 mg chol., 278 mg sodium, 2 g carbo., 0 g fiber, 34 g pro.

Plum preserves and Marsala add a tantalizing touch of sweetness to this basil-accented, down-home medley of beef and vegetables.

WINE-GLAZED POT ROAST

1	3- to 4-pound boneless beef chuck pot roast
4	medium potatoes, peeled and cut lengthwise into sixths
4	medium carrots, peeled and cut in half lengthwise and crosswise
1	rutabaga, peeled and cut into 1-inch chunks (about 1 pound)
1	medium onion, cut into large wedges
½	cup plum preserves or plum jam
⅓	cup water
⅓	cup sweet Marsala
2	teaspoons dried basil, crushed
1	teaspoon garlic salt
½	teaspoon black pepper
3	tablespoons cornstarch
3	tablespoons cold water

PREP:
30 minutes

COOK:
Low 11 hours, High 5½ hours

MAKES:
8 to 10 servings

SLOW COOKER:
5- to 7-quart

1 Trim fat from meat. In a 5- to 7-quart slow cooker combine potatoes, carrots, rutabaga, and onion. Place meat on vegetables. In a small bowl stir together plum preserves, the ⅓ cup water, the Marsala, basil, garlic salt, and pepper; pour over meat.

2 Cover and cook on low-heat setting for 11 to 12 hours or on high-heat setting for 5½ to 6 hours.

3 Transfer meat and vegetables to a serving platter, reserving cooking juices. Cover meat with foil to keep warm.

4 For gravy, skim fat from cooking juices. In a medium saucepan stir together cornstarch and the 3 tablespoons cold water until smooth; stir into juices in saucepan. Cook and stir until thickened and bubbly; cook and stir for 2 minutes more. Serve gravy with meat and vegetables.

Per serving: 375 cal., 6 g total fat (2 g sat. fat), 101 mg chol., 268 mg sodium, 37 g carbo., 4 g fiber, 39 g pro.

Black bean garlic sauce, a staple in Chinese cuisine, gives a rich, exotic flavor to pot roast. Look for the sauce in the supermarket's Asian foods section or in Asian food stores.

ASIAN-STYLE POT ROAST

PREP:
30 minutes

COOK:
Low 10 hours, High 5 hours; plus 15 minutes on High

MAKES:
6 servings

SLOW COOKER:
4- to 5½-quart

1	2-pound boneless beef chuck pot roast
1	tablespoon cooking oil
1½	cups hot water
¼	cup black bean garlic sauce
1	teaspoon instant beef bouillon granules
1	tablespoon sugar (optional)
8	ounces fresh green beans, trimmed
1	medium red sweet pepper, cut into thin strips
½	of a medium onion, cut into thin strips
3	tablespoons cornstarch
3	tablespoons cold water
	Hot cooked brown rice (optional)

1 Trim fat from meat. If necessary, cut meat to fit in a 4- to 5½-quart slow cooker. In a large skillet heat oil over medium-high heat. Brown meat in hot oil, turning to brown evenly. Drain off fat.

2 In the slow cooker stir together the 1½ cups water, the black bean garlic sauce, bouillon granules, and, if desired, sugar. Add green beans, sweet pepper, and onion. Place meat on top of vegetables.

3 Cover and cook on low-heat setting for 10 to 12 hours or on high-heat setting for 5 to 6 hours.

4 Transfer meat and vegetables to a serving platter, reserving cooking juices; cover meat with foil to keep warm.

5 If using low-heat setting, turn to high-heat setting. For sauce, in a small bowl combine cornstarch and the 3 tablespoons cold water; stir into cooking juices in slow cooker. Cover and cook about 15 minutes more or until sauce is slightly thickened.

6 Using 2 forks, separate meat into serving-size pieces. Serve meat with the vegetables, sauce, and, if desired, hot cooked brown rice.

Per serving: 261 cal., 9 g total fat (2 g sat. fat), 89 mg chol., 470 mg sodium, 10 g carbo., 2 g fiber, 34 g pro.

Shredded reduced-fat cheddar cheese and light dairy sour cream make great low-fat toppers for this cold-weather favorite.

HEARTY BEEF CHILI

1½	pounds beef chuck roast
2	cups low-sodium vegetable juice or tomato juice
2	large onions, chopped
2	15- to 16-ounce cans black beans, red kidney beans, and/or garbanzo beans (chickpeas), rinsed and drained
1	14½-ounce can no-salt-added diced tomatoes, undrained
2	medium green sweet peppers, chopped
1	10-ounce can diced tomatoes and green chile peppers, undrained
3	cloves garlic, minced
1	teaspoon ground chipotle chile pepper
1	teaspoon ground cumin
1	teaspoon dried oregano, crushed

1 Trim fat from meat. Cut meat into 1-inch cubes. In a 4½- to 6-quart slow cooker combine meat, vegetable juice, onions, beans, undrained no-salt-added tomatoes, sweet peppers, undrained tomatoes and green chile peppers, garlic, ground chipotle chile pepper, cumin, and oregano.

2 Cover and cook on low-heat setting for 9 to 10 hours or on high-heat setting for 4½ to 5 hours.

Per serving: 226 cal., 4 g total fat (1 g sat. fat), 50 mg chol., 467 mg sodium, 27 g carbo., 8 g fiber, 26 g pro.

PREP:
20 minutes

COOK:
Low 9 hours, High 4½ hours

MAKES:
8 to 10 servings

SLOW COOKER:
4½- to 6-quart

Chipotle peppers in adobo sauce are doubly delicious. The smoky flavor of the dried jalapeño chiles adds a direct hit of heat, while the adobo sauce produces a slow burn. Together they flavor this chili with a richness that can only be developed during slow cooking.

BEEF & RED BEAN CHILI

PREP:
20 minutes

STAND:
1 hour

COOK:
Low 10 hours, High 5 hours

MAKES:
8 servings

SLOW COOKER:
3½- or 4-quart

1 cup dry red beans or dry kidney beans

2 pounds boneless beef chuck roast

1 tablespoon olive oil

1 large onion, coarsely chopped

1 14-ounce can beef broth

1 or 2 canned chipotle chile peppers in adobo sauce, finely chopped* plus 2 teaspoons adobo sauce

2 teaspoons dried oregano, crushed

1 teaspoon ground cumin

⅛ teaspoon salt

1 14½-ounce can diced tomatoes and green chile peppers, undrained

1 15-ounce can tomato sauce

¼ cup snipped fresh cilantro

1 medium red sweet pepper, chopped

1 Rinse beans. Place beans in a large saucepan or Dutch oven. Add enough water to cover by 2 inches. Bring to boiling; reduce heat. Simmer, uncovered, for 10 minutes. Remove from heat. Cover; let stand for 1 hour.

2 Meanwhile, trim fat from meat. Cut meat into 1-inch cubes. In a large skillet heat oil over medium-high heat. Add half of the meat and the onion; cook until meat is light brown. Transfer to a 3½- or 4-quart slow cooker. Repeat with remaining meat. Add broth, chipotle peppers and adobo sauce, oregano, cumin, and salt to slow cooker. Pour undrained tomatoes and tomato sauce over all; stir to combine. Drain and rinse beans; stir beans into meat mixture in slow cooker.

3 Cover and cook on low-heat setting for 10 to 12 hours or on high-heat setting for 5 to 6 hours. Top individual servings with cilantro and sweet pepper.

Per serving: 278 cal., 6 g total fat (2 g sat. fat), 67 mg chol., 708 mg sodium, 23 g carbo., 6 g fiber, 31 g pro.

*NOTE: Because chile peppers contain volatile oils that can burn your skin and eyes, avoid direct contact with them as much as possible. When working with chile peppers, wear plastic or rubber gloves. If your bare hands do touch the peppers, wash your hands and nails well with soap and warm water.

Barley adds both a chewy texture and a nutty flavor to this stick-to-the-ribs soup.
Look for barley next to the rice at your supermarket.

BEEF & BARLEY SOUP

12	ounces boneless beef chuck roast
	Nonstick cooking spray
4	cups water
1	10½-ounce can condensed French onion soup
2	medium carrots, shredded
½	cup regular barley (not quick cooking)
1	teaspoon dried thyme or oregano, crushed
	Salt
	Black pepper

1 Trim fat from meat. Cut meat into ½-inch pieces. Lightly coat an unheated large skillet with nonstick cooking spray. Preheat skillet over medium heat. Brown meat in hot skillet; drain off fat.

2 In a 3½- to 4½-quart slow cooker combine meat, the water, French onion soup, carrots, barley, and thyme.

3 Cover and cook on low-heat setting for 7 to 8 hours or on high-heat setting for 3½ to 4 hours. Season to taste with salt and pepper.

Per serving: 252 cal., 5 g total fat (1 g sat. fat), 52 mg chol., 684 mg sodium, 29 g carbo., 5 g fiber, 22 g pro.

PREP:
15 minutes

COOK:
Low 7 hours, High 3½ hours

MAKES:
4 servings

SLOW COOKER:
3½- to 4½-quart

Strong brewed coffee contributes to the fabulous flavor overtones in this steak dish.

SWISS STEAK CAFÉ

PREP:
20 minutes

COOK:
Low 8 hours, High 4 hours

MAKES:
6 servings

SLOW COOKER:
3½- or 4-quart

2   pounds boneless beef round steak, cut ¾ inch thick

1   tablespoon cooking oil

3   medium onions, cut into wedges

4   teaspoons quick-cooking tapioca

2   tablespoons soy sauce

2   cloves garlic, minced

2   bay leaves

½   teaspoon dried oregano, crushed

1   cup strong brewed coffee

1 Trim fat from meat. Cut meat into serving-size pieces. In a 12-inch skillet heat oil over medium-high heat. Brown meat pieces on all sides in hot oil (add more oil, if necessary during cooking). Drain off fat.

2 Place onions in a 3½- or 4-quart slow cooker. Add meat. Sprinkle with tapioca. Add soy sauce, garlic, bay leaves, and oregano. Pour coffee over all.

3 Cover and cook on low-heat setting for 8 to 10 hours or on high-heat setting for 4 to 5 hours.

4 Remove meat and onions to a serving platter. Discard bay leaves. Spoon some of the cooking juices over meat and onions.

Per serving: 256 cal., 9 g total fat (3 g sat. fat), 72 mg chol., 399 mg sodium, 6 g carbo., 1 g fiber, 35 g pro.

All it takes is 15 minutes to get the steak and vegetables into a slow cooker, and you're on your way to a great meal.

SO-EASY PEPPER STEAK

2 pounds boneless beef round steak, cut ¾ to 1 inch thick

Salt

Black pepper

1 14½-ounce can Italian-style stewed tomatoes, undrained*

3 tablespoons Italian-style tomato paste*

1 tablespoon quick-cooking tapioca

1 teaspoon Worcestershire sauce

1 16-ounce package frozen (yellow, green, and red) peppers and onion stir-fry vegetables

Hot cooked noodles

1 Trim fat from meat. Cut meat into 6 serving-size pieces; sprinkle lightly with salt and pepper. Transfer to a 3½- or 4-quart slow cooker.

2 In a medium bowl stir together undrained stewed tomatoes, tomato paste, tapioca, and Worcestershire sauce; pour over meat in slow cooker. Top with frozen vegetables.

3 Cover and cook on low-heat setting for 7 to 8 hours or on high-heat setting for 3½ to 4 hours. Serve meat, vegetables, and cooking juices over hot cooked noodles.

Per serving: 374 cal., 8 g total fat (2 g sat. fat), 114 mg chol., 377 mg sodium, 32 g carbo., 3 g fiber, 39 g pro.

*NOTE: If you can't find Italian-style stewed tomatoes and tomato paste at your supermarket, buy regular tomato products and add 1 teaspoon dried Italian seasoning, crushed.

PREP:
15 minutes

COOK:
Low 7 hours, High 3½ hours

MAKES:
6 servings

SLOW COOKER:
3½- or 4-quart

Dill mustard adds tremendous flavor to this round steak. Experiment with a different type of mustard, such as a horseradish variety, for a whole new take on the dish.

MUSTARD-SAUCED ROUND STEAK

PREP:
20 minutes

COOK:
Low 6 hours, High 3 hours; plus 15 minutes on High

MAKES:
4 servings

SLOW COOKER:
3½- or 4-quart

2	pounds boneless beef round steak, cut ¾ inch thick
½	teaspoon black pepper
¼	teaspoon salt
2	medium fennel bulbs, trimmed and cut into wedges
½	cup reduced-sodium beef broth
3	tablespoons dill mustard
½	cup fat-free half-and-half
1	tablespoon cornstarch

1 Trim fat from meat. Sprinkle both sides of meat with pepper and salt. Cut meat into 4 serving-size pieces. Place fennel in a 3½- or 4-quart slow cooker. Arrange meat on top of fennel. In a small bowl combine broth and mustard. Pour over meat.

2 Cover and cook on low-heat setting for 6 to 8 hours or on high-heat setting for 3 to 4 hours.

3 Transfer meat and fennel to a serving platter, reserving cooking juices in slow cooker. Cover meat with foil to keep warm.

4 If using low-heat setting, turn to high-heat setting. For sauce, in a small bowl combine half-and-half and cornstarch. Stir into juices in slow cooker. Cover and cook about 15 minutes more or until thickened. Serve sauce with meat and fennel.

Per serving: 237 cal., 7 g total fat (2 g sat. fat), 87 mg chol., 438 mg sodium, 7 g carbo., 1 g fiber, 36 g pro.

The sweet-tart blend of vinegar and molasses brings out the flavor of the beef in this stew.

BEEF-MUSHROOM STEW

2   pounds boneless beef chuck steak

3   tablespoons all-purpose flour

2   tablespoons cooking oil

6   medium carrots, cut into ½-inch-thick slices

2   medium onions, chopped

1   14½-ounce can diced tomatoes, undrained

¼   cup cider vinegar

2   tablespoons mild-flavored molasses

½   teaspoon salt

½   teaspoon celery salt

¼   teaspoon black pepper

¼   teaspoon ground ginger

12   ounces assorted fresh mushrooms
      (such as button, shiitake, oyster, and/or brown), halved

¼   cup raisins

     Hot cooked noodles, rice, or mashed potatoes (optional)

1 Trim fat from meat. Cut meat into 1-inch cubes. Place flour in a large resealable plastic bag. Add meat cubes, a few at a time, shaking to coat meat cubes. In an extra-large skillet heat 1 tablespoon of the oil over medium-high heat. Brown half of the meat in hot oil. Remove from skillet. Brown remaining meat in remaining 1 tablespoon oil.

2 Place carrots and onions in a 4- to 5-quart slow cooker. Add browned meat. In a medium bowl combine undrained tomatoes, cider vinegar, molasses, salt, celery salt, pepper, and ginger; pour over meat.

3 Cover and cook on low-heat setting for 8 hours or on high-heat setting for 4 hours.

4 If using low-heat setting, turn to high-heat setting. Stir in mushrooms and raisins. Cover and cook for 1 hour more. If desired, serve over hot cooked noodles, rice, or mashed potatoes.

Per serving: 263 cal., 9 g total fat (2 g sat. fat), 67 mg chol., 444 mg sodium, 20 g carbo., 3 g fiber, 27 g pro.

PREP:
40 minutes

COOK:
Low 8 hours, High 4 hours;
plus 1 hour on High

MAKES:
8 servings

SLOW COOKER:
4- to 5-quart

Canned soup makes this stew extra simple. The hardest part is cutting up the meat and mushrooms.

EASY BEEF BURGUNDY

PREP:
15 minutes

COOK:
Low 8 hours, High 4 hours

MAKES:
6 servings

SLOW COOKER:
3½- or 4-quart

1   10¾-ounce can condensed cream of onion soup

1   10¾-ounce can reduced-fat and reduced-sodium condensed cream of mushroom soup

¾   cup Burgundy or other dry red wine

1½   pounds beef stew meat cut into 1-inch cubes

8   ounces fresh mushrooms, quartered (3 cups)

1   medium onion, sliced

6   ounces whole wheat pasta or multigrain pasta, cooked and drained

1 In a 3½- or 4-quart slow cooker combine cream of onion soup, cream of mushroom soup, and Burgundy. Stir in meat, mushrooms, and onion.

2 Cover and cook on low-heat setting for 8 to 10 hours or on high-heat setting for 4 to 5 hours. Serve over hot cooked pasta.

Per serving: 354 cal., 9 g total fat (2 g sat. fat), 73 mg chol., 647 mg sodium, 33 g carbo., 2 g fiber, 30 g pro.

A can of your favorite beer is the zesty foundation for this hearty stew. Preshredded cole slaw mix keeps prep quick and simple.

BEEF & CABBAGE STEW

1   pound beef stew meat cut into 1-inch pieces

4   cups packaged shredded cabbage with carrot (coleslaw mix)

3   tablespoons quick-cooking tapioca

1   envelope (½ of a 2½-ounce package) dry onion soup mix

3   cups water

1   12-ounce can beer

1 In a 3½- or 4-quart slow cooker combine meat and cabbage with carrot. Sprinkle with tapioca and dry onion soup mix. Pour the water and beer over all.

2 Cover and cook on low-heat setting for 7 to 8 hours or on high-heat setting for 3½ to 4 hours.

Per serving: 242 cal., 4 g total fat (1 g sat. fat), 67 mg chol., 476 mg sodium, 19 g carbo., 2 g fiber, 26 g pro.

PREP:
10 minutes

COOK:
Low 7 hours, High 3½ hours

MAKES:
4 servings

SLOW COOKER:
3½- or 4-quart

A ragout is a rich, well-seasoned stew. Beans and beef star in this tasty version.

BEEF & BEAN RAGOUT

PREP:
10 minutes

COOK:
Low 8 hours, High 4 hours

MAKES:
6 servings

SLOW COOKER:
3½- or 4-quart

1   pound beef stew meat cut into 1-inch pieces

1   16-ounce can kidney beans, rinsed and drained

1   15-ounce can tomato sauce with onion and garlic

1   14½-ounce can Italian-style stewed tomatoes, undrained

½   of a 28-ounce package (about 4 cups) loose-pack frozen
     diced hash brown potatoes with onion and peppers

1 In a 3½- or 4-quart slow cooker combine meat, beans, tomato sauce, undrained tomatoes, and frozen potatoes.

2 Cover and cook on low-heat setting for 8 to 10 hours or on high-heat setting for 4 to 5 hours.

Per serving: 247 cal., 4 g total fat (1 g sat. fat), 45 mg chol., 634 mg sodium, 31 g carbo., 6 g fiber, 23 g pro.

Some dishes always seem to taste better made at home rather than at a restaurant.
Beef stew is one. Tangy Worcestershire sauce boosts the oomph in this version.

OLD-TIME BEEF STEW

1	tablespoon cooking oil
1½	pounds lean beef stew meat cut into 1-inch pieces
3	medium potatoes, cut into 1-inch chunks
4	medium carrots, cut into ¾-inch-thick slices
½	of a 16-ounce package (about 2 cups) frozen small whole onions
3	tablespoons quick-cooking tapioca
2	tablespoons Worcestershire sauce
1	tablespoon snipped fresh thyme or 1 teaspoon dried thyme, crushed
¼	teaspoon salt
¼	teaspoon black pepper
2	bay leaves
2	14-ounce cans beef broth

1 In a large skillet heat oil over medium-high heat. Brown meat, half at a time, in hot oil. Drain off fat.

2 In a 3½- to 5-quart slow cooker combine potatoes, carrots, and frozen onions. Add meat. Sprinkle with tapioca, Worcestershire sauce, dried thyme (if using), salt, and pepper. Add bay leaves. Pour broth over all.

3 Cover and cook on low-heat setting for 9 to 11 hours or on high-heat setting for 4½ to 5½ hours.

4 Discard bay leaves. Stir in fresh thyme, if using.

Per serving: 310 cal., 8 g total fat (2 g sat. fat), 53 mg chol., 593 mg sodium, 27 g carbo., 4 g fiber, 31 g pro.

PREP:
30 minutes

COOK:
Low 9 hours, High 4½ hours

MAKES:
6 servings

SLOW COOKER:
3½- to 5-quart

With this easy-does-it recipe you can make hearty, old-fashioned beef soup without spending hours working in the kitchen.

VEGETABLE-BEEF SOUP

PREP:
20 minutes

COOK:
Low 8 hours, High 4 hours

MAKES:
6 servings

SLOW COOKER:
4- to 5-quart

1½	pounds beef stew meat cut into 1-inch pieces
1	large potato, chopped
1	large onion, chopped
2	carrots, chopped
1½	cups loose-pack frozen whole kernel corn
1	cup loose-pack frozen cut green beans
1	stalk celery, chopped
4	cups reduced-sodium beef broth
1	teaspoon chili powder
¼	teaspoon black pepper

1 In a 4- to 5-quart slow cooker combine meat, potato, onion, carrots, frozen corn, frozen green beans, and celery. Add broth, chili powder, and pepper; stir to combine.

2 Cover and cook on low-heat setting for 8 to 10 hours or on high-heat setting for 4 to 5 hours.

Per serving: 239 cal., 5 g total fat (1 g sat. fat), 67 mg chol., 394 mg sodium, 21 g carbo., 3 g fiber, 29 g pro.

Cincinnati chili parlors offer chili spooned over spaghetti. This totable version has the consistency of a casserole, and with ziti (thick tube shapes) or gemelli (short twists), it's easily spooned up from the potluck table.

CINCINNATI-STYLE CHILI CASSEROLE

2	pounds lean ground beef
2	large onions, chopped
1	26-ounce jar garlic pasta sauce
1	15-ounce can red kidney beans, rinsed and drained
½	cup water
2	tablespoons chili powder
2	tablespoons semisweet chocolate pieces
1	tablespoon vinegar
1	teaspoon ground cinnamon
1	teaspoon instant beef bouillon granules
¼	teaspoon cayenne pepper
¼	teaspoon ground allspice
1	pound dried cut ziti or gemelli pasta

PREP:
25 minutes

COOK:
Low 8 hours, High 4 hours

MAKES:
16 servings

SLOW COOKER:
4- to 5-quart

1 In a 12-inch skillet cook ground beef and onions until meat is brown. Drain off fat. Transfer meat mixture to a 4- to 5-quart slow cooker. Stir in pasta sauce, beans, the water, chili powder, semisweet chocolate pieces, vinegar, cinnamon, bouillon granules, cayenne pepper, and allspice.

2 Cover and cook on low-heat setting for 8 to 10 hours or on high-heat setting for 4 to 5 hours.

3 Cook pasta according to package directions; drain well. Add cooked pasta to meat mixture in slow cooker; toss gently to combine.

Per serving: 257 cal., 7 g total fat (2 g sat. fat), 36 mg chol., 277 mg sodium, 33 g carbo., 4 g fiber, 17 g pro.

Toasting the buns keeps them from getting soggy when the barbecue is added.

DOWN-SOUTH BARBECUE

PREP:
20 minutes

COOK:
Low 10 hours, High 5 hours

MAKES:
*16 sandwiches
(about 1/3 cup meat mixture
per sandwich)*

SLOW COOKER:
3 1/2- or 4-quart

1	1½-pound boneless pork shoulder roast
1	1½-pound boneless beef chuck pot roast
1	6-ounce can tomato paste
½	cup no-calorie, heat-stable granulated sugar substitute (Splenda®)
¼	cup cider vinegar
¼	cup water
2	tablespoons chili powder
2	teaspoons Worcestershire sauce
1	teaspoon dry mustard
½	teaspoon salt
16	whole grain hamburger buns, split and toasted

1 Trim fat from pork and beef roasts. If necessary, cut roasts to fit into a 3½- or 4-quart slow cooker. Place meat in slow cooker. In a small bowl combine tomato paste, sugar substitute, vinegar, the water, chili powder, Worcestershire sauce, dry mustard, and salt. Pour tomato paste mixture over meat in cooker.

2 Cover and cook on low-heat setting for 10 to 12 hours or on high-heat setting for 5 to 6 hours.

3 Remove meat from slow cooker, reserving sauce. Use 2 forks to shred meat. Stir together shredded meat and reserved sauce in slow cooker. Using a slotted spoon, spoon meat mixture onto buns.

Per sandwich: 241 cal., 7 g total fat (2 g sat. fat), 53 mg chol., 430 mg sodium, 23 g carbo., 2 g fiber, 22 g pro.

A savory blend of seeds—anise, fennel, caraway, dill, and celery—creates a crustlike coating for this ultra tender pork roast. Apple juice in the cooking liquid lends a pleasantly subtle sweetness.

SEEDED PORK ROAST

1   2½- to 3-pound boneless pork shoulder roast

1   tablespoon soy sauce

2   teaspoons anise seeds, crushed

2   teaspoons fennel seeds, crushed

2   teaspoons caraway seeds, crushed

2   teaspoons dill seeds, crushed

2   teaspoons celery seeds, crushed

½   cup beef broth

⅔   cup apple juice or apple cider

1   tablespoon cornstarch

1 Remove netting, if present, from meat; trim fat from meat. If necessary, cut meat to fit in a 3½- to 5-quart slow cooker. Brush meat with soy sauce. On a large piece of foil combine anise seeds, fennel seeds, caraway seeds, dill seeds, and celery seeds. Roll meat in seeds to coat.

2 Place meat in slow cooker. Pour broth and ⅓ cup of the apple juice around meat.

3 Cover and cook on low-heat setting for 9 to 11 hours or on high-heat setting for 4½ to 5½ hours.

4 Transfer meat to a serving platter. Cover meat with foil to keep warm.

5 For gravy, strain cooking juices and skim off fat. Transfer juices to a small saucepan. In a small bowl combine remaining ⅓ cup apple juice and the cornstarch; add to juices in saucepan. Cook and stir until thickened and bubbly. Cook and stir for 2 minutes more. Pass gravy with meat.

Per serving: 220 cal., 9 g total fat (3 g sat. fat), 92 mg chol., 285 mg sodium, 5 g carbo., 0 g fiber, 29 g pro.

PREP:
25 minutes

COOK:
Low 9 hours, High 4½ hours

MAKES:
8 servings

SLOW COOKER:
3½- to 5-quart

Savory and slightly sweet, this pork roast is a surefire family pleaser.

APPLE PORK ROAST & VEGETABLES

PREP:
20 minutes

COOK:
*Low 10 hours, High 5 hours;
plus 30 minutes on High*

MAKES:
6 servings

SLOW COOKER:
3½- or 4-quart

1 2- to 2½-pound boneless pork shoulder roast

3 medium parsnips, peeled and cut into 1-inch pieces (2 cups)

3 medium carrots, peeled and cut into 1-inch pieces

2 stalks celery, cut into 1-inch pieces

3 tablespoons quick-cooking tapioca

1 6-ounce can or ½ of a 12-ounce can frozen apple juice concentrate (¾ cup), thawed

¼ cup water

1 teaspoon instant beef bouillon granules

¼ teaspoon black pepper

Salt

Black pepper

1 large green sweet pepper, cut into 1-inch-wide strips

1 Trim fat from meat. If necessary, cut meat to fit into a 3½- or 4-quart slow cooker. In slow cooker combine parsnips, carrots, and celery. Sprinkle with tapioca. Add apple juice concentrate, the water, bouillon granules, and the ¼ teaspoon black pepper. Place meat on top of vegetables. Sprinkle meat lightly with salt and additional black pepper.

2 Cover and cook on low-heat setting for 10 to 12 hours or on high-heat setting for 5 to 6 hours.

3 If using low-heat setting, turn to high-heat setting. Add sweet pepper strips to slow cooker, stirring into juices. Cover and cook for 30 minutes more.

4 To serve, transfer meat and vegetables to a serving platter. Slice meat. Strain cooking juices into a serving bowl. Drizzle some of the cooking juices over the sliced meat; pass the remaining cooking juices.

Per serving: 330 cal., 9 g total fat (3 g sat. fat), 98 mg chol., 398 mg sodium, 29 g carbo., 4 g fiber, 31 g pro.

Corn bread sticks or muffins are a tasty accompaniment to this inviting sage- and cardamom-seasoned medley.

SAGE, PORK & SWEET POTATO STEW

1½	pounds boneless pork shoulder
1	tablespoon cooking oil
4	medium sweet potatoes (about 1½ pounds), peeled and cut into 1-inch pieces
1	large onion, cut into thin wedges
½	cup dried apples
2	tablespoons quick-cooking tapioca
1	clove garlic, minced
½	teaspoon dried sage, crushed
¼	teaspoon ground cardamom
¼	teaspoon black pepper
1	14-ounce can chicken broth
1¼	cups apple juice or apple cider

PREP:
25 minutes

COOK:
Low 7 hours, High 3½ hours

MAKES:
6 servings

SLOW COOKER:
3½- or 4-quart

1 Trim fat from meat. Cut meat into 1-inch cubes. In a large skillet heat oil over medium-high heat. Brown meat, half at a time, in hot oil. Drain off fat.

2 In a 3½- or 4-quart slow cooker layer sweet potatoes, onion, and dried apples. Add meat. Sprinkle with tapioca, garlic, sage, cardamom, and pepper. Pour broth and apple juice over all.

3 Cover and cook on low-heat setting for 7 to 8 hours or on high-heat setting for 3½ to 4 hours.

Per serving: 373 cal., 10 g total fat (3 g sat. fat), 74 mg chol., 391 mg sodium, 44 g carbo., 5 g fiber, 25 g pro.

A light, sage-infused sauce makes this stew an elegant evening meal. Ladle it over rice, egg noodles, or fluffy mashed potatoes.

PORK & MUSHROOM STEW

PREP:
25 minutes

COOK:
Low 6 hours, High 3 hours

MAKES:
5 servings

SLOW COOKER:
3½- or 4-quart

1½   pounds lean boneless pork
     Nonstick cooking spray
1   16-ounce package frozen small whole onions, thawed
12   ounces whole mushrooms, quartered
1   10¾-ounce can condensed cream of mushroom soup
     with roasted garlic
½   teaspoon ground sage

1 Trim fat from meat. Cut meat into ¾-inch pieces. Lightly coat an unheated 12-inch skillet with nonstick cooking spray. Preheat skillet over medium heat. Brown meat, half at a time, in hot skillet; drain off fat.

2 In a 3½- or 4-quart slow cooker combine meat, thawed onions, and mushrooms. In a small bowl combine cream of mushroom soup and sage. Pour over meat and vegetables in slow cooker.

3 Cover and cook on low-heat setting for 6 to 7 hours or on high-heat setting for 3 to 3½ hours.

Per serving: 271 cal., 9 g total fat (3 g sat. fat), 77 mg chol., 481 mg sodium, 15 g carbo., 3 g fiber, 33 g pro.

The flavors of India emerge when you mix lamb, potatoes, and tomatoes with garam masala. You'll find garam masala—an Indian spice mix—at ethnic grocers, and many supermarkets stock it too.

INDIAN-FLAVORED LAMB STEW

2	pounds lean boneless lamb
1	tablespoon garam masala
3	cups chopped peeled potatoes (3 medium)
¼	teaspoon salt
¼	teaspoon black pepper
1	14½-ounce can diced tomatoes with garlic and onion, undrained
¼	cup water
¾	cup plain yogurt (optional)

1 Trim fat from meat. Cut meat into 1-inch cubes. In a large bowl toss meat with garam masala. In a 3½- or 4-quart slow cooker combine seasoned meat and potatoes. Sprinkle with salt and pepper. Pour undrained tomatoes and the water over all.

2 Cover and cook on low-heat setting for 8 to 10 hours or on high-heat setting for 4 to 5 hours. If desired, top individual servings with yogurt.

Per serving: 282 cal., 8 g total fat (3 g sat. fat), 97 mg chol., 538 mg sodium, 18 g carbo., 1 g fiber, 33 g pro.

PREP:
15 minutes

COOK:
Low 8 hours, High 4 hours

MAKES:
6 servings

SLOW COOKER:
3½- or 4-quart

Green onions sprinkled on just before serving add color and zip.

SAUCY CHICKEN & VEGETABLES

PREP:
15 minutes

COOK:
Low 7 hours, High 3½ hours

MAKES:
6 servings

SLOW COOKER:
3½- or 4-quart

2   cups bias-sliced carrots

2   tablespoons quick-cooking tapioca

2   to 2½ pounds meaty chicken pieces
     (breast halves, thighs, and drumsticks)

1   8-ounce can tomato sauce

½   cup plum jam or plum preserves

2   tablespoons rice vinegar

1   teaspoon ground ginger

½   teaspoon ground cinnamon

1   6-ounce package frozen pea pods, thawed

3   cups hot cooked rice

¼   cup bias-sliced green onions

1 Place carrots in a 3½- or 4-quart slow cooker; sprinkle with tapioca. Arrange chicken pieces on top of carrots.

2 In a small bowl combine tomato sauce, plum jam, vinegar, ginger, and cinnamon. Pour tomato sauce mixture over chicken.

3 Cover and cook on low-heat setting for 7 to 8 hours or on high-heat setting for 3½ to 4 hours. Stir in thawed pea pods.

4 Arrange chicken over rice on serving platter. Skim fat from cooking juices; pour cooking juices over chicken. Sprinkle with sliced green onions.

Per serving: 324 cal., 3 g total fat (1 g sat. fat), 51 mg chol., 271 mg sodium, 52 g carbo., 3 g fiber, 19 g pro.

Serve the flavorful cooking juices of this exotic chicken dish with a side of hot cooked rice or couscous.

MOROCCAN-SPICED CHICKEN

1½	teaspoons ground cumin
1	teaspoon salt
½	teaspoon ground cinnamon
½	teaspoon ground coriander
¼	teaspoon ground turmeric
¼	teaspoon black pepper
3½	to 4 pounds meaty chicken pieces (breast halves, thighs, and drumsticks), skinned
½	cup chicken broth

1 In a small bowl stir together cumin, salt, cinnamon, coriander, turmeric, and pepper. Sprinkle evenly over chicken; rub in with your fingers. Place chicken in a 3½- or 4-quart slow cooker. Pour broth over chicken.

2 Cover and cook on low-heat setting for 6 to 8 hours or on high-heat setting for 3 to 4 hours.

Per serving: 230 cal., 9 g total fat (2 g sat. fat), 108 mg chol., 567 mg sodium, 1 g carbo., 0 g fiber, 35 g pro.

PREP:
10 minutes

COOK:
Low 6 hours, High 3 hours

MAKES:
6 servings

SLOW COOKER:
3½- or 4-quart

Enjoy the tantalizing mix of citrus juices and chili powder in this homey dish.

LEMON-LIME CHILI CHICKEN

PREP:
15 minutes

COOK:
Low 5 hours, High 2½ hours

MAKES:
6 to 8 servings

SLOW COOKER:
4- to 5-quart

2 tablespoons chili powder

1 teaspoon salt

½ teaspoon black pepper

3 to 3½ pounds meaty chicken pieces
   (breast halves, thighs, and drumsticks), skinned

1 medium zucchini or yellow summer squash,
   halved lengthwise and cut into 1-inch pieces

1 medium onion, cut into wedges

¼ cup reduced-sodium chicken broth

¼ cup lime juice

¼ cup lemon juice

2 cloves garlic, minced

1 In a small bowl stir together chili powder, salt, and pepper. Sprinkle evenly over chicken; rub in with your fingers. Place chicken in a 4- to 5-quart slow cooker. Arrange zucchini and onion over chicken. In a small bowl stir together broth, lime juice, lemon juice, and garlic. Pour over chicken and vegetables.

2 Cover and cook on low-heat setting for 5 to 6 hours or on high-heat setting for 2½ to 3 hours. Transfer chicken and vegetables to a serving platter or serving plates; discard cooking liquid.

Per serving: 156 cal., 4 g total fat (1 g sat. fat), 76 mg chol., 525 mg sodium, 6 g carbo., 1 g fiber, 24 g pro.

Spicy red pepper pasta sauce is the flavor of choice for this recipe. If you can't find it, use one of your favorite varieties.

SPICY CHICKEN WITH PEPPERS & OLIVES

2½ to 3 pounds meaty chicken pieces
(breast halves, thighs, and drumsticks), skinned

Salt

Black pepper

1 small yellow sweet pepper, coarsely chopped

½ cup sliced, pitted ripe olives and/or pimiento-stuffed green olives

1 26-ounce jar spicy red pepper pasta sauce

Hot cooked whole wheat pasta (optional)

PREP:
20 minutes

COOK:
Low 6 hours, High 3 hours

MAKES:
6 servings

SLOW COOKER:
3½- or 4-quart

1 Place chicken in a 3½- or 4-quart slow cooker. Sprinkle lightly with salt and black pepper. Add sweet pepper and olives to slow cooker. Pour pasta sauce over chicken mixture in slow cooker.

2 Cover and cook on low-heat setting for 6 to 7 hours or on high-heat setting for 3 to 3½ hours. If desired, serve chicken and sauce over hot cooked pasta.

Per serving: 239 cal., 10 g total fat (2 g sat. fat), 77 mg chol., 592 mg sodium, 10 g carbo., 3 g fiber, 27 g pro.

Its comforting flavor makes this chowder a welcome choice any night of the week.

NACHO CHEESE CHICKEN CHOWDER

PREP:
10 minutes

COOK:
Low 4 hours, High 2 hours

MAKES:
6 servings

SLOW COOKER:
3¹/₂- or 4-quart

1 pound skinless, boneless chicken breast halves, cut into ¹/₂-inch pieces

2 14¹/₂-ounce cans Mexican-style stewed tomatoes, undrained

1 10³/₄-ounce can condensed fiesta nacho cheese soup

1 10-ounce package frozen whole kernel corn

¹/₃ cup shredded taco cheese or cheddar cheese

1 In a 3¹/₂- or 4-quart slow cooker combine chicken, undrained tomatoes, fiesta nacho cheese soup, and corn.

2 Cover and cook on low-heat setting for 4 to 5 hours or on high-heat setting for 2 to 2¹/₂ hours. Sprinkle individual servings with cheese.

Per serving: 244 cal., 6 g total fat (3 g sat. fat), 55 mg chol., 647 mg sodium, 24 g carbo., 2 g fiber, 23 g pro.

Two doses of cheese make this dish extra rich. Four cloves of garlic make the flavors soar.

CHEESY GARLIC CHICKEN

2	pounds skinless, boneless chicken breast halves, cut into 1½-inch pieces
1½	cups cauliflower florets
¾	cup reduced-sodium chicken broth
4	cloves garlic, minced
2	tablespoons quick-cooking tapioca
¼	teaspoon salt
1½	cups loose-pack frozen cut green beans
½	of an 8-ounce package reduced-fat cream cheese (Neufchâtel), cubed
⅔	cup chopped plum tomatoes (2 medium)
½	cup shredded part-skim mozzarella cheese (2 ounces)

1 In a 3½- or 4-quart slow cooker combine chicken, cauliflower, broth, garlic, tapioca, and salt.

2 Cover and cook on low-heat setting for 3½ to 4½ hours or on high-heat setting for 1½ to 2 hours.

3 If using low-heat setting, turn to high-heat setting. Stir frozen green beans into chicken mixture in slow cooker. Cover and cook for 30 minutes more.

4 Remove liner from slow cooker, if possible, or turn off slow cooker. Stir cream cheese into chicken mixture in slow cooker. Cover and let stand for 10 minutes. Remove cover and gently stir until cream cheese is melted and sauce is smooth. Sprinkle individual servings with tomatoes and mozzarella cheese.

Per serving: 283 cal., 8 g total fat (4 g sat. fat), 108 mg chol., 393 mg sodium, 10 g carbo., 2 g fiber, 41 g pro.

PREP:
20 minutes

COOK:
Low 3½ hours, High 1½ hours; plus 30 minutes on High

STAND:
10 minutes

MAKES:
6 servings

SLOW COOKER:
3½- or 4-quart

Apricot and mustard flavors come together in this chicken dish. Soak up the flavorful juices with servings of brown rice.

APRICOT CHICKEN

PREP:
25 minutes

COOK:
Low 8 hours, High 4 hours

MAKES:
8 servings

SLOW COOKER:
3½- or 4-quart

1	tablespoon cooking oil
2½	pounds skinless, boneless chicken thighs
2	cups loose-pack frozen small whole onions, thawed
4	medium carrots, bias-cut into ½-inch-thick slices
	Salt
	Black pepper
½	cup chicken broth
⅓	cup low-sugar apricot spread
2	tablespoons quick-cooking tapioca, ground if desired
1	to 2 tablespoons Dijon-style mustard
⅛	teaspoon ground allspice
	Hot cooked brown rice (optional)

1 In an extra large skillet heat oil over medium heat. Brown chicken, half at a time, in hot oil. (Add more oil, if necessary.) Set aside.

2 In a 3½- or 4-quart slow cooker combine onions and carrots. Arrange chicken over vegetables. Sprinkle chicken with salt and pepper. In a small bowl stir together chicken broth, apricot spread, tapioca, mustard, and allspice. Pour over chicken and vegetables in slow cooker.

3 Cover and cook on low-heat setting for 8 to 9 hours or on high-heat setting for 4 to 4½ hours. Serve chicken and vegetables with some of the cooking juices. If desired, serve with hot cooked brown rice.

Per serving: 247 cal., 8 g total fat (2 g sat. fat), 113 mg chol., 234 mg sodium, 13 g carbo., 2 g fiber, 29 g pro.

Use a wire whisk to incorporate the sour cream-cornstarch mixture into the cooking liquid and to make the sauce smooth.

SMOKY PAPRIKA CHICKEN THIGHS

1	tablespoon smoked paprika or paprika
1	teaspoon salt
¼	teaspoon garlic powder
¼	teaspoon black pepper
3	pounds chicken thighs, skinned
½	cup chicken broth
1	tablespoon tomato paste
1	8-ounce carton light dairy sour cream
2	tablespoons cornstarch

1 In a small bowl stir together paprika, salt, garlic powder, and pepper. Sprinkle evenly over chicken thighs; rub in with your fingers. Place chicken in a 4½- to 5½-quart slow cooker. In another small bowl whisk together chicken broth and tomato paste. Pour over chicken.

2 Cover and cook on low-heat setting for 6 to 7 hours or on high-heat setting for 3 to 3½ hours. Transfer chicken to a serving platter, reserving cooking juices in slow cooker. Cover chicken with foil to keep warm.

3 If using low-heat setting, turn to high-heat setting. For sauce, in a small bowl stir together sour cream and cornstarch; whisk into cooking juices in slow cooker until smooth. Cover and cook about 15 minutes more or until slightly thickened. Spoon sauce over chicken.

Per serving: 164 cal., 6 g total fat (2 g sat. fat), 90 mg chol., 439 mg sodium, 5 g carbo., 0 g fiber, 21 g pro.

PREP:
20 minutes

COOK:
Low 6 hours, High 3 hours; plus 15 minutes on High

MAKES:
8 servings

SLOW COOKER:
4½- to 5½-quart

Deep-colored, rich hoisin sauce imparts a sweet-and-spicy flavor to the chicken. Look for hoisin sauce in the Asian food section of the supermarket.

PLUM-SAUCED CHICKEN IN TORTILLAS

PREP:
15 minutes

COOK:
Low 4 hours, High 2 hours

MAKES:
6 servings

OVEN:
350°F

SLOW COOKER:
3½- or 4-quart

1   30-ounce can whole unpitted purple plums, drained

1   cup hot-style vegetable juice

¼   cup hoisin sauce

4½   teaspoons quick-cooking tapioca

2   teaspoons grated fresh ginger

¼   teaspoon salt

½   teaspoon five-spice powder*

⅛   to ¼ teaspoon cayenne pepper

1¼   pounds skinless, boneless chicken thighs, cut into bite-size strips

6   7- to 8-inch flour tortillas, warmed**

2   cups packaged shredded broccoli (broccoli slaw mix) or packaged shredded cabbage with carrot (coleslaw mix)

1 Remove pits from drained plums. Place plums in a blender or food processor. Cover and blend or process until smooth. Transfer plums to a 3½- or 4-quart slow cooker. Stir in vegetable juice, hoisin sauce, tapioca, ginger, salt, five-spice powder, and cayenne pepper. Stir chicken into plum mixture in slow cooker.

2 Cover and cook on low-heat setting for 4 to 5 hours or on high-heat setting for 2 to 2½ hours. Remove chicken from slow cooker, reserving cooking juices.

3 Spoon about ⅓ cup of the chicken mixture onto each warm tortilla just below the center. Drizzle with some of the reserved juices. Top each with ⅓ cup of the shredded broccoli. Roll up tortillas.

Per serving: 331 cal., 4 g total fat (1 g sat. fat), 55 mg chol., 575 mg sodium, 47 g carbo., 3 g fiber, 26 g pro.

*****NOTE:** You can use Homemade Five-Spice Powder (see recipe on page 73) or purchased five-spice powder.

******NOTE:** To warm tortillas, preheat oven to 350°F. Wrap tortillas tightly in foil. Heat in the oven about 10 minutes or until heated through.

You can count on basic old favorites, such as this chicken soup, to please again and again. The thyme lends an aromatic, fresh-from-the-garden quality.

CHUNKY **CHICKEN-VEGETABLE SOUP**

1¼   pounds skinless, boneless chicken thighs, cut into ½- to ¾-inch pieces

1   20-ounce package refrigerated diced potatoes with onions

1   16-ounce package loose-pack frozen broccoli, cauliflower, and carrots

2   14-ounce cans reduced-sodium chicken broth

1¾   cups water

1   10¾-ounce can reduced-fat and reduced-sodium condensed cream of chicken soup

1   teaspoon dried thyme, crushed

1 In a 4½- to 6-quart slow cooker combine chicken, potatoes, frozen vegetables, broth, the water, cream of chicken soup, and thyme.

2 Cover and cook on low-heat setting for 7 to 8 hours or on high-heat setting for 3½ to 4 hours.

Per serving: 201 cal., 3 g total fat (1 g sat. fat), 60 mg chol., 662 mg sodium, 22 g carbo., 3 g fiber, 19 g pro.

PREP:
15 minutes

COOK:
Low 7 hours, High 3½ hours

MAKES:
8 servings

SLOW COOKER:
4½- to 6-quart

Slices of mushrooms, slivers of bok choy, and chunks of turkey mingle in a soy- and ginger-scented broth, creating a savory soup with stir-fry flavors.

ASIAN TURKEY & RICE SOUP

PREP:
25 minutes

COOK:
Low 7 hours, High 3½ hours; plus 10 minutes on High

MAKES:
6 servings

SLOW COOKER:
3½- or 4-quart

1   pound turkey breast tenderloin or skinless, boneless chicken breast halves, cut into 1-inch pieces

2   cups sliced fresh mushrooms (such as shiitake or button)

2   14-ounce cans reduced-sodium chicken broth

1½   cups water

2   medium carrots, cut into thin bite-size strips

1   medium onion, chopped

2   tablespoons reduced-sodium soy sauce

2   teaspoons grated fresh ginger

4   cloves garlic, minced

1½   cups sliced bok choy

1   cup instant brown rice

1 In a 3½- or 4-quart slow cooker combine turkey, mushrooms, broth, the water, carrots, onion, soy sauce, ginger, and garlic.

2 Cover and cook on low-heat setting for 7 to 8 hours or on high-heat setting for 3½ to 4 hours.

3 If using low-heat setting, turn to high-heat setting. Stir in bok choy and uncooked brown rice. Cover and cook for 10 to 15 minutes more or until rice is tender.

Per serving: 166 cal., 2 g total fat (0 g sat. fat), 45 mg chol., 572 mg sodium, 15 g carbo., 2 g fiber, 22 g pro.

A down-home favorite goes uptown. Here smoked salmon and dill add a gourmet touch to creamed turkey and mushrooms.

CREAMED TURKEY & SMOKED SALMON

2   pounds turkey breast tenderloins, cut into 1-inch pieces

8   ounces fresh mushrooms, quartered

⅓   cup water

1   teaspoon salt

½   teaspoon dried dill, crushed

¼   teaspoon black pepper

¾   cup fat-free half-and-half

2   tablespoons cornstarch

4   ounces smoked salmon (not lox-style), skinned and flaked

¼   cup sliced green onions

1 In a 3½- or 4-quart slow cooker combine turkey and mushrooms. Stir in the water, salt, dill, and pepper.

2 Cover and cook on low-heat setting for 3½ hours or on high-heat setting for 1½ hours.

3 If using low-heat setting, turn to high-heat setting. In a small bowl combine half-and-half and cornstarch. Stir into turkey mixture in slow cooker. Cover and cook for 15 minutes more. Stir in smoked salmon and green onions.

Per serving: 227 cal., 2 g total fat (0 g sat. fat), 104 mg chol., 628 mg sodium, 7 g carbo., 0 g fiber, 42 g pro.

PREP:
20 minutes

COOK:
Low 3½ hours, High 1½ hours; plus 15 minutes on High

MAKES:
6 servings

SLOW COOKER:
3½- or 4-quart

Serve these saucy vegetables and turkey with a side of nutritionally rich baked sweet potatoes.

CREAMY TARRAGON TURKEY

PREP:
15 minutes

COOK:
Low 5 hours, High 2½ hours; plus 15 minutes on High

MAKES:
6 servings

SLOW COOKER:
3½- or 4-quart

2   medium fennel bulbs, cored and cut into thin wedges (2 cups)

1   large onion, cut into thin wedges

3   turkey breast tenderloins (about 2¼ pounds total)

½   cup reduced-sodium chicken broth

1   tablespoon Dijon-style mustard

½   teaspoon dried tarragon, crushed

¼   teaspoon salt

¼   teaspoon black pepper

¼   cup fat-free half-and-half

4   teaspoons cornstarch

2   ounces goat cheese (chèvre), crumbled (½ cup)

¼   cup snipped fresh parsley

1 In a 3½- or 4-quart slow cooker combine fennel and onion. Add turkey. In a small bowl combine broth, mustard, tarragon, salt, and pepper. Pour over turkey in slow cooker.

2 Cover and cook on low-heat setting for 5 to 6 hours or on high-heat setting for 2½ to 3 hours.

3 Transfer turkey to a serving platter, reserving fennel mixture in slow cooker. Cover turkey with foil to keep warm.

4 If using low-heat setting, turn to high-heat setting. In a small bowl combine half-and-half and cornstarch. Stir into fennel mixture in slow cooker. Cover and cook about 15 minutes more or until thickened.

5 To serve, cut turkey into serving-size pieces. Spoon fennel mixture over turkey pieces. Sprinkle with goat cheese and parsley.

Per serving: 258 cal., 5 g total fat (2 g sat. fat), 106 mg chol., 347 mg sodium, 8 g carbo., 1 g fiber, 43 g pro.

The punch of cranberries joins the kick of chili sauce for a knockout combination.

CRANBERRY-SAUCED TURKEY THIGHS

1	16-ounce can jellied cranberry sauce
½	cup bottled chili sauce
1	tablespoon vinegar
¼	teaspoon pumpkin pie spice
2½	to 3 pounds turkey thighs (2 or 3 thighs), skinned

1 In a 3½- or 4-quart slow cooker combine cranberry sauce, chili sauce, vinegar, and pumpkin pie spice. Place turkey thighs, meaty sides down, on sauce mixture.

2 Cover and cook on low-heat setting for 9 to 10 hours or on high-heat setting for 4½ to 5 hours.

3 Transfer turkey to a serving dish. Skim fat from cooking juices. Serve cooking juices with turkey.

Per serving: 388 cal., 5 g total fat (2 g sat. fat), 145 mg chol., 300 mg sodium, 46 g carbo., 2 g fiber, 37 g pro.

PREP:
10 minutes

COOK:
Low 9 hours, High 4½ hours

MAKES:
4 to 6 servings

SLOW COOKER:
3½- or 4-quart

Instead of ordering out, declare clam chowder a Friday night tradition at your house. Fragrant dill gives this mild version a dash of color. Serve the chowder in warm bowls.

CREAMY CLAM CHOWDER

PREP:
10 minutes

COOK:
Low 6 hours, High 3 hours; plus 15 minutes on High

MAKES:
6 servings

SLOW COOKER:
3½- or 4-quart

3 6½-ounce cans minced clams

3 cups chopped, peeled potatoes (3 medium)

1 10¾-ounce can condensed cream of onion soup

½ teaspoon dried dill

2 to 3 cups fat-free half-and-half

1 Drain clams, reserving liquid. Cover clams and refrigerate until needed. If necessary, add water to reserved clam liquid to measure 1¾ cups total liquid.

2 In a 3½- or 4-quart slow cooker combine clam liquid and potatoes. Stir in cream of onion soup and dill. Cover and cook on low-heat setting for 6 to 8 hours or on high-heat setting for 3 to 4 hours.

3 If using low-heat setting, turn to high-heat setting. Stir in clams and enough of the half-and-half to make desired consistency. Cover and cook about 15 minutes more or until heated through.

Per serving: 280 cal., 4 g total fat (1 g sat. fat), 68 mg chol., 547 mg sodium, 28 g carbo., 1 g fiber, 28 g pro.

Red, white, and black beans make this meatless chili both colorful and tasty.
A drizzle of chocolate adds an exotic note.

THREE-BEAN VEGETARIAN CHILI

1   15-ounce can no-salt-added red kidney beans, rinsed and drained

1   15-ounce can small white beans, rinsed and drained

1   15-ounce can low-sodium black beans, rinsed and drained

1   14½-ounce can diced tomatoes and green chile peppers, undrained

1   cup beer or chicken broth

3   tablespoons chocolate-flavored syrup

1   tablespoon chili powder

2   teaspoons salt-free Cajun seasoning

    Fat-free or light dairy sour cream (optional)

1 In a 3½- or 4-quart slow cooker combine kidney beans, white beans, black beans, undrained tomatoes and green chile peppers, beer or broth, chocolate-flavored syrup, chili powder, and Cajun seasoning.

2 Cover and cook on low-heat setting for 6 to 8 hours or on high-heat setting for 3 to 4 hours. If desired, top individual servings with sour cream.

Per serving: 309 cal., 1 g total fat (0 g sat. fat), 0 mg chol., 625 mg sodium, 59 g carbo., 19 g fiber, 20 g pro.

PREP:
15 minutes

COOK:
Low 6 hours, High 3 hours

MAKES:
4 servings

SLOW COOKER:
3½- or 4-quart

Goulash is typically a meaty dish well-seasoned with paprika and served with noodles. This caraway-accented variation skips the meat.

MUSHROOM GOULASH

PREP:
25 minutes

COOK:
Low 8 hours, High 4 hours

MAKES:
6 servings

SLOW COOKER:
3½- or 4-quart

16   ounces fresh baby portobello mushrooms, sliced

1   tablespoon dried minced onion

3   cloves garlic, minced

1   14½-ounce can no-salt-added diced tomatoes, undrained

1   14-ounce can vegetable broth

1   6-ounce can no-salt added tomato paste

2   tablespoons paprika

1   teaspoon dried oregano, crushed

1   teaspoon caraway seeds

¼   teaspoon salt

¼   teaspoon black pepper

½   cup light dairy sour cream

8   ounces dried egg noodles

1 In a 3½- or 4-quart slow cooker combine mushrooms, dried minced onion, and garlic. Stir in undrained tomatoes, broth, tomato paste, paprika, oregano, caraway seeds, salt, and pepper.

2 Cover and cook on low-heat setting for 8 to 9 hours or on high-heat setting for 4 to 4½ hours.

3 Cook noodles according to package directions; drain well. To serve, stir sour cream into mushroom mixture in slow cooker. Spoon over hot cooked noodles.

Per serving: 251 cal., 5 g total fat (2 g sat. fat), 43 mg chol., 443 mg sodium, 43 g carbo., 5 g fiber, 12 g pro.

Tofu is the main protein source in this meatless main dish. It's a good recipe for introducing your family to this healthful ingredient.

NOODLE CASSEROLE

2½	cups water
1	10¾-ounce can reduced-fat and reduced-sodium condensed cream of mushroom soup
1	14½-ounce can no-salt-added diced tomatoes, undrained
2	stalks celery, sliced
2	medium carrots, sliced
1	large onion, chopped
2	cloves garlic, minced
1½	teaspoons dried Italian seasoning, crushed
¼	teaspoon salt
¼	teaspoon black pepper
8	ounces dried extra-wide noodles
1	16-ounce package extra-firm tofu (fresh bean curd), drained, if necessary, and cubed
½	cup shredded reduced-fat cheddar cheese (2 ounces)

1 In a 3½- or 4-quart slow cooker whisk together the water and cream of mushroom soup until combined. Add undrained tomatoes, celery, carrots, onion, garlic, Italian seasoning, salt, and pepper; stir to combine.

2 Cover and cook on low-heat setting for 7 to 8 hours or high-heat setting for 3½ to 4 hours.

3 If using low-heat setting, turn to high-heat setting. Stir in uncooked noodles; cover and cook for 20 to 30 minutes more or until noodles are tender, stirring once halfway through cooking.

4 Remove liner from slow cooker, if possible, or turn off slow cooker. Gently stir tofu cubes into mixture in slow cooker. Sprinkle with cheese. Cover and let stand until cheese is melted.

Per serving: 316 cal., 8 g total fat (2 g sat. fat), 44 mg chol., 447 mg sodium, 42 g carbo., 4 g fiber, 17 g pro.

PREP:
25 minutes

COOK:
Low 7 hours, High 3½ hours; plus 20 minutes on High

MAKES:
6 servings

SLOW COOKER:
3½- or 4-quart

The blend of spices in garam masala can include cinnamon, nutmeg, cloves, coriander, cumin, cardamom, black pepper, dried chile peppers, fennel, and mace.

SPICED SQUASH & LENTIL SOUP

PREP:
25 minutes

COOK:
Low 8 hours, High 4 hours

MAKES:
5 or 6 servings

SLOW COOKER:
3½- or 4-quart

2½ cups coarsely chopped butternut squash

1 cup brown lentils, rinsed and drained

1 medium onion, chopped

1 medium carrot, chopped

1 stalk celery, chopped

1 teaspoon garam masala

2 cloves garlic, minced

4 cups chicken broth or vegetable broth

1 In a 3½- or 4-quart slow cooker combine squash, lentils, onion, carrot, and celery. Sprinkle with garam masala and garlic. Pour broth over all.

2 Cover and cook on low-heat setting for 8 to 9 hours or on high-heat setting for 4 to 4½ hours.

Per serving: 199 cal., 2 g total fat (0 g sat. fat), 0 mg chol., 639 mg sodium, 31 g carbo., 13 g fiber, 16 g pro.

5-INGREDIENT MAIN DISHES

7

Sassy and lively, just like the classic cocktail, this easy-fixing steak is sensational served with torn greens and steamed yellow summer squash.

BLOODY MARY STEAK

PREP:
20 minutes

COOK:
Low 8 hours, High 4 hours

MAKES:
6 servings

SLOW COOKER:
2½- to 3½-quart

2	pounds beef round steak, cut ¾ inch thick
	Nonstick cooking spray
¾	cup hot-style tomato juice
2	cloves garlic, minced
¼	cup water
4	teaspoons cornstarch
2	tablespoons cold water
2	teaspoons prepared horseradish

1 Trim fat from meat. Cut meat into 6 serving-size pieces. Lightly coat an unheated large skillet with nonstick cooking spray. Preheat skillet over medium-high heat. Add meat; cook until brown, turning once. Place meat in a 2½- to 3½-quart slow cooker. Add tomato juice, garlic, and the ¼ cup water.

2 Cover and cook on low-heat setting for 8 to 9 hours or on high-heat setting for 4 to 4½ hours.

3 Transfer meat to a serving platter, reserving cooking juices. If desired, slice meat. Cover meat and keep warm.

4 For gravy, pour cooking juices into a glass measuring cup; skim off fat. Measure juices; add water if necessary to measure 1½ cups total liquid. In a small saucepan combine cornstarch and the 2 tablespoons cold water; stir in cooking juices. Cook and stir over medium heat until thickened and bubbly. Cook and stir for 2 minutes more. Stir in horseradish. Season to taste with *salt* and *black pepper*. Serve meat with gravy.

Per serving: 196 cal., 4 g total fat (1 g sat. fat), 85 mg chol., 292 mg sodium, 3 g carbo., 0 g fiber, 35 g pro.

COUNT FIVE

In calculating the five ingredients for each recipe in this chapter, the following items were not counted:
• Water
• Nonstick cooking spray
• Items listed as optional
• Salt and black pepper

When the weather forecast is wicked, hole up at home with board games and thick socks, and put this dish in the slow cooker.

EASY BEEF STROGANOFF

2   pounds boneless beef round steak

2   10¾-ounce cans condensed golden mushroom soup

1   medium onion, sliced

1   8-ounce container dairy sour cream chive dip

3   cups hot cooked noodles

1 Trim fat from meat. Cut meat into 1-inch cubes. In a 3½- or 4-quart slow cooker stir together meat, golden mushroom soup, and onion.

2 Cover and cook on low-heat setting for 8 to 10 hours or on high-heat setting for 4 to 5 hours.

3 Stir in sour cream chive dip. Serve over hot cooked noodles.

Per serving: 450 cal., 16 g total fat (7 g sat. fat), 131 mg chol., 1,155 mg sodium, 33 g carbo., 2 g fiber, 42 g pro.

PREP:
15 minutes

COOK:
Low 8 hours, High 4 hours

MAKES:
6 servings

SLOW COOKER:
3½- or 4-quart

Plan this Irish classic for St. Patrick's Day or any time you're in the mood for a bit of the green (though the beef itself sports a purple hue). Enjoy it with a mug of cold beer.

CORNED BEEF & CABBAGE

PREP:
15 minutes

COOK:
Low 10 hours, High 5 hours

MAKES:
6 servings

SLOW COOKER:
5- to 6-quart

1	3- to 4-pound corned beef brisket with spice packet
½	of a small head cabbage, cut into 3 wedges
4	medium carrots, peeled and cut into 2-inch pieces
2	medium yellow potatoes, cut into 2-inch pieces
1	medium onion, quartered
¾	cup water

1 Trim fat from meat. If necessary, cut meat to fit in a 5- to 6-quart slow cooker. Sprinkle spices from packet evenly over meat; rub in with your fingers. Place cabbage, carrots, potatoes, and onion in the slow cooker. Pour the water over vegetables. Top with meat.

2 Cover and cook on low-heat setting for 10 to 12 hours or on high-heat setting for 5 to 6 hours.

3 Transfer meat to a cutting board. Thinly slice meat across the grain. Serve vegetables using a slotted spoon.

Per serving: 458 cal., 27 g total fat (7 g sat. fat), 115 mg chol., 1,557 mg sodium, 16 g carbo., 3 g fiber, 35 g pro.

Here's a decadent party-pleaser that's easy on the hosts. Those who love Reubens will applaud you.

REUBENS FROM A CROCK

1   2- to 3-pound corned beef brisket with spice packet
1   16-ounce jar sauerkraut, drained
½   cup bottled Thousand Island salad dressing
16   slices rye swirl bread, toasted
8   ounces Swiss cheese, sliced
     Bottled Thousand Island salad dressing (optional)

1 Trim fat from meat. If necessary, cut meat to fit in a 3½- or 4-quart slow cooker. Place meat in slow cooker. Sprinkle spices from packet evenly over meat; rub in with your fingers. Spread sauerkraut over meat. Drizzle the ½ cup salad dressing over all.

2 Cover and cook on low-heat setting for 4 to 6 hours or on high-heat setting for 2 to 3 hours.

3 Transfer meat to a cutting board. Thinly slice meat across the grain. Return sliced meat to the slow cooker and stir to combine with the cooking juices. Using a slotted spoon, spoon meat mixture onto 8 slices of the toasted bread. Top with cheese. If desired, top with additional salad dressing. Top with remaining bread.

Per sandwich: 564 cal., 34 g total fat (10 g sat. fat), 89 mg chol., 2,101 mg sodium, 35 g carbo., 4 g fiber, 29 g pro.

PREP:
15 minutes

COOK:
Low 4 hours, High 2 hours

MAKES:
8 sandwiches

SLOW COOKER:
3½- or 4-quart

Plum sauce, rice vinegar, and grated fresh ginger are your passports to this exotic dish.
A side dish of steamed rice absorbs the extra sauce.

ASIAN BEEF SHORT RIBS

PREP:
25 minutes

COOK:
Low 6 hours, High 3 hours

MAKES:
6 servings

SLOW COOKER:
3¹/₂- or 4-quart

3 pounds boneless beef short ribs

1 7.6-ounce jar plum sauce

²/₃ cup ketchup

1 tablespoon rice vinegar

2 teaspoons grated fresh ginger

1 In a large nonstick skillet cook ribs over medium-high heat until browned, turning to brown evenly.

2 Place ribs in a 3¹/₂- or 4-quart slow cooker. In a medium bowl stir together plum sauce, ketchup, rice vinegar, and ginger. Pour over ribs.

3 Cover and cook on low-heat setting for 6 to 8 hours or on high-heat setting for 3 to 4 hours.

4 Using a slotted spoon, transfer ribs to a serving platter. Skim fat from cooking juices; spoon some of the cooking juices over the ribs.

Per serving: 245 cal., 8 g total fat (3 g sat. fat), 53 mg chol., 538 mg sodium, 25 g carbo., 0 g fiber, 18 g pro.

Here's a stick-to-your ribs meal with a nifty twist. Bottled plum or hoisin sauce and beef gravy make a delectable sauce for the meat and vegetables.

SIMPLE SHORT RIB STEW

Nonstick cooking spray

2 pounds boneless beef short ribs, trimmed and cut into 1½-inch pieces

1 pound tiny new potatoes, halved

5 carrots, cut into 1-inch pieces

1 12-ounce jar beef gravy

½ cup bottled plum sauce or hoisin sauce

PREP:
35 minutes

COOK:
Low 7 hours, High 3½ hours

MAKES:
6 servings

SLOW COOKER:
3½- or 4-quart

1 Lightly coat an unheated 12-inch skillet with nonstick cooking spray. Preheat over medium heat. In hot skillet cook ribs, half at a time, until brown. Drain off fat.

2 In a 3½- or 4-quart slow cooker combine potatoes and carrots. Arrange ribs on top of vegetables. In a medium bowl stir together beef gravy and plum sauce; pour over ribs and vegetables in slow cooker.

3 Cover and cook on low-heat setting for 7 to 8 hours or on high-heat setting for 3½ to 4 hours. Before serving, skim fat from surface of stew.

Per serving: 621 cal., 26 g total fat (11 g sat. fat), 173 mg chol., 670 mg sodium, 30 g carbo., 3 g fiber, 62 g pro.

A native of Hungary, goulash features the zest of tomatoes, garlic, and oregano. Serve this quick version the traditional way with buttered noodles.

SHORTCUT GOULASH

PREP:
20 minutes

COOK:
Low 6 hours, High 3 hours

STAND:
5 minutes

MAKES:
4 servings

SLOW COOKER:
3½- or 4-quart

1   pound lean ground beef

½   of a 24-ounce package loose-pack frozen diced hash brown potatoes with onions and peppers (about 3½ cups)

1   15-ounce can tomato sauce

1   14½-ounce can diced tomatoes with basil, garlic, and oregano, undrained

½   cup shredded cheddar cheese (2 ounces)

1 In a large skillet cook ground beef over medium heat until brown. Drain off fat.

2 In a 3½- or 4-quart slow cooker combine meat, frozen potatoes, tomato sauce, and undrained tomatoes.

3 Cover and cook on low-heat setting for 6 to 8 hours or on high-heat setting for 3 to 4 hours.

4 Remove liner from slow cooker, if possible, or turn off slow cooker. Sprinkle meat mixture with cheese. Let stand for 5 minutes or until cheese melts.

Per serving: 535 cal., 33 g total fat (14 g sat. fat), 109 mg chol., 1,371 mg sodium, 34 g carbo., 4 g fiber, 27 g pro.

Shaped so that it doesn't touch the edge of the slow cooker, this simple meat loaf lifts out easily so you can place it on a platter before serving.

ITALIAN MEAT LOAF

1   egg
1   8-ounce can pizza sauce
½   cup seasoned fine dry bread crumbs
2   pounds lean ground beef
¼   cup shredded Monterey Jack cheese,
      mozzarella cheese, or Parmesan cheese
      (1 ounce)

PREP:
15 minutes
COOK:
Low 5 hours, High 2½ hours
STAND:
10 minutes
MAKES:
6 to 8 servings
SLOW COOKER:
3½- or 4-quart

1 In a large bowl beat egg with a fork. Stir in ½ cup of the pizza sauce and the bread crumbs. Add ground beef; mix well. Cover and refrigerate remaining pizza sauce until meat loaf is ready to serve.

2 On waxed paper, shape meat mixture into a 6-inch round loaf. Crisscross three 18×2-inch foil strips. Place meat loaf in center of strips. Bringing up foil strips, lift and transfer meat and foil to a 3½- or 4-quart slow cooker. Press meat away from side of slow cooker to avoid burning.

3 Cover and cook on low-heat setting for 5 to 6 hours or on high-heat setting for 2½ to 3 hours.

4 Using foil strips, carefully lift meat loaf from the slow cooker and transfer to a serving plate. Spoon remaining pizza sauce over meat; sprinkle with cheese. Let stand for 10 minutes before slicing.

Per serving: 327 cal., 17 g total fat (7 g sat. fat), 135 mg chol., 541 mg sodium, 11 g carbo., 1 g fiber, 31 g pro.

This is a kid favorite that adults like too. Sweet pickle slices taste great on top of the meat.

CHEESY SLOPPY JOES

PREP:
20 minutes

COOK:
Low 4½ hours, High 2 hours

MAKES:
16 servings

SLOW COOKER:
3½- or 4-quart

2½   pounds lean ground beef

1   large onion, chopped

2   10¾-ounce cans condensed fiesta nacho cheese soup

¾   cup ketchup

16   hamburger buns, split and toasted

1 In a 12-inch skillet cook ground beef and onion over medium heat until meat is brown and onion is tender; drain off fat.

2 In a 3½- or 4-quart slow cooker combine meat mixture, fiesta nacho cheese soup, and ketchup.

3 Cover and cook on low-heat setting for 4½ to 5 hours or on high-heat setting for 2 to 2½ hours. Serve meat mixture in toasted buns.

Per serving: 389 cal., 22 g total fat (9 g sat. fat), 63 mg chol., 680 mg sodium, 29 g carbo., 2 g fiber, 17 g pro.

This dish is for those who crave homey foods. If you like, sprinkle with a bit of shredded cheddar.

BEEFY SHEPHERD'S PIE

2   pounds lean ground beef

1   large onion, chopped

1   16-ounce package frozen mixed vegetables

2   10¾-ounce cans condensed tomato soup

8   servings refrigerated or frozen mashed potatoes

1 In a large skillet cook ground beef and onion until meat is brown and onion is tender; drain off fat.

2 In a 3½- or 4-quart slow cooker combine meat mixture, frozen vegetables, and tomato soup.

3 Cover and cook on low-heat setting for 6 to 8 hours or on high-heat setting for 3 to 4 hours.

4 Meanwhile, prepare mashed potatoes according to package directions. Serve meat mixture with potatoes.

Per serving: 575 cal., 27 g total fat (13 g sat. fat), 106 mg chol., 836 mg sodium, 51 g carbo., 7 g fiber, 32 g pro.

PREP:
20 minutes

COOK:
Low 6 hours, High 3 hours

MAKES:
8 servings

SLOW COOKER:
3½- or 4-quart

The hollows of the colorful sweet peppers provide a crisp, cool complement to their contents: warm ground meat, spicy cheese, and zesty salsa. Use a combo of green, red, and yellow peppers to impress guests with a pretty presentation.

MEXICAN STUFFED SWEET PEPPERS

PREP:
25 minutes

COOK:
Low 6 hours, High 3 hours

MAKES:
4 servings

SLOW COOKER:
4½- or 5-quart

4   medium green, red, and/or yellow sweet peppers

1   pound lean ground beef or ground pork

1   16-ounce jar black bean salsa or chunky salsa

1   cup instant white rice

6   ounces Monterey Jack cheese with jalapeño chile peppers or Monterey Jack cheese, shredded (1½ cups)

1   cup water

1 Remove tops of sweet peppers; scoop out membranes and seeds. Set peppers aside. For filling, in a large skillet cook meat until brown; drain off fat. Stir salsa, the uncooked rice, and 1 cup of the cheese into meat in skillet. Spoon filling into peppers, mounding tops as needed. Cover and refrigerate remaining cheese until peppers are ready to serve.

2 Pour the water into a 4½- or 5-quart slow cooker. Arrange stuffed peppers, filling sides up, in slow cooker.

3 Cover and cook on low-heat setting for 6 to 7 hours or on high-heat setting for 3 to 3½ hours.

4 Transfer stuffed peppers to a serving platter. Top with remaining ½ cup of the cheese.

Per serving: 513 cal., 24 g total fat (12 g sat. fat), 109 mg chol., 1,060 mg sodium, 38 g carbo., 2 g fiber, 37 g pro.

Chili sauce spikes the cranberry glaze for this tender roast. Prepare to dish out seconds.

CRANBERRY PORK ROAST

Nonstick cooking spray
1 2½- to 3-pound boneless pork shoulder roast
1 16-ounce package loose-pack frozen stew vegetables
1 16-ounce can whole cranberry sauce
½ cup bottled chili sauce

1 Lightly coat an unheated large skillet with nonstick cooking spray. Preheat over medium heat. In hot skillet brown meat on all sides; drain off fat.

2 Place meat in a 3½- or 4-quart slow cooker. Top with frozen vegetables. In a small bowl stir together cranberry sauce and chili sauce. Pour over meat and vegetables in slow cooker.

3 Cover and cook on low-heat setting for 8 to 9 hours or on high-heat setting for 4 to 4½ hours. Transfer meat and vegetables to a serving platter. Cover with foil and keep warm.

4 Strain cooking juices and skim off fat. Transfer cooking juices to a medium saucepan; bring cooking juices to boiling. Reduce heat. Simmer, uncovered, about 20 minutes or until cooking juices are thickened and volume is reduced by half. Serve with meat and vegetables.

Per serving: 494 cal., 16 g total fat (5 g sat. fat), 140 mg chol., 833 mg sodium, 44 g carbo., 2 g fiber, 41 g pro.

PREP:
15 minutes
COOK:
Low 8 hours, High 4 hours; plus 20 minutes on range top
MAKES:
6 servings
SLOW COOKER:
3½- or 4-quart

This tender shredded pork smothered in a tasty, sweet-hot sauce has an attractive deep red color. Don't skip the dried apricots (they're key to the full flavor). For sandwiches, pile the meat onto crusty Kaiser rolls or wrap it in a tortilla.

APRICOT PULLED PORK

PREP:
20 minutes

COOK:
Low 8 hours, High 4 hours

MAKES:
6 to 8 servings

SLOW COOKER:
3½- or 4-quart

Nonstick cooking spray

1   3- to 3½-pound boneless pork shoulder roast

1   10-ounce jar apricot spreadable fruit

1   cup bottled hot-style barbecue sauce

1   medium sweet onion
(such as Vidalia, Maui, or Walla Walla), chopped

½   cup snipped dried apricots

1 Lightly coat a 3½- or 4-quart slow cooker with nonstick cooking spray. Trim fat from meat. If necessary, cut meat to fit in slow cooker. Place meat in prepared cooker. In a medium bowl combine spreadable fruit, barbecue sauce, onion, and dried apricots. Pour over meat in slow cooker.

2 Cover and cook on low-heat setting for 8 to 10 hours or on high-heat setting for 4 to 5 hours.

3 Transfer meat to a cutting board. Using 2 forks, gently shred the meat. In a large bowl combine shredded meat and some of the cooking juices from the cooker. Pass remaining cooking juices.

Per serving: 535 cal., 19 g total fat (7 g sat. fat), 166 mg chol., 513 mg sodium, 42 g carbo., 2 g fiber, 49 g pro.

Cola and dry onion soup mix simmer together to form a full-flavored sauce that gives an appealing spin to old-fashioned pot roast and veggies.

COLA-PORK STEW

1   2- to 2½-pound boneless pork shoulder roast

1   16-ounce package peeled baby carrots

1   pound turnips, peeled and cut into 1-inch pieces

1   12-ounce can cola (do not use diet cola)

1   envelope (½ of a 2-ounce package) dry onion soup mix

1 Trim fat from meat. Cut meat into 1-inch pieces. Place meat in a 4½- or 5-quart slow cooker. Top with carrots, turnips, cola, and dry onion soup mix.

2 Cover and cook on low-heat setting for 10 to 12 hours or on high-heat setting for 5 to 6 hours. Season to taste with *salt* and *black pepper*.

Per serving: 286 cal., 9 g total fat (3 g sat. fat), 98 mg chol., 400 mg sodium, 18 g carbo., 1 g fiber, 31 g pro.

PREP:
25 minutes

COOK:
Low 10 hours, High 5 hours

MAKES:
6 servings

SLOW COOKER:
4½- or 5-quart

Pick up corn muffins at the supermarket to serve with these tender, thyme-flavored chops.

FRUITED PORK CHOPS

PREP:
15 minutes

COOK:
Low 4 hours, High 2 hours

MAKES:
6 servings

SLOW COOKER:
3½- or 4-quart

6   boneless pork loin chops, cut 1 inch thick

1   teaspoon dried thyme, crushed

2   7-ounce packages mixed dried fruit

1   medium red or yellow sweet pepper, seeded and sliced

1   cup bottled barbecue sauce

1 Trim fat from chops. Place chops in a 3½- or 4-quart slow cooker. Sprinkle with thyme. Add dried fruit and sweet pepper to slow cooker. Pour barbecue sauce over all.

2 Cover and cook on low-heat setting for 4 to 4½ hours or on high-heat setting for 2 to 2½ hours.

3 Transfer chops to a serving platter. Skim fat from the cooking juices. Spoon some of the juices over chops; pass remaining cooking juices.

Per serving: 450 cal., 11 g total fat (4 g sat. fat), 92 mg chol., 421 mg sodium, 49 g carbo., 3 g fiber, 40 g pro.

Tender meat and potatoes nestle in a brown mushroom gravy seasoned with apple juice and caraway seeds—classic flavor complements to pork that work just as well with beef. Try this stew in the fall with a fresh apple pie for dessert.

GERMAN-STYLE PORK STEW

2   to 2¼ pounds boneless pork shoulder or beef chuck
      Nonstick cooking spray

1   16- to 20-ounce package refrigerated diced potatoes

2   12-ounce jars mushroom gravy

1½   cups apple juice or apple cider

2   teaspoons caraway seeds

1 Trim fat from meat. Cut meat into ¾-inch cubes. Lightly coat an unheated 12-inch skillet with nonstick cooking spray. Preheat over medium heat. Add meat; cook and stir until light brown. Drain off fat.

2 In a 3½- or 4-quart slow cooker stir together meat, refrigerated potatoes, mushroom gravy, apple juice, and caraway seeds.

3 Cover and cook on low-heat setting for 7 to 8 hours or on high-heat setting for 3½ to 4 hours.

Per serving: 462 cal., 16 g total fat (5 g sat. fat), 101 mg chol., 1,150 mg sodium, 44 g carbo., 3 g fiber, 34 g pro.

PREP:
25 minutes

COOK:
Low 7 hours, High 3½ hours

MAKES:
4 servings

SLOW COOKER:
3½- or 4-quart

Classic burgoo, a thick stew of various meats, includes whatever the hunter catches that day. This version mixes pork and chicken with cayenne pepper for sass.

EASY BURGOO

PREP:
15 minutes

COOK:
Low 4 hours, High 2 hours

MAKES:
6 servings

SLOW COOKER:
3½- or 4-quart

1¼   pounds lean boneless pork

Nonstick cooking spray

2   10¾-ounce cans condensed chicken gumbo soup

1   16-ounce package frozen succotash, thawed*

2   cups loose-pack frozen diced hash brown potatoes with onion and peppers

2   cups water

¼   teaspoon cayenne pepper

1 Trim fat from meat. Cut meat into ¾-inch pieces. Lightly coat an unheated large skillet with nonstick cooking spray. Preheat over medium heat. In hot skillet cook meat, half at a time, until brown. Drain off fat.

2 In a 3½ or 4-quart slow cooker combine meat, chicken gumbo soup, thawed succotash, frozen potatoes, the water, and cayenne pepper.

3 Cover and cook on low-heat setting for 4 to 6 hours or on high-heat setting for 2 to 3 hours.

Per serving: 310 cal., 8 g total fat (3 g sat. fat), 57 mg chol., 994 mg sodium, 32 g carbo., 5 g fiber, 28 g pro.

*NOTE: You can substitute one 10-ounce package frozen lima beans, thawed, and 1 cup frozen whole kernel corn, thawed, for the succotash.

For a less spicy version, use regular vegetable juice rather than hot-style juice.

SPICY HAM & GARBANZO BEAN SOUP

1½   cups cubed cooked ham (about 8 ounces)

1   15-ounce can garbanzo beans (chickpeas),
     rinsed and drained

4   medium carrots, sliced

2   stalks celery, sliced

4   cups hot-style vegetable juice

1   cup water

PREP:
15 minutes

COOK:
Low 7 hours, High 3½ hours

MAKES:
6 servings

SLOW COOKER:
3½- to 4½-quart

1 In a 3½- to 4½-quart slow cooker combine ham, garbanzo beans, carrots, and celery. Pour vegetable juice and the water over all.

2 Cover and cook on low-heat setting for 7 to 9 hours or on high-heat setting for 3½ to 4½ hours.

Per serving: 187 cal., 5 g total fat (1 g sat. fat), 22 mg chol., 1,272 mg sodium, 23 g carbo., 5 g fiber, 12 g pro.

This golden-yellow casserole is like macaroni and cheese without the macaroni. Kids will like its rosy ham, soft potatoes, and rich cheese flavor. Roasted red sweet peppers add flavor and color.

HAM & POTATOES AU GRATIN

PREP:
15 minutes

COOK:
Low 7 hours, High 3½ hours

MAKES:
6 servings

SLOW COOKER:
3½- or 4-quart

Nonstick cooking spray

2 5½-ounce packages dry au gratin potato mix

2 cups diced cooked ham (10 ounces)

¼ cup bottled roasted red sweet peppers, drained and chopped

3 cups water

1 10¾-ounce can condensed cheddar cheese soup

1 Lightly coat a 3½- or 4-quart slow cooker with nonstick cooking spray. Place au gratin potato mixes with contents of seasoning packets, the ham, and roasted red sweet peppers in the prepared cooker. In a large bowl stir together the water and cheddar cheese soup. Pour over potato mixture in slow cooker.

2 Cover and cook on low-heat setting for 7 to 8 hours or on high-heat setting for 3½ to 4 hours.

Per serving: 255 cal., 7 g total fat (3 g sat. fat), 29 mg chol., 2,087 mg sodium, 45 g carbo., 3 g fiber, 15 g pro.

Some say the secret of good cooking is good ingredients. Here you'll find four Greek classics: chicken, feta, olives, and the flavor of pine nuts.

GREEK CHICKEN WITH COUSCOUS

2   pounds skinless, boneless chicken breast halves,
    cut into ½-inch pieces

2   14½-ounce cans diced tomatoes with basil, oregano,
    and garlic, undrained

1½ cups water

2   6-ounce packages couscous with toasted pine nut mix

1   cup crumbled feta cheese (4 ounces)

½   cup pitted kalamata olives, coarsely chopped

PREP:
15 minutes

COOK:
Low 5 hours, High 2½ hours

STAND:
5 minutes

MAKES:
8 servings

SLOW COOKER:
3½- or 4-quart

1 Place chicken in a 3½- or 4-quart slow cooker. Add undrained tomatoes and the water.

2 Cover and cook on low-heat setting for 5 to 6 hours or on high-heat setting for 2½ to 3 hours.

3 Stir in couscous. Remove liner from slow cooker, if possible, or turn off slow cooker. Cover and let stand for 5 minutes. Fluff couscous-chicken mixture with a fork. Sprinkle individual servings with feta cheese and olives.

Per serving: 377 cal., 8 g total fat (4 g sat. fat), 82 mg chol., 1,226 mg sodium, 41 g carbo., 3 g fiber, 36 g pro.

This rice with the flamboyant name—jambalaya—hails from New Orleans. The spicy Cajun flavor is sure to put a zip in your day.

CHICKEN JAMBALAYA

PREP:
15 minutes

COOK:
Low 5 hours, High 2½ hours; plus 45 minutes on High

MAKES:
6 servings

SLOW COOKER:
3½- or 4-quart

1 16-ounce package frozen (yellow, green, and red) peppers and onion stir-fry vegetables

8 ounces skinless, boneless chicken breast halves, cut into ½-inch-wide strips

8 ounces smoked turkey sausage, halved lengthwise and cut into ½-inch-thick slices

2 cups water

1 14½-ounce can diced tomatoes with jalapeño chile peppers, undrained

1 8-ounce package jambalaya rice mix

1 Place frozen stir-fry vegetables in a 3½- or 4-quart slow cooker. Top with chicken strips and turkey sausage. Add water, undrained tomatoes, and, if present, the seasoning packet from rice mix.

2 Cover and cook on low-heat setting for 5 to 6 hours or on high-heat setting for 2½ to 3 hours.

3 Stir in uncooked rice mix. If using low-heat setting, turn to high-heat setting. Cover and cook about 45 minutes more or until most of the liquid is absorbed and the rice is tender.

Per serving: 265 cal., 4 g total fat (1 g sat. fat), 47 mg chol., 1,118 mg sodium, 37 g carbo., 2 g fiber, 19 g pro.

The secrets of this recipe come from unexpected sources: the hot dog stand for the mustard and the breakfast table for the preserves.

FINGER LICKIN' BARBECUE CHICKEN

2½   to 3 pounds chicken drumsticks, skinned if desired

1   cup bottled barbecue sauce

⅓   cup apricot or peach preserves

2   teaspoons yellow mustard

1 Place chicken in a 3½- or 4-quart slow cooker. In a small bowl stir together barbecue sauce, preserves, and mustard. Pour over chicken.

2 Cover and cook on low-heat setting for 6 to 8 hours or on high-heat setting for 3 to 4 hours. Transfer chicken to a serving dish. Cover with foil and keep warm.

3 If desired, transfer cooking juices from slow cooker to a medium saucepan. Bring mixture to boiling; reduce heat. Simmer, uncovered, about 10 minutes or until desired consistency. Serve with chicken.

Per serving: 456 cal., 17 g total fat (4 g sat. fat), 154 mg chol., 963 mg sodium, 37 g carbo., 2 g fiber, 38 g pro.

PREP:
10 minutes

COOK:
Low 6 hours, High 3 hours

MAKES:
4 to 6 servings

SLOW COOKER:
3½- or 4-quart

Rice and steamed Brussels sprouts make taste-tempting partners for this savory fruited chicken. For a change of pace, prepare your favorite recipe for rice pilaf to substitute for the plain rice.

CRANBERRY CHICKEN

PREP:
15 minutes

COOK:
Low 5 hours, High 2½ hours

MAKES:
6 servings

SLOW COOKER:
3½- or 4-quart

2½ to 3 pounds chicken thighs and/or drumsticks, skinned

1 16-ounce can whole cranberry sauce

2 tablespoons dry onion soup mix

2 tablespoons quick-cooking tapioca

3 cups hot cooked rice

1 Place chicken in a 3½- or 4-quart slow cooker. In a small bowl stir together cranberry sauce, dry onion soup mix, and tapioca. Pour over chicken.

2 Cover and cook on low-heat setting for 5 to 6 hours or on high-heat setting for 2½ to 3 hours. Serve chicken and cooking juices over hot cooked rice.

Per serving: 357 cal., 4 g total fat (1 g sat. fat), 89 mg chol., 268 mg sodium, 55 g carbo., 1 g fiber, 23 g pro.

Here's a mild sweet-sour chicken flavored with a mango chutney and chili sauce. Serve rice alongside to soak up the rosy sauce.

GINGERED CHUTNEY CHICKEN

½   cup mango chutney

¼   cup bottled chili sauce

2   tablespoons quick-cooking tapioca

1½ teaspoons grated fresh ginger or ½ teaspoon ground ginger

12 chicken thighs, skinned (about 4 pounds)

1 Cut up any large pieces of fruit in the chutney. In a 4- to 5-quart slow cooker combine mango chutney, chili sauce, tapioca, and ginger. Add chicken, turning to coat.

2 Cover and cook on low-heat setting for 5 to 6 hours or on high-heat setting for 2½ to 3 hours.

Per serving: 264 cal., 7 g total fat (2 g sat. fat), 143 mg chol., 494 mg sodium, 16 g carbo., 1 g fiber, 34 g pro.

PREP:
20 minutes

COOK:
Low 5 hours, High 2½ hours

MAKES:
6 servings

SLOW COOKER:
4- to 5-quart

The meatballs hail from Italy, but the spicy sauce is definitely Mexican. Eat this culturally blended stew with a side of warm corn bread.

MEXICAN MEATBALL STEW

PREP:
10 minutes

COOK:
Low 6 hours, High 3 hours

MAKES:
8 to 10 servings

SLOW COOKER:
4- to 5-quart

2   14½-ounce cans Mexican-style stewed tomatoes, undrained

2   12-ounce packages frozen cooked turkey meatballs (24), thawed

1   15-ounce can black beans, rinsed and drained

1   14-ounce can chicken broth with roasted garlic

1   10-ounce package frozen corn, thawed

1 In a 4- to 5-quart slow cooker combine undrained tomatoes, thawed meatballs, beans, broth, and thawed corn.

2 Cover and cook on low-heat setting for 6 to 7 hours or on high-heat setting for 3 to 3½ hours.

Per serving: 268 cal., 10 g total fat (3 g sat. fat), 66 mg chol., 1,328 mg sodium, 30 g carbo., 8 g fiber, 20 g pro.

Have a craving for kraut? With sausage and potatoes, this dish will soon have you fed and happy.

COUNTRY-STYLE SAUSAGE & SAUERKRAUT

10   to 12 tiny new potatoes, quartered (about 1 pound)

1   medium onion, cut into thin wedges

1   pound smoked turkey sausage, cut into 1-inch pieces

1   14- to 15-ounce can Bavarian-style sauerkraut (with caraway seeds)*

⅓   cup water

1   tablespoon Dijon-style mustard

1 In a 3½- or 4-quart slow cooker place potatoes and onion wedges. Top with sausage and undrained sauerkraut.

2 In a small bowl whisk together the water and mustard; pour over sauerkraut.

3 Cover and cook on low-heat setting for 6 to 8 hours or on high-heat setting for 3 to 4 hours.

Per serving: 317 cal., 10 g total fat (2 g sat. fat), 76 mg chol., 3,472 mg sodium, 37 g carbo., 2 g fiber, 21 g pro.

*NOTE: If Bavarian-style sauerkraut is not available, substitute one 14½-ounce can sauerkraut plus 2 tablespoons packed brown sugar and ½ teaspoon caraway seeds.

PREP:
15 minutes

COOK:
Low 6 hours, High 3 hours

MAKES:
4 servings

SLOW COOKER:
3½- or 4-quart

Chunks of cod or whitefish get a flavorful kick in this creamy, zesty chowder. Serve with a basket of blue corn tortilla chips and cold Mexican beer.

MEXICAN-STYLE FISH CHOWDER

PREP:
15 minutes

COOK:
Low 3 hours, High 1½ hours; plus 1 hour on High

MAKES:
6 to 8 servings

SLOW COOKER:
3½- or 4-quart

Nonstick cooking spray

2　10¾-ounce cans condensed cream of celery soup

1　16- to 20-ounce package frozen whole kernel corn

1½　cups milk

1　pound fresh or frozen cod or other white fish fillets

2　14½-ounce cans Mexican-style stewed tomatoes, undrained

1 Lightly coat a 3½- or 4-quart slow cooker with nonstick cooking spray. In the prepared cooker combine cream of celery soup, frozen corn, and milk.

2 Cover and cook on low-heat setting for 3 to 4 hours or on high-heat setting for 1½ to 2 hours.

3 Meanwhile, thaw fish, if frozen. Rinse fish; pat dry with paper towels. If using low-heat setting, turn to high-heat setting. Stir corn mixture in slow cooker. Place fish on top of mixture in slow cooker. Cover and cook for 1 hour more. Stir in undrained tomatoes.

Per serving: 293 cal., 8 g total fat (3 g sat. fat), 39 mg chol., 1,296 mg sodium, 36 g carbo., 2 g fiber, 21 g pro.

Seasoned tomatoes and marinara sauce flavor the cheese tortellini. Ground sausage-style meat substitute boosts the protein.

CHEESY TORTELLINI CASSEROLE

Nonstick cooking spray

2   15-ounce containers refrigerated marinara sauce

2   14½-ounce cans diced tomatoes with basil, oregano, and garlic, undrained

1   12-ounce package frozen cooked and crumbled ground sausage-style meat substitute (soy protein)

1   9-ounce package refrigerated cheese-filled tortellini

1   cup shredded mozzarella cheese (4 ounces)

1 Lightly coat a 3½- or 4-quart slow cooker with nonstick cooking spray. In the prepared cooker stir together marinara sauce, undrained tomatoes, and ground meat substitute.

2 Cover and cook on low-heat setting for 7 to 8 hours or on high-heat setting for 3½ to 4 hours.

3 If using high-heat setting, turn to low-heat setting. Stir in tortellini. Cover and cook for 15 to 20 minutes more or until tortellini are tender.

4 Remove liner from slow cooker, if possible, or turn off slow cooker. Sprinkle mixture in slow cooker with mozzarella cheese. Cover and let stand about 10 minutes or until cheese is melted.

Per serving: 298 cal., 10 g total fat (3 g sat. fat), 23 mg chol., 1,377 mg sodium, 34 g carbo., 2 g fiber, 21 g pro.

PREP:
5 minutes

COOK:
Low 7 hours, High 3½ hours; plus 15 minutes on Low

STAND:
10 minutes

MAKES:
8 servings

SLOW COOKER:
3½- or 4-quart

Looking for something to eat when comfort food sounds too heavy and soup sounds too light? This soup, with its substantial pasta and creamy sauce, is an attractive in–between solution.

TORTELLINI ALFREDO SOUP

PREP:
15 minutes

COOK:
Low 5 hours, High 2½ hours; plus 1 hour on High

MAKES:
4 servings

SLOW COOKER:
3½- or 4-quart

1   28-ounce jar or two 16-ounce jars Alfredo pasta sauce

2   14-ounce cans vegetable broth

1   medium onion, chopped

1   2-ounce jar sliced pimientos, drained and chopped

1   6- to 8-ounce package dried cheese-filled tortellini

1 In a 3½- or 4-quart slow cooker combine pasta sauce, broth, onion, and pimientos.

2 Cover and cook on low-heat setting for 5 to 6 hours or on high-heat setting for 2½ to 3 hours.

3 If using low-heat setting, turn to high-heat setting. Stir in tortellini. Cover and cook for 1 hour more.

Per serving: 544 cal., 34 g total fat (16 g sat. fat), 114 mg chol., 2,247 mg sodium, 47 g carbo., 2 g fiber, 14 g pro.

Here's a meatless dish you can really sink your teeth into. The eggplant sauce is rich in tomato, onions, and olives. Whole wheat pasta adds variety and the goodness of whole grains.

EGGPLANT SAUCE WITH PASTA

Nonstick cooking spray

1 medium eggplant, cut into 1-inch pieces (5½ cups)

1 large onion, cut into thin wedges

1 2¼-ounce can sliced pitted ripe olives, drained

1 28-ounce jar roasted garlic pasta sauce

12 ounces dried whole wheat penne or rotini pasta

Shredded Parmesan cheese (optional)

1 Coat a 3½- or 4-quart slow cooker with nonstick cooking spray. In the prepared cooker combine eggplant, onion, and olives. Stir in pasta sauce.

2 Cover and cook on low-heat setting for 3 to 4 hours.

3 Cook pasta according to package directions; drain. Serve sauce over hot cooked pasta. If desired, sprinkle with Parmesan cheese.

Per serving: 316 cal., 4 g total fat (0 g sat. fat), 0 mg chol., 512 mg sodium, 60 g carbo., 8 g fiber, 10 g pro.

PREP:
15 minutes

COOK:
Low 3 hours

MAKES:
6 servings

SLOW COOKER:
3½- or 4-quart

Chowder applies to any thick, chunky soup—and this one certainly meets those standards. The vegetables and chicken with rice soup complement the Italian-seasoned tomatoes.

CHEESY CHICKEN-RICE CHOWDER

PREP:
10 minutes

COOK:
Low 5 hours, High 2½ hours

MAKES:
5 or 6 servings

SLOW COOKER:
3½- or 4-quart

1 26-ounce can condensed chicken with rice soup

2 cups water

2 cups loose-pack frozen peas and carrots

1 14½-ounce can diced tomatoes with Italian herbs, undrained

4 ounces American cheese, shredded (1 cup)

½ cup half-and-half, light cream, or milk

1 In a 3½- or 4-quart slow cooker combine chicken with rice soup, the water, frozen peas and carrots, and undrained tomatoes.

2 Cover and cook on low-heat setting for 5 to 6 hours or on high-heat setting for 2½ to 3 hours. Stir in cheese until melted. Stir in half-and-half.

Per serving: 250 cal., 12 g total fat (7 g sat. fat), 39 mg chol., 1,577 mg sodium, 23 g carbo., 3 g fiber, 13 g pro.

This recipe is a hodgepodge of flavor and texture: savory-sweet with zing from the jalapeño peppers and crunch from the almonds.

CURRIED COUSCOUS WITH VEGETABLES

1	large onion, cut into thin wedges
2	cups coarsely chopped yellow summer squash and/or zucchini
2	14½-ounce cans diced tomatoes with jalapeño chile peppers, undrained
2	cups water
2	5.7-ounce packages curry-flavored couscous mix
1	cup chopped slivered almonds, toasted
½	cup raisins (optional)

PREP:
15 minutes

COOK:
Low 4 hours, High 2 hours

STAND:
5 minutes

MAKES:
8 servings

SLOW COOKER:
3½- or 4-quart

1 In a 3½- or 4-quart slow cooker combine onion, summer squash and/or zucchini, undrained tomatoes, the water, and seasoning packets from couscous mixes.

2 Cover and cook on low-heat setting for 4 to 6 hours or on high-heat setting for 2 to 3 hours.

3 Stir in couscous. Remove liner from slow cooker, if possible, or turn off slow cooker. Cover and let stand for 5 minutes. Fluff couscous mixture with a fork. Sprinkle individual servings with almonds and, if desired, raisins.

Per serving: 280 cal., 9 g total fat (1 g sat. fat), 0 mg chol., 842 mg sodium, 43 g carbo., 6 g fiber, 10 g pro.

Curly rotini and chunky green or yellow beans crowd into this red brothy soup. Top each bowl with Parmesan cheese for a creamy-sharp tang. Hunks of chunky bread taste great dunked in the broth.

VEGETABLE MINESTRONE

PREP:
10 minutes

COOK:
Low 6 hours, High 3 hours; plus 15 minutes on High

MAKES:
4 to 6 servings

SLOW COOKER:
3½- to 5-quart

2   9-ounce packages frozen cut green and/or yellow wax beans

2   teaspoons spicy pizza seasoning

2   14-ounce cans vegetable broth (3½ cups)

3   cups vegetable juice

1½   cups dried rotini pasta

     Grated Parmesan cheese (optional)

1 Place frozen beans in a 3½- to 5-quart slow cooker. Sprinkle with pizza seasoning. Pour broth and vegetable juice over all.

2 Cover and cook on low-heat setting for 6 to 7 hours or on high-heat setting for 3 to 3½ hours.

3 If using low-heat setting, turn to high-heat setting. Stir in uncooked pasta. Cover and cook for 15 to 20 minutes more or until pasta is tender. If desired, sprinkle individual servings with Parmesan cheese.

Per serving: 201 cal., 2 g total fat (0 g sat. fat), 0 mg chol., 1,414 mg sodium, 42 g carbo., 6 g fiber, 9 g pro.

Traditional Greek seasonings—onion, garlic, oregano, and mint—impart a zesty, fresh flavor that is pleasing with lentils. Toasted pita wedges, sliced green onion, chopped tomato, and sour cream are great serve-alongs.

GREEK-SEASONED LENTILS

2 cups dry brown lentils

Nonstick cooking spray

3 14-ounce cans vegetable broth

4 medium carrots, shredded

1 large onion, chopped

2 teaspoons Greek seasoning

PREP:
25 minutes

COOK:
Low 6 hours, High 3 hours

MAKES:
6 to 8 servings

SLOW COOKER:
3½- to 5-quart

1 Rinse lentils; drain well. Lightly coat a 3½- to 5-quart slow cooker with nonstick cooking spray. In the prepared slow cooker combine lentils, vegetable broth, carrots, onion, and Greek seasoning.

2 Cover and cook on low-heat setting for 6 to 7 hours or on high-heat setting for 3 to 3½ hours. Serve lentils using a slotted spoon.

Per serving: 260 cal., 2 g total fat (0 g sat. fat), 0 mg chol., 874 mg sodium, 45 g carbo., 21 g fiber, 20 g pro.

Spunky Cajun seasoning, velvety black beans, and colorful vegetables keep this lively, loaded gumbo interesting. There's plenty of saucy liquid to ladle over the rice.

CAJUN-SEASONED VEGETARIAN GUMBO

PREP:
10 minutes

COOK:
Low 6 hours, High 3 hours

MAKES:
6 servings

SLOW COOKER:
3¹/₂- to 4¹/₂-quart

2   15-ounce cans black beans, rinsed and drained

1   28-ounce can diced tomatoes, undrained

1   16-ounce package frozen (yellow, green, and red) peppers and onion stir-fry vegetables

2   cups loose-pack frozen cut okra

2   to 3 teaspoons Cajun seasoning

Hot cooked white or brown rice (optional)

1 In a 3¹/₂- to 4¹/₂-quart slow cooker combine beans, undrained tomatoes, frozen stir-fry vegetables, frozen okra, and Cajun seasoning.

2 Cover and cook on low-heat setting for 6 to 8 hours or on high-heat setting for 3 to 4 hours. If desired, serve over hot cooked rice.

Per serving: 153 cal., 0 g total fat (0 g sat. fat), 0 mg chol., 639 mg sodium, 31 g carbo., 10 g fiber, 12 g pro.

SIDE DISHES

8

Pineapple affords these lively baked beans a hint of sweetness.

HAWAIIAN PINEAPPLE BAKED BEANS

PREP:
15 minutes

COOK:
Low 7 hours, High 3½ hours

MAKES:
16 servings

SLOW COOKER:
5- to 6-quart

8   ounces ground beef

1   cup chopped onion

2   15- or 16-ounce cans pork and beans in tomato sauce

2   15-ounce cans chili beans with chili gravy

1   20-ounce can pineapple tidbits (juice pack), drained

1   cup ketchup

1   cup bottled hot-style barbecue sauce

1 In a large skillet cook ground beef and onion until meat is brown and onion is tender; drain off fat. In a 5- to 6-quart slow cooker combine ground beef mixture, pork and beans, chili beans, drained pineapple, ketchup, and barbecue sauce.

2 Cover and cook on low-heat setting for 7 to 9 hours or on high-heat setting for 3½ to 4½ hours or until heated through.

Per serving: 189 cal., 3 g total fat (1 g sat. fat), 13 mg chol., 762 mg sodium, 35 g carbo., 6 g fiber, 9 g pro.

FOR A 3½- OR 4-QUART SLOW COOKER:
Use 6 ounces ground beef, ½ cup onion, 1 can pork and beans in tomato sauce, 1 can chili beans with chili gravy, 1 cup drained pineapple tidbits, ½ cup ketchup, and ½ cup barbecue sauce. Makes 8 servings.

Per serving: 193 cal., 3 g total fat (1 g sat. fat), 17 mg chol., 810 mg sodium, 34 g carbo., 6 g fiber, 10 g pro.

Need a dish to tote to a potluck, picnic, or family reunion? These molasses-flavored beans will be a crowd-pleaser.

BEANS WITH GINGER SAUCE

2	31-ounce cans pork and beans with tomato sauce
¾	cup finely crushed gingersnaps (10 cookies)
½	cup ketchup
¼	cup molasses
1	tablespoon dried minced onion

1 In a 3½- to 5-quart slow cooker stir together pork and beans, gingersnaps, ketchup, molasses, and dried minced onion.

2 Cover and cook on low-heat setting for 5 to 6 hours or on high-heat setting for 2½ to 3 hours.

Per serving: 198 cal., 2 g total fat (1 g sat. fat), 10 mg chol., 796 mg sodium, 41 g carbo., 7 g fiber, 8 g pro.

PREP:
15 minutes

COOK:
Low 5 hours, High 2½ hours

MAKES:
12 servings

SLOW COOKER:
3½- to 5-quart

An intriguing variation of classic baked beans, this version gets a hint of saucy sweetness from apricot preserves. Show it off at your next picnic; it's great with grilled chicken or burgers.

APRICOT-BACON BEANS

PREP:
15 minutes

COOK:
Low 8 hours, High 4 hours

MAKES:
12 to 16 servings

SLOW COOKER:
3½- or 4-quart

2   28-ounce cans beans with brown sugar
    or baked beans or four 15- to 16-ounce cans
    Great Northern, lima, and/or pinto beans

8   slices peppered bacon, crisp-cooked, drained,
    and crumbled

1   10- to 12-ounce jar apricot preserves

2   stalks celery, chopped

½   cup packed brown sugar

1 If using beans with brown sugar or baked beans, do not rinse or drain. If using Great Northern, lima, or pinto beans, rinse and drain beans.

2 In a 3½- or 4-quart slow cooker combine beans, bacon, apricot preserves, celery, and brown sugar.

3 Cover and cook on low-heat setting for 8 to 10 hours or on high-heat setting for 4 to 5 hours.

Per serving: 343 cal., 9 g total fat (4 g sat. fat), 19 mg chol., 631 mg sodium, 53 g carbo., 7 g fiber, 9 g pro.

Curry powder and apples give ordinary baked beans a deliciously unexpected flavor twist.

CURRIED BEANS & APPLES

2 31-ounce cans pork and beans in tomato sauce

2 medium cooking apples
   (such as Granny Smith or Rome Beauty), peeled,
   cored, and cut into bite-size pieces

½ cup bottled chili sauce

¼ cup packed brown sugar or mild-flavored molasses

1 tablespoon curry powder

¼ cup sliced green onions
   Crumbled, crisp-cooked bacon (optional)

1 If you prefer a less saucy bean mixture, drain one of the cans of pork and beans. In a 3½- or 4-quart slow cooker combine pork and beans, apples, chili sauce, brown sugar or molasses, and curry powder.

2 Cover and cook on low-heat setting for 5 to 6 hours or on high-heat setting for 2½ to 3 hours. Before serving, stir in green onions and, if desired, sprinkle with crumbled bacon.

Per serving: 184 cal., 2 g total fat (1 g sat. fat), 10 mg chol., 781 mg sodium, 39 g carbo., 8 g fiber, 8 g pro.

PREP:
15 minutes

COOK:
Low 5 hours, High 2½ hours

MAKES:
12 servings

SLOW COOKER:
3½- or 4-quart

The traditional mix of corn and lima beans joins onions in this full-bodied side dish.

CHEESY SUCCOTASH

PREP:
15 minutes

COOK:
Low 7 hours, High 3½ hours

MAKES:
12 servings

SLOW COOKER:
4- or 4½-quart

2   16-ounce packages frozen whole kernel corn

1   16-ounce package frozen lima beans

1   cup loose-pack frozen small whole onions

1   10¾-ounce can condensed cream of celery soup

1   8-ounce tub cream cheese with chive and onion

¼   cup water

1 In a 4- or 4½-quart slow cooker combine frozen corn, frozen lima beans, and frozen onions. In a medium bowl stir together cream of celery soup, cream cheese, and the water. Stir soup mixture into vegetables in slow cooker.

2 Cover and cook on low-heat setting for 7 to 8 hours or on high-heat setting for 3½ to 4 hours. Stir before serving.

Per serving: 211 cal., 8 g total fat (5 g sat. fat), 19 mg chol., 296 mg sodium, 29 g carbo., 4 g fiber, 6 g pro.

Tender potatoes and crisp green beans achieve elegance in a mustard-dill sauce that's just right for Sunday dinner's roast, chicken, or salmon. No one needs to know how simple it is to make.

SAUCY GREEN BEANS & POTATOES

2   pounds tiny new potatoes

1   pound fresh green beans, trimmed and halved crosswise

1   10¾-ounce can condensed cream of celery soup

¾   cup water

¼   cup Dijon-style mustard

¾   teaspoon dried dill

1 In a 3½- or 4-quart slow cooker combine potatoes and green beans. In a medium bowl stir together cream of celery soup, the water, mustard, and dill. Pour over vegetables in slow cooker; stir gently to combine.

2 Cover and cook on low-heat setting for 6 to 8 hours or on high-heat setting for 3 to 4 hours. Stir gently before serving.

Per serving: 95 cal., 2 g total fat (1 g sat. fat), 1 mg chol., 313 mg sodium, 17 g carbo., 3 g fiber, 3 g pro.

PREP:
20 minutes

COOK:
Low 6 hours, High 3 hours

MAKES:
12 servings

SLOW COOKER:
3½- or 4-quart

This cheesy bean combo is ideal for family gatherings or potluck dinners. To transport the beans, wrap the slow cooker in a thick towel. Once you arrive, remove the towel, plug in the slow cooker, and keep the beans warm on the low-heat setting. Be sure to serve them within two hours.

SMOKY GREEN BEAN CASSEROLE

PREP:
20 minutes

COOK:
Low 3½ hours, High 2 hours

MAKES:
12 servings

SLOW COOKER:
4- to 5-quart

4	14½-ounce cans cut green beans, drained
1	cup bottled roasted red sweet peppers, drained and cut into strips
1	8-ounce can sliced water chestnuts, drained
1	10¾-ounce can condensed cream of mushroom soup
1	cup shredded smoked Gouda or cheddar cheese (4 ounces)
¼	cup milk
2	tablespoons coarse-grain mustard
1⅓	cups canned cheddar-flavored French-fried onions or plain French-fried onions

1 In a large bowl stir together green beans, sweet pepper strips, and water chestnuts; set aside. In a medium bowl stir together cream of mushroom soup, cheese, milk, and mustard; add to bean mixture and toss to coat. Spoon half of the bean mixture into a 4- to 5-quart slow cooker. Top with half of the onions. Repeat layers.

2 Cover and cook on low-heat setting for 3½ to 4½ hours or on high-heat setting for 2 to 2½ hours.

Per serving: 139 cal., 8 g total fat (2 g sat. fat), 9 mg chol., 622 mg sodium, 15 g carbo., 2 g fiber, 4 g pro.

Here's a luscious way to celebrate the beet harvest from your garden or farmer's market. The cran-apple drink is an unexpectedly good pairing with sweet beets and apple pie spice .

CRANBERRY-APPLE SPICED BEETS

3	pounds medium beets, peeled and quartered
½	teaspoon apple pie spice
1	tablespoon quick-cooking tapioca
1	cup cranberry-apple drink
2	tablespoons butter or margarine (optional)

1 Place beets in a 3½- or 4-quart slow cooker. Sprinkle with apple pie spice and tapioca; pour cranberry-apple drink over all. If desired, dot with butter.

2 Cover and cook on low-heat setting for 6 to 7 hours or on high-heat setting for 3 to 3½ hours. To serve, remove beets from slow cooker; spoon some of the sauce over beets.

Per serving: 75 cal., 0 g total fat (0 g sat. fat), 0 mg chol., 85 mg sodium, 17 g carbo., 3 g fiber, 2 g pro.

PREP:
25 minutes

COOK:
Low 6 hours, High 3 hours

MAKES:
8 to 10 servings

SLOW COOKER:
3½- or 4-quart

Caraway and cabbage are a classic flavor combo. Pair them in your slow cooker for a side dish that complements roasted beef, pork, lamb, or chicken.

CARAWAY CABBAGE IN CREAM

PREP:
10 minutes

COOK:
Low 6 hours, High 3 hours

MAKES:
8 servings

SLOW COOKER:
4- to 5-quart

1	cup chicken broth
2	tablespoons quick-cooking tapioca
2	teaspoons caraway seeds, crushed
½	teaspoon salt
¼	teaspoon black pepper
1	large head red cabbage (about 2 pounds), coarsely chopped (12 cups)
½	cup half-and-half or light cream
2	tablespoons prepared horseradish

1 In a small bowl combine broth, tapioca, caraway seeds, salt, and pepper. Pour broth mixture into a 4- to 5-quart slow cooker. Add cabbage. Toss to coat.

2 Cover and cook on low-heat setting for 6 hours or on high-heat setting for 3 hours. Add half-and-half and horseradish to cabbage mixture in slow cooker; stir until coated.

Per serving: 68 cal., 2 g total fat (1 g sat. fat), 6 mg chol., 312 mg sodium, 12 g carbo., 3 g fiber, 2 g pro.

Carrots and onions are irresistible when sauced with a combo of apple jelly and dill.

SWEET BABY CARROTS

2   16-ounce packages peeled baby carrots

1   pound boiling onions (about 16), peeled, or one
    16-ounce package frozen small whole onions

½   teaspoon dried dill

¾   cup water

1   cup apple jelly

1 In a 4½- to 5½-quart slow cooker combine carrots and onions. Sprinkle with dill. Pour the water over all.

2 Cover and cook on low-heat setting for 6 to 7 hours or on high-heat setting for 3 to 3½ hours.

3 Using a slotted spoon, remove carrots and onion from slow cooker. For sauce, gently stir apple jelly into mixture in slow cooker; let stand for 2 to 3 minutes or until jelly is melted. Stir mixture. Return carrots and onions to slow cooker. Stir gently to coat vegetables. Serve with a slotted spoon.

Per serving: 178 cal., 0 g total fat (0 g sat. fat), 0 mg chol., 53 mg sodium, 43 g carbo., 5 g fiber, 2 g pro.

PREP:
10 minutes

COOK:
Low 6 hours, High 3 hours

STAND:
2 minutes

MAKES:
8 to 10 servings

SLOW COOKER:
4½- to 5½-quart

For an extra spicy kick, use Monterey Jack cheese with jalapeño peppers.

SPICY CREAMED CORN

PREP:
15 minutes

COOK:
Low 5 hours, High 2½ hours

STAND:
10 minutes

MAKES:
12 servings

SLOW COOKER:
3½- or 4-quart

2   16-ounce packages frozen white whole kernel corn (shoe peg), thawed

1   14¾-ounce can cream-style corn

2   cups shredded Monterey Jack cheese (8 ounces)

1   cup chopped tomato

⅓   cup chopped onion

1   4½-ounce can diced green chile peppers, undrained

1½ teaspoons chili powder

½   teaspoon salt

1   16-ounce container dairy sour cream

2   tablespoons snipped fresh cilantro

1 In a 3½- or 4-quart slow cooker combine thawed whole kernel corn, cream-style corn, shredded cheese, tomato, onion, undrained chile peppers, chili powder, and salt.

2 Cover and cook on low-heat setting for 5 to 6 hours or on high-heat setting for 2½ to 3 hours.

3 Gently stir in sour cream and cilantro. Let stand for 10 minutes.

Per serving: 250 cal., 15 g total fat (9 g sat. fat), 33 mg chol., 350 mg sodium, 25 g carbo., 2 g fiber, 9 g pro.

Ratatouille (ra-tuh-TOO-ee) is a favorite dish from the French region of Provence. Eggplant, tomatoes, onions, herbs, and garlic are typically simmered together to create a delicious medley. It's great as a side dish or as an appetizer topper for bread or crackers.

RATATOUILLE

1½	cups chopped onions
1	6-ounce can tomato paste
1	tablespoon olive oil or cooking oil
1	tablespoon sugar
2	cloves garlic, minced
1½	teaspoons dried basil, crushed, or 1 tablespoon snipped fresh basil
1	teaspoon salt
1	teaspoon dried thyme, crushed
¼	teaspoon black pepper
4	medium tomatoes, peeled and coarsely chopped
2	medium zucchini, halved lengthwise and sliced
1	small eggplant, peeled and cubed (about 3 cups)
1	12-ounce loaf baguette-style French bread, cut into ½-inch-thick slices and toasted

1 In a 3½- or 4-quart slow cooker combine onions, tomato paste, olive oil, sugar, garlic, dried basil (if using), salt, thyme, and pepper. Add tomatoes, zucchini, and eggplant.

2 Cover and cook on low-heat setting for 7 to 8 hours or on high-heat setting for 3½ to 4 hours. Stir in fresh basil (if using). Stir before serving. Serve hot, cold, or at room temperature with bread slices.

Per serving: 198 cal., 3 g total fat (1 g sat. fat), 0 mg chol., 727 mg sodium, 37 g carbo., 5 g fiber, 7 g pro.

PREP:
20 minutes

COOK:
Low 7 hours, High 3½ hours

MAKES:
8 servings

SLOW COOKER:
3½- or 4-quart

Greens for dinner may seem old-fashioned, but this version gets a bold flavor update from a zesty blend of molasses, balsamic vinegar, and hot pepper sauce.

SPICY SUNDAY DINNER GREENS

PREP:
30 minutes

COOK:
Low 7 hours

MAKES:
8 to 10 servings

SLOW COOKER:
5- to 6-quart

2	pounds fresh collard greens, trimmed and coarsely torn
3½	cups water
1	large onion, chopped
3	slices bacon or turkey bacon, coarsely chopped
¼	cup mild-flavored molasses
2	tablespoons balsamic vinegar
4	cloves garlic, minced
1	teaspoon bottled hot pepper sauce
1	teaspoon celery salt
½	teaspoon salt
¼	teaspoon black pepper

1 In a 5- to 6-quart slow cooker combine collard greens, the water, onion, bacon, molasses, balsamic vinegar, garlic, hot pepper sauce, celery salt, salt, and black pepper (cooker will be full). Cover and cook on low-heat setting for 7 to 8 hours, stirring once after 4 hours of cooking.

2 Using a slotted spoon, transfer greens to a serving dish, reserving cooking juices. If desired, pass cooking juices to spoon over individual servings.

Per serving: 83 cal., 2 g total fat (1 g sat. fat), 3 mg chol., 413 mg sodium, 15 g carbo., 3 g fiber, 3 g pro.

This decadent dish is a luscious celebration of flavor—mashed potatoes, cream cheese, sour cream, and garlic.

SUPER CREAMY MASHED POTATOES

Nonstick cooking spray

3 20-ounce packages refrigerated mashed potatoes or 8 cups leftover mashed potatoes

1 8-ounce package cream cheese, cut up

1 8-ounce container dairy sour cream onion or chive dip

¼ teaspoon garlic powder

1 Coat a 4- or 4½-quart slow cooker with nonstick cooking spray. Place two-thirds (2 packages) of the potatoes in slow cooker. Top with cream cheese and sour cream dip. Sprinkle with garlic powder. Top with remaining package of the mashed potatoes.

2 Cover and cook on low-heat setting for 3½ to 4 hours. Stir before serving.

Per serving: 214 cal., 11 g total fat (6 g sat. fat), 21 mg chol., 409 mg sodium, 22 g carbo., 1 g fiber, 5 g pro.

PREP:
10 minutes

COOK:
Low 3½ hours

MAKES:
12 to 14 servings

SLOW COOKER:
4- or 4½-quart

Looking for please-all, post-game party fare? Try these creamy, extra-thick, slow-cooked new potatoes.

CREAMY POTATO WEDGES

PREP:
10 minutes

COOK:
Low 3½ hours, High 1¾ hours

MAKES:
8 servings

SLOW COOKER:
3½- or 4-quart

2 8-ounce containers dairy sour cream chive dip

1 cup finely shredded Asiago cheese (4 ounces)

1 3-ounce package cream cheese, cut up

½ cup mayonnaise or salad dressing

2 20-ounce packages refrigerated new potato wedges

1 In a 3½- or 4-quart slow cooker combine sour cream dip, Asiago cheese, cream cheese, and mayonnaise. Stir in potatoes.

2 Cover and cook on low-heat setting for 3½ to 4½ hours or on high-heat setting for 1¾ to 2¼ hours. Stir gently before serving.

Per serving: 415 cal., 31 g total fat (14 g sat. fat), 55 mg chol., 835 mg sodium, 23 g carbo., 4 g fiber, 10 g pro.

These creamy potatoes are a delicious partner for roast beef, pork, or chicken.

LEMON PESTO NEW POTATOES

3   pounds tiny new potatoes, halved or quartered

1   16-ounce jar Alfredo pasta sauce

⅓   cup purchased basil pesto

1   tablespoon finely shredded lemon peel

¼   to ½ teaspoon coarsely ground black pepper

    Finely shredded Parmesan cheese

1 Place potatoes in a 4- to 5-quart slow cooker. Stir in the Alfredo sauce, pesto, lemon peel, and pepper. Toss to coat.

2 Cover and cook on low-heat setting for 5 to 6 hours.

3 Using a slotted spoon, transfer potatoes from slow cooker to serving dish. Whisk mixture in slow cooker and pour over potatoes. Sprinkle with Parmesan cheese.

Per serving: 252 cal., 14 g total fat (4 g sat. fat), 29 mg chol., 431 mg sodium, 26 g carbo., 2 g fiber, 7 g pro.

PREP:
15 minutes

COOK:
Low 5 hours

MAKES:
10 to 12 servings

SLOW COOKER:
4- to 5-quart

Creamy, thick, and rich, this is the kind of asparagus dish you expect to find at an elegant brunch. Serve it with hot scrambled eggs and sliced fresh fruit.

SWISS POTATOES & ASPARAGUS

PREP:
15 minutes

COOK:
Low 5 hours plus 15 minutes

MAKES:
10 to 12 servings

SLOW COOKER:
3½- or 4-quart

Nonstick cooking spray

1 10¾-ounce can condensed cream of asparagus soup

8 ounces process Swiss cheese, cut into ½-inch pieces

1 8-ounce carton dairy sour cream

1 32-ounce package loose-pack frozen diced hash brown potatoes, thawed

1 10-ounce package frozen cut asparagus, thawed

1 Lightly coat a 3½- or 4-quart slow cooker with nonstick cooking spray. In the slow cooker stir together cream of asparagus soup, Swiss cheese, and sour cream. Stir in thawed potatoes.

2 Cover and cook on low-heat setting for 5 to 6 hours. Stir in thawed asparagus. Cover; cook for 15 to 25 minutes more or until heated through.

Per serving: 237 cal., 12 g total fat (7 g sat. fat), 32 mg chol., 311 mg sodium, 22 g carbo., 2 g fiber, 11 g pro.

Crisp greens provide a pleasing contrast to tangy sweet-sour potatoes laced with bacon.

HOT ITALIAN-STYLE POTATO SALAD

1	28-ounce package loose-pack frozen diced hash brown potatoes with onions and peppers
½	cup water
½	cup bottled balsamic vinaigrette salad dressing
¼	teaspoon crushed red pepper
4	slices bacon, crisp-cooked and crumbled
8	cups torn mixed salad greens
¼	cup sliced green onions
	Shaved Parmesan cheese

1 Place frozen potatoes in a 3½- to 5-quart slow cooker. Stir in the water, salad dressing, and crushed red pepper. Cover and cook on low-heat setting for 8 to 10 hours or on high-heat setting for 4 to 5 hours. Gently stir in bacon.

2 Serve warm potato mixture over greens. Top individual servings with green onions and Parmesan cheese.

Per serving: 160 cal., 8 g total fat (2 g sat. fat), 7 mg chol., 345 mg sodium, 19 g carbo., 3 g fiber, 5 g pro.

PREP:
10 minutes

COOK:
Low 8 hours, High 4 hours

MAKES:
8 servings

SLOW COOKER:
3½- to 5-quart

Take a break from the usual candied sweet potatoes—serve these golden slices instead.

ORANGE-SAGE SWEET POTATOES

PREP:
15 minutes

COOK:
Low 5 hours, High 2½ hours

MAKES:
10 to 12 servings

SLOW COOKER:
5- to 6-quart

4   pounds sweet potatoes, peeled and cut into ¼-inch-thick slices (about 10 cups)

½   cup frozen orange juice concentrate, thawed

3   tablespoons packed brown sugar

1½ teaspoons salt

½   teaspoon dried leaf sage, crushed

½   teaspoon dried thyme, crushed

2   tablespoons butter or margarine, cut up

4   slices bacon, crisp-cooked and crumbled

1 Place sweet potato slices in a 5- to 6-quart slow cooker. In a small bowl stir together thawed orange juice concentrate, brown sugar, salt, sage, and thyme. Pour over sweet potato slices; toss to coat. Dot with butter.

2 Cover and cook on low-heat setting for 5 to 6 hours or on high-heat setting for 2½ to 3 hours. Before serving, stir to coat with orange juice mixture and sprinkle with crumbled bacon.

Per serving: 189 cal., 4 g total fat (2 g sat. fat), 10 mg chol., 509 mg sodium, 36 g carbo., 4 g fiber, 4 g pro.

Dried cherries, apple, ginger, maple syrup, and spices dress up sweet potatoes in this seasonal delight.

MAPLE HARVEST SWEET POTATOES

2	pounds sweet potatoes, peeled and cut into bite-size pieces (about 6 cups)
1	medium tart cooking apple, peeled and chopped (about 1 cup)
¼	cup dried cherries or dried cranberries
¼	cup packed brown sugar
1½	teaspoons finely shredded fresh ginger
½	teaspoon salt
½	teaspoon ground cinnamon
¼	teaspoon ground nutmeg
⅛	teaspoon black pepper
½	cup water
½	cup pure maple syrup or maple-flavored syrup
¼	cup whipping cream

PREP:
25 minutes

COOK:
Low 7 hours, High 3½ hours

MAKES:
8 servings

SLOW COOKER:
3½- or 4-quart

1 In a 3½- or 4-quart slow cooker combine sweet potatoes, apple, dried cherries or cranberries, brown sugar, ginger, salt, cinnamon, nutmeg, and pepper. Pour the water and syrup over sweet potato mixture.

2 Cover and cook on low-heat setting for 7 to 8 hours or on high-heat setting for 3½ to 4 hours. Turn off heat and gently stir in whipping cream. Use a slotted spoon to serve.

Per serving: 236 cal., 3 g total fat (2 g sat. fat), 10 mg chol., 167 mg sodium, 51 g carbo., 4 g fiber, 2 g pro.

Tender cubed squash with onion and thyme immersed in a cherry sauce renders a sweet and savory surprise. Try it with grilled or roasted meats, or as part of a holiday buffet.

WINTER SQUASH IN CHERRY SAUCE

PREP:
20 minutes

COOK:
Low 8 hours, High 4 hours

MAKES:
6 to 8 servings

SLOW COOKER:
3½- or 4-quart

1   21-ounce can cherry pie filling

2   pounds butternut or other winter squash, peeled, seeded, and cut into ¾-inch pieces (about 4½ cups)

1   medium onion, cut into wedges

½   teaspoon dried thyme, crushed

½   cup chopped pecans, toasted

1 In a 3½- or 4-quart slow cooker combine pie filling, squash, onion, and thyme.

2 Cover and cook on low-heat setting for 8 to 9 hours or on high-heat setting for 4 to 4½ hours. Cool slightly before serving. Sprinkle individual servings with pecans.

Per serving: 223 cal., 7 g total fat (1 g sat. fat), 0 mg chol., 23 mg sodium, 40 g carbo., 3 g fiber, 3 g pro.

Onions plus two other root veggies—turnips and parsnips—team up for a warming side dish.

TURNIPS & PARSNIPS

2   pounds turnips, peeled and cut into 1-inch pieces

2   medium parsnips, peeled and cut into 1-inch pieces

2   medium onions, cut into thin wedges

1   10¾-ounce can condensed cream of celery soup

2   tablespoons water

1   teaspoon dried thyme, crushed

¼   teaspoon garlic salt

⅛   teaspoon black pepper

1 In a 3½- or 4-quart slow cooker combine turnips, parsnips, and onions. Add cream of celery soup, the water, thyme, garlic salt, and pepper; stir to coat.

2 Cover and cook on low-heat setting for 6 to 7 hours or on high-heat setting for 3 to 3½ hours.

Per serving: 98 cal., 2 g total fat (0 g sat. fat), 2 mg chol., 370 mg sodium, 18 g carbo., 4 g fiber, 2 g pro.

PREP:
30 minutes

COOK:
Low 6 hours, High 3 hours

MAKES:
8 to 10 servings

SLOW COOKER:
3½- or 4-quart

A jar of brown gravy makes these cream-of-the-crop sherried vegetables super simple to assemble.

VEGETABLES IN SHERRY SAUCE

PREP:
20 minutes

COOK:
Low 2 hours

MAKES:
10 servings

SLOW COOKER:
3½- or 4-quart

4   cups fresh button, cremini, or baby portobello mushrooms (about 14 ounces)

20   to 24 white and/or red pearl onions (about 10 ounces)

1   large red sweet pepper, cut into 1-inch pieces (about 1½ cups)

1   12-ounce jar brown gravy

⅓   cup dry sherry

2   teaspoons Dijon-style mustard

1   teaspoon dried thyme, crushed

¼   teaspoon black pepper

1 Halve any large mushrooms. In a 3½- or 4-quart slow cooker combine mushrooms, pearl onions, and sweet pepper pieces. In a medium bowl combine gravy, dry sherry, mustard, thyme, and black pepper. Pour over vegetables.

2 Cover and cook on low-heat setting for 2 to 3 hours.

Per serving: 53 cal., 1 g total fat (0 g sat. fat), 0 mg chol., 213 mg sodium, 7 g carbo., 1 g fiber, 2 g pro.

If you like, turn this creamy vegetable-and-rice side dish into a main dish by stirring in a cup of chopped cooked chicken or cubed ham.

CALIFORNIA VEGETABLE CASSEROLE

1   16-ounce package loose-pack frozen California-blend vegetables (cauliflower, broccoli, and carrots)

1   10¾-ounce can condensed cream of mushroom soup

1   cup instant white rice

1   cup milk

½   of a 15-ounce jar (about ¾ cup) cheese dip

1   small onion, chopped

¼   cup water

2   tablespoons butter or margarine, cut up

1 Place frozen vegetables in a 3½- or 4-quart slow cooker. In a medium bowl combine cream of mushroom soup, uncooked rice, milk, cheese dip, onion, the water, and butter. Pour soup mixture over the vegetables in slow cooker.

2 Cover and cook on low-heat setting for 4 to 5 hours or on high-heat setting for 2 to 2½ hours or until vegetables and rice are tender. Stir before serving.

Per serving: 209 cal., 12 g total fat (7 g sat. fat), 36 mg chol., 717 mg sodium, 21 g carbo., 2 g fiber, 6 g pro.

PREP:
15 minutes

COOK:
Low 4 hours, High 2 hours

MAKES:
8 servings

SLOW COOKER:
3½- or 4-quart

If a friend or family member is having a "turkey and all the trimmings" dinner and wisely asks your help in bringing the trimmings, take this out-of-the-ordinary dish!

WILD RICE WITH PECANS & CHERRIES

PREP:
20 minutes

COOK:
Low 5 hours

STAND:
10 minutes

MAKES:
15 servings

SLOW COOKER:
3½- or 4-quart

3   14-ounce cans chicken broth

2½   cups wild rice, rinsed and drained

2   medium carrots, coarsely shredded

1   4½-ounce jar (drained weight) sliced mushrooms, drained

2   tablespoons butter or margarine, melted

2   teaspoons dried marjoram, crushed

¼   teaspoon salt

¼   teaspoon black pepper

⅔   cup dried tart cherries

⅔   cup sliced green onions

½   cup coarsely chopped pecans, toasted

1 In a 3½- or 4-quart slow cooker combine broth, uncooked wild rice, carrots, drained mushrooms, melted butter, marjoram, salt, and pepper.

2 Cover and cook on low-heat setting for 5 to 6 hours. Remove liner from slow cooker, if possible, or turn off slow cooker. Stir in dried cherries and green onions. Cover and let stand for 10 minutes.

3 Just before serving, sprinkle with pecans. Serve with a slotted spoon.

Per serving: 169 cal., 5 g total fat (1 g sat. fat), 4 mg chol., 423 mg sodium, 27 g carbo., 3 g fiber, 5 g pro.

Winter squash and oranges boost the nutrients in this pilaf. It's a nice match for fish or chicken.

WILD RICE PILAF WITH SQUASH

2   large oranges

3   cups peeled, seeded butternut or other winter squash cut into bite-size pieces

2   4.1- to 4.5-ounce packages long grain and wild rice mix with herbs (not quick-cooking)

¼   cup packed brown sugar

2   14-ounce cans chicken broth

PREP:
20 minutes

COOK:
Low 4 hours, High 2 hours

MAKES:
8 to 10 servings

SLOW COOKER:
3½- or 4-quart

1 Finely shred the peel from one of the oranges. Measure 1 teaspoon finely shredded orange peel; set aside. Squeeze juice from both oranges. Measure ⅔ cup orange juice; set aside.

2 In a 3½- or 4-quart slow cooker combine squash pieces, rice mix and contents of both rice seasoning packets, and brown sugar. Add orange peel and orange juice. Pour broth over all. Stir to combine.

3 Cover and cook on low-heat setting for 4 to 5 hours or on high-heat setting for 2 to 3 hours. Stir gently before serving.

Per serving: 170 cal., 1 g total fat (0 g sat. fat), 0 mg chol., 931 mg sodium, 37 g carbo., 1 g fiber, 4 g pro.

This full-flavored dressing boasts a Southern flair. If you're serving a crowd at a big holiday feast, borrow another slow cooker so you also can offer Raisin-Herb Seasoned Dressing (see recipe, page 363).

SAUSAGE & CORN BREAD DRESSING

PREP:
20 minutes

COOK:
Low 4 hours

MAKES:
12 servings

SLOW COOKER:
3½- to 4½-quart

Nonstick cooking spray
1   pound bulk pork sausage
1   large onion, chopped
1   16-ounce package corn bread stuffing mix
3   cups chicken broth
½   cup butter or margarine, melted

1 Lightly coat a 3½- to 4½-quart slow cooker with nonstick cooking spray; set aside.

2 In a large skillet cook sausage and onion until meat is brown and onion is tender. Drain off fat.

3 In the prepared cooker combine sausage mixture, dry stuffing mix, broth, and butter. Toss gently to mix well.

4 Cover and cook on low-heat setting for 4 to 5 hours.

Per serving: 466 cal., 30 g total fat (13 g sat. fat), 57 mg chol., 1,214 mg sodium, 37 g carbo., 0 g fiber, 11 g pro.

When it's holiday time and your oven is full, put a slow cooker on dressing duty. This savory herb-onion version gets a sweet note from raisins.

RAISIN-HERB SEASONED DRESSING

Nonstick cooking spray

1   16-ounce package herb-seasoned stuffing mix

1   cup golden and/or dark raisins

1   medium onion, chopped

1½   cups water

1   10¾-ounce can condensed golden mushroom soup

1   8-ounce carton dairy sour cream

1 Lightly coat a 3½- or 4-quart slow cooker with nonstick cooking spray. In the prepared cooker combine dry stuffing mix, raisins, and onion. In a medium bowl combine the water, golden mushroom soup, and sour cream. Pour soup mixture over stuffing mixture in slow cooker; stir gently to combine.

2 Cover and cook on low-heat setting for 5 to 6 hours or on high-heat setting for 2½ to 3 hours.

Per serving: 377 cal., 9 g total fat (4 g sat. fat), 14 mg chol., 1,105 mg sodium, 65 g carbo., 6 g fiber, 9 g pro.

PREP:
20 minutes

COOK:
Low 5 hours, High 2½ hours

MAKES:
8 to 10 servings

SLOW COOKER:
3½- or 4-quart

Slices of this spunky steamed bread are the perfect serve-along for spaghetti and meatballs or lasagna.

PARMESAN CHEESE BREAD

PREP:
15 minutes

COOK:
High 1¾ hours

COOL:
10 minutes

MAKES:
12 servings

SLOW COOKER:
4- to 6-quart

1¾ cups packaged biscuit mix

¼ cup grated Parmesan cheese

1 teaspoon dried basil, crushed

2 slightly beaten eggs

⅓ cup milk

2 tablespoons snipped oil-packed sun-dried tomatoes, well drained

1 Well grease two 1-pint straight-sided, wide-mouth canning jars; flour the greased jars. Set aside.

2 In a medium bowl combine biscuit mix, Parmesan cheese, and basil. In a small bowl combine eggs and milk; add to flour mixture and stir just until moistened. Stir in tomatoes.

3 Divide mixture between prepared jars. Cover jars tightly with greased foil, greased side down. Place jars in a 4- to 6-quart slow cooker. Pour ½ cup warm water into slow cooker around jars.

4 Cover and cook on high-heat setting about 1¾ hours or until a wooden skewer inserted in center of each comes out clean. Remove jars from slow cooker. Cool for 10 minutes on a wire rack. Remove bread from jars. Cool completely before slicing.

Per serving: 96 cal., 4 g total fat (1 g sat. fat), 37 mg chol., 260 mg sodium, 12 g carbo., 0 g fiber, 3 g pro.

Try this fluffy corn side dish instead of dressing with chicken or turkey.

CORNY SPOON BREAD

Nonstick cooking spray

4 slightly beaten eggs

2 8½-ounce packages corn muffin mix

1 14¾-ounce can cream-style corn

¾ cup milk

1 medium red sweet pepper, seeded and chopped

1 4-ounce can diced green chile peppers, undrained

½ cup shredded Mexican cheese blend (2 ounces)

1 Lightly coat a 3½- or 4-quart slow cooker with nonstick cooking spray; set aside.

2 In a large bowl stir together eggs, corn muffin mix, cream-style corn, milk, sweet pepper, and undrained chile peppers. Spoon egg mixture into prepared slow cooker.

3 Cover and cook on low-heat setting about 4 hours or until a toothpick inserted near the center comes out clean. Remove liner from slow cooker, if possible, or turn off slow cooker. Sprinkle top of spoon bread with cheese. Cover and let stand for 30 to 45 minutes before serving.

Per serving: 360 cal., 12 g total fat (2 g sat. fat), 114 mg chol., 713 mg sodium, 54 g carbo., 1 g fiber, 11 g pro.

PREP:
15 minutes

COOK:
Low 4 hours

COOL:
30 minutes

MAKES:
8 to 10 servings

SLOW COOKER:
3½- or 4-quart

Bread in the slow cooker? You bet. Serve this sweet bread with soft-style cream cheese.

APPLE BREAD

PREP:
20 minutes

COOK:
High 1¾ hours

COOL:
10 minutes

MAKES:
2 loaves (6 servings per loaf)

SLOW COOKER:
4- to 6-quart

1	cup all-purpose flour
1½	teaspoons baking powder
1	teaspoon apple pie spice
¼	teaspoon salt
½	cup packed brown sugar
2	tablespoons cooking oil or melted butter
2	slightly beaten eggs
½	cup applesauce
½	cup chopped walnuts, toasted

1 Well-grease two 1-pint straight-side wide-mouth canning jars; flour the greased jars. Set aside.

2 In a medium bowl combine the 1 cup flour, the baking powder, apple pie spice, and salt. Make a well in the center of the flour mixture; set aside.

3 In a small bowl combine brown sugar, oil, eggs, and applesauce; mix well. Add applesauce mixture all at once to flour mixture. Stir just until moistened. Stir in walnuts.

4 Divide mixture between the prepared canning jars. Cover jars tightly with greased foil, greased sides in. Place jars in a 4- to 6-quart slow cooker. Pour ½ cup warm water into slow cooker around jars.

5 Cover and cook on high-heat setting for 1¾ to 2 hours or until a long wooden skewer inserted near the centers comes out clean. Remove jars from slow cooker; cool for 10 minutes on a wire rack. Carefully remove bread from jars. Serve warm.

Per serving: 146 cal., 7 g total fat (1 g sat. fat), 35 mg chol., 113 mg sodium, 20 g carbo., 1 g fiber, 3 g pro.

DESSERTS

9

Underneath the fluffy cake layer, you'll find a treasure trove of luscious berries.

TRIPLE BERRY PUDDING CAKE

PREP:
20 minutes

COOK:
High 2½ hours

STAND:
1 hour

MAKES:
8 servings

SLOW COOKER:
3½- or 4-quart

Nonstick cooking spray
1½ cups loose-pack frozen blueberries
1½ cups loose-pack frozen red raspberries
½ cup fresh cranberries
1 cup all-purpose flour
⅔ cup sugar
1½ teaspoons baking powder
½ teaspoon ground cinnamon
¼ teaspoon salt
½ cup milk
2 tablespoons butter, melted
1 teaspoon vanilla
¾ cup boiling water
⅓ cup sugar
½ cup sliced almonds, toasted

1 Lightly coat a 3½- or 4-quart slow cooker with nonstick cooking spray. In the prepared slow cooker combine frozen blueberries, frozen raspberries, and cranberries; set aside.

2 For batter, in a medium bowl combine flour, the ⅔ cup sugar, the baking powder, cinnamon, and salt. Stir in milk, melted butter, and vanilla. Spoon batter over berries in slow cooker; carefully spread batter over berries.

3 In a small bowl combine boiling water and the ⅓ cup sugar; stir to dissolve sugar. Pour evenly over batter in slow cooker. Cover and cook on high-heat setting for 2½ to 3 hours or until a toothpick inserted near center comes out clean. Remove liner from slow cooker, if possible, or turn off slow cooker. Let stand, uncovered, for 1 hour to cool slightly before serving. Sprinkle individual servings with almonds.

Per serving: 260 cal., 8 g total fat (2 g sat. fat), 9 mg chol., 146 mg sodium, 45 g carbo., 4 g fiber, 4 g pro.

With caramel apple "pudding" on the bottom and a moist walnut cake layer on top, this dessert has an irresistibly homespun appeal.

DUTCH APPLE PUDDING CAKE

Nonstick cooking spray

1 20- or 21-ounce can apple pie filling

½ cup dried cherries, dried cranberries, or raisins

1 cup all-purpose flour

¼ cup granulated sugar

1 teaspoon baking powder

¼ teaspoon salt

½ cup milk

2 tablespoons butter or margarine, melted

½ cup chopped walnuts, toasted

1¼ cups apple juice or apple cider

⅓ cup packed brown sugar

1 tablespoon butter or margarine

1 recipe Sweetened Whipped Cream (optional)

1 Lightly coat a 3½- or 4-quart slow cooker with nonstick cooking spray; set aside. In a small saucepan bring apple pie filling to boiling. Stir in dried cherries. Transfer apple mixture to prepared slow cooker.

2 For batter, in a medium bowl stir together flour, granulated sugar, baking powder, and salt. Add milk and melted butter; stir just until combined. Stir in nuts. Spread batter over apple mixture in slow cooker.

3 In the same small saucepan combine apple juice, brown sugar, and the 1 tablespoon butter. Bring to boiling. Boil gently, uncovered, for 2 minutes. Carefully pour apple juice mixture over batter in slow cooker.

4 Cover and cook on high-heat setting for 2 to 2½ hours or until a toothpick inserted into center of cake comes out clean. Remove liner from slow cooker, if possible, or turn off slow cooker. Let stand, uncovered, for 30 to 45 minutes to cool slightly before serving.

5 To serve, spoon warm cake and sauce into dessert dishes. If desired, top individual servings with Sweetened Whipped Cream.

SWEETENED WHIPPED CREAM: Chill a small bowl and the beaters of an electric mixer. In chilled bowl combine ½ cup whipping cream and 2 teaspoons packed brown sugar. Beat with an electric mixer on medium speed until soft peaks form (tips curl).

Per serving: 435 cal., 13 g total fat (5 g sat. fat), 18 mg chol., 284 mg sodium, 77 g carbo., 3 g fiber, 5 g pro.

PREP:
25 minutes

COOK:
High 2 hours

STAND:
30 minutes

MAKES:
6 to 8 servings

SLOW COOKER:
3½- or 4-quart

If you love warm, rich desserts, this pudding cake is sure to become one of your favorites. Enjoy it even more with a scoop of vanilla ice cream on top.

GINGERBREAD PUDDING CAKE

PREP:
15 minutes

COOK:
High 2 hours

STAND:
45 minutes

MAKES:
8 servings

SLOW COOKER:
3½- or 4-quart

Nonstick cooking spray

1   14½-ounce package gingerbread mix

½   cup milk

½   cup raisins

2¼   cups water

¾   cup packed brown sugar

¾   cup butter or margarine

Vanilla ice cream (optional)

1 Lightly coat a 3½- or 4-quart slow cooker with nonstick cooking spray; set aside.

2 For batter, in a medium bowl stir gingerbread mix and milk together until moistened. Stir in raisins (batter will be thick). Spread batter evenly in the bottom of prepared slow cooker.

3 In a medium saucepan combine the water, brown sugar, and butter; bring to boiling. Carefully pour mixture over batter in slow cooker.

4 Cover and cook on high-heat setting for 2 hours (center may appear moist but will set up upon standing). Remove liner from slow cooker, if possible, or turn off slow cooker. Let stand, uncovered, for 45 minutes to cool slightly before serving.

5 To serve, spoon warm cake into dessert dishes; spoon pudding over cake.

Per serving: 501 cal., 24 g total fat (13 g sat. fat), 50 mg chol., 548 mg sodium, 70 g carbo., 1 g fiber, 4 g pro.

Thanks to this recipe, you can have your cake and pudding too. Rich chocolate flavor runs through this blend of soft cake and pudding. For a decadent dessert, serve it with ice cream, whipped cream, or thawed frozen raspberries in juice.

BROWNIE PUDDING CAKE

Nonstick cooking spray

1   19.8-ounce package brownie mix

½   cup butter or margarine, melted

2   eggs

¼   cup water

¾   cup sugar

¾   cup unsweetened cocoa powder

3   cups boiling water

PREP:
15 minutes

COOK:
High 2 hours

STAND:
30 minutes

MAKES:
8 servings

SLOW COOKER:
3½- or 4-quart

1 Lightly coat a 3½- or 4-quart slow cooker with nonstick cooking spray; set aside.

2 For batter, in a medium bowl stir together brownie mix, melted butter, eggs, and the ¼ cup water until batter is nearly smooth. Spread brownie batter evenly in the bottom of prepared slow cooker.

3 In another bowl combine sugar and cocoa powder. Gradually stir the boiling water into the sugar-cocoa mixture. Pour evenly over batter in slow cooker.

4 Cover and cook on high-heat setting for 2 hours (center may appear moist but will set up upon standing). Remove liner from slow cooker, if possible, or turn off slow cooker. Let stand, uncovered, for 30 to 45 minutes to cool slightly before serving.

5 To serve, spoon warm cake into dessert dishes; spoon pudding over cake.

Per serving: 534 cal., 25 g total fat (10 g sat. fat), 86 mg chol., 355 mg sodium, 76 g carbo., 0 g fiber, 6 g pro.

This comforting fall dessert gets its incredible flavor from a liberal sprinkling of pumpkin pie spice.

NUTTY PUMPKIN-PIE PUDDING

PREP:
20 minutes

COOK:
High 2½ hours

STAND:
30 minutes

MAKES:
8 servings

SLOW COOKER:
3½- or 4-quart

Nonstick cooking spray

1   15-ounce can pumpkin

1   5-ounce can (⅔ cup) evaporated milk

⅓   cup sugar

2   tablespoons pumpkin pie spice

1   1-layer-size yellow cake mix

1   cup pecans or walnuts, toasted and chopped

¼   cup butter, melted

Frozen whipped dessert topping, thawed (optional)

1 Coat a 3½- or 4-quart slow cooker with nonstick cooking spray. In the prepared cooker combine pumpkin, evaporated milk, sugar, and 1 tablespoon of the pumpkin pie spice. Spread batter evenly in the bottom of prepared slow cooker.

2 In a medium bowl combine cake mix, nuts, and remaining 1 tablespoon pumpkin pie spice. Sprinkle mixture evenly on top of pumpkin mixture in slow cooker. Drizzle melted butter over cake mix mixture.

3 Cover and cook on high-heat setting for 2½ hours. Remove liner from slow cooker, if possible, or turn off slow cooker. Let stand, uncovered, for 30 to 45 minutes to cool slightly before serving.

4 To serve, spoon warm pudding into bowls. If desired, top individual servings with whipped dessert topping.

Per serving: 349 cal., 20 g total fat (5 g sat. fat), 21 mg chol., 278 mg sodium, 42 g carbo., 3 g fiber, 4 g pro.

Before beginning this recipe, check to make sure that the dish or casserole you plan to use fits into your slow cooker.

CRUSTLESS LEMONY CHEESECAKE

Nonstick cooking spray

12 ounces cream cheese, softened

½ cup sugar

2 teaspoons finely shredded lemon peel (set aside)

2 tablespoons lemon juice

1 tablespoon all-purpose flour

½ teaspoon vanilla

½ cup dairy sour cream

3 beaten eggs

1 cup warm water

Fresh or frozen raspberries (optional)

PREP:
15 minutes

COOK:
High 1¾ hours

CHILL:
4 to 24 hours

MAKES:
8 servings

SLOW COOKER:
3½- to 5-quart

1 Lightly coat a 1-quart soufflé dish or casserole with nonstick cooking spray. Tear off an 18×12-inch piece of heavy foil; cut in half lengthwise. Fold each piece lengthwise into thirds. Crisscross the foil strips and place the dish in the center of the crisscross; set aside.

2 For filling, in a large mixing bowl beat cream cheese, sugar, lemon juice, flour, and vanilla with an electric mixer on medium speed until combined. Beat in sour cream until smooth. Beat in eggs with mixer on low speed just until combined. Stir in lemon peel. Pour filling mixture into prepared dish. Cover dish tightly with foil. Pour warm water into a 3½- to 5-quart slow cooker. Bringing up the foil strips, lift the ends of the strips to transfer the dish and foil to the slow cooker. Leave foil strips under dish.

3 Cover and cook on high-heat setting for 1¾ to 2 hours or until center is set. Carefully lift with foil strips to remove the dish; discard foil strips. Cool completely on a wire rack. Cover and chill for 4 to 24 hours before serving. If desired, serve with raspberries.

Per serving: 253 cal., 19 g total fat (11 g sat. fat), 131 mg chol., 159 mg sodium, 15 g carbo., 0 g fiber, 6 g pro.

Although traditional spoon bread is savory, this sweet variation has the same delightful texture as the classic.

PINEAPPLE SPOON BREAD

PREP:
15 minutes

COOK:
Low 3 hours

STAND:
1 hour

MAKES:
10 to 12 servings

SLOW COOKER:
3½- or 4-quart

Nonstick cooking spray
½   cup butter, softened
1½ cups granulated sugar
1   teaspoon baking soda
2   eggs
2   cups all-purpose flour
1   20-ounce can crushed pineapple, undrained
¾   cup chopped walnuts or pecans, toasted
¾   cup packed brown sugar

1 Lightly coat a 3½- or 4-quart slow cooker with nonstick cooking spray; set aside.

2 In a large mixing bowl beat butter with an electric mixer on medium speed for 30 seconds.

3 Beat in the granulated sugar and baking soda until well mixed. Beat in eggs. Beat in as much of the flour as you can with the mixer. Using a wooden spoon, stir in any remaining flour (batter will be stiff). Stir in undrained pineapple and the walnuts. Spoon into prepared slow cooker. Sprinkle with brown sugar.

4 Cover and cook on low-heat setting for 3 to 3½ hours or until edges are set (cakelike) and temperature of center registers 175°F when tested with an instant-read thermometer. Center of cake will appear wet.

5 Remove liner from slow cooker, if possible, or turn off slow cooker. Let stand, uncovered, for 1 hour to cool slightly before serving.

Per serving: 442 cal., 16 g total fat (7 g sat. fat), 67 mg chol., 213 mg sodium, 71 g carbo., 2 g fiber, 5 g pro.

Spoon into this irresistible dessert and you'll find nuggets of apricots and almonds nestled in the cardamom-seasoned pudding.

WHITE CHOCOLATE-APRICOT BREAD PUDDING

1½ cups half-and-half or light cream

½ of a 6-ounce package white chocolate baking squares (with cocoa butter), coarsely chopped

⅓ cup snipped dried apricots

2 eggs

½ cup sugar

½ teaspoon ground cardamom

4½ slices white bread, cut into ½-inch cubes, dried* (3 cups dry)

¼ cup coarsely chopped almonds

1 cup warm water

Whipped cream (optional)

Grated white chocolate baking squares (optional)

PREP:
30 minutes

COOK:
Low 4 hours, High 2 hours

MAKES:
6 servings

SLOW COOKER:
3½- to 5-quart

1 In a small saucepan heat half-and-half over medium heat until very warm but not boiling. Remove from heat; add chopped white chocolate and apricots. Stir until white chocolate is melted.

2 In a bowl beat eggs with a fork; whisk in sugar and cardamom. Whisk in half-and-half mixture. Gently stir in bread cubes and almonds. Pour mixture into a 4- to 5-cup soufflé dish (dish may be full). Cover dish tightly with foil.

3 Pour warm water into a 3½- to 5-quart slow cooker. Tear off an 18×12-inch piece of heavy foil. Tear in half lengthwise. Fold each foil piece lengthwise into thirds. Crisscross the foil strips and place the soufflé dish in the center of the crisscross. Bringing up the foil strips, lift the ends of the strips to transfer the dish and foil to the slow cooker. Leave foil strips under dish.

4 Cover and cook on low-heat setting for 4 hours or on high-heat setting for 2 hours.

5 Using the foil strips, carefully lift soufflé dish out of slow cooker. Serve pudding warm. If desired, serve with whipped cream and sprinkle with grated white chocolate.

Per serving: 345 cal., 17 g total fat (8 g sat. fat), 98 mg chol., 191 mg sodium, 42 g carbo., 2 g fiber, 8 g pro.

*NOTE: To make dry bread cubes, preheat oven to 300°F. Spread fresh bread cubes in a single layer in a 15×10×1-inch baking pan. Bake, uncovered, for 10 to 15 minutes or until dry, stirring twice; cool.

Have mugs of coffee and glasses of milk ready to accompany this treat. If the kids in your life have yet to taste bread pudding, introduce them to this one. They'll love its creamy, rich chocolate flavor.

SEMISWEET-CHOCOLATE BREAD PUDDING

PREP:
25 minutes

COOK:
Low 2½ hours

STAND:
30 minutes

MAKES:
8 servings

SLOW COOKER:
3½- or 4-quart

Nonstick cooking spray

3 cups milk

¾ cup semisweet chocolate pieces

¾ cup presweetened cocoa powder

3 slightly beaten eggs

5 cups Hawaiian sweet bread or cinnamon swirl bread (no raisins) cut into ½-inch cubes, dried* (about 6½ ounces bread)

Whipped cream (optional)

1 Lightly coat a 3½- or 4-quart slow cooker with nonstick cooking spray; set aside.

2 In a medium saucepan heat milk just until simmering; remove from heat. Add chocolate pieces and presweetened cocoa powder (do not stir); let stand for 5 minutes. Whisk until chocolate is melted and smooth. Cool slightly (about 10 minutes). Transfer chocolate mixture to a large bowl; whisk in eggs. Gently stir in dried bread cubes. Pour chocolate-bread mixture into prepared cooker.

3 Cover and cook on low-heat setting about 2½ hours or until puffed and a knife inserted near center comes out clean. Remove liner from cooker, if possible, or turn off cooker. Let stand, uncovered, for 30 to 45 minutes to cool slightly before serving (pudding will fall during cooling). If desired, serve with whipped cream.

Per serving: 360 cal., 12 g total fat (6 g sat. fat), 95 mg chol., 214 mg sodium, 62 g carbo., 4 g fiber, 9 g pro.

*NOTE: To make dry bread cubes, preheat oven to 300°F. Spread fresh bread cubes in a single layer in a 15×10×1-inch baking pan. Bake, uncovered, for 10 to 15 minutes or until dry, stirring twice; cool.

Chunky apple pie filling and cinnamon-raisin bread are the main attractions in this luscious dessert. If you don't have cinnamon-raisin bread, use white bread, ⅓ cup raisins, and ⅛ teaspoon cinnamon in its place.

APPLE PIE BREAD PUDDING

Nonstick cooking spray

3 eggs

2 cups milk, half-and-half, or light cream

½ cup sugar

1 21-ounce can chunky apple pie filling (with more fruit)

9 slices cinnamon-raisin bread, cut into ½-inch cubes, dried* (4½ cups dry)

Whipped cream or vanilla ice cream (optional)

PREP:
10 minutes

COOK:
Low 3 hours

STAND:
30 minutes

MAKES:
10 servings

SLOW COOKER:
3½- or 4-quart

1 Lightly coat a 3½- or 4-quart slow cooker with nonstick cooking spray; set aside.

2 In a large bowl beat eggs with a wire whisk. Whisk in milk and sugar. Gently stir in pie filling and dried bread cubes. Pour egg mixture into prepared slow cooker.

3 Cover and cook on low-heat setting about 3 hours or until a knife inserted near center comes out clean (mixture will be puffed). Remove liner from slow cooker, if possible, or turn off slow cooker. Let stand, uncovered, for 30 to 45 minutes to cool slightly before serving (pudding will fall as it cools). If desired, serve with whipped cream or ice cream.

Per serving: 328 cal., 3 g total fat (1 g sat. fat), 67 mg chol., 77 mg sodium, 68 g carbo., 5 g fiber, 10 g pro.

***NOTE:** To make dry bread cubes, preheat oven to 300°F. Spread fresh bread cubes in a single layer in a 15×10×1-inch baking pan. Bake, uncovered, for 10 to 15 minutes or until dry, stirring twice; cool.

Slow cookers are much loved in the winter months because they're great for simmering soups, stews, and hearty meat dishes. But they make great sense in summer too. You can have a sweet fruit cobbler without heating up your kitchen!

CHERRY-RHUBARB COBBLER

PREP:
20 minutes

COOK:
High 2 hours

STAND:
30 minutes

MAKES:
8 to 10 servings

SLOW COOKER:
3¹/₂- or 4-quart

Nonstick cooking spray

1   cup all-purpose flour

²/₃ cup packed brown sugar

¹/₂ teaspoon ground cinnamon

¹/₂ teaspoon baking powder

¹/₄ teaspoon baking soda

¹/₄ teaspoon salt

2   eggs

3   tablespoons butter or margarine, melted

2   tablespoons milk

5   cups fresh or frozen sliced rhubarb

1   30-ounce can cherry pie filling

¹/₃ cup packed brown sugar

¹/₄ teaspoon ground cinnamon

1   tablespoon granulated sugar

¹/₄ teaspoon ground cinnamon

Vanilla ice cream (optional)

1 Lightly coat a 3¹/₂- or 4-quart slow cooker with nonstick cooking spray; set aside.

2 For batter, in a medium bowl combine flour, the ²/₃ cup brown sugar, the ¹/₂ teaspoon cinnamon, the baking powder, baking soda, and salt. In a small bowl beat eggs with a fork; stir in melted butter and milk. Add egg mixture to flour mixture; stir just until combined. Set aside.

3 In a large saucepan combine rhubarb, cherry pie filling, the ¹/₃ cup brown sugar, and ¹/₄ teaspoon cinnamon. Cook and stir until fruit mixture comes to boiling. Transfer hot fruit mixture to prepared slow cooker. Immediately spoon batter over top of fruit mixture. In a small bowl combine the granulated sugar and ¹/₄ teaspoon cinnamon; sprinkle on top of batter.

4 Cover and cook on high-heat setting about 2 hours or until a toothpick inserted into center of cake comes out clean. Remove liner from slow cooker, if possible, or turn off slow cooker. Let stand, uncovered, for 30 to 45 minutes to cool slightly before serving. If desired, serve with ice cream.

Per serving: 374 cal., 6 g total fat (3 g sat. fat), 66 mg chol., 235 mg sodium, 76 g carbo., 3 g fiber, 4 g pro.

Mellow cooked fruit and fluffy iced cinnamon rolls are the perfect partners in this easy cobbler.

PINEAPPLE-PEACH COBBLER

Nonstick cooking spray

2   21-ounce cans pineapple pie filling

1   6- or 7-ounce package dried peaches, snipped

½   cup orange juice

1   17½-ounce package (5) refrigerated large cinnamon rolls

Vanilla ice cream (optional)

1 Lightly coat a 3½- or 4-quart slow cooker with nonstick cooking spray. In prepared slow cooker stir together the pie filling, dried peaches, and orange juice.

2 Cover and cook on high-heat setting about 1½ hours or until fruit mixture is hot and bubbly; stir fruit mixture. Place cinnamon rolls on a cutting board, cinnamon sides up (set icing packet aside). Cut each roll in half crosswise. Place roll halves on top of fruit mixture in slow cooker, cinnamon sides up.

3 Cover and cook on high-heat setting about 1 hour more or until rolls are fluffy all the way through. Remove liner from cooker, if possible, or turn off cooker. Let stand, uncovered, for 30 to 45 minutes to cool slightly before serving. Spread icing over rolls. If desired, serve with ice cream.

Per serving: 373 cal., 6 g total fat (2 g sat. fat), 0 mg chol., 395 mg sodium, 77 g carbo., 1 g fiber, 3 g pro.

PREP:
15 minutes

COOK:
High 1½ hours plus 1 hour

STAND:
30 minutes

MAKES:
10 servings

SLOW COOKER:
3½- or 4-quart

Tart cooking apples offer a pleasing contrast to the sweet blueberries in this homey cobbler that's topped with an irresistible whole wheat-almond mixture.

APPLE-BLUEBERRY COBBLER

PREP:
25 minutes

COOK:
Low 3 hours, High 1½ hours; plus 1 hour on High

STAND:
1 hour

MAKES:
8 servings

SLOW COOKER:
3½- or 4-quart

Nonstick cooking spray

4   cups thinly sliced peeled cooking apples (such as Granny Smith)

1   21-ounce can blueberry pie filling

½   cup water

⅓   cup sugar

1   tablespoon quick-cooking tapioca

2   teaspoons finely shredded lemon peel

½   teaspoon almond extract

¾   cup sugar

½   cup whole wheat flour

¼   cup all-purpose flour

¼   cup ground toasted almonds

1   teaspoon baking powder

¼   teaspoon salt

2   slightly beaten eggs

3   tablespoons cooking oil

2   tablespoons milk

1 Lightly coat a 3½- or 4-quart slow cooker with nonstick cooking spray. In the prepared slow cooker stir together apples, pie filling, the water, the ⅓ cup sugar, the tapioca, lemon peel, and almond extract. Cover and cook on low-heat setting for 3 to 4 hours or on high-heat setting for 1½ to 2 hours (mixture should be bubbly).

2 In a medium bowl stir together the ¾ cup sugar, the whole wheat flour, all-purpose flour, almonds, baking powder, and salt. In a small bowl stir together eggs, oil, and milk. Add egg mixture to flour mixture; stir just until moistened. Spoon batter evenly over fruit mixture in slow cooker.

3 If using low-heat setting, turn to high-heat setting. Cover; cook about 1 hour more or until a toothpick inserted in topping comes out clean.

4 Remove liner from slow cooker, if possible, or turn off slow cooker. Let stand, uncovered, for 1 hour to cool slightly before serving.

Per serving: 356 cal., 9 g total fat (1 g sat. fat), 53 mg chol., 171 mg sodium, 67 g carbo., 5 g fiber, 4 g pro.

Because it uses frozen and dried fruits, this cobbler is easy to prepare any time of the year.

RASPBERRY-PEACH COBBLER

Nonstick cooking spray

1 16-ounce package unsweetened frozen peach slices

1 12-ounce package frozen raspberries

¾ cup sugar

½ cup cranberry juice

¼ cup dried cranberries or snipped dried cherries

2 tablespoons quick-cooking tapioca

1 cup all-purpose flour

¾ cup sugar

1 teaspoon baking powder

1 teaspoon finely shredded orange peel

¼ teaspoon salt

2 slightly beaten eggs

3 tablespoons cooking oil

2 tablespoons milk

Vanilla ice cream (optional)

1 Lightly coat a 3½- or 4-quart slow cooker with nonstick cooking spray. In the prepared slow cooker stir together frozen peaches, frozen raspberries, ¾ cup sugar, the cranberry juice, dried cranberries, and tapioca. Cover and cook on low-heat setting for 3 to 4 hours or on high-heat setting for 1½ to 2 hours (mixture should be bubbly).

2 For batter, in a medium bowl stir together flour, ¾ cup sugar, the baking powder, orange peel, and salt. In a small bowl stir together eggs, oil, and milk. Add egg mixture to flour mixture; stir just until moistened. Stir fruit mixture in slow cooker. Spoon batter in mounds over fruit mixture.

3 If using low-heat setting, turn to high-heat setting. Cover; cook about 1 hour more or until a toothpick inserted in topping comes out clean.

4 Remove liner from slow cooker, if possible, or turn off slow cooker. Let stand, uncovered, for 1 hour to cool slightly before serving. If desired, serve with ice cream.

Per serving: 336 cal., 7 g total fat (1 g sat. fat), 53 mg chol., 123 mg sodium, 67 g carbo., 4 g fiber, 4 g pro.

PREP:
10 minutes

COOK:
Low 3 hours, High 1½ hours; plus 1 hour on High

STAND:
1 hour

MAKES:
8 servings

SLOW COOKER:
3½- or 4-quart

The coconut, dried fruit bits, and crunchy granola take this crisp to bold flavor heights.

TROPICAL APRICOT CRISP

PREP:
10 minutes

COOK:
Low 2½ hours

STAND:
30 minutes

MAKES:
6 servings

SLOW COOKER:
3½- or 4-quart

Nonstick cooking spray

2 21-ounce cans apricot pie filling

1 7-ounce package tropical blend mixed dried fruit bits

1 cup granola

⅓ cup coconut, toasted

Vanilla ice cream

1 Lightly coat a 3½- or 4-quart slow cooker with nonstick cooking spray. In prepared slow cooker combine pie filling and dried fruit bits.

2 Cover and cook on low-heat setting for 2½ hours.

3 Remove liner from slow cooker, if possible, or turn off slow cooker. In a small bowl combine granola and coconut. Sprinkle over fruit mixture in slow cooker. Let stand, uncovered, for 30 minutes to cool slightly before serving. Serve with ice cream.

Per serving: 587 cal., 13 g total fat (8 g sat. fat), 45 mg chol., 144 mg sodium, 109 g carbo., 7 g fiber, 6 g pro.

For an extra-special touch, serve this ginger-spiced dessert with butter pecan or praline ice cream.

CHERRY-BERRY CRISP

Nonstick cooking spray
6 cups frozen blueberries
1 21-ounce can cherry pie filling
⅓ cup granulated sugar
¼ cup water
1 tablespoon quick-cooking tapioca
½ teaspoon ground ginger
¾ cup quick-cooking rolled oats
½ cup all-purpose flour
½ cup packed brown sugar
¼ cup butter

PREP:
20 minutes

COOK:
Low 3½ hours, High 1½ hours

MAKES:
8 servings

SLOW COOKER:
3½- or 4-quart

1 Lightly coat a 3½- or 4-quart slow cooker with nonstick cooking spray. In the prepared slow cooker combine blueberries, cherry pie filling, granulated sugar, the water, tapioca, and ginger.

2 In a medium bowl stir together oats, flour, and brown sugar. Using a pastry blender, cut in butter until crumbly. Sprinkle oats mixture over berry mixture in slow cooker.

3 Cover and cook on low-heat setting for 3½ to 4 hours or on high-heat setting for 1½ to 2 hours or until bubbly around edges. Cool slightly. Serve warm.

Per serving: 338 cal., 7 g total fat (4 g sat. fat), 15 mg chol., 61 mg sodium, 68 g carbo., 5 g fiber, 3 g pro.

This cinnamony blend of cherries, pineapple, peaches, and apricots boasts a buttery oatmeal topper.

MIXED FRUIT CRISP

PREP:
15 minutes

COOK:
Low 3 hours, High 1½ hours

STAND:
30 minutes

MAKES:
8 servings

SLOW COOKER:
3½- or 4-quart

Nonstick cooking spray

1   21-ounce can cherry pie filling

1   20-ounce can pineapple chunks, drained

1   15- to 16-ounce can sliced peaches, drained

1   15-ounce can unpeeled apricot halves in light syrup, undrained

½   teaspoon ground cinnamon

3   envelopes instant oatmeal (with maple and brown sugar)

3   tablespoons butter, melted

1 Lightly coat a 3½- or 4-quart slow cooker with nonstick cooking spray. In prepared slow cooker combine pie filling, drained pineapple chunks, drained peaches, undrained apricots, and cinnamon. In a small bowl stir together oatmeal and butter, being sure to break up any sugar clumps in the oatmeal. Sprinkle over fruit mixture in slow cooker.

2 Cover and cook on low-heat setting for 3 hours or on high-heat setting for 1½ hours or until bubbly at edges.

3 Remove liner from slow cooker, if possible, or turn off slow cooker. Let stand, uncovered, for 30 minutes to cool slightly before serving. Serve warm.

Per serving: 308 cal., 5 g total fat (3 g sat. fat), 11 mg chol., 195 mg sodium, 64 g carbo., 3 g fiber, 3 g pro.

The granola-and-coconut topper adds a nice crunch to this warm, comforting tropical pleaser.

GRANOLA-TOPPED MANGO-PEAR CRUNCH

Nonstick cooking spray

1 24-ounce jar refrigerated mango slices

5 medium pears, peeled, cored, and sliced

¼ cup sugar

2 cups granola

½ cup shredded or flaked coconut, toasted

1 Lightly coat a 5- to 6-quart slow cooker with nonstick cooking spray; set aside. Drain mango slices, reserving ½ cup of the liquid. Coarsely chop mango slices. In prepared slow cooker combine mango, reserved mango liquid, sliced pears, and sugar.

2 Cover and cook on low-heat setting for 3 to 4 hours or on high-heat setting for 1½ to 2 hours.

3 Remove liner from slow cooker, if possible, or turn off slow cooker. Let stand, uncovered, for 30 minutes before serving. To serve, divide warm fruit mixture among 8 dessert bowls. Top with granola and coconut.

Per serving: 255 cal., 6 g total fat (3 g sat. fat), 0 mg chol., 21 mg sodium, 50 g carbo., 5 g fiber, 3 g pro.

PREP:
20 minutes

COOK:
Low 3 hours, High 1½ hours

STAND:
30 minutes

MAKES:
8 servings

SLOW COOKER:
5- to 6-quart

If you have the time, make your own granola using the recipe below to sprinkle on top of this spiced apple-and-date medley. Enjoy the leftover granola with milk for breakfast or out of hand as a snack.

ALMOND GRANOLA-TOPPED APPLESAUCE

PREP:
25 minutes

COOK:
Low 5 hours, High 2½ hours

OVEN:
300°F

MAKES:
10 servings

SLOW COOKER:
4- to 6-quart

3½ to 4 pounds cooking apples (such as Granny Smith), peeled, cored, and cut into chunks

¼ cup orange juice

¼ cup apple juice or apple cider

½ cup packed brown sugar

1½ teaspoons apple pie spice

1 8-ounce package chopped dates or 1 cup dried cherries or raisins

⅔ cup Almond Granola or purchased granola cereal

1 Place apples in a 4- to 6-quart slow cooker. Add orange juice, apple juice, brown sugar, and apple pie spice. Toss to coat apples. Cover and cook on low-heat setting for 5 to 6 hours or on high-heat setting for 2½ to 3 hours (apples should be very tender).

2 Using a potato masher or an immersion blender mash or blend apple mixture to desired consistency. Stir in dates. Serve warm topped with Almond Granola.

ALMOND GRANOLA: Preheat oven to 300°F. In a large bowl combine 2 cups regular rolled oats, 1½ cups sliced almonds, ¼ cup toasted wheat germ, and 1 teaspoon ground cinnamon. In a small bowl stir together ½ cup honey and 2 tablespoons butter, melted; stir honey mixture into oat mixture. Spread evenly in a greased 15×10×1-inch baking pan. Bake, uncovered, for 30 to 35 minutes or until lightly browned, stirring once. Spread on a large piece of foil to cool. Store in an airtight container at room temperature for up to 1 week or place in a freezer container and freeze for up to 3 months. Makes 5 cups.

Per serving: 223 cal., 2 g total fat (0 g sat. fat), 1 mg chol., 9 mg sodium, 54 g carbo., 6 g fiber, 2 g pro.

A mix of chocolate milk and cream gives a velvety richness to this home-style dessert.

CHOCOLATE RICE PUDDING

Nonstick cooking spray

½ cup sugar

½ teaspoon salt

4½ cups chocolate milk

2 cups half-and-half or light cream

1⅔ cups converted rice (do not substitute long grain rice)

1 teaspoon vanilla

1 cup whipping cream, whipped

Miniature semisweet chocolate pieces

1 Lightly coat a 3½- or 4-quart slow cooker with nonstick cooking spray. In prepared slow cooker stir together sugar and salt. Whisk in chocolate milk and half-and-half. Stir in uncooked rice.

2 Cover and cook on low-heat setting for 5 hours (do not stir during cooking).

3 Stir in vanilla. Remove liner from slow cooker, if possible, or turn off slow cooker. Cover and let stand for 30 minutes to cool slightly. Fold in whipped cream.

4 Serve warm or cover and chill up to 2 days before serving. Top individual servings with chocolate pieces.

Per serving: 315 cal., 14 g total fat (9 g sat. fat), 49 mg chol., 177 mg sodium, 41 g carbo., 0 g fiber, 7 g pro.

PREP:
10 minutes

COOK:
Low 5 hours

STAND:
30 minutes

MAKES:
12 servings

SLOW COOKER:
3½- or 4-quart

Cardamom adds a tantalizingly exotic note to this creamy pudding flecked with colorful dried fruit.

TROPICAL RICE PUDDING

PREP:
15 minutes

COOK:
Low 6 hours

STAND:
30 minutes

MAKES:
10 to 12 servings

SLOW COOKER:
3½- or 4-quart

4	cups half-and-half or light cream
2½	cups whole milk
⅔	cup sugar
1⅔	cups converted rice (do not substitute long grain rice)
½	teaspoon ground cardamom
¼	teaspoon salt
1	7-ounce package tropical mixed dried fruit bits
1	teaspoon vanilla
	Milk (optional)
1	3-ounce jar macadamia nuts, chopped (optional)

1 In a 3½- or 4-quart slow cooker stir together half-and-half, the 2½ cups milk, the sugar, uncooked rice, cardamom, and salt. Cover and cook on low-heat setting for 6 hours (do not stir).

2 Stir in fruit bits and vanilla. Remove liner from slow cooker, if possible, or turn off slow cooker. Cover and let stand for 30 minutes to cool slightly before serving. If necessary, stir in additional milk to reach desired consistency. Top individual servings with nuts.

Per serving: 396 cal., 14 g total fat (9 g sat. fat), 42 mg chol., 147 mg sodium, 61 g carbo., 1 g fiber, 7 g pro.

Enjoy this cinnamony vanilla pudding either warm or cool.

TAPIOCA PUDDING

8 cups whole milk

1 cup sugar

½ cup small pearl tapioca (not quick-cooking)

½ teaspoon ground cinnamon

4 eggs

1 tablespoon vanilla

1 In a 4- to 5-quart slow cooker combine milk, sugar, pearl tapioca, and cinnamon. Cover and cook on low-heat setting for 5 to 6 hours or on high-heat setting for 2½ to 3 hours.

2 In a medium bowl slightly beat eggs. Stir tapioca mixture in slow cooker. Remove about 1 cup of the tapioca mixture and gradually whisk into eggs. Stir egg mixture into tapioca mixture in slow cooker.

3 If using low-heat setting, turn to high-heat setting. Cover and cook for 30 minutes more.

4 Transfer to a serving bowl. Stir in vanilla. Cover and let stand for 45 minutes to cool slightly before serving.

Per serving: 210 cal., 7 g total fat (4 g sat. fat), 87 mg chol., 89 mg sodium, 29 g carbo., 0 g fiber, 7 g pro.

MAKE-AHEAD DIRECTIONS: Prepare as directed. Cover and store in the refrigerator for up to 3 days.

PREP:
15 minutes

COOK:
Low 5 hours, High 2½ hours; plus 30 minutes on High

STAND:
45 minutes

MAKES:
12 servings

SLOW COOKER:
4- to 5-quart

It takes only three ingredients to make this incredibly rich yet simple chocolate treat.

S'MORE FONDUE

PREP:
10 minutes

COOK:
Low 1½ hours

MAKES:
16 servings

SLOW COOKER:
3½-quart

15 ounces milk chocolate, chopped

1 10-ounce package large marshmallows

½ cup half-and-half or light cream

Graham cracker snack sticks; graham cracker squares, halved; and/or large marshmallows

1 In a 3½-quart slow cooker stir together chocolate, the 10-ounce package marshmallows, and half-and-half.

2 Cover and cook on low-heat setting for 1½ to 2 hours, stirring once during cooking. Whisk until smooth before serving.

3 Serve immediately or keep warm, covered, on low-heat setting for up to 2 hours. Serve with graham cracker snack sticks, graham cracker squares, and/or additional marshmallows for dipping.

Per ¼ cup fondue: 404 cal., 19 g total fat (11 g sat. fat), 12 mg chol., 54 mg sodium, 63 g carbo., 3 g fiber, 4 g pro.

This scrumptious peanutty apple-caramel sauce is also wonderful over slices of pound cake.

PEANUT BUTTER-CARAMEL APPLES

Nonstick cooking spray

1   12-ounce jar caramel ice cream topping

½   cup peanut butter

½   cup water

2½ pounds cooking apples (such as Granny Smith), peeled, cored, and sliced into ½-inch-thick wedges

Vanilla ice cream (optional)

Purchased nut topping (optional)

1 Lightly coat a 3½- or 4-quart slow cooker with nonstick cooking spray. In the prepared slow cooker combine caramel topping, peanut butter, and the water, whisking until smooth. Add apples; toss to coat. Cover and cook on low-heat setting for 3 to 4 hours.

2 If desired, serve warm apple mixture over ice cream and top individual servings with nut topping.

Per serving: 297 cal., 8 g total fat (2 g sat. fat), 0 mg chol., 189 mg sodium, 53 g carbo., 5 g fiber, 4 g pro.

PREP:
20 minutes

COOK:
Low 3 hours

MAKES:
8 to 10 servings

SLOW COOKER:
3½- or 4-quart

Prepared in the slow cooker, this classic, old-fashioned dessert is still a real family-pleaser.

STUFFED APPLES

PREP:
20 minutes

COOK:
Low 5 hours, High 2½ hours

MAKES:
4 servings

SLOW COOKER:
3½- or 4-quart

4   medium, tart baking apples (such as Granny Smith)

⅓   cup snipped dried figs, golden raisins, or raisins

¼   cup packed brown sugar

½   teaspoon apple pie spice or ground cinnamon

¼   cup apple juice or apple cider

1   tablespoon butter or margarine, cut into 4 pieces

1 Core apples; peel a strip from the top of each apple. Place apples, top sides up, in a 3½- or 4-quart slow cooker. In a small bowl combine figs, brown sugar, and apple pie spice. Divide mixture among apples, spooning into centers of apples and patting in with a knife or thin metal spatula. Pour apple juice around apples in slow cooker. Top each apple with a piece of the butter.

2 Cover and cook on low-heat setting for 5 hours or on high-heat setting for 2½ hours.

3 Use a large spoon to transfer apples to shallow bowls or dessert dishes. Spoon juices from slow cooker over apples. Serve warm.

Per serving: 200 cal., 3 g total fat (2 g sat. fat), 8 mg chol., 31 mg sodium, 45 g carbo., 5 g fiber, 1 g pro.

Warm pears drizzled with caramel and sprinkled with cashews—that's a dessert lover's delight!

CARAMEL-SPICED PEARS

8	pears (7 to 8 ounces each) peeled if desired, cored, and halved
1	teaspoon ground cinnamon
¼	teaspoon ground cloves
¾	cup apple juice or apple cider
2	tablespoons lemon juice
1	12-ounce jar caramel ice cream topping
½	cup chopped lightly salted cashews or honey-roasted cashews

1 Place pears in a 4- to 6-quart slow cooker. Sprinkle evenly with cinnamon and cloves. Pour apple juice and lemon juice over pears.

2 Cover and cook on low-heat setting for $3\frac{1}{2}$ to 4 hours or on high-heat setting for $1\frac{1}{2}$ to 2 hours.

3 Using a slotted spoon, transfer pears to individual serving dishes. Drizzle with caramel topping; sprinkle with cashews.

Per serving: 286 cal., 4 g total fat (1 g sat. fat), 0 mg chol., 130 mg sodium, 63 g carbo., 7 g fiber, 2 g pro.

PREP:
20 minutes

COOK:
Low $3\frac{1}{2}$ hours, High $1\frac{1}{2}$ hours

MAKES:
8 servings

SLOW COOKER:
4- to 6-quart

Orange juice and marmalade blend into a pretty syrup for cooking the pear halves. Whipped cream adds a bit of richness, and, if you like, a sprig of fresh mint makes an attractive, fragrant garnish.

CREAM-TOPPED PEARS IN ORANGE SAUCE

PREP:
15 minutes

COOK:
Low 4 hours, High 2 hours

STAND:
30 minutes

MAKES:
8 servings

SLOW COOKER:
3½- or 4-quart

¾ cup orange juice

6 tablespoons orange marmalade

2 teaspoons quick-cooking tapioca

8 small to medium ripe yet firm pears, peeled, cored, and quartered

1 cup whipping cream

1 In a 3½- or 4-quart slow cooker combine orange juice, 4 tablespoons of the marmalade, and the tapioca. Add pears. Toss gently to coat.

2 Cover and cook on low-heat setting for 4 to 5 hours or on high-heat setting for 2 to 2½ hours.

3 Remove liner from slow cooker, if possible, or turn off slow cooker. Let stand, uncovered, for 30 minutes to cool slightly before serving.

4 In a chilled medium mixing bowl combine whipping cream and the remaining 2 tablespoons marmalade; beat until soft peaks form (tips curl).

5 To serve, spoon pears and sauce into dessert dishes. Top with whipped cream mixture.

Per serving: 221 cal., 12 g total fat (7 g sat. fat), 41 mg chol., 20 mg sodium, 31 g carbo., 3 g fiber, 1 g pro.

Serve these fruits as a dessert soup or over ice cream to make a sundae.

SPICED PEACH COMPOTE

2	29-ounce cans peach slices
½	cup dried tart cherries
½	cup dried apricots
½	cup dried figs, stems removed
½	cup orange juice
3	2-inch-long cinnamon sticks

PREP:
10 minutes

COOK:
Low 5 hours, High 2½ hours

MAKES:
8 servings

SLOW COOKER:
3½-quart

1 Drain one of the cans of peach slices; discard liquid. In a 3½-quart slow cooker stir together drained peaches, peaches with juice, dried cherries, dried apricots, dried figs, orange juice, and cinnamon sticks.

2 Cover and cook on low-heat setting for 5 to 6 hours or on high-heat setting for 2½ to 3 hours. Discard cinnamon sticks.

Per serving: 246 cal., 0 g total fat (0 g sat. fat), 0 mg chol., 20 mg sodium, 60 g carbo., 4 g fiber, 3 g pro.

When the weather is cold and dreary, make this triple-fruit dessert to remind you of spring.

MIXED BERRY COMPOTE

PREP:
10 minutes

COOK:
Low 6 hours, High 3 hours

MAKES:
4 cups compote

SLOW COOKER:
3¹/₂- or 4-quart

4 cups frozen unsweetened raspberries

2 cups frozen blueberries

2 cups frozen dark sweet cherries

¹/₃ cup sugar

¹/₄ cup frozen orange juice concentrate

2 tablespoons quick-cooking tapioca

Angel food cake slices or vanilla ice cream

1 In a 3¹/₂- or 4-quart slow cooker combine raspberries, blueberries, cherries, sugar, orange juice concentrate, and tapioca.

2 Cover and cook on low-heat setting for 6 to 8 hours or on high-heat setting for 3 to 4 hours. Cool slightly. Serve warm over cake or ice cream.

Per ¹/₃ cup compote: 388 cal., 16 g total fat (9 g sat. fat), 115 mg chol., 160 mg sodium, 58 g carbo., 3 g fiber, 5 g pro.

Your family will love crispy French toast sticks smothered with a peachy blueberry sauce.

PEACH & BLUEBERRY DESSERT

6 cups sliced, peeled fresh peaches or unsweetened frozen peach slices

1 3-ounce package (⅔ cup) dried blueberries

½ cup white grape-peach juice or white grape juice

¼ cup sugar

1 tablespoon quick-cooking tapioca

1 teaspoon vanilla

1 18.8-ounce package (24) frozen French toast sticks

Frozen whipped dessert topping, thawed (optional)

PREP:
25 minutes

COOK:
Low 4 hours, High 2 hours

STAND:
1 hour

MAKES:
8 servings

SLOW COOKER:
3½- or 4-quart

1 In a 3½- or 4-quart slow cooker combine peaches, dried blueberries, juice, sugar, and tapioca.

2 Cover and cook on low-heat setting for 4 to 5 hours or on high-heat setting for 2 to 2½ hours.

3 Remove liner from slow cooker, if possible, or turn off slow cooker. Stir in vanilla. Let stand, uncovered, for 1 hour to cool slightly before serving.

4 Prepare frozen French toast sticks according to package directions; separate into sticks. (Discard maple syrup cups or save for another use.)

5 To serve, place 3 toast sticks in each of 8 dessert dishes. Spoon warm peach-blueberrry mixture over the sticks. If desired, serve with whipped topping.

Per serving: 307 cal., 4 g total fat (1 g sat. fat), 3 mg chol., 236 mg sodium, 66 g carbo., 3 g fiber, 3 g pro.

This dessert is a real treat when rhubarb and strawberries are in season, yet it's just as wonderful made with frozen fruit.

STRAWBERRY-RHUBARB SAUCE

PREP:
20 minutes

COOK:
Low 5½ hours, High 2½ hours; plus 15 minutes on High

MAKES:
10 servings

SLOW COOKER:
3½- or 4-quart

6   cups fresh rhubarb cut into 1-inch pieces (about 2 pounds) or two 16-ounce packages frozen unsweetened sliced rhubarb

1   cup sugar

½   cup white grape juice or apple juice

½   teaspoon finely shredded orange peel

¼   teaspoon ground ginger

3   inches stick cinnamon

2   cups fresh strawberries, halved

    Vanilla ice cream or frozen yogurt

1 Place rhubarb in a 3½- or 4-quart slow cooker. Stir in sugar, grape juice, orange peel, ginger, and stick cinnamon.

2 Cover and cook on low-heat setting for 5½ to 6 hours or on high-heat setting for 2½ to 3 hours.

3 Remove stick cinnamon. If using low-heat setting, turn to high-heat setting. Stir in strawberries. Cover and cook for 15 minutes more.* Serve the warm sauce over ice cream or frozen yogurt.

Per serving: 236 cal., 8 g total fat (4 g sat. fat), 29 mg chol., 58 mg sodium, 41 g carbo., 2 g fiber, 3 g pro.

***NOTE:** If desired, transfer sauce to a freezer container and freeze for up to 3 months.

INDEX

D–G

METRIC MEASUREMENTS

The charts on this page provide a guide for converting measurements from the U.S. customary system, which is used throughout this book, to the metric system.

Product Differences

Most of the ingredients called for in the recipes in this book are available in most countries. However, some are known by different names. Here are some common American ingredients and their possible counterparts:

- **All-purpose flour** is enriched, bleached or unbleached white household flour. When self-rising flour is used in place of all-purpose flour in a recipe that calls for leavening, omit the leavening agent (baking soda or baking powder) and salt.
- **Baking soda** is bicarbonate of soda.
- **Cornstarch** is cornflour.
- **Golden raisins** are sultanas.
- **Green, red, or yellow sweet peppers** are capsicums or bell peppers.
- **Light-colored corn syrup** is golden syrup.
- **Powdered sugar** is icing sugar.
- **Sugar** (white) is granulated, fine granulated, or castor sugar.
- **Vanilla** or vanilla extract is vanilla essence.

Volume and Weight

The United States traditionally uses cup measures for liquid and solid ingredients. The chart below shows the approximate imperial and metric equivalents. If you are accustomed to weighing solid ingredients, the following approximate equivalents will be helpful.

- 1 cup butter, castor sugar, or rice = 8 ounces = $\frac{1}{2}$ pound = 250 grams
- 1 cup flour = 4 ounces = $\frac{1}{4}$ pound = 125 grams
- 1 cup icing sugar = 5 ounces = 150 grams

Canadian and U.S. volume for a cup measure is 8 fluid ounces (237 ml), but the standard metric equivalent is 250 ml.

1 British imperial cup is 10 fluid ounces.

In Australia, 1 tablespoon equals 20 ml, and there are 4 teaspoons in the Australian tablespoon.

Spoon measures are used for smaller amounts of ingredients. Although the size of the tablespoon varies slightly in different countries, for practical purposes and for recipes in this book, a straight substitution is all that's necessary. Measurements made using cups or spoons always should be level unless stated otherwise.

Common Weight Range Replacements

Imperial / U.S.	Metric
$\frac{1}{2}$ ounce	15 g
1 ounce	25 g or 30 g
4 ounces ($\frac{1}{4}$ pound)	115 g or 125 g
8 ounces ($\frac{1}{2}$ pound)	225 g or 250 g
16 ounces (1 pound)	450 g or 500 g
$1\frac{1}{4}$ pounds	625 g
$1\frac{1}{2}$ pounds	750 g
2 pounds or $2\frac{1}{4}$ pounds	1,000 g or 1 Kg

Oven Temperature Equivalents

Fahrenheit Setting	Celsius Setting*	Gas Setting
300°F	150°C	Gas Mark 2 (very low)
325°F	160°C	Gas Mark 3 (low)
350°F	180°C	Gas Mark 4 (moderate)
375°F	190°C	Gas Mark 5 (moderate)
400°F	200°C	Gas Mark 6 (hot)
425° as Mark 8 (very hot)		
475°F	240°C	Gas Mark 9 (very hot)
500°F	260°C	Gas Mark 10 (extremely hot)
Broil	Broil	Grill

*Electric and gas ovens may be calibrated using Celsius. However, for an electric oven, increase Celsius setting 10 to 20 degrees when cooking above 160°C. For convection or forced air ovens (gas or electric), lower the temperature setting 25°F/10°C when cooking at all heat levels.

Baking Pan Sizes

Imperial / U.S.	Metric
9×1$\frac{1}{2}$-inch round cake pan	22- or 23×4-cm (1.5 L)
9×1$\frac{1}{2}$-inch pie plate	22- or 23×4-cm (1 L)
8×8×2-inch square cake pan	20×5-cm (2 L)
9×9×2-inch square cake pan	22- or 23×4.5-cm (2.5 L)
11×7×1$\frac{1}{2}$-inch baking pan	28×17×4-cm (2 L)
2-quart rectangular baking pan	30×19×4.5-cm (3 L)
13×9×2-inch baking pan	34×22×4.5-cm (3.5 L)
15×10×1-inch jelly roll pan	40×25×2-cm
9×5×3-inch loaf pan	23×13×8-cm (2 L)
2-quart casserole	2 L

U.S. / Standard Metric Equivalents

$\frac{1}{8}$ teaspoon = 0.5 ml	
$\frac{1}{4}$ teaspoon = 1 ml	
$\frac{1}{2}$ teaspoon = 2 ml	
1 teaspoon = 5 ml	
1 tablespoon = 15 ml	
2 tablespoons = 25 ml	
$\frac{1}{4}$ cup = 2 fluid ounces = 50 ml	
$\frac{1}{3}$ cup = 3 fluid ounces = 75 ml	
$\frac{1}{2}$ cup = 4 fluid ounces = 125 ml	
$\frac{2}{3}$ cup = 5 fluid ounces = 150 ml	
$\frac{3}{4}$ cup = 6 fluid ounces = 175 ml	
1 cup = 8 fluid ounces = 250 ml	
2 cups = 1 pint = 500 ml	
1 quart = 1 litre	

HEALTHY, FAST & FLAVORFUL RECIPES

FOR NO-HASSLE MEALS!

THE BIGGEST BOOK SERIES INCLUDES:

30-Minute Meals
Bread Machine Recipes
Casseroles
Diabetic Recipes
Slow Cooker Recipes
Slow Cooker Recipes Volume 2
Soups & Stews

Available where quality books are sold.

FAMILY-FRIENDLY RECIPES
TO SATISFY EVERY APPETITE.

ADT0144_0406